THE CIVIL WAR 1922-23

Eoin Neeson

First published 1966 by
The Mercier Press

This edition published 1989 by
Poolbeg Press Ltd.
Knocksedan House,
Swords, Co. Dublin, Ireland.

© Eoin Neeson 1966, 1989

ISBN1 85371 013

Cover design by John Short
Typeset by Print-Forme,
62 Santry Close, Dublin 9.
Printed by The Guernsey Press Ltd.,
Vale, Guernsey, Channel Islands.

THE CIVIL WAR 1922-23

POOLBEG

Eoin Neeson was born and reared in Cork. He was educated in Cork and at Newbridge College. He has written many works of fiction, history and drama. Under the pseudonym of Donal O'Neill he is currently writing a seven-volume work on the Irish people, *March of a Nation,* of which the first three volumes have been published. He has also been prominent in journalism broadcasting and TV and was head of the Government Information Bureau. He lives in Dublin and is Director of Special Projects with the Forestry Division of the Department of Energy.

Books by Eoin Neeson

Life Has No Price (Desmond O'Neill) 1957.

Red Diamonds (Desmond O'Neill) 1959.

The First Book of Irish Myths and Legends, 1965.

The Second Book of Irish Myths and Legends, 1966.

The Life and Death of Michael Collins, 1968.

Crucible (Donal O'Neill), 1986.

Of Gods and Men (Donal O'Neill), 1987.

Sons of Death (Donal O'Neill), 1988.

Plays

Cuchulain, 1947.

A Voice in Rama, 1954.

Public Enemy, 1961.

In memory of my parents,

Seán and Geraldine Neeson

CONTENTS

PART THREE — THE GUERILLA WAR

INTRODUCTION TO 1989 EDITION

When this book was first published in 1966 it was the pioneer account of the Irish Civil War. Prior to this those twelve formative months, from March 1922 to March 1923, the bitter legacy of which so profoundly dominated the social and political life of the State for the following forty years, remained unchronicled.

Much had been written about the War of Independence and the Treaty, but such published information as existed relating to the Civil War period consisted of long-forgotten contemporary newspaper reports; occasional articles or pamphlets on specific persons or incidents; some general histories — Dorothy Macardle's *Irish Republic* being the most useful for the period — biographies and accounts of political events leading up to the outbreak of hostilities, and little else other than unpublished material: none of it, of course, was collated. But in general the subject was skirted and published historical narrative lurched from the spring of 1922 (often earlier) to the summer of 1923, or later, as if intervening events had no place on the highroad of history. A notable exception was *Peace by Ordeal*, Frank Pakenham's — necessarily limited — study of the political situation leading up to and resulting from the Civil War.

Civil War 1922-23 is the first comprehensive and detached assessment of the period, in particular of the military history. Additional detail has come to light since its first publication (mainly through the publication of Cabinet documents by both the Irish and British governments, and important papers such as the Mulcahy collection), but nothing that would alter the broad scope and thrust of this account.

Several books about the period have also been published, notably (in 1968) Calton Younger's *The Irish Civil War*, a popularised treatment, and, more recently, academic studies such as Sheila Lawlor's *Britain and Ireland, 1914-1923* and Michael Hopkinson's *Green Against*

Green, an important study and source book. This book, however, remains the essential chronology of the events of the Civil War.

Prior to 1960 jaded Civil War issues were still being offered to an impatient electorate more anxious about matters of immediate concern. For the (largely post-Civil War) electorate the Civil War was history and they rightly demanded a dynamic more appropriate to the times of which they were the children. They eagerly welcomed the approach of the 'rising tide that raises all vessels'. When that was seen to be happening, the interest of the public in the Civil War — as history — reawakened. It had been an uneasy, closeted — and sometimes sinister — skeleton for too long.

While there have been several remarkable social changes in the State since then, and not always for the better, there is one outstanding issue (with which, ironically, the Civil War was not directly concerned) that seemed — as remarked in the original Introduction — in danger of going by default, namely the question of the six counties of Northern Ireland and the reunification of the country. That objective seems no nearer.

THE NORTH

Notwithstanding the assurances — both those in respect of the Treaty and of the Constitution — given by the British leaders to the Irish delegations, it is long since evident that there was no intention on the part of the British of acceding to any reduction in size of the proposed northern state, and that the inducements offered to the Irish on this score were false.

In the interim the situation in what emerged as the Six Counties of Northern Ireland has also changed in a number of ways, many of them profound and some of them social as well as political. But violence has continued there to the lamentable point where it seems to be virtually endemic, although its character and purpose also appear to have changed.

There is an evident major alteration so far as idealism, such as it may be, and the motivation of those conducting campaigns of violence in the North are concerned. Those who believed they could sustain the claim, with whatever improbable legitimacy, that under the banner of the IRA they, as heirs of the Second Dáil, carried on in the North the struggle against English imperialism, have, for much more than a decade, passed

2

into history and have been succeeded by men and women with no such claim, whose sole authority is that of the bomb, the bullet and terrorism as an end in itself.

Insofar as they proclaim any political creed it does not derive from the War of Independence or from the high motives and ideals that inspired it. Rather they demonstrate a species of theoretic and untested socialism that, not infrequently, is a hallmark of the modern terrorist who — often unwittingly — can become the manipulated tool of greater and subtler powers. There is a vast — and unbridgeable — gulf between the men who fought the War of Independence and brought honour and distinction to the name of the Irish Republican Army and who, as one of them (Sean Moylan, a distinguished brigadier in the War of Independence and subsequently minister in several Fianna Fáil administrations) wrote: 'were associated in an adventure of high honour' in 'the struggle for our nation's independence', and the abominable evildoers who today horrify the world by their despicable actions — and yet presume to lay claim to and usurp the noble and dignified mantle of that great generation and their vision of a free, peaceful Ireland and a unified and harmonious people.

Moylan and his comrades would have recoiled at the ruthless actions of those who today attempt to misappropriate that ideal and birthright of the whole nation. Some measure of the difference between them may be judged from the fact that the chivalrous behaviour on the battlefield of Moylan and his comrades of the IRA to which *they* belonged was the subject of favourable comment and admiration in the British House of Commons during the height of the War of Independence.

In the late 1950s I recall discussing aspects of 'republican' tactics with certain leaders of the then IRA. They announced their intention of seeking assistance from the international Communist movement: 'We will use it for our own ends as long as it suits us'. It struck me as being naive on their part that it did not seem to occur to them that the boot might be on the other foot; or that the other foot was more experienced and cunning (to say nothing of its resources) in such games of Russian roulette. Nor did they think the question worth more than a laugh.

It may be asked why this point was not made in the introduction to the earlier edition. The IRA campaign in the 1950s did not compare with the current campaign. The present situation in the North is very different. If today's leaders of the movement calling itself the IRA can justifiably claim any dominant tradition it does not derive from the

3

Second Dáil, or the motives that brought it about.

Today the so-called IRA's 'offensive' policy consists of acts of violence, murder and terrorism coupled with a so-called 'community defence policy' (that may have a vestigial validity, given the continued threat of racial and sectarian violence in the North and the inadequacy of the Crown forces in dealing with it). But they are also deeply involved in established anti-social, and criminal, activities which, in the last analysis, alienate them from all right-thinking people however oppressed and which – paradoxically – are absolutely counter-productive of their declared purpose or the means of achieving it. The organizations they have created have the appearance of a kind of self-perpetuating, psychotic, multicamerate, viviparous and uncontrollable Frankenstein monster, related more to the crime syndicates of Chicago in the Roaring Twenties or to the anarchic brigades of the twilight zone of international 'liberation' fronts, than to any motivations which gave rise to the movement for national self-determination at the beginning of the century, or its achievements.

On the other side of the divide, the Unionist (Protestant) para-military organizations have acted in similar fashion, at times indulging in orgies of sectarian murders directly related to feelings of outrage arising from the threat they feel directed against their perceived entitlements, namely the position of power and privilege they held, or believed they held, for generations, to which they had become accustomed and which they felt they held as of superior right, blood, breeding and religion: an attitude, of course, encouraged by earlier British colonial interests, and which they now seek to disown. These paramilitary groups also own and control major criminal activities.

But there were social and political changes in the North too. To a considerable extent the hitherto institutionalised position of power and privilege enjoyed by the Unionist sector has been corrected (though not entirely), on a basis of improved social and democratic rights for the nationalist sector: more significantly, in an internal and revealing change, much of the control of Unionist privilege has appeared to pass from the hands of the industrialists and great landowners who had held it for centuries to those of the middle and working classes. This happened mainly because the latter groups were dissatisfied with the manner in which they felt their old leaders were jeopardising their traditional rights and privileges. It occurred in 1974 when, following the Sunningdale Agreement, the intention of the British Government to

4

introduce power-sharing, with or without Unionist approval, was opposed 'insufficiently' by the Unionist leadership to satisfy their following. This phenomenon also produced — if in somewhat diluted form — an additional change of internal Unionist structure. Social differences tended to separate Anglicans and Non-conformists. Historically, power and authority in Ireland from the 17th century was in the hands of the Establishment, religiously represented by the Anglican Church of Ireland and temporally represented by the landowners and professional classes who tended to belong to that Church and enjoyed the special status reserved for it. Both Catholics and Non-conformists were subordinated by it, sometimes with severe penal laws. Although Anglicans were in a minority in the country, north and south, they concentrated most of the power and wealth in their hands. That was the case at the beginning of the century. One effect of Partition was to throw Anglican and Non-conformist, especially in the North, closer together than before and close ranks against a common 'enemy'. Nonetheless it remained the case that power was concentrated to a significant extent in Anglican, landowning and professional classes in the North until 1974.

A general (intimidatory) strike, which they called a 'constitutional stoppage', was organized by working-class Unionists. Faced with it the British (Labour) Government backed down, power sharing was 'deterred', and effective leadership of Unionist affairs passed, to a very large extent, into the hands of Non-conformists, primarily Presbyterians — working-class, business people and prosperous farmers in the main.

It was interesting also because, for a moment in history, Northern Unionists, adrift in the heart of the problem, seemed to lack any sense of identity as old allegiances failed. Perhaps it was time for them to be encouraged to seek an Irish one. Crawford (*Depopulation Not Necessary*) puts it succinctly when writing of the plantations and settlements in Ulster from 1600 onwards.

When we find a hardy, industrious race transplanted to a country under the sanction and by the authority of the Crown, protected and favoured by the laws and ruling authority of the State, placed under fostering landlords who exhibit a paternal care, and then permitted to hold their farms under a custom which practically gave them a lease in perpetuity, it would be a strange thing indeed if prosperity were not the result.

Add to that, corruption of the franchise and administrative systems so that power was vested and remained in their hands, and an understanding of, if not a sympathy for, Unionists' anxieties and fears about loss of privilege is possible.

These people, although originally of the same ethnic stock — they were descendants of the Irish or 'Scots' who colonised and eponymously gave their name to the new country – and with similar traditions were, nevertheless, as 'Planters' both alien and privileged in the land, homes and territories of those they had dispossessed and persecuted. Moreover they subscribed to a variant sect. Throughout the succeeding centuries they preserved and developed an artificial sense of identity, redolent of 16th and 17th century Europe, conferred by these sectarian and 'acquired rights' differences. They maintained power and privilege (though admittedly at second-hand through the great Unionist landowners, professional classes and industrialists who exploited their unthinking allegiance and commitment as of right) until the 1974 Strike. Thereafter, while the power-base was changed, the bitter struggle to retain and hold privilege remained. More recent unrest in the North which started in 1968 on the basis of human rights was extended, mainly by extremists from both sectors of the community locked into this historical anachronism, into that sectarian/political violence virtually endemic in the North for over a hundred years. It is little secret that, leaving aside strategic and economic questions, the social problems of Northern Ireland derive essentially — however ill-founded or however artificially stimulated they may be — from Ulster Protestant loathing, fear and misunderstanding of Catholicism, and their refusal to associate with their Catholic neighbours on an equal footing. *If* they did so then they could address the question of their identity in logical and modern terms. Until they do so they will remain isolated and out of their time. In the meantime horrendous acts of violence by both sides result in hysterical retaliation and counter retaliation to the point where violence becomes a cause in itself.

THE ANGLO-IRISH AGREEMENT

The situation in Northern Ireland is a major issue of concern to all in these islands. Every sane and sensible person supports the cause of peace and an enduring basis for unity and reconciliation in the North — with justice and honour.

In 1978, as a result of long behind-the-scenes negotiations, another proposed formula for peace, The Anglo-Irish Agreement, was negotiated. It received considerable applause both in the Republic and in Britain. But it also received considerable opposition, from both Unionists and Irish (mainly Opposition – Fianna Fáil, at that time) political leaders. The Unionists were most vociferous and bitter, accusing the British Government of (again) betraying them by not 'consulting' with them before signing the Agreement. (This was an ill-founded criticism as they had refused to participate in preliminary discussions.) Nevertheless as a formula for peace in the North the effectiveness of the Agreement seems doubtful if not impossible without their support — which has, indeed, proved to be the case since it came into effect.

Since, in any case, its effectiveness depends also on the 'goodwill' of British governments, it is endemically suspect. Since, thirdly, it purports to recognition as a document of international status between sovereign governments, it appears also to contain elements of unconstitutionality, if it is not, in fact, unconstitutional.

The subsequent Fianna Fáil Government, while preserving their original stand on the matter, agreed to accept it, *de facto*, as the only available *via media* of joint operations with the British Government on the Northern question.

By and large the situation in the North is usually presented as being essentially sectarian, which is simplistic. The issues are both deeper and less complicated than one of Northern Ireland being the home of a Protestant versus Catholic anachronistic extension into the 20th century of the Thirty Years' War, with roots and aspirations so deep and so powerful that, it is held, the surgery required to correct the disease could prove fatal.

The fact is that sectarianism was deliberately stimulated and employed as a political instrument by the Tories at the time of Gladstone's Home Rule proposals a hundred years ago — not from any love of Ulster Protestantism, but as a power-base for Toryism when they lost their home ground in England.

But the notion of a sectarian quagmire has been encouraged and fostered so that it obscures the reality by developing a dynamic of its own and has almost become the cause instead of being seen as a manipulated smoke screen. The phrase 'politically manoeuvred sectarianism' well describes the position. During the Stuart plantations of Ulster, Scottish (and some English) colonists — many of them

7

Dissenters persecuted at home — were 'planted' in Ulster on the lands of dispossessed Irish landowners. Thus was one set of 'troublemakers' employed to subdue another. In one fashion or another this ploy has been used by the British in Ireland as an aspect of the piratical imperial policy of divide and conquer. While the strategic relevance of Ireland vis à vis England has marginally altered — some might allege diminished — the strategic policy of Whitehall has not. Meanwhile the false and residual sectarian bias remains. The irony is that it was these very Non-conformists who introduced republicanism to Ireland in the 18th century and who guided its destinies in the first republican rebellion in 1798. What is not, apparently, clearly — or well — understood in Whitehall is that the strategic value of a friendly, unified Ireland on Britain's western approaches would far outweigh the present unsettled situation. But it should also be recognized that the position regarding NATO involvement and submarine intelligence gathering are, of course, major limiting *de facto* considerations in substituting existing policy for any notional improvement so far as Whitehall is concerned.[1]

The 'isolation' of the Northern Unionist people is partly their own doing and partly that of British policy. They continue to be fuelled, irrationally, on a diet of virulent anti-Catholicism, bigotry of a type today found only in the Third World, remote backwoods pockets of the West or in South Africa. It is tribal and emotional and owes nothing to reason or civilisation. It is rooted in fear and hatred and finds expression in the most bizarre and inexplicable occurrences — an apparently otherwise undemonstrative bank clerk suddenly jumping onto her desk and dancing with hysterical glee at the (false) news that Ian Paisley and his supporters are marching on the area; a worker (employed by a Catholic) stating seriously that his feelings, if he saw a Catholic in his house, would be the same as if he saw a rat there.

The Catholic population as a whole have responded to the continuous triumphalist and oppressive, often violent, hostility from their Protestant fellows (who, for decades, denied them the elementary rights of fellow citizens) by developing a siege mentality, which produced its own violence. This induced the paradoxical situation of a siege within a siege, for the essence of the Northern 'Protestant' outlook is that of the besieged. Their references and the community dynamic return again and again to the Siege of Derry (1689) for inspiration. Here is the illogical reality.

As Crawford pointed out, it would be 'a strange thing indeed' if

8

prosperity did not result from the protection, privilege and encouragement given the 'planted' settlers who ousted the Irish from their lands in the 16th century. But more than that resulted — in particular an absolute bartering to Britain of an identity of their own in return for these privileges. They were Protestant and British, and so they have remained. But there is a difference. They were planted to become British first and 'Protestant' second. Because of the manipulated hatred necessary to maintain this alien outlook the extremists became, as the years passed, Protestant first and British second — a state of affairs, for instance, which enabled them to seek guns and assistance from Germany in 1913 to be used, if necessary, against Britain if Home Rule ('Home Rule means Rome Rule') was introduced for all-Ireland. The great enemy was no longer Britain's enemy, the primary interest no longer Britain's interest; they had been metamorphosed, respectively, into Catholicism and the Protestant (non-conformist) ethic. Today the same irrational bigotry, again politically manipulated, has left them with another crisis of identity. For the fact is that these people have no identity except their strange brand of archaic puritan Protestantism, as has been amply demonstrated. And yet, when outside Ireland, they are proud to call themselves Irish. It is only in Ireland that they blench at this. What they are apparently terrified of is that by acknowledging themselves Irish in Ireland they are in mortal danger from two unforgivable sins — firstly of admitting to share something (even something as vague as Irishness) on an equal basis with Irish Catholics, and secondly of being swamped in a bog of 'idolatrous' popery (and, of course, of losing the position and privileges to which they had grown accustomed — though it must be pointed out that, until recently, the material benefits of these, in fact, applied to the community leaders and to a very limited extent to the urban worker, militant or otherwise, who usually benefited only notionally or, perhaps, in kind. The limitations on his benefits, of course, in no way diminished the virulence of the worker). Yet the fact is that they are Irish and have been for hundreds of years.

Until they acknowledge that fact and live by it — or leave — there can be no solution to the problem in the North. To help them maintain their position they claim that they will not be forced into an Irish Republic. That, however, is not the issue. No one — except the lunatic fringe on the other side responding in kind — would make any such claim. Irishness does not necessarily mean an all-Ireland republic. There are many other forms of association, all of them to the advantage of all communities, which might resolve the problem. But none of them can be attempted until the Northern Unionists face up to their nationality. Not all the crawthumping, hearkening back to Dissenter origins or blinkered hysteria in the world, is going to alter that. They are Irish whether they like it or not. And they share the island with those who were here first, whether they like that or not.

Only the Unionists can solve the problems of the North. They can solve them only by facing the facts and realities of today rather than by trying to live according to a way of life that ended elsewhere in the modern world more than two centuries ago.

Britain knows this, but is so engrossed in the archaic and convoluted policies accumulated in the files of her civil service that change can be achieved only by drastic decisions, which they are reluctant to make. The North of Ireland remains strategically important to Britain. The question which is becoming increasingly interesting is to what extent a friendly and co-operative de-partitioned Ireland is of more value to Britain than an unstable, expensive and potentially disruptive partitioned one. There are more ways of securing a strategic objective than by occupying it.

Gradualism cannot work so long as Britain underwrites the position of the Northern Unionists who — ironically — would reject Britain and the British in the morning without a qualm if promised the support of, say, South Africa.

What are the prospects for the six counties of the North of Ireland, still occupied by Britain 66 years after the Treaty, which was to lead in time to the unity of Ireland?

The continued occupation does, certainly, affect the community problem, but the community problem is not — nor has it ever been — England's principal concern, which is simply stated by the old adage — 'England has neither friends nor enemies, only interests.' England, though she is adept at propagandising the opposite view, has seldom been swayed by moral principle in such matters. An apparent, but incorrect, motive may obscure the real one, and England has successfully promoted and used sectarianism in Northern Ireland to obscure the real, political, issue, at a terrible cost to the whole Irish community, but especially in the North.

The essential factor governing Britain's continued occupation of Northern Ireland is not concern for the people who live there, but strategy.

The Tudor Conquest of Ireland was conducted at (then) enormous effort and expense for only one reason: to protect England's western approaches. The North Atlantic sea-routes, then as later, were the highways that enabled England, poised on the threshold of that expansion into piracy of several levels — trade, colonisation, statecraft — to exert a powerful influence on world events for over four hundred years and to adopt the piratical policy which also enabled her to control the balance of power in Europe.

During that time protection of the western approaches — additionally vulnerable because of the prevailing westerly winds — against the Spanish, against the Dutch, against the French, against the Americans, against the Germans — was a continuous preoccupation of both the War and Foreign Offices on Whitehall. Therefore Ireland was of vital strategic value to Britain in any war situation. That strategic value, so far as the policies of these great English offices of State are concerned, has not diminished, and was re-inforced following the handing over of the ports by Prime Minister Chamberlain in 1938 followed by the Second World War, when they badly wanted them back.

In the early and mid-1970s Britain had so many regular troops committed in Northern Ireland that she could not fulfil her NATO obligations. To appease public opinion and her NATO allies Britain devised the 'Ulsterization' policy under which half the regular troops in Northern Ireland were pulled out, and replaced by paramilitary forces recruited from amongst the local Unionist population. The RUC was re-armed and trebled in size, while the UDR was expanded and given new responsibilities.

The significance of 'Ulsterization' in producing and exacerbating the violence in Northern Ireland was trenchantly made by Professor R. E. Rowthorn of Cambridge (*Irish Times*, April 1988):

From the British point of view this policy has been a brilliant success. Thousands of troops were released for duty elsewhere. . . For the Irish, however, the policy has been a disaster. By its very nature Ulsterization is divisive . . . and has made the task of reconciliation more difficult than ever . . . The spectacle of Irish people killing each other only confirms the British in their complacent belief that Britain is merely an honest broker trying to keep the mad Irish apart . . .

11

Nevertheless if, for whatever reason, the government of Britain did bring about a situation where withdrawal from the North and reunification of the country were feasible, would it not be to their enormous advantage in the long run? At a social level it would enable the confused and disoriented Unionist community of Northern Ireland to discover for themselves a logical and appropriate identity of which they could be proud and institutions to which they could contribute in an important way. On a strategic level it would secure England's western approaches by having there a friendly and allied Ireland in a manner not before possible secured, perhaps, by a treaty, *entente cordiale*.

Leaving all enlightened constitutional or moral considerations aside, even within the terms of the pragmatic adage already quoted, would not such an Ireland seem to be far more in England's interest than the present situation of slow and corrupting attrition? But supposing this question were seriously contemplated, how might England's great ally to the west react? Unfavourably, one must conclude.

It is doubtful if America would permit it unless some accommodation were also provided under which Britain was enabled readily to continue monitoring America's Atlantic defences.

A united Ireland so independent as to be open to extreme socialist government (by force or not, from without or within) would be a substantial threat to United States policy and interests and to NATO.

An Ireland committed to neutrality — which, if it means anything, means the right and the freedom of a nation to decide an issue of principle without duress or coercion — however benevolent and appropriate and desirable from an Irish viewpoint, would seem to be insufficient in the eyes of the great power blocs in present world circumstances; what might be called an unacceptable risk factor for world powers as sensitive and vulnerable to the nuances of international power-play as those controlling our destinies today.

Accordingly it seems that, as things now stand, Britain either (a) does not want the Agreement to achieve what she claims she wants it to achieve, or (b) would agree to a unified Ireland only with conditions doubtfully acceptable to the Republic.

It is futile to ignore the fact that Britain created, and has contributed to, the continuance of the problem of complicated and often violently confrontational social, religious and political conditions that exist in Northern Ireland. Nor is it unreasonable to look to Britain to take the initiative in justly solving it.

POLITICAL CONSEQUENCES OF THE CIVIL WAR

It is ironic that although the Civil War achieved absolutely nothing not capable of being achieved constitutionally, it nevertheless affected parliamentary and electoral forms and procedures in an enduring way.

1. It polarised and fixed for decades attitudes that would otherwise have been absorbed into the political system quite differently. For instance from then on the vast bulk of anti-Treaty support, both civil and army, acquired, willy-nilly, a species of left-wing, socialist colouring that had not been earlier so apparent. The opposite happened with pro-Treaty supporters. In neither case had it very much to do with the political philosophies involved. In the main it simply reflected additional and readily identifiable political platforms of existing polarisation and also had something to do with the momentum of events, both outside and inside the country, that carried participants along. An accident of time or place was sometimes the only basis of initial commitment in the Civil War, and often gave rise to lasting and sometimes inexplicable passions and loyalties.

2. Even before hostilities broke out in 1922 it was no longer simply a case of two factions of Sinn Fein and the army in confrontation. After the Truce with England, and particularly during the period of the Treaty Debates in the Dáil, the Establishment as a whole, with small concern for the issues dividing the main protagonists, unreservedly thrust their power and support behind the Treaty and, later, behind the Provisional and Free State governments. As has been said of Collins: 'The party slipped out from under him.'[2]

The emergence of what up to now has been, for all practical purposes, a two-party State is a direct consequence of the Civil War. The two major political parties, Fianna Fáil and Fine Gael (both now slightly left of centre, with Fine Gael, perhaps, closest), were formed by those who took opposing sides in the Civil War. It is some indication of where sentiment lay that Fianna Fáil, the party of the anti-Treaty element, took office exactly ten years after the Civil War began and was then, and has remained, the largest and most powerful political influence in the country. It is also, perhaps, some indication of how the issues have faded that in the 1970s, for the first time in over forty years, Fine Gael began to look as if it might successfully seek and obtain a mandate from the electorate on its own, on social and economic policies. What is undeniable is that no party other than one or the other has ever, since the foundation of the State, been in a position to even think of forming a government on its own, much less doing so. There have been some attempts to establish a party in the middle-ground between the two, notably Clann na Poblachta in the late 1940s and the Progressive Democrats in 1986. Clann na Poblachta joined in coalition with Fine Gael, thereby sacrificing, fatally, the support and commitment of those who genuinely hoped for a middle-ground party. The Progressive Democrats, founded in 1986 with much the same purpose, do not appear to have achieved the objective.

Today, contrary to the situation that lingered when this book was first published, the electorate, from whatever source allegiance may derive (and in rural areas in particular it tends to be familial and handed down), is presented with current rather than past issues (although some politicians do not seem yet to be familiar with the fact that whereas until the 1960s economics was simply one element of political policy, today politics is, first and last, an instrument of global economic policies).

A postscript to the paperback edition (Mercier 1969) provided an assessment of certain British Cabinet papers relating to the period which had been released since first publication. Although much of what these papers disclosed has since been thoroughly analysed it was in that paperback edition that they were first related to the overall context.

What they reveal about the period March to July 1922, particularly in relation to the Collins/de Valera Pact of May and the drafting of the Constitution of the Irish Free State, is important, and for that reason an abridgement of the assessment follows. It is included here, encapsulated, for the convenience of the reader, rather than being integrated into the general text which deals principally with other dominant issues.

THE PACT AND THE CONSTITUTION

Any consideration of what was happening in Ireland during the six months between the Treaty Debate in the Dáil and the outbreak of hostilities in 1922 must take into account what effect the Pact and the alignment it was expected to produce in Ireland was likely to have on the English domestic political scene.

The British Government of the time was hanging on to power. Indeed it was toppled from power not many months later largely on foot of what was happening in Ireland. The British Government of the day well understood that the outcome of Irish domestic affairs might seal its own fate; none knew better how to manipulate matters in such a way as to try to force an Irish decision which would best suit itself. This it proceeded to do with ruthlessness and tenacity.

When the Collins/de Valera Pact was announced the British Cabinet were furious and alarmed. They regarded the Pact as 'a betrayal by Collins . . . ' (Terence de Vere White, *Kevin O'Higgins*). Evacuation of British troops from Ireland was temporarily halted. Their alarm was due to the apparition of a united and Republican Sinn Féin which the terms of the Pact proposed. Even though the Treaty had already been signed the prospect alarmed them for three main reasons:

1 The Unionist vote for Northern Ireland (at all times a Conservative vote), clearly supported their present policy and therefore, in the delicate situation in which they found themselves, could hold the balance of power. Nothing should be done to alienate it (a point of particular significance in view of Lloyd George's undertaking about Northern Ireland).

2. The Irish Constitution, which was subordinate to the Treaty in some respects, was not yet drafted. It was clearly capable of two interpretations, one favourable to Ireland, one to England. If a united Sinn Féin regained control of the political destinies of the Twenty-Six Counties the Constitution which eventually emerged was likely to be very different to the one which did in fact emerge.

3. Finally, a united Sinn Féin would be a potent force to deal with, particularly in respect of the Northern Ireland situation which still remained to be clarified, and would ensure that the implicit terms of the Treaty in this regard, together with the explicit undertakings of Churchill and Birkenhead that they would make 'a four county Government impossible' (P.S. O'Hegarty. *A History of Ireland Under the Union 1801-1922*), were observed.

This would alienate the Unionist vote in Westminster and down would come that British Government. The Pact as a threat to Northern Ireland was not an ethical worry to London, but as a threat to the survival of the administration and to the unity of the Empire — another electoral consideration — it was another matter altogether. The British

15

Government took immediate steps to ensure that the Pact would not survive. The minutes of the British Cabinet meetings of the time show how it was proposed to achieve this.

In secret Cabinet session Lloyd George, after hearing the views of the other ministers, outlined the method he proposed to adopt. It was this: he argued that to oppose the Pact directly would mean making an issue of Northern Ireland (because of the factors listed above). But, he pointed out, the new Irish Constitution was still in the process of being drafted by the Irish. Quite clearly, he argued, they would present to the British Cabinet for agreement (since the Constitution was subordinate to the Treaty this was a requirement) a constitution which would be most favourable to the Irish. This, Lloyd George proposed, was the ground on which the Pact might be defeated.

He argued that by insisting on a constitution which was radically British in interpretation they could produce a document which the anti-Treatyites could not accept. Thus there would be no Coalition and so the Pact would be broken.

Even before the May Pact the British displayed uneasiness on this score. The following summary of a note by Churchill, then Secretary of State for the Colonies with special responsibility for Ireland, was submitted to a Cabinet meeting on 5 April 1922. Churchill did not wish the entire document to be entered in the minutes, hence the 'note'.

The date is significant and occurs a few days after the capture of *Upnor* (see pp. 97-100). Churchill's note indicates British Cabinet reaction to these events.

1. The situation in Ireland has now taken a turn in which various important contingencies must be considered. There is no reason to doubt the good faith of the Provisional Government nor the goodwill of the Treaty Party who support them in the Dáil. There is every reason to believe that a great mass of people in Ireland will gladly vote for the Treaty and the Free State. On the other hand the Irish Republican Army which we have not recognized, but to which we have been forced to hand over a number of barracks (on the assurance that it will obey the Provisional Government) now appears to be largely unreliable, and the Provisional Government appears to be incapable of withstanding the extremists.

2. Upon review of all the circumstances it seems clear that there may be a strong effort to overthrow the present Provisional Government

before the elections under the Treaty can take place in Ireland.

3. It must be understood that we should not recognize or parley with an Irish Republican Government in any circumstances, and that the mere fact of its being brought into being would constitute a state of war between it and the British Empire.

4. His Majesty's Government stand fast by the Treaty as their full and firm offer, neither adding to nor detracting from those provisions.

5. It is imperative that the action we should take on the various foreseen and imaginable contingencies should now be carefully thought out by the military, naval and aviation authorities.

6. A *coup d'état* might take one of at least three possible forms:

(i) A *coup d'état* might be made in Dublin with the object of forcibly overthrowing the Provisional Government and setting up a Republican Government. In that contingency the General Officer Commanding in Chief (Macready) will at once proclaim martial law, attack the Republican Government and seize all persons taking part in the conspiracy for its establishment. This should be done irrespective of the view taken by the Provisional Government. The present garrison of Dublin is believed to be adequate for all purposes so far as Dublin and its immediate surroundings are concerned. It can be reinforced with great rapidity from England.

(ii) A Republican Government might be set up outside Dublin. In that event we should at once call upon the Provisional Government to take effective steps to wage war upon the Republican forces. Such a *coup d'état* would open up the following alternatives:

(a) It might be resisted by the Provisional Government and other loyal elements. In that event an endeavour should be made to rally the North and all elements in the country favourable to the Treaty on our side and form an army out of them wherewith to march against and attack the Republican forces. It is not improbable that the North would assist, but it is doubtful if the Provisional Government would consent to fight alongside the North for the Treaty.

(b) A *coup d'état* in the provinces, on the other hand, might not be met by an effective protest on the part of the Provisional Government and other loyal elements. If the whole of the Twenty-Six Counties

17

quietly accepted the Republic and no serious attempt was made to resist it, we should be confronted with a different situation.

There would not then be civil war between the Treaty party and the Republicans, but only a Republic in which the people of the whole country will have acquiesced, and in all probability civil war between Northern Ireland and the Southern Republic. In that event the British Army should not invade except where convenient the territories of the Republic.

Dublin and possibly certain other ports should be held. Flying columns should attack the centre of Irish Republican Government wherever set up, but speaking broadly there should be no permanent occupation of towns in southern Ireland. For the protection of Ulster the British Army should also hold the Ulster boundary (presumably the line from Dundalk to Ballyshannon).

7. Aerodromes should presumably be established both in the north of Ireland and in the neighbourhood of Dublin in order that hostile concentrations might be dealt with from the air or retaliatory measures taken in case of aggressive attack upon the British forces.

8. A cessation of intercourse with the disaffected counties would be proclaimed and foreign powers would be notified of their effective blockade.

9. In the preparation of plans to meet the foregoing hypothetical contingencies the following further points should be taken into account:

(a) The judicial condition of a conflict between the British Government and an Irish Republic would be, broadly speaking, those between the Union Government and the Confederate States; that is there would be military recognition for persons in uniform. They would not be treated as rebels if they belonged to the army forces of the republic, but there would be no recognition on our part capable of admitting their rights to recognition by other nations.

(b) In such hostilities we should enjoy the advantage of no longer having direct responsibility for the welfare of the people of Southern Ireland, but we should have heavy responsibilities to refugees. There are 300,000 Unionists living in the Twenty-Six Counties whose position might at any time become grave. Veiled threats have already been directed against them at recent Republican meetings. They may be compelled to fly to Dublin or the sea. The aid of the Navy may have to be invoked to remove them from certain points off the coast.

(c) In the event of a collision between British Forces and the Republican Government or upon the mere establishment of a Republican Government, serious outrage might take place in this country. Against these also precautionary measures must be put in train.

* * *

On the same day (April 5th) it was decided 'to agree to instructions to the Commander-in-Chief in Ireland' in accordance with Churchill's memorandum. It was also decided that the Admiralty should put two destroyers in the river at Dublin in accordance with a request from Macready.

Inferences which may be drawn from these proposals of Churchill's give an entirely new aspect to the Irish domestic turmoil. It is clear that the thinking in the British Cabinet at this stage was projected along two main lines; the first (and from their point of view more desirable) one was that hostilities might break out in Ireland before the election as a consequence of non-acceptance of the Treaty provisions by the Republicans and the efforts to implement them by the Provisional Government backed up by their supporters in Ireland, in which case the British proposed to support the Provisional Government if an attempt to establish a rival Republican Government materialised.

Moreover, they laid emphasis on holding Dublin, irrespective of the wishes of the Provisional Government.

They foresaw a situation in which the pro-Treaty element of Sinn Féin would co-operate with the Republicans in forming such a government and they formulated lines of action to adopt if a Republican Government was established and accepted by the country.[3]

What they did not appear to foresee (and this, in turn, is significant of their approach to the question) was that the republican constitutionalists would not set up such a government so long as the Dáil existed. However it is clear from what Churchill proposed that British interference in Irish affairs even at this time would have been extensive . . . *but* that, in the event of a Republican Government being formed with general support, it would have been far less than the threatened 'immediate and

19

terrible war'. What does emerge clearly is that Northern Ireland was their special interest and concern. They were determined, at all costs, to retain this bastion of Empire in Ireland for which purpose lip-service to the so-called rights of minorities provided a useful camouflage. The deceptions concerning the North put over on Griffith and Collins were no more than political manoeuvring without substance other than immediate tactical gain for British statesmen. A further extract from these series of minutes illustrates the more prosaic attitude of the British Cabinet in its approach to the matter of Ireland North and Ireland South.

As late as 29 June 1922, a conference of Northern Irish and British officers was held at Kesh, Co. Fermanagh (on the question of agreement on the extent and policing of a 'neutral zone'). Churchill urged Sir James Craig (then premier of Northern Ireland as established under the Government of Ireland Act) to accept a request from the Provisional Government in Dublin that 'all officially supplied arms' should be withdrawn from the affected area, adding, 'The British forces can be trusted to afford protection to all Specials in charge of Northern territory within their zone . . . I trust that in view of the efforts we are making to assist you (the Northern government) that you will meet my wishes in this matter. Very serious events may occur in the South in the near future . . . ' This was a direct reference to the Civil War which, in fact, had begun on June 28, the previous day.

That Winston Churchill was contemplating seizing Free State territory in the event of the Provisional Government failing to take the field against the ant-Treaty IRA is, according to Dr Eamon Phoenix (*Irish Times* 3 January 1986), confirmed in a secret memo. issued by Colonel Taylor, Director of Operations, RUC, on June 30th. (However, as we have seen, this information is already well-established from the British Cabinet Papers released in 1968, the relevant portions of which were published in previous editions of this book). The memorandum referred to by Phoenix was circulated (following a Cabinet decision some time earlier) to Craig and his police and military commanders informing them that, in the event of occupation of Free State territory by the British, 'the Northern Ireland Border is to be protected by the military occupation of an outpost zone, mainly beyond the Border. The troops occupying this zone will ensure that no raids from the Free State on a large scale take place, or that armed parties do not assemble in the vicinity of the frontier with a view to making raids . . . '

'In a two-pronged operation', says Phoenix, 'British troops were to occupy "the new line" which would stretch from Derry to Ballyshannon and then eastwards through Belturbet to Dundalk. The C1 Specials — a reserve force — were to be mobilised for maintaining internal order in Belfast' (as were the A and notorious B Specials).

This suggests that the British did not, at this time in any case, intend a full scale re-occupation of the country or resumption of the war.

In answer to a claim by Craig for full compensation for malicious damages resulting from the War of Independence, in which he asked for £2,000,000 on account of a claim for £6,000,000, the following was given:

> The Secretary of State for the Colonies (Churchill), in reply to the Chancellor of the Exchequer, states that the Cabinet had already agreed that Ulster should not receive in this matter terms less favourable than were granted to the rest of Ireland. He proposed first to settle with the Free State on the basis of each side paying its own damages *and to conclude this settlement in such a way as to debar the Free State from making fresh claims to equal treatment with the Northern Parliament when a settlement was made with the latter . . .* CAB 23/29/6/6 (author's italics).

It should be borne in mind that, according to P. S. O'Hegarty and others, Churchill was one of those who had given the guarantee to Collins that he (Churchill) would see to it that the North would consist of only four counties which could not survive as an economic unit.

The British, who up to April of 1922 had been corresponding exclusively with Griffith, then began to deal (with corresponding exclusivity) with Collins, whom they recognized as the key to the developing situation in Ireland.

The catalyst which produced this change was, once again, the pattern of circumstances in Ireland in March–April and the British Cabinet meeting on 5 April at which future policy was determined. Having approved Churchill's proposals and the Prime Minister's (Lloyd George) proposition that the British Government could not allow the republican flag to fly in Ireland, it was decided that 'a point might come when it would be necessary to tell Mr Collins that if he was unable to deal with the situation the British Government would have to do so'.

Clearly what is here meant is 'if he was unable to deal with the situation *to the satisfaction of the British Government . . .*'

And what next happened was not at all to the satisfaction of the British Government: that was the Collins/de Valera Pact which seemed to bring about the very rapprochement the British most dreaded .

What stirred them most and brought them fully alive to the situation which Collins was trying to achieve was the pre-Pact "Truce" between both sides in Ireland in which a group of Army officers, representing both the IRB and the IRA from anti- and pro-Treaty units, attempted to hammer out a basis for national agreement.

At a Cabinet meeting on 16 May, Churchill reported on the Irish situation. He deplored the weakness of the Provisional Government and said 'there appears to be little chance of a free election being held.' By which he meant an election in which the Treaty would be the issue.

He went on to say: 'There is really none too much difference between the Free State and the Republican parties and there is general reluctance to kill one another . . .' In which regretful expression of disappointment he was not only correct, it was something of an understatement (and it well illustrated the pig-headed stupidity and ignorance of Ireland and Irish issues by English statesmen of the period). Collins had already (on April 2) written to his friend, Paddy Daly: 'I am in sympathy with a majority of the IRA. I would wish to continue now and finish the fight. I want to help them to do so. To postpone the struggle for fifteen to twenty years would be a forlorn consolation . . . '

Churchill went on:

We have good reason to complain of our treatment by the Provisional Government. We have handed over to them authority, arms and property, and treated them with generosity and patience. They have given the Irish people no chance to express an opinion upon the Treaty. Last week when the Truce between the two parties showed signs of breaking down Mr Collins sent me a message to the effect that the Provisional Government intended to fight. He asked that he might be supplied with 10,000 additional rifles as well as guns, mortars and other military equipment to enable the Provisional Government to take action against the rebels . . .

Churchill opposed giving the arms unless an attack were made on Dublin Republicans first. He gave as his reason the efforts to effect the Pact. Undoubtedly, though for quite the wrong reason, this was a sound stance by Churchill.

22

Collins's request for arms had more to do with preparing for a renewal of war with the English (in the North, certainly) than with making war against his fellow soldiers in the IRA. He was at that time actively engaged in providing the anti-Treaty forces with weapons newly supplied by the British; in exchange for which they supplied an equal number of weapons for immediate shipment to Northern units. (The purpose, of course, being to prevent identification of recently supplied weapons of British origin should they be captured in the North. Shades of Hugh O'Neill and the lead he acquired from England ostensibly for the roof of his castle at Dungannon, but which was turned into bullets instead.)

Collins had repeatedly given as his principal reason for supporting the Treaty and opposing a continuation of the war with England, shortage of arms. Had he been given the arms he asked for, that situation would have been radically altered.

Continuing his report, Churchill said:
I understand that the Provisional Government have entertained the idea that an agreed election should be held. I have written to Mr Collins and pointed out to him that such an election would be received with world-wide reprobation.

An agreed election was, of course, the proposed outcome of the Pact. The British Cabinet required an election on the Treaty issue because they were well aware that, given the volume of old Irish Party members in the country, the Southern Unionists, the Church, Press and other interests, to say nothing of those in Sinn Féin who supported the Treaty, the election would most likely go in favour of the Treaty. But were the Treaty not an issue the outcome would almost certainly be a coalition uniformly Republican and even inimical to British interests.

Churchill continued:
I have been much concerned to learn that General Macready has recently lost confidence in the intentions of the Provisional Government to act. Recruiting in the Free State Army[4] (sic) is only open to members of the IRA, although it was in theory an anti-Republican (sic) body.

'Ex-servicemen are not', he went on, 'officially allowed to join the army or to occupy important positions in it.' He referred, of course, to the Beggar's Bush force. (That situation altered rapidly once hostilities

23

broke out when recruitment for the pro-Treaty forces reached a thousand men a week, many of them from recently disbanded Irish regiments of the British Army.)

He pointed out that the draft Irish constitution was expected in London the following week. The Lord Chancellor, Lord FitzAlan, warned of difficulties that might arise in it. He said that they (the Provisional Government) wanted to diminish the powers of the King's representative. 'It must be remembered', he said, 'that they were Republicans in sentiment, and that probably the constitution would contain many provisions which His Majesty's government were unable to accept.'

Churchill's advice was: 'if there is to be a break (in the truce) we should make sure that there would be a real fight with the Republicans, while if the truce was continued we should see that it was not on a Republican basis.'

Because of the proposed Pact the British were becoming increasingly uneasy with regard to Collins and his intentions. Churchill was instructed to write to the Provisional Government — the letter to Collins referred to above – formally calling attention to the very serious state of affairs in Ireland and asking how they proposed to deal with it.'

Collins and Griffith had already been summoned to London by Churchill to answer for the Pact prior to going over with the Constitution. British tactics on how to deal with the 'deplored' Pact situation now emerged.

As noted, the Constitution was capable of two clear interpretations, one which was British and imperialist in outlook and one which was Irish in outlook. It goes without saying that the draft which the Irish brought to London was Irish in outlook; it also goes without saying that the British, who conceivably might have accepted all or portion of it had it not been for the Pact, now rejected it as an adequate interpretation of the 'Treaty, framed with meticulous ambiguity' (Frank Gallagher, *King and Constitution*).

Briefly, the British denounced the Pact, insisted that whatever ministers were chosen in Ireland must conform to Article 17 of the Treaty specifically, and that the Constitution would be brought within the Treaty where there was any difference between the two.

There were several meetings between various members of the British Cabinet and the Irish representatives during the next three days, at which the British attacked the Pact, the Constitution and the general behaviour of the Provisional Government. During these discussions, according to Lloyd George, Chamberlain got the impression that Collins was behind the IRA activity in the north.

All in all the British took a very tough line. At a Cabinet meeting on 30 May, Churchill denounced the Pact saying that he believed it was the intention to make de Valera one of the ministers. If he and the three other (Coalition) ministers of the anti-Treaty faction took office, said Churchill, the Treaty would be definitely violated. This had been impressed on Collins and Griffith.

Collins had replied to Churchill that without the Pact there could be no election. The reason adduced, and explained by Churchill to his own Cabinet, was that:

The Provisional Government which resulted from the election would be elected in accordance with the statutory forms which we (the British) had required. But it was equally the Third Republican Dáil and that was its only sanctity in the eyes of the Irish (Cabinet Meeting, 30 May 1922).

The meeting was unanimous on the question of the Irish Draft Constitution (Draft 'B', largely prepared by Collins) that it was 'a negation of the Treaty'. They had given the Irish representatives their observations on it and the Irish leaders said that they would make the Constitution conform to the Treaty.

Churchill went on to say that there were three main factors:

1. The Constitution adjusted to our view might prove insuperable to them when they returned to Ireland.
2. Disorder — (resulting from this) in the South.
3. Disorder . . . . North.

Lloyd George, with his customary farsightedness and political brilliance, made the following summary:

If we make their constitution conform to our view de Valera will not be able to accept and the Pact will be broken. On the other hand, if the Constitution is not made to conform to the Treaty then we will be confronted with a large issue of the Republic versus the Empire.

He felt, he went on, that Collins was trying to manoeuvre them into a position where their case was weak. The fate of the Pact was being sealed by a British Cabinet.

But it looked at one stage as if it might have a last minute reprieve. There had been an undertaking given by Collins and Griffith to the Sinn Féin Ard Fheis that the Constitution would be published ten days before the election in order that the public might have time to consider it. This now became impossible, as the re-drafting began to take more time than had been anticipated. In fact the Constitution was not published until the morning of the election and, clearly, many people — particularly those in areas other than Dublin — had no chance at all of studying it, little as people in Dublin had. Consequently, it might be argued, the Constitution could not affect the election at all.

But two days before the election Collins made a speech in Cork in breach of the Pact. Why? Once again we must turn to what was happening in Britain to find the answer. On 1 June 1922 it was stated in the British Cabinet that the draft Constitution was 'purely Republican in character and but thinly veiled'. It was also stated that this draft was being kept secret because 'It would put them (the Irish representatives) in an impossible position if it leaked out that they had come over with one constitution and gone back with another.'

Quite clearly Collins, even in the face of his own Cabinet's disagreement, was still striving to preserve the Republican ideal; equally clearly Lloyd George was not going to allow anything to get in the way of ensuring that the expression of this ideal was prevented. Had the draft Constitution been published — and it might well have been a weapon of some political significance in England to have it published at that time — the uproar in Ireland when it was found that the original had been thrown out for something much less favourable *might* have produced Churchill's *coup d'état*. It might on the other hand have given even greater significance to the unifying influence of the Pact when the anti-Treatyites realized how far the pro-Treatyites had hoped to go in accommodating Republican ideals and principals.

Thus, in spite of the support publication and denunciation might have won for himself in Britain and in Northern Ireland, Lloyd George suppressed publication of the draft Constitution because of the contrary effect it might have in Ireland, and to ensure the Pact would be broken.

He again chose Collins as his instrument. No one else would do; unless and until Collins himself broke the Pact, the Pact would survive. Griffith had made known his dislike of it, Darrell Figgis, a prominent member of the Sinn Féin Standing Committee, had openly attacked it within a week of its announcement. The Church, the Press, the power-interests, were all critical of it. Still it remained. Unless Collins rejected it, or unless de Valera did so, the Pact would remain. Lloyd George knew this. Therefore, even though acknowledging Collins's dedication to unity (asked for example in his own Cabinet if the Irish leaders did not realize that the time had come for them to choose between de Valera and the Treaty, Lloyd George said 'Perhaps Mr Griffith does, but Mr Collins appears to think he can carry the others along with him'), Lloyd George decided that Collins was the instrument he would use to destroy the Pact.

The day before Collins made his speech against the Pact in Cork he attended a conference in London with Lloyd George. At that stage, no matter when the Constitution was published, a coalition Cabinet seemed out of the question, thanks to Lloyd George's adroitness. Whether or not the final Constitution was published in time for the election it would hardly prove acceptable to the Republicans and the outcome of the election would therefore not be a Coalition. Accordingly, was there any purpose at this stage in holding to the Pact on the eve of the election?

Collins was in a difficult situation. He had been outmanoeuvred; there seemed no way out but to make, for the moment, what best use he could of the situation and gather as much power as possible into his own hands. Was it in this frame of mind, and after such an interview with Lloyd George, that he returned to Ireland and went to Cork to make his speech?

Note: It is important, here, to clarify something that, while unquestioned in Ireland, may elsewhere be misinterpreted.

The mindless violence of the paramilitaries (from both communities in Northern Ireland) is condemned and rejected by most Irish men and women. At the same time few of them would dissent from the fundamental principle of national unity. Accordingly, insofar as some paramilitary groups hold to the same principle, it is an important factor shared in common with the vast majority of the Irish people.

27

ADDENDA

British Cabinet notes on Irish Draft Constitution, 27 May 1922 at 6 p.m.

Present:

British Representatives – Lloyd George, Sir Austen Chamberlain, Winston Churchill, Lord Birkenhead, Sir L. Worthington Evans, Sir Hamar Greenwood.

Irish Representatives – Arthur Griffith, Michael Collins, Eamon Duggan, W. T. Cosgrave.

Secretaries: British – Thomas Jones, Lionel Curtis, T. St. Quentin Hill. Irish – O'Hegarty.

1. Considerable discussion took place in regard to the draft Irish Constitution (S.F. (c)34, the British representatives maintaining that this document was an evasion and a negation of the Treaty of 6 December 1921 by the spirit and letter of which the British Government stood. The Irish representatives replied that they too stood by the spirit and letter of the Treaty and that if it could be shown that the draft constitution did not conform to the Treaty they were ready to alter it.

The conference agreed: that further discussions should be adjourned until a statement showing the objections of the British Government to the draft constitution had been communicated to the Irish representatives.

2. The conference next discussed the issuing of a proclamation and writs to enable the Irish elections to proceed in accordance with the law. Objections were raised by the British representatives to these preliminary steps being taken at a time when the Constitution was still under debate.

The Irish representatives maintained that if there were any delays in proceeding with the election their position in Ireland would become impossible and they might as well abandon the attempt to carry on an administration.

It was pointed out that by issuing the necessary proclamation and the writs the British Government would lay themselves open to the accusation of condoning the Collins/de Valera agreement which they regarded as a breach of the Treaty. In particular the Collins/de Valera agreement was criticized on the grounds that it provided that four ministers of the new Irish Government should be members of de Valera's party, although according to Article 17 of the Treaty of 6 December 1922 (which provided for the acceptance in writing by members of the Provisional Government formed until the constitution of a parliament of the Free State) every member of the Government was required to signify in writing his or her acceptance of the Treaty.

To this the Irish representatives replied that they had not regarded the written acceptance of the Treaty by all ministers as necessary since the government would be a coalition one and coalition did not involve a sacrifice of principles. Coalition government was necessary in Ireland in order to enable the elections to be held. Without it there would be no chance of a fair election. It was intended that the Irish Government should be in existence and that the four ministers referred to should be extra ministers concerned with certain internal departments.

It was also pointed out that there could be no breach of the Treaty under the Collins/de Valera agreement until parliament had met and some definite step taken in regard to these ministers.

After considerable discussion during the course of which it was stated by the British representatives that whatever ministers were chosen by the Provisional Government they must conform with the most specific proviso of Article 17 of the Treaty, the conference agreed:

That the necessary instruction should be given immediately by the British Government for the issue of a proclamation and writs for the forthcoming Irish election on the understanding that such action did not commit the British Government in any way to countenancing the Collins/de Valera agreement and on the understanding and definite assurance of the Irish representatives that they proposed that the Constitution should be brought within the Treaty where there was a difference between the two.

* * *

Extracts from a letter from Arthur Griffith to Lloyd George dated 2 June 1922, which is in reply to a letter from Lloyd George to Griffith putting six specific questions relating to the proposed Irish Constitution. In reply Griffith refers to Lloyd George's letter, quoting extracts from it

29

and also quoting the six questions to which he gives replies. It is therefore not necessary to include Lloyd George's original letter in full here. It may be summarized in the following extract taken from his letter, dated 1 June:

> His Majesty's Government therefore press for an early and explicit declaration that the Draft Constitution will be amended so as to conform with the Treaty in the several particulars in which as shown in the memorandum the present draft differs from it and in particular for a clear answer to each of the following questions . . .

Griffith's reply may be adequately summarized:

> Your first question is: Is it intended by the Irish representatives that the Irish Free State shall be within the Empire on the basis of common citizenship or merely associated with it? My answer is that it is intended that the Irish Free State shall be not merely associated with, but a member of and within the community of nations known as the British Empire and on the basis of common citizenship as explicitly provided by the Treaty.
>
> Your second question: Is the position of the Crown to be the same in Ireland as it is in Canada, Australia, New Zealand and South Africa? [Griffith discussed this at some length. He summed up by saying] (It) raises the issue upon which some difference of view has appeared . . . Let me therefore say that in all matters in which the Crown is constitutionally effective (and consideration shows these to be matters arising out of the relationship of the community of nations) the position of the Crown is beyond question to be the same in Ireland as it is in Canada, Australia, New Zealand and South Africa . . .
>
> Your third question: Is the Treaty-making power of the Irish Free State to be the same as that of Canada? Is capable of a simple answer, namely that it is. We should be glad to have it pointed out to us in what respect we are supposed to have exceeded that position. We do not seek to do so.
>
> Your fourth question: Are the Courts of the Irish Free State to stand in the same relation to the King in Council (The judicial committee of the Privy Council) as do the Courts of the Dominion of Canada? Raises a matter of no small delicacy in Ireland. (He pointed out that appeals to Privy Council were objected to all over the dominions – particularly objected to were the personnel of the

30

judicial committee – members of which had taken an anti-Irish stand in politics. Irish people could not look on them as impartial.) We did not think that their appeal was a necessary incident of the Treaty position . . . He wants to know how far Lloyd George is insistent on this.

Your fifth question: Is the oath set forth in the Treaty to be incorporated in the Constitution as the oath required of members of the Irish Free State parliament? — does not present any difficulty. If your government is not satisfied that the oath is sufficiently incorporated in the Constitution by the fact that the Constitution will enact the Treaty as law, the oath will be expressly set forth in the Constitution as the oath required of members of the parliament.

You are entitled to an affirmative answer to your sixth question — Will all members of the Irish Provisional Government be required to sign the declaration under Article 17 of the Treaty?

EVENTS OF 1988

An extraordinary sequence of events in 1988 affected Anglo-Irish relations. It began with the 'Stalker Affair', as it came to be called — the hounding and black-balling of a Deputy Chief Constable from England, investigating an alleged 'Shoot-to-Kill' policy (official or otherwise) amongst members of the RUC, when he was about to conclude his investigations with interviews at the top: and reached an incredible apogee with the 'execution' by British security forces outside due process of the law, of three unarmed and unsuspecting IRA alleged 'terrorists' in Gibraltar, one of them a woman, an event defended by the British government as being effected in the name of law and order — a logic impossible to follow.

The attitude of the British seems to be that they want their problems in Northern Ireland solved by others (in this case 'the Irish'), but to the satisfaction of no one but the English: an impossible proposition.

Note: The details and implications of the Pact, the Constitution and Collins's predicament are dealt with extensively in the author's forthcoming *Michael Collins*. See especially Introduction.

1. See Clause 1/., British offer of July 1921, p. 306.

2. Lt. Gen. M. J. Costello, private conversation, 1985.

3. See *Michael Collins*.

4. This statement is very previous in its use of the term 'Free State', which did not come into existence until the following December. The final part of the sentence well illustrates the seemingly endemic inability of British statesmen to see other than their own point of view. From what other source than the IRA were the Provisional Government expected to recruit an army at that time?

INTRODUCTION
(1966 edition)

The Civil War in Ireland of 1922-23 was the biggest single influence in modern Irish history and in the development of contemporary Irish politics, yet, up to the present, no detailed account of it has been published, largely because of the political situation that developed from the war.

Before the Civil War there was only one major political party in the south of Ireland. This was Sinn Féin, which secured a 90 per cent poll in the 1920 election and provided the vast majority of Dáil (Republican Parliament) deputies, the Cabinet of the Republic and the military leaders. After four years of guerilla fighting with the occupying forces of the British Government, Lloyd George, the Prime Minister of Great Britain, sought a truce with the Irish Republican Army and asked that negotiations should begin with representatives of the Dáil Cabinet. These negotiations were opened in July 1921 and, in December, choice of accepting the British proposals (which gave to a partitioned Ireland a considerable measure of autonomy, but reserved to England the custody of the Irish ports and enforced a declaration of allegiance to the British monarch with the partitioning of Ireland into separate northern and southern states) or the threatened alternative of 'immediate and terrible war' was offered to the Irish delegation. The delegation accepted the proposals without further reference to their Cabinet. On this issue, in December 1921-January 1922, the Cabinet and the country split and Civil War ensued.

Those opposed to the signed Articles of Agreement, called the Treaty for convenience, held that the Republic of Ireland could not constitutionally accept articles that did not acknowledge the existence of the Republic. Those in favour of accepting the articles said that acceptance did not preclude future Republican status. The latter mustered a majority of seven members in the Dáil and voted into existence a provisional Government which could constitutionally accept the articles and administer on that basis. Six months later, when negotiations and an election — the 'Pact' election — had not resolved differences, Civil War began.

Two major political parties emerged after the Civil War. One, the pro-Treaty party, now known as Fine Gael, successful in the Civil War, the other, Fianna Fáil, the party of the anti-Treaty element. Until recently party leaders have, almost without exception, been Civil War veterans of either side. Over the years they have reiterated the arguments of 1922-23 until they became political doctrines. Briefly, the reasons why these issues lingered as the primary force in Irish politics may be outlined as follows:

1. Sinn Féin, as united and homogeneous as any political party could be before the Civil War, gave birth to divergent and bitterly opposed parties whose methods were different but whose ultimate objective – a united country – was identical.

2. Supporters of these parties were identified, and on election day identified themselves with, the opposing sides during the Civil War. But there was also a third block vote in the electorate – a kind of national vote unattached to either party and consisting of those who had been neutral, of the old Home Rule party, and of those who, as individuals, were politically progressive without being unified – which had to be played for largely on an idealistic level over and above normal political or economic considerations. This vote very often became the deciding factor in an election and for that reason idealistic as distinct from economic policies became the commonplace of Irish party politics.

3. (a) The Unity of Ireland, desired by both parties, has not been achieved and no practical policy for achieving it has emerged. There seems to be a very real danger of the question going by default.

   (b) Confusion on the question of Partition was at the time one of the principal causes of the Civil War, though little was heard of it thanks to Lloyd George's masterful manipulation of the issue. Avoidance of a clear statement of policy on this question weakened the faith of a great many people in both major political parties.

4. Because of political frustration in the youth of the country who had heard the story of Ireland's fight for independence from childhood, some young aspirants took the responsibility for illegally declaring 'war' on the forces preventing a united Ireland, in the name of what was done during the War of Independence.

5. The Civil War achieved nothing that could not have been achieved by constitutional means. Pre-war issues were still there – with added bitterness — after the Cease Fire.

New generations have only recently begun to believe in constructive politics, in their own power and authority or in a secure future. Politicians in Ireland recently not only had the problem of winning the allegiance of the younger generation, they first had to restore its faith in politics; a much more difficult task.

The desire for national independence in Ireland was traditional and intellectual and was not, as with colonists of America, of economic growth. Because of this and other factors, large numbers of the middle class did not actively support the patriotic movement; indeed, because of political developments within the preceding hundred years, many of them opposed any form of nationalism which envisaged military action, an attitude in which they had the full support of the Churches. Nevertheless, alliance of labour and national forces made the separatist movement stronger, and democratic processes of election looked, before the outbreak of the 1914-18 war, as if they might win Home Rule . . . or even Dominion status. A minority in the north-east, fomenting religious bigotry, opposed this and were apparently prepared to fight anyone who sought to bring it about. Armed with guns from Germany, they called themselves the Ulster Volunteers and looked to the Kaiser to help them. War postponed the Home Rule Act already on the Statute Book and, when the Home Rule leaders supported recruiting for the British Army in Ireland, a group of nationalists who stood for complete independence and who had recruited volunteers in opposition to the Ulster Volunteers, resolved to rise against British rule in Ireland. They were the Irish Volunteers and Labour's Citizen Army, later — collectively — called Sinn Féiners. On Easter

Monday 1916 they made their effort, believing that, even if the Rising failed, a baptism of blood was needed to revive the national spirit. With some 800 men the Rising began in Dublin and lasted a week. It has been reasonably well documented, particularly by Desmond Ryan in his book *The Rising*.

During the 1917-21 period it was possible to conduct a successful guerilla war against the occupying British troops for four years: against terror, victimization, wholesale murder, rapine, arson, reprisals and the ultimate horror of the uncontrolled Black and Tans.

In 1921 came the Truce, Treaty negotiations, the offer, the split in January 1922 and, six months later, Civil War.

Why Civil War? One point, not generally known and on which the fate of the Irish cause may well have turned, is that before the delegation went from Dublin for the final meeting with the British representatives they were already divided in opinion to such an extent that they travelled in two groups by different routes.

This book is concerned not with justifying or condemning either side, but with describing, as accurately as possible, what happened. The complex question of Northern Ireland since 1914, a vital part of the political structure of Ireland, should be dealt with separately and fully elsewhere.

A minister[1] of the Provisional Government of the period said to the author that 'all countries must have a civil war, social or political, in their evolution. It's as necessary as an economic depression and the sooner over the better'.

Immediately post Civil War, in June 1923, emerged the two political groups which have shaped the political destiny of Ireland and have dominated Irish politics ever since[2].

There is no doubt that Lloyd George deliberately misled the Irish delegation on the Partition question, giving them the impression that it was a temporary expedient, and there is little doubt that the renewed fear of a re-uniting Sinn Féin party in June 1922, when six months had passed without Civil War beginning or the issues being otherwise resolved, prompted the ultimatum from Downing Street to the Irish Cabinet to attack their 'recalcitrant' comrades in their Four Courts headquarters. Why that attack and the subsequent war took place this book hopes to show.

How men, who had just spent four years as comrades in arms, fighting side by side against the British, came to turn their guns on each other, succeeding generations are entitled to ask. It is for these generations principally, therefore, that this book was attempted; that, avoiding bitterness themselves, they may give to the country the same united effort of their fathers in Sinn Féin and yet understand and sympathize with the tragedy that overtook those earnest men.

[1] Earnan de Blaghd.
[2] The part played by the 1939-45 war in binding a growing electorate to a political party guiding the country through the shoal waters of neutrality is, of course, important.

ACKNOWLEDGMENTS

For many reasons I do not publish a list of those whose generous help made this work possible, principally because most of those who helped me with information requested anonymity.

Nevertheless, to the extent that it is a true record, I hope that those from both sides who gave me assistance will look on this as their book.

To my late father, Seán Neeson, to the late Lieutenant General M. J. Costello, Cathal O Seanain, Liam Deasy and Florence O'Donoghue, who read the typescript and helped me avoid many pitfalls, and to the late Dr F. X. Bourke who made available newspapers and periodicals of the period from his magnificent library, and to my late friend and colleague Noel McGrath, whose help in preparing the index to much of the original material was invaluable, I owe a deep debt of gratitude.

(The reasons for the reluctance of those who offered so much invaluable help and information when this book was first published have long since been overcome by time. But I do not feel at liberty to break the trust and confidence vested in me when this pioneer work was begun. E. N. 1989).

FOREWORD

On the first of August 1915, at the graveside of the Fenian leader
O'Donovan Rossa in Glasnevin Cemetery, Dublin, Padraic Pearse, to
be executed less than a year later for his part in the Dublin Rising of
1916, said:

> . . . we know only one definition of freedom: it is Tone's definition: it
> is Mitchell's definition. It is Rossa's definition. Let no man
> blaspheme the cause that the dead generations of Ireland served by
> giving it any other name and definition than their name and
> definition.

Seven years later, on the twenty-eight of June 1922, at seven minutes
past four in the morning, 'blasphemy,' in the shape of the Civil War,
broke out in Dublin because the name and definition of freedom were in
dispute.

The Civil War and the Partition of Ireland which is associated with it
are two of the most controversial subjects in Ireland. There are
thousands of men and women who have first-hand knowledge of many
of the incidents described in this book and whom it has been impossible,
for obvious reasons, to consult. Therefore many details will be criticized
and, perhaps, challenged. In a pioneer work of this nature that is
inevitable, but care has been taken to ensure that the broad outlines of
the story and the details, where given, are accurate.

Partisanship has been deliberately avoided. The respective parties
involved are well able to look after that aspect for themselves. A certain
romantic sympathy with the anti-Treaty party — very evident nowadays,
though conspicuously absent in the bulk of the population during the
war — had to be guarded against, as had a tendency to accept the
successes — and popularity — of the pro-Treaty party as demonstrable
evidence of being in the right.

The facts, and the circumstances surrounding them, have been given

37

without attempting to white-wash either side. Both sides made tragic blunders, but the onus and responsibility of taking national control fell on the shoulders of the pro-Treaty party, and, consequently, it is they who must first be measured against the aphorism: 'power corrupts, absolute power corrupts absolutely.'

Official documents of the Civil War are generally incomplete, unobtainable or have been destroyed. Though some authorities may claim otherwise, there is no complete and reliable collection of Civil War documents available up to now. For details of battles and operations memory alone, in most cases, has been the guide. This is bound to lead to contradictions. Signals, logs and reports were either not kept at all, or only in a desultory fashion. Most anti-Treaty documents were destroyed at the time of the Cease Fire. Many vital pro-Treaty documents were destroyed just prior to the first change of Government in 1932. For these reasons the record of the Civil War lacks the shape and definition of more formal encounters.

Through the very generous help of many of those who took part in the campaign I have been given access to unpublished diaries, accounts, letters, signals, orders and private papers which cover almost every facet of this complicated period. With this assistance I have been able to construct what I believe to be a just account of the war, of its characters and effect.

Eoin Neeson,
Dublin 1966

CHRONOLOGY OF EVENTS LEADING TO
CIVIL WAR

Date

July 1921 — De Valera has preliminary talks with Lloyd George during Truce in Anglo-Irish war.

29 *September* 1921 — Decision to negotiate on the basis of Lloyd George's 'Gairloch formula'.

5 *November* 1921 — Griffith gives Lloyd George assurances, during Treaty negotiations, which he could not keep without overstepping his authority.

Lloyd George's successful use of 'Divide and Conquer' policy.

3 *December* 1921 — Divided delegation returns to London from Dublin Cabinet meeting to negotiate with Lloyd George.

6 *December* 1921 — Treaty signed by delegates without reference to Dublin in spite of instructions to the contrary.

1 *January* 1922 — De Valera abstains from Provisional Parliament as it has no mandate but does not provide alternative for an anxious populace.

January-June 1922 — Volunteer Army of IRA begins to split following political division: danger of Civil War. Paid force set up in Dublin by Provisional Government. Re-arming of both sides.

March 1922 — Armed crisis in Limerick.

May-June 1922 — Collins/de Valera Coalition Pact to avoid Civil War.

June 1922 — Lloyd George's fear of Pact and of a United Southern Ireland. British pressure on Griffith and Collins.

14 *June* 1922 — Collins repudiates Pact.

16 *June* 1922 — General Election.

18 *June* 1922 — Split in Republican (anti-Treaty) military executive when huge minority favour immediate war on British troops in Ireland in hopes of unity in a common cause.

22 *June* 1922 — Sir Henry Wilson shot in London . . .
Lloyd George holds 'Republicans' responsible.

23 *June* 1922 — British ultimatum to Collins to attack Four Courts, Republican HQ in Dublin, rejected by Collins.

24 *June* 1922 — Macready, British GOC in Ireland, ordered to attack Four Courts.

25 *June* 1922 — Macready's orders revoked.

26 *June* 1922 — Renewal of ultimatum to Collins and Griffith (who did not approve Pact).

28 *June* 1922 — Four Courts attacked: breach in Republican ranks healed; Civil War.

PART ONE

PRELUDE TO WAR

1

TRUCE OVERTURES

The birth pangs of modern Ireland began at ten o'clock on a sunny April morning in Dublin. Nelson, from his lofty pedestal in the hub of the city, towered over small groups of armed men — many of them wearing an unfamiliar green uniform and slouch hat — marching purposefully through the holiday thoroughfares. It was Easter Monday morning, 1916.

Ireland was part of the British Empire. Controlled from Dublin Castle, the seat of English Government in Ireland, it was occupied by an English Army, 66,000 strong, of which a militarized police force, the Royal Irish Constabulary (RIC), was the eyes and ears. The maintenance of English rule in Ireland had never been a peaceful matter. The 800 men marching so determinedly on that Easter Monday were in arms for the independence of their country. A pathetic yet magnificent failure, without the 1916 Rising there might have been no subsequent success. One group marched through the principal street — O'Connell Street (formerly Sackville Street) — and swung into the General Post Office. The staff was ordered out at gun point, windows were barricaded and the Tricolour — the green, white and orange standard of the Republic about to be proclaimed — was raised on the flag pole on top of the building.

One of the leaders of the insurrection, a poet and scholar who has joined the legendary heroes of Ireland — Padraic Pearse, a tall, soldierly figure with fine, clear features and broad shoulders — came out of the GPO and, bareheaded, read to an indifferent crowd, who idly watched the proceedings, the proclamation of the Irish Republic.

James Connolly, joint leader with him, who, wounded and strapped in a chair, was to be executed with him within a few weeks, clasped Pearse's hand as he finished and said: 'Thanks be to God, Pearse, that we have lived to see this day.'

The Proclamation, then posted up outside the building for the public to read, is one of the great documents of Irish history:

Poblacht na h-Éireann
The Provisional Government
of the
Irish Republic

To the people of Ireland

Irishmen and Irishwomen: In the name of God and of the dead generations from which she received her old tradition of manhood, Ireland, through us, summons her children to her flag and strikes for her freedom.

Having organized and trained her manhood through her secret revolutionary organization, the Irish Republican Brotherhood, and through her open military organizations, the Irish Volunteers and the Irish Citizen Army, having patiently perfected her discipline, having resolutely waited for the right moment to reveal itself, she now seizes that moment and, supported by her exiled children in America and by gallant allies in Europe, but relying first on her own strength, she strikes in full confidence of victory.

We declare the right of the people of Ireland to the ownership of Ireland and to the unfettered control of Irish destinies, to be sovereign and indefeasible. The long usurpation has not extinguished the right, nor can it ever be extinguished except by the destruction of the Irish people. In every generation of the Irish people they have asserted their right to national freedom and sovereignty; six times during the past three hundred years they have asserted it in arms. Standing on that fundamental right and again asserting it in arms in the face of the world, we hereby proclaim the Irish Republic as a Sovereign Independent State, and we pledge our lives and the lives of our comrades–in–arms to the cause of its freedom, of its welfare and of its exaltation among nations.

The Irish Republic is entitled to, and hereby claims, the allegiance of every Irishman and Irishwoman. The Republic guarantees religious and civil liberty, equal rights and equal opportunities to all citizens and declares its resolve to pursue the happiness and prosperity of the whole nation equally and oblivious of the differences carefully fostered by an alien government, which have divided a minority from the majority in the past.

Until our arms have brought the opportune moment for the establishment of a permanent National Government, representative of the whole people of Ireland, and elected by the suffrages of all her men and women, the Provisional Government, hereby constituted, will administer the civil and military affairs of the Republic, in trust for her people. We place the cause of the Irish Republic under the protection of the Most High God, Whose blessings we invoke upon our arms, and we pray that no one who serves that cause will dishonour it by cowardice, inhumanity or rapine. In this supreme hour the Irish nation must, by its valour and discipline and by the readiness of its children to sacrifice themselves for the common good, prove itself worthy of the august destiny to which it is called.

Signed on behalf of the Provisional Government, *Thomas J. Clarke, Sean Mac Diarmada, P. H. Pearse, James Connolly, Thomas Mac Donagh, Eamonn Ceannt, Joseph Plunkett.*

The most inspired and tragic attempt to break free of English rule in Ireland in more than a hundred years found its first public expression that morning. *At the same time The Republic of Ireland was proclaimed in the name of the people.*

At that time and in the weeks to follow there was understanding and sympathy from only a few; the vast majority of the Irish people were apathetic, derisive or openly contemptuous of what this handful of men were attempting, and did not seem to care much whether they belonged to an independent and sovereign state or not. The savage executions of the leaders a few weeks later shocked them out of their complacency. Wholesale arrests, the influx of more and more British soldiers and the increasing frequency of reprisals, instead of intimidating the people, fanned their latent nationalism, so that when the Black and Tans were finally let loose their attitude was hardened and even former Unionists were shocked by the lawless campaign of authorized murder, torture, looting and rapine into full and complete support of the principles stated in the Proclamation.

The principal result of the 1916 Rising and of the subsequent executions in which sixteen men were shot, was the sweeping success of the new party, Sinn Féin, constituted in 1904 and re–adopted in 1917. In the general election of December 1918 Sinn Féin won an overwhelming — 73 out of 105 — majority. The declared objective of the party was the establishment of the Republic proclaimed in 1916. No English party had ever received from the people of Great Britain such an overwhelming majority. Such was the *volte face* performed by a majority of the Irish people in thirty–one months. The Unionist historian, Ronald McNeill, later Lord Cushendun, wrote, 'The General Election of 1918 had gone over with foot, horse and artillery, with bag and baggage, from the camp of the so–called Constitutional Home Rule, to the Sinn Féiners, who made no pretence that their aim was anything short of complete and independent sovereignty for Ireland.'

The Sinn Féin Constitution[1] was fundamentally, one might almost say, a pacifist document. Its adoption by the nationalists as a whole in 1917, and the election manifesto which followed this, brought together militant and constitutional nationalists with deeply held differences of opinion, who were agreed, to quote from the manifesto, on 'securing the establishment of the (Irish) Republic: 1. By withdrawing the Irish Representation from the British Parliament . . . 2. By using every means to render impotent the power of England to hold Ireland in subjugation by military force or otherwise . . . 3. By the establishment of a constituent assembly . . And who stood less for a political party than for a Nation . . . re–asserting the inalienable right of the Irish Nation to sovereign independence . . .'

Every elected Sinn Féin candidate was entitled to a seat at Westminster, yet one plank of the Sinn Féin platform had been that they would not go there. And they did not go there. Instead they implemented the third point above. Point No. 2 came a few weeks later.

On 7 January 1919, twenty six Sinn Féin representatives met in Dublin's Mansion House — the Lord Mayor's establishment — and made arrangements to convene the first Dáil Éireann (Assembly of Ireland i.e parliament). On 21 January this national parliament met. On the same day, at a place called Soloheadbeg in County Tipperary a local IRA leader, Dan Breen, commandeered arms and gelignite, shooting two of the Royal Irish Constabulary dead while doing so. These shootings were one of the first in the War of Independence which, thus begun, lasted with mounting intensity for two and a half years.

At the first Dáil meeting Ireland's Declaration of Independence[2] was read: '. . . we, the elected representatives of the Ancient Irish People in National Parliament assembled, do, in the name of the Irish nation, ratify the establishment of the Irish Republic and pledge ourselves and our people to make this declaration effective by every means at our command . . .'

Cathal Brugha, 1916 leader and founder member of Sinn Féin, was elected President in the absence of Eamon de Valera, who was automatically to assume office when he was released from Lincoln prison where he had been imprisoned without trial when deported the previous May for anti–conscription activities. Also in jail were elder statesmen of the Home Rule and National movements, Arthur Griffith (later President of the Republic and leader of the pro–Treaty party in the Civil War) and William Cosgrave (successor to Collins on the latter's death in 1922).

A French historian, present with foreign press on the occasion, realized, as the British authorities apparently did not, the full significance of what was happening. He wrote: 'Those who knew it, partisans or adversaries, divined that a new epoch was beginning, and one that would be terrible.'

There is a relentless irony in that last phrase.

The war against the occupying forces grew in pace until one of the most efficient underground armies the world has ever seen[3] began to gain the upper hand in spite of the enormous military machine which opposed it, in spite of the terrorist methods of the Black and Tans.[4] The Irish Republican Army fought this war against the forces of a mighty empire and, with their civilian supporters, made Ireland impossible to govern by any civilized means.

By 1920 public opinion in England and America, particularly among the Labour and Liberal groups, was perturbed by continuous accounts of conditions in Ireland, most of which was under strict martial law and curfew at the time. The report of a Labour Commission to Ireland led to an attempt on the part of the astute 'Welsh Wizard', Lloyd George, then Prime Minister of Great Britain, to foist a dual government on Ireland, so dividing the 'Orange' north–east from the 'Green' south: The Government of Ireland Act of 1920 was put in the Statute Book. Momentarily, in the face of world opinion, Lloyd George repudiated war and sought to hold by guile what he could not keep by force.

Lloyd George turned to that policy, traditional with English statesmen to restless and subject peoples, divide and conquer. This policy was so successful that it later unnaturally divided a country with an expressed common purpose and drove a wedge between the fighting men opposing him, bringing Civil War in its wake.

The Government of Ireland Act was supposed to come into force in

47

May 1921, when elections for the proposed separate parliaments for north and south would be held. But, as late as April, the questions uppermost in the minds of the English MPs were: Would the Irish resistance be broken by then? Would the people repudiate Sinn Féin, the party of the illegal Dáil Éireann? Would the Volunteers of the IRA lay down their arms as repentant rebels to the King of England? They were doubtful, and with just cause. The whole of southern Ireland was, at the time, at the mercy of military governors who unleashed the Black and Tan terror on a defenceless populace. Murder was commonplace, and whole villages were razed to the ground.

Instead of laying down their arms, men like Tom Barry and Séan Moylan in the south, Kilroy and Brennan in Mayo and Clare, Séan MacEoin in the Midlands, Frank Aiken in the North, Richard Mulcahy and Cathal Brugha in Dublin, Dan Breen in Tipperary, redoubled their efforts.

So ruthless were the methods of the undisciplined Black and Tans that Britain's General F. P. Crozier resigned his command in disgust. So unlimited was their power that Lloyd George could say in the Houses of Parliament of this policy: 'Six months ago the Irish Republican organization had all the symbols and all the realities of a Government . . . Sinn Féin courts were held openly . . . Sinn Féin soldiers patrolled the towns . . . Now patrols, military and police are gone. The Courts have disappeared into cellars.'

But this optimism was premature. Within a few months he was having pressure brought to bear on Pope Benedict to have the IRA outlawed. When that failed the first tentative overtures — unofficial feelers through Cardinal Logue, and others — began to filter through to de Valera, now President of Sinn Féin. These overtures were rejected by de Valera who required any negotiations to be made openly and officially to the Executive of Dáil Éireann.

The election — which, inevitably, has come to be called the Partition Election — was due to take place in the southern twenty–six counties on 17 May and in the northern six on 24 May. Its aim was simple, to split, internally, the tremendous unity of spirit and purpose evident, through Sinn Féin, in the country and prevent, at all costs, the Republican ideal from fructifying. Sectarianism was to be the lever.

In April Lloyd George said to English churchmen officially protesting at reports of brutalities in Ireland: . . .'So long as Sinn Féin demands a Republic the present evils must go on. So long as the leaders of Sinn

Féin stand in this position, and receive the support of their countrymen, settlement is, in my judgement, impossible.'

Yet, throughout April and May he probed for peace — or a means of bringing it about — on his own terms.

Significant in juxtaposition to the subsequent signing of the Articles of Agreement is the following, taken from Macardle's *Irish Republic*, which is quoted from the *Philadelphia Public Ledger*, whose correspondent, Carl Ackerman, interviewed Collins:

Collins: Lloyd George has a chance of showing himself to be a great statesman by recognizing the Irish Republic.

Ackerman: Do you mean a Republic within the British Commonwealth of Nations, or outside?

Collins: No, I mean an Irish Republic.

Ackerman: So you are still opposed to a compromise?

Collins: When I saw you before I said that the same effort which could get us Dominion Home Rule would get us a Republic. I am still of that opinion and we have never had so many peace moves as we have had since last autumn. Our army is becoming stronger, every day, its morale is improving and efficiency is increasing.

De Valera, asked if an offer of Dominion Home Rule on Canadian lines would be acceptable, said: 'The essence of Dominion Home Rule as it exists in Canada and in New Zealand is the fact that the Dominions are part of the British Empire of their own free will.'

In May 1921, the same month the southern Parliament should have come into existence, Lloyd George sent his message: 'I will meet Mr de Valera, or any of the Irish leaders without condition on my own part, and without exacting promises from them. It is the only way a conclusion can be reached. The conference will lead to an exchange of opinions out of which we may find common ground upon which we can refer to our respective people for a settlement.' From this point onward the drama and suspense which led up to the Civil War began.

Almost immediately came the general election. In every constituency the Republican candidates were returned unopposed. Of 128 seats they won 124, the four oppositions being unopposed in Trinity College. In the northern election, in spite of violent intimidation and campaign wrecking — during which Nationalists and Republican voters and agents were attacked and beaten — Sinn Féin won twelve of the fifty-two seats, an insignificant return measured against the sentiments of the populace. Nevertheless, the Unionists said that 'too many Sinn

Féin votes had been cast ' — in spite of the measures they had taken to prevent it, and that 'they would drive Sinn Féin, bag and baggage, out of the Six Counties'. Almost immediately a pogrom of murder and violence began in which more than a hundred victims, many of them women and children, were murdered and thousands were driven from their homes.

In England the election results were recognized as a sweeping victory for Sinn Féin. Lloyd George said: 'Two-thirds of the population of Ireland demand the setting up of an Independent Republic in that island. Every effort I have made, publicly or otherwise, to secure a modification of that demand has failed. They have emphatically stated they will agree to nothing else.'

To the British statesman, fighting for power and prestige at home, and to the blindly embittered, month-old 'Prime Minister' of the newly-created Northern Parliament, Sir Edward Carson, trying to maintain a 'Quisling' sub-state against the wishes of the overwhelming majority of the people of Ireland, no trick of politics; no threat; no deceit; no ruthlessness; no dishonour was too vicious, no promise or undertaking free from ambiguity (to put it mildly) in their dealings with the Republican representatives.

The election, by establishing the Government of Ireland Act as law in Ireland, brought the six-county State into being. In spite of the wishes of the Irish people it was now a *fait accompli*. This unnatural division was part of the British answer to the Republican successes. The rest of that answer, to use the words of Winston Churchill spoken in the Commons, was: 'The most unlimited exercise of rough-handed force — a tremendous onslaught.'

Winston Churchill's proposed solution was: 'A hundred thousand new special troops and police, thousands of armoured cars and the provinces closely laced with cordons of block-houses and barbed wire' in addition to the troops already in occupation. This was agreed to and improved on to the extent of a decision that if the southern parliament — to which, of course, none but the four representatives from Trinity College had turned up — was not in force by 12 July, martial law would be extended to the whole country. The question of peace negotiations was again held in abeyance. It is clear that, whatever else the policy of Lloyd George and his Cabinet towards Ireland may have been, it certainly was not consistent.

This wavering was the result of trying to please an unsteady following at home and it finally came to an end the following year when Lloyd George tumbled in the 1922 General Election, largely because of his mishandling of 'The Irish Situation'.

Throughout May and June 1921 the war continued with mounting ferocity until the country and her people were scourged as never before. All the time, in contradiction to his war and his Black and Tans, Lloyd George was sending out feelers to try if limited conditions of independence would satisfy the Republicans. Then, dramatically, came an opening. On 22 June King George V spoke in Belfast to the Northern Parliament:

I speak from a full heart when I pray that my coming to Ireland today may prove to be the first step towards the end of strife among her people, whatever their race or creed. In that hope I appeal to all Irishmen to pause, to stretch out the hand of forbearance and conciliation, to forgive and forget, and to join in making for the land they love a new era of peace, contentment and goodwill.

It is my earnest desire that in Southern Ireland, too, there may, ere long, take place a parallel to what is passing in this hall; that there a similar occasion may present itself, and a similar ceremony be performed. For this the parliament of the United Kingdom has in the fullest measure provided the powers. For this the parliament of Ulster is pointing the way.

The future lies in the hands of my Irish people themselves. May this historic gathering be the prelude of the day in which the Irish people, North and South, under one parliament or two as these parliaments may themselves decide, shall work together in common love for Ireland upon the common ground of mutual justice and respect.

The same day de Valera was arrested in Dublin in a surprise raid. Twenty-four hours later, to the bewilderment of the country, he was released. The mystery was explained two days later when he had a letter from Lloyd George asking him to come to London for a conference with Sir James Craig, the Northern Prime Minister, and himself 'to explore the possibilities of a settlement'.

As acceptance of Partition was an implied condition to such a meeting, de Valera refused. He arranged, however, a meeting between himself and 'representatives of the political minority' in Ireland. This meeting was held in the Mansion House, Dublin, from 4 July to 8 July.

Craig refused to attend. On 8 July, the day this meeting ended, de Valera telegraphed his willingness to meet Lloyd George in London on 14 July.

In Dublin a truce was agreed on between de Valera and General Macready, Commander-in-Chief of the British troops in Ireland. With the exception of minor 'incidents' not uncommon in such truces, British guns were not heard again in Dublin, until, on loan — or hastily secured on credit — from British military to one of the opposed Irish forces, eighteen-pounder field guns roared across Dublin's River Liffey on a June morning almost exactly one year later — the first shots of the Civil War.

---

¹ Statements and Documents P. 333.

² Statements and Documents P. 304. This ratification was subsequently denounced by some pro-Treaty authorities on the grounds that it 'nailed our colours to the mast' and left no room for manoeuvre.

³ In this connection it is interesting to note that partisan armies, such as those which operated in France, Norway, Greece and Yugoslavia during World War II and in India, Israel, Algiers, Cyprus, etc., more recently, adopted a pattern of guerilla warfare blueprinted by the Irish Republican Army.

⁴ It is worth remembering, though too frequent reference to their atrocities may tend to make readers think stories about the Black and Tans exaggerated, that they carved for themselves a hated and rightful place in the world of horror beside the Gestapo, the OGPU and the Kempeitai. Many, if not all of them, were convicted criminals — even murderers — released from penal institutions in England to become Black and Tans in Ireland. They were a heavily armed, uncontrollable mob for whom no service accepted direct responsibility. The Auxiliaries, like the Black and Tans a special para-military supplementary police force, were equally loathed by the Irish people and for similar reasons. The difference between the Black and Tans and the Auxiliary Cadets — as they were euphemistically called; a number of them, for example, had held brigadier rank in the war — was that the Auxiliaries were a force of ex-officers. As such they received pay of one pound a day and became, it is said, the highest paid force of its kind in the world of that time. Their commanding officer, Brigadier General F. P. Crozier, resigned his command in disgust at their activities.

2

THE TREATY

The uneasy truce between the Volunteers and the British Forces which came in to effect on 11 July 1921 tottered unsteadily beneath the threat of 'might is right'.

It was with this threat over him and the knowledge that: 'Compromise, surrender of the Republic and the acceptance of some form of Home Rule, or else a resumption by England of aggression were certain to be the alternatives presented to Ireland's representatives'[1] before him, that de Valera went to London to meet Lloyd George and Sir James Craig. Together with Austin Stack, Arthur Griffith, Count Plunkett, Robert Barton and Erskine Childers, he met Lloyd George for the first time at 10 Downing Street on 14 July.

The meeting was friendly and a general atmosphere of cordiality prevailed. But, after separate talks with Lloyd George, Sir James Craig published a statement in which he said 'that it was only necessary for Mr de Valera and Lloyd George to come to terms regarding that area outside of that of which I am Prime Minister'.

This statement, implying, as it did, Partition as final and de facto preliminary to the negotiations, drew a sharp protest from de Valera to Lloyd George. In a statement of his own, de Valera said: 'If peace is to come, the negotiations must be conducted between nation and nation.'

On the day following these contradictory statements, when Lloyd George's proposals for a treaty were handed to de Valera, it was clear that this was not the view taken by the English Prime Minister.

His offer was an invitation to Ireland 'to take her place in the great association of free nations over which His Majesty reigns', and then proceeded to impose limits on the 'freedom' it purported to offer.[2] It demanded naval, air and military facilities; rights of recruitment, restrictions on Irish armed forces, a contribution from Ireland to Britain's war debt, full recognition of the Six-County parliament and an oath of allegiance to the King of Great Britain. This offer, not even of

Dominion status, was rejected by de Valera. Lloyd George threatened unrestricted resumption of 'immediate and terrible war' but this bluff was called at that time. The Cabinet in Dublin subsequently confirmed de Valera's rejection of the English proposals and, because of this, Craig refused to have any further discussions with de Valera until the latter recognized the Northern parliament, which de Valera could not do.

At a meeting of the Dáil on 16 August President de Valera said that their first duty was to make the Republic they had established a *de facto* as well as a *de jure* Republic. Arthur Griffith also spoke in the following significant words: that it was every member's ambition to work for the independence of his country, and that no body of men had ever been brought together for the task who had worked in such complete harmony . . . They were all absolutely united and ready, he said, in their efforts to secure a sovereign Republic . . . . Ireland was ready, he said, to negotiate on the basis of these principles.[3] At the same meeting de Valera said: 'It is as a separate nation that we are talking . . . and if negotiations are to be continued it is as such that we must enter into them.' Lord Birkenhead's reply to these affirmations of the Republic's position was a threat of 'hostilities on a scale never hitherto undertaken by this country against Ireland'. In the face of that threat the Dáil confirmed the rejection of the British proposals.

At the Dáil meeting which rejected the British terms, de Valera, nominated for re-election as President, told the meeting that he was no longer to be regarded merely as a party leader. He said he would keep himself free to consider each question as it arose, and, as President, would act simply as the head of the Government of any country would act.[4]

He went on: 'My position is that, when such a time comes, I will be in a position, having discussed the matter with the Cabinet, to come forward with such proposals as we think wise and right. It will be then for you to either accept the recommendations of the Ministry or reject them. You would then be creating a definite active opposition.'

On 26 August de Valera was re-elected President on the proposal of Commandant (later General, and opposition candidate in 1959 to de Valera for the Presidency of the Irish Republic) Seán MacEoin, seconded by General Richard Mulcahy. Both men subsequently fought against de Valera in the Civil War, Mulcahy becoming Commander-in-Chief and Minister for Defence of the Free State Government. He was succeeded as head of the Fine Gael political party by Mr James Dillon; subsequently by Mr Liam Cosgrave.

The Cabinet elected at the same meeting was as follows: Arthur Griffith (Foreign Affairs), Austin Stack (Home Affairs), Cathal Brugha (Defence), Michael Collins (Finance), W. T. Cosgrave (Local Government), Robert Barton (Economic Affairs).

Ministers outside the Cabinet were: Count Plunkett (Fine Arts) and Kevin O'Higgins.

Britain would not agree to a meeting on the basis 'Between nation and nation', and, pointing out that Irish leaders in the past had asked less than Britain had already offered, renewed the threats of force. The Irish leaders in turn pointed out that historical references were fallacious and misleading, that the present was the reality with which they had to deal; that the Irish people, relying on their fundamental rights, had declared for and set up a Republic and had confirmed that action twice. Only on the basis of 'government by consent of the governed' was there any hope of reconciling the divergent views.

The difficulties of trying to act on any basis, satisfactory to both governments, persisted during August and September.

After further correspondence, with the ever-present danger of a break and the resumption of war, the following formula on which Treaty negotiations could take place was agreed on: 'How the association of Ireland with the community of nations known as the British Empire may be best reconciled with Irish National aspirations.' This formula, so far as the Irish leaders were concerned, was capable of an interpretation which appeared to surrender nothing; neither did it commit Britain, at that stage, to the recognition of the Republic. This proposal, which came from Lloyd George, was accepted by de Valera on 30 September 1921. It is called 'The Gairloch Formula'.

Draft proposals for a Treaty, based on external association with the British Commonwealth, had even been prepared, principally by de Valera, George Gavan Duffy — a lawyer — and Erskine Childers, an Englishman and a British ex-soldier and diplomat who had espoused the Irish cause. It is known as 'Draft Treaty A.'[5]

When the Irish Cabinet met to appoint delegates who would negotiate with the British, it was taken for granted, not only by the Cabinet, but by the Dáil and by the Irish people, that de Valera would be one of them. He was recognized as a most skilful negotiator with a remarkable talent for getting his own way. But de Valera disagreed. He

55

referred to the principle mentioned earlier, saying that in time of crisis the place of the head of State was at home.

He has been much criticized for giving away a considerable advantage; for not, as the foremost and most persuasive Irish leader, going himself as a negotiator, and for over-emphasizing the importance of impressing Lloyd George instead of concentrating on what Lloyd George might be made to do if de Valera again confronted him. However, Griffith supported de Valera's views and it was agreed that the delegation would keep in close touch with Dublin — where the final proposals were to be decided on.

Five delegates to the conference were chosen. They were Michael Collins, Minister for Finance; Arthur Griffith, Minister for Foreign Affairs; Robert Barton, Minister for Economic Affairs, and two legal advisers, George Gavan Duffy and Eamonn Duggan. The secretaries were Erskine Childers, Fionan Lynch, Diarmuid O'Hegarty and John Chartres.

The credentials given to the Irish delegates were:

> In virtue of the authority vested in me by Dáil Éireann I hereby appoint Arthur Griffith, TD[6] Minister for Foreign Affairs ; Michael Collins, TD Minister for Finance; Robert C. Barton, TD Minister for Economic Affairs; Edmund J. Duggan, TD and George Gavan Duffy, TD as Envoys Plenipotentiary of the Republic of Ireland to negotiate *and conclude on behalf of Ireland,* with the representatives of His Majesty George V, a treaty or treaties of settlement, association and accommodation between Ireland and the community of nations known as the British Commonwealth. In witness whereof I hereunder subscribe my name as President.

> Eamon de Valera

The following written instructions were also given to the delegates:

(1) The Plenipotentiaries have full powers as defined in their credentials.

(2) It is understood, before decisions are finally reached on a main question, that a dispatch notifying the intention to make these decisions will be sent to members of the Cabinet in Dublin, and that a reply will be awaited by the Plenipotentiaries before the final decision is made.

(3) It is also understood that a complete text of the draft Treaty

about to be signed will be submitted to Dublin, and reply awaited.

(4) In case of a break, the text of the final proposals from our side will be similarly submitted.

(5) It is understood that the Cabinet in Dublin will be kept regularly informed of the progress of the negotiations.

The credentials and the written instructions to the plenipotentiaries were apparently contradictory, the words 'conclude on behalf of Ireland' giving the impression that the delegates had full plentipotentiary powers. Their instructions, on the other hand, made it clear that they had no such power. The fault lay in the wording of the credentials which should have included a phrase such as 'conclude on behalf of Ireland and *with the approval of the Irish Cabinet'*. However, in spite of the importance that was attached to them during the heated Treaty debates, these credentials were never presented.

In the crisis the delegates did not observe sections two or three of their instructions. This negligence led ultimately to Civil War.

Summing up the attitude of the people, of the Dáil, of the Cabinet and of their delegates, Cathal O'Shannon, Vice-President of the Irish Labour Party (later Labour Court Judge), during the debate over the choice of delegates said: 'Sinn Féin cannot compromise. If Liberty is not complete Liberty, it is not Liberty at all, and besides the Dáil has been specially returned to defend the Republican ideal.'

Negotiations opened on 11 October, when the Irish and British delegates met at 10 Downing Street. As if to give support to the Republican ideal, Lloyd George, in the early negotiations, offered a 'benevolent neutrality' on any efforts of the Dáil to induce the Northern Nationalists to unite with the rest of Ireland, thus encouraging the hope that the Irish suggestion of federation in an all-Ireland parliament might be successful.

In London on 24 October, the preliminary skirmishing nearly over, the Irish presented their first proposals to the British, but not referring separately to the north. The question of the Six Counties they declared to be a domestic matter for Ireland, to be settled by agreement with elected representatives of that area or by national elections. Realizing that the Irish were as determined as ever in their demands and could not be shaken by open discussion, Lloyd George now tried a new tactic. He proposed that he and Winston Churchill meet Arthur Griffith and

Michael Collins in private conference. He chose the most dynamic and impressionable of the Irish delegation for his purpose. The Irish delegation never sat in the conference room as a delegation again until the Treaty was signed.

One result of Lloyd George's tactics was that when de Valera repeated to the delegates his instructions regarding the basis for negotiating a treaty, all five protested, saying that he was tying their hands. This indication of tension among the delegates worried him.

Meantime, English pressure for allegiance to the Crown, inclusion in the Empire, naval, military and air force facilities — in spite of the 'benevolent neutrality' — and acceptance of the Northern Government as a *fait accompli* were being pressed on Griffith and Collins. The Irish were standing firmly against Partition. The Cabinet in Dublin were satisfied that the proposals they had given to the delegates represented the limit of concession to which the delegates would go and, fearing the British would not come to meet them, prepared for the only alternative, renewal of war.

De Valera, speaking at the Sinn Féin Ard Fheis at the Mansion House on 28 October, said: 'Ireland's representatives will never call upon the people to swear allegiance to the English King, but they would, perhaps, be forced to call on them to face an "abomination of persecution again". (Our delegates) may come back having found what seems to them a way and recommend it to us . . . the worst thing that could happen would be that we should not be tolerant of honest differences of opinion.

'I believe that if such differences of opinion arose and were carried to the country it would mean disaster for our hopes. *As sure as the nation is divided, the nation will be tricked.*'

In this speech, which was hailed enthusiastically in Dublin, de Valera reiterated that under no circumstances would Sinn Féin agree to allegiance to the Crown or to Partition.

At this time a decision to be of vital importance in the future was made by the IRA Executive. The Executive had been the controlling authority of the Army (the IRA) up to the time that the Oath of Allegiance to the Dáil had been taken in August 1919. Some confusion had risen in the minds of some Volunteers regarding authority after this. Now the Executive, so that there could be no ambiguity as to proper authority, dissolved itself. Three members of the Executive, including Mr Seán Mac Entee,[7] opposed this course as being premature.

Had their views been taken the army split which precipitated the Civil War might have been avoided.

Early in November Lloyd George found himself faced with serious political crises, not the least of which was a note of censure in the Commons, and an attack by the National Unionist Party, both based on his handling of the 'Irish Question': at that moment the 'Irish Question', because of the refusal of the delegates to moderate their final proposals, was as far from peaceful solution as ever; yet Lloyd George was equal to the occasion.

He extracted from Arthur Griffith assurances which, during the temporary period of crisis, seemed to imply that the Irish delegates would accept allegiance to the Crown and inclusion in the Empire and used these to try to persuade the Unionists of north-east Ireland to consider local autonomy under an all-Ireland parliament.

These assurances prevented a breakdown of negotiations which would inevitably have brought down Lloyd George and his Cabinet, and were won by Lloyd George's argument that a new Cabinet under Bonar Law would be even more hostile to Irish interests.

Griffith, assured by Lloyd George that the latter wanted a united and friendly Ireland, and foreseeing the advantages of Unionist approval, however implicit, in the concept of an all-Ireland parliament, gave the requested assurances in a letter which read:

> 22 Hans Place,
> London, S.W.,
> 2nd November, 1921.

The Right Hon. Lloyd George,
10 Downing Street,
LONDON.

Sir,

In our personal conversation on Sunday night you stated that three things are vital — our attitude to the British Commonwealth, the Crown and Naval Defence, and you ask me whether, provided I was satisfied on other points, I would give you personal assurances in regard to these matters.

I assured you in reply that, provided I was so satisfied, I was prepared to recommend a free partnership of Ireland with the other States associated in the British Commonwealth. The formula defining the partnership to be arrived at in a later discussion. I was, on the same condition, prepared to recommend that Ireland should consent to a recognition of the Crown as head of the proposed association of free states.

As to Naval Defence, I noted the assurance contained in your memorandum of October 27th to the effect that:

The objects of the British Government in regard to the Navy and the Air Force are, and will remain, purely defensive. None of their stipulations is intended in the smallest degree to afford either armed occupation or political control of any part of Ireland; and I agreed consequently to recommend that the British Navy should be afforded such coastal facilities as may be necessary pending an agreement similar to these made with the Dominions providing for the assumption by Ireland of her own coastal defence.

I stated that this attitude of mine was conditional on the recognition of the essential unity of Ireland. As to the North–East of Ireland, while reserving for further discussion the question of area, I would agree to any necessary safeguards and to the maintenance of existing parliamentary powers, and would agree that its industrial life should not be hampered or discriminated against in any way.

With reference to the question of financial relations between the two nations, I am willing to let adjustment of this matter rest in the hands of the agreed arbitrator.

To de Valera, Griffith wrote:

They assure me that if 'Ulster' proves unreasonable they are prepared to resign rather than use force against us. In such an event no English Government is capable of formation on a war policy against Ireland.

Doubtless Griffith hoped to use Lloyd George's domestic difficulties to his own advantage, but he forgot that one needs a long spoon to sup with the devil.

Erskine Childers, Gavan Duffy and Robert Barton were tempted to resign from the delegation on the head of the private conferences which only Griffith and Collins attended, but were reassured, as de Valera and his fellow Ministers were, by the belief that any final decision must come from Dublin and that nothing could happen in London that would prejudice the claims of the Republic.

On 5 November, a new, vital and insidious danger threatened the

60

Irish delegation without their being aware of it. Up till that time they had won their duels, individually and collectively. They had conceded nothing of the Republican aim — Griffith's letter was not, in itself, a concession — and they had been warned that if a break had to come in the negotiations, that break must be on the question of a united Ireland. It was to be all or nothing. So far they had kept in a position to ensure one or the other. On 5 November, from Thomas Jones, one of the British secretaries, came the proposal for a Boundary Commission.

It was made at a time when Lloyd George's proposal of a Northern Parliament subordinate to an all–Ireland one had been rejected by Craig, upon which Lloyd George threatened to resign and retire from public life. Jones, pointing out that this would mean military rule in Ireland under Bonar Law, made the Boundary Commission suggestion. For the first time the shortness of Griffith's spoon began to show. He, naturally, expected to gain from the findings of an independent commission and wrote to de Valera: 'This would give us most of Tyrone, Fermanagh, part of Armagh, Down, etc.' The argument was that what remained would, of economic necessity, be forced to join the rest of Ireland.

But on 9 November, Lloyd George was proposing that a Twenty–Six–County Parliament be set up, and 'a Boundary Commission to de–limit the Six–County area be established'.

Yet the 'devil' had still a further, and even more potent, mouthful for Griffith's little spoon.

Already Griffith had agreed not to repudiate Lloyd George when he said (a) that settlement within the Empire with allegiance to the Crown seemed not unattainable, and (b) that the Delegation's consent to Partition might be won, in an effort to win the northern Unionists to acceptance of an all–Ireland parliament.

The effort was not successful. Lloyd George met with a flat refusal from Craig to consider an all–Ireland parliament. Lloyd George then turned again to Griffith and told him of a last proposal he intended to make to Craig — which he was sure the latter would refuse, thus forfeiting English sympathy.

He, Birkenhead and Chamberlain were prepared to risk their political careers over this proposal before a huge Unionist meeting at Liverpool the same week. But they would present it only if they could say that the Irish Delegation would not repudiate it.

Griffith had doubts. He was being asked to support a proposal which made Partition a possibility, yet he gave Lloyd George the assurance he wanted. He wrote to de Valera:

> . . . (They) are offering to create an all–Ireland Parliament, Ulster to have the right to vote itself out within twelve months, but, if it does, a Boundary Commission to be set up to de–limit the area, and the part that remains after the Commission has acted to be subject to equal financial burdens with England. Lloyd George intimated that this would be their last word to Ulster. If they refused, as he believed they would, he would fight, summon Parliament, appeal to it against Ulster, dissolve or pass an Act establishing the all–Ireland Parliament.

It is hard to avoid the suspicion of collusion between Lloyd George and Craig — a suspicion subsequent events would reinforce. Griffith said that while Lloyd George was fighting the Unionists he would 'help' by not repudiating him. If the Unionists accepted he would not guarantee to accept. Lloyd George got Thomas Jones to write down what had been agreed between Griffith and himself. Jones later showed the paper to Griffith who agreed that it was correct. He may also have signed it. One way or the other, it cost him the advantage he held up till then, and cost him what he spent a lifetime fighting for and two months negotiating for. That paper is one of the milestones on the road leading to Civil War, indicating clearly the immense political foresight and adroitness of Lloyd George who even at that time, could plot for and foresee that Civil War in Ireland could emerge from this Treaty.

Craig did not reply until 29 November. Meanwhile further proposals from both Great Britain and Ireland brought the crisis nearer. The Irish had rejected a tentative offer of Dominion Status, while Britain rejected Ireland's latest offer — a still further modification of Draft Treaty A. On 25 November Collins and Griffith crossed to Dublin for a Cabinet meeting. Two facts of vital significance emerged from that meeting. One was a formula which enabled the Republic to accept the Crown. It was: 'Ireland shall recognize the British Crown for the purposes of the Association (with the Commonwealth) as the symbol and accepted head of the combination of Associated States.'

At the same meeting, when Brugha objected to the concession that an annual sum be voted to the King's Civil List, he was told by Collins that the proposal had already been sent to Downing Street . . . This was the first indication that the delegates were taking any kind of independent action without consulting the Cabinet.

English counter–proposals to those resulting from this meeting based on the status of Canada brought another Cabinet meeting in Dublin on 3 December.

The proposals included an oath of allegiance to the King as head of the State, coastal defence to be exclusively British, Britain to have whatever facilities she required during wartime, Northern Ireland, if she wished, to be excluded from the Irish Free State (title of new state). It was at this meeting that the first effects of Lloyd George's wedges, so skilfully splitting the solid front of Sinn Féin, were to be seen. Already, because of the private nature of the discussions between Collins, Griffith and their British opposite numbers, Gavan Duffy, Barton and Duggan were uneasy. Childers, once a British Diplomat himself, was frantic and is said to have felt that the Republic was almost irretrievably compromised. Eamon Duggan, who, in all fairness, may be said to have been well out of his depth — even the others were struggling to find bottom — had confidence in the two most dynamic personalities on the delegation, Griffith and Collins.

When the Cabinet in Dublin began, on 3 December, to discuss these final British proposals, the delegation was already divided in spirit. It was soon clear that it was also divided in opinion.

Griffith said that the Treaty would almost recognize the Republic. He felt that a break on the oath would satisfy Sinn Féin. He was in favour of getting it accepted by Craig, and of signing. There was no need for the Cabinet to accept it. The Dáil was the body to decide for or against war.[8] He did not like the document, he said, but he did not think it dishonourable.

Eamonn Duggan was in favour of acceptance, believing that more concessions could be obtained. Collins thought the Treaty should be recommended to the Electorate; that many concessions could be won; that non–acceptance of the oath should also be recommended. Gavan Duffy was against acceptance. He believed the Irish proposals could yet succeed. Barton was against acceptance as there was no guarantee against Partition. Erskine Childers, consulted, was against acceptance as the Treaty offered Ireland no national status and made neutrality impossible.

It was clear that, whatever the outcome of the Cabinet meeting, the delegation was well and truly divided. The Cabinet, however, was almost at one in rejection of the proposals.[9]

Barton appealed to de Valera to join the delegation in London for the final negotiations, pointing out, quite properly, that it was not fair to ask Griffith to lead a delegation which might have to choose war, when he himself was already satisfied. For a moment de Valera was inclined to agree.

But Cathal Brugha helped to make up de Valera's mind. Leaning over to Griffith, Brugha asked: 'Do you realize that to sign such proposals would split the nation?' Impressed with the truth of this, Griffith gave an undertaking that he would not accept the Crown as a symbol of the Head of State and would not sign an acceptance of allegiance to the King. He would not sign anything without referring it to the Dáil and if, necessary, to the people (see Note ii at end of chapter).

Comradeship in the delegation had been severed so much that Barton, Gavan Duffy and Childers returned to London from Dublin's North Wall, while Griffith, Collins and Duggan went by Dunlaoghaire (Kingstown). It seems clear that the delegation as a whole believed that rejection might mean war, but were divided in opinion as to whether the end of bargaining had been reached. Griffith, Collins and Duggan felt that it had while Duffy, Barton and Childers — backed by the Cabinet — felt that the British had not yet dealt the final hand.

The issue before the delegates was by no means clear-cut. They had instructions to break, if a break came, on the Six Counties issue. But they had not been directed what to do if these instructions could not be carried out. They were not able to break on the Six Counties. Britain, as was expected, again dismissed the idea of a Republic. The delegates were given no time to return to Dublin for further consultation. On 4 December, the day after the Cabinet meeting in Dublin, Childers, Barton and Gavan Duffy in London prepared a fresh draft of the Irish proposals as outlined in Dublin. But Collins and Griffith, dissatisfied with proposals which — after their long negotiations with the opposite side — they felt sure would be rejected, refused to present them and were supported by Duggan. They said it was for those who wanted a break to present them.

Finally Griffith, seeing that Barton and Gavan Duffy were determined to go and realizing the danger of their going alone — clearly showing to the British the split in the delegation — decided to accompany them.

The proposals were treated by the British as hopelessly inadequate. Griffith, who had been so loath to come, fought for and defended the Irish proposals with sheer brilliance, but with no result and the Irish Delegation returned to their hotel convinced that negotiations had, after all, finally broken down.

Machiavelli writes: 'How laudable it is for a prince to keep faith and live with integrity, and not with astuteness, everyone knows. Still, experience shows princes to have done great things who have little regard for good faith, and have been able by astuteness to confuse men's brains, and who have ultimately overcome these who have made loyalty their foundation.'

Lloyd George arranged, with some difficulty, to see Collins early the following morning. At that Monday meeting at 9.30 a.m., Lloyd George could see that Collins, 'disgusted at what seemed the unrealistic attitude of his friends in the Cabinet and the delegation, but with all the horrors of a split before him . . . had resigned himself to the duty of war.'[10]

Lloyd George was reasonably sure that Collins would accept Dominion Status in preference to war. He became certain of it at the meeting, for Collins never objected to the Dominion clause in the British proposal.[11] Lloyd George was able to reassure Collins on the Six Counties, the Oath, Defence and Trade.

The third achievement of the 'Welsh Wizard' was to get Collins to agree to a further discussion that afternoon between the full negotiating bodies — on the basis of Dominion Status for Ireland — in the belief that Collins (and Griffith) would, in the last resort, accept the British terms.[12]

The meeting was at three o'clock. The Ulster Parliament was to meet the next day and 'from the first moment the clouds of impending war hovered over the Council Chamber and weighed down the spirits of all'.[13]

Collins had succeeded in drafting a form of oath which was ambiguous enough to satisfy English demands and Irish aspirations, he felt. The oath, with minor alterations, became the Treaty Oath.[14]

But beyond that point the Irish — Griffith in particular – remained firm in their determination that, if a break must come, it must come on the Six Counties question. Lloyd George was furious. Then he remembered the undertaking Griffith had given earlier and frantically the house was searched for it. It was retyped and an envelope with a corner of the paper sticking out was shown to Griffith.

Lloyd George reminded Griffith that he had promised not to let him down. Shaking his pencil across the table, Griffith said: 'I have never let a man down in my whole life and I never will.' Then he agreed to abandon the attempt to break on the Six Counties — blinded, perhaps, to the fact that he was letting down his Cabinet colleagues.

Lloyd George pressed his advantage. He bluntly stated 'that the British could concede no more and debate no further. The Irish delegates must settle now.'[15]

Griffith, already torn to shreds, accepted the ultimatum with — to all appearances — his customary imperturbability. What his thoughts were can only be conjectured. Hating war, he chose peace.

'"I will give the answer of the Irish delegation tonight at nine: but, Mr Prime Minister, I will personally sign this agreement and will recommend it to my countrymen."'

'"Do I understand, Mr Griffith,' said Lloyd George, 'that though everyone else refuses to sign you will nevertheless agree to sign?"'

'Yes, that is so, Mr Prime Minister,' replied this quiet little man of great heart and purpose.

'Michael Collins rose, looking as though he were going to shoot someone, preferably himself. In all my life I never saw so much passion and suffering in restraint.'[16]

'Both Michael Collins and Arthur Griffith saw the shadow of doom clouding over that fateful paper . . . '[17]

In Dublin there were rumours that the negotiations had broken down. The Black and Tans and the Auxiliaries were swaggering around the streets and threatening civilians in violation of the Truce. The Cabinet waited for the message from London . . . which never came. Lloyd George dominated the scene in the Council Chamber. A great, white–headed Nemesis he must have seemed to the five Irishmen before him.

He warned them that he had a special train waiting with steam up to catch a destroyer at Holyhead which would go to Belfast. Outside was an emissary, Geoffrey Shakespeare, ready to take one of two letters to Sir James Craig.

One letter said: 'Peace, the negotiations are successful.'

The other said: 'War in three days, the negotiations have failed.'

Peace — at a price — or war. These were the alternatives offered the Irishmen in the British ultimatum.

Collins asked for four hours in which to consider. Four hours passed. Six hours, and the Englishmen still waited for the Irish delegates. It was more than seven hours later, after midnight, that the Irish delegates returned to Downing Street. During that time, first Duggan, then Collins, agreed to sign with Griffith. When Collins agreed, the position of the other two was hopeless. Barton agreed to sign when it was pointed out to him that otherwise he made himself responsible for bringing war on Ireland. Gavan Duffy, though he did not believe the threat of war — which had been made many times during the negotiations — could not take sole responsibility. He agreed to sign. It is inexplicable that before the final decision not one of them considered telephoning Dublin.

The Treaty was signed by the delegates at 2.15 a.m. on the morning of Tuesday, 6 December 1921. A major factor in Collins's agreeing to sign was that he believed from Lloyd George that the Boundary Commission would give large territories — 'Tyrone, Fermanagh, parts of Derry, Armagh and Down' — to the democracy and that 'Ulster' — reduced to an uneconomic unit — would, before long, be forced to become part of a United Ireland again.

It was Collins's decision to sign, more than that of Griffith, which swayed Duggan, Gavan Duffy and, most important of the three, Barton, because — like Collins and Griffith — he too was a Cabinet Minister.

Collins was desperately unsure of the ability of the Army to continue the fight against the British. It seems clear that he set peace above External Association. He was a realist, in the sense that to him a bird in the hand was worth more than two in the bush, however rightfully his. Yet he would have been glad to go on fighting, 'until the surviving soldiers of the Republic dug themselves into the Aran Islands, fighting to the last,'[18] but his instructions did not tell him to do that. They told him to negotiate, and that is what he tried to do. There is little doubt that Collins intended, whatever settlement was reached, to see that it was greatly amplified in Ireland's favour as soon as possible. A famous sentence of his during the Treaty debate says: 'The Treaty gives us freedom, not the ultimate freedom that all nations desire and develop to, but the freedom to achieve it.'

While Griffith was the architect of Irish acceptance of the Treaty, it would hardly have been accepted by either Cabinet or Dáil on his recommendation alone — it was Collins who was the final arbiter. Without him neither Barton nor Duffy would have signed; without his vote a majority of the Cabinet would not have recommended the Treaty to the Dáil, and without his recommendation the Dáil would not have voted in its favour. It is virtually certain that, were it not for his influence, the IRB — which really decided the issue — would have rejected it. The Republic and the Treaty which had been signed could not exist together.

Peace had been the aim of these negotiations and peace was the one thing this Treaty could not bring to Ireland. Winston Churchill, speaking in the British House of Commons on 14 December, said: 'Sinn Féin Ireland demanded an independent Sovereign Republic for the whole of Ireland, including Ulster. We insisted upon allegiance to the Crown, partnership in the Empire, facilities and securities for the Navy, and complete option for Ulster. Every one of these conditions is embodied in the Treaty.'

A few hours before the Treaty was signed de Valera, speaking in Limerick, said: 'This is a separate nation and never, till the end of time, will they get from this nation allegiance to their rulers.' When he heard that an agreement had been signed he came back jubilant to Dublin under the impression that the Irish proposals had been accepted. When the evening papers came out he received a shock! They contained details of the agreement. It had been decided in London — without reference to the Irish Cabinet — to publish these simultaneously in London and Dublin. British and Irish newspapers knew the terms of the agreement before the President of the Irish Republic and his full Cabinet.

Notes:

(i) The exchange of correspondence leading up to the first negotiations is vitally significant, but extremely tedious and already well–documented (Dorothy Macardle, Piaras Beaslai, etc.). Its essentials are that Lloyd George refused to negotiate with Irish Representatives of a *sovereign State,* while de Valera maintained the *de jure* existence of the Republic. Nevertheless it is clear enough that the rock of an independent, sovereign and totally separate Republic was recognized, by this time, as unattainable and, indeed, impractical.

The dangers of oversimplifying a complex situation are, in this context, primarily those of injustice; nevertheless the attempt must be made. In retrospect the issue between Britain and Ireland appears to have been that of an occupied dependent people seeking sovereign independence from the aggressor; and that it was the failure of the resulting compromise to satisfy these aspirations which brought about Civil War. The position, more accurately, seems to have been this: that acceptance of the Gairloch formula, to — 'meet your delegates as spokesmen of the people whom you represent with a view to ascertaining how the association of Ireland with the community of nations known as the British Empire may best be reconciled with Irish national aspirations' — paved the way, not for a totally sovereign Republic — which Britain would never have conceded under the circumstances at the time — but for a form of (External) Association with the British Empire; as de Valera himself said, the same relation as Cuba (then had) with the United States would have been satisfactory.

Yet, although the Cabinet had acclaimed the principle of External Association when he coined the phrase in July 1921, the nature of that association when he put it forward — after the Treaty was already signed — was (a) argued to be unattainable; (b) held only to be a rhetorical substitute for the Republic; (c) called a formula of dissimulation without positive merit; (d) condemned as a sacrificing of real substantial economic aspects of independence — e.g. tariffs, acceptance of National Debt responsibilities to a degree greater than contained in the Articles of Agreement as signed — in favour of an abstract ideal.

It was also held to be a formula which could do all he claimed for it and for the country. It seems likely that it came too soon; when it was easily misunderstood, at a time when freedom meant only one thing and traditional imperialism was still overt. It is nevertheless true that it is substantially this formula which today forms the basis for the relationship between India and Britain, for example.

It must also be emphasized that Partition was not a major issue — though it became a major cause — at this time. Both Irish sides believed Lloyd George when he said that the north–east could not be an economic unit and would be forced to join the remainder of the country after the Boundary Commission. He, alone, it seems, foresaw — and plotted — that Civil War in Ireland could be the outcome of these particular Articles of Agreement. De Valera accepted Lloyd George at his face value when he gave the assurance that Ulster would not be coerced. (Letter to Lloyd George, 10 August 1921; Lloyd George's reply 13 August.)

(ii) Nevertheless the recorded decisions of this Cabinet meeting include one which states: 'The President shall not go to London at this stage of the negotiations.' Implicit in this decision are the assumptions (a) that further and final negotiations were anticipated by the Cabinet and (b) that de Valera might attend these.

[1] Dorothy Macardle, *The Irish Republic*, p. 477.
[2] For full text see Statements and Documents, p. 306.
[3] According to Dorothy Macardle, Griffith himself, months later, in the bitter Dáil Treaty Debates, said: 'To say that we went (to London) to get a Republic and nothing else is false and maligning . . .'
[4] His adherence to principle later on during the Treaty negotiations suggests that the abstract principle itself, more than the material objective, sometimes took first place with de Valera. Having assumed a stand on what he conceived to be a matter of principle, even modification of the rules of conduct governing that principle were intolerable to him.
[5] See Statements and Documents, p. 310.

⁶ Teachta Dála — Parliamentary Deputy, the title of a member of the Irish Parliament.

⁷ Cabinet Minister in each Fianna Fáil Government since 1932. Retired 1965.

⁸ This and the following paragraphs are based on pp. 577–80 of *The Irish Republic* by Dorothy Macardle, in which she was indebted to Robert Barton, Austin Stack and Colm O'Murchada as well as to 'other participants'; Pakenham's *Peace by Ordeal,* and subsequent statements by both parties.

⁹ A form of oath, acceptable to the Republican ideal as he saw it, yet compatible with External Association, was outlined by de Valera.

¹⁰ Frank Pakenham, *Peace by Ordeal.* p. 283.

¹¹ Authority: Pakenham.

¹² Pakenham's impartial account is by far the most satisfactory.

¹³ There are five personal accounts of this meeting, one by Lloyd George, one by Chamberlain — both in the *Daily Telegraph* — one by Winston Churchill in *Aftermath,* one by Barton and one by Griffith.

¹⁴ See Note 11, p. 86.

¹⁵ Winston Churchill.

¹⁶ Winston Churchill. *Aftermath.*

¹⁷ David Lloyd George, *Is it Peace?*

¹⁸ Alasdair MacCaba.

3

THE SPLIT

The announcement that the Treaty was signed was the signal for tremendous rejoicing — even by people not directly affected. In those days when imperialism was still a *modus vivendi*, there was yet a new spirit of Liberalism and Democracy abroad; and the 'Irish Question' had become a test case from which all cases might benefit. Telegrams and messages of congratulations poured in applauding, jointly, both the Irish and the British. The national press of both countries hailed the settlement and praised the Treaty, moulding public opinion as they did so. Only by a section of the populace in Ireland was the Treaty considered a disaster.

'The Treaty', says Pakenham, 'signed as it was, must always have divided Ireland with bitter discord, torn her with conflict between cruel existing loyalties and so preserved her for a space for the British Commonwealth with an economy of British lives.'

The delegates were summoned by telegram to Dublin for a Cabinet meeting. There can be no doubt that they — Griffith in particular — must have anticipated a difficult — even a stormy — meeting and an eventful Dáil session.

The Treaty, though signed, had not yet been approved by the Dáil. The Dáil was entitled to reject it. All might have been well for the future if it had been left at that. But Griffith, feeling, perhaps, that he had put himself and the delegates in a false position, began to defend and consolidate his position as far as possible. Thus he agreed to publish details of the Agreement in the Press before his own Cabinet had seen them. As a peaceful settlement it was bound to win enormous support from the conservative Irish newspapers and from a large proportion of the Irish public.

The only criticism there might be from the British Press and public would not worry the Irish, as it was to be directed at the British leaders and it was not very widespread. For example: 'The document discloses an abandonment and betrayal of British powers and British friends in Ireland. We cannot see our way to join in the finely orchestrated chorus which greets alleged settlement in Ireland.'[1]

In order to secure further public support, especially from America, Griffith issued the following statement before coming to Dublin for the Cabinet meeting: 'These proposals do give Ireland control of her destinies. They put our future in our own hands — enable us to stand on our feet, develop our own civilization and national distinctiveness. In short, we have won liberty after the struggle of centuries.'

Meanwhile de Valera had asked the Cabinet to repudiate the Agreement and to remove from the Cabinet those who had signed it. But William Cosgrave, later head of the Free State Government, asked him to give the delegates an opportunity to explain their actions. At a five–hour Cabinet meeting the circumstances of the signing were debated over and over again. Griffith would not admit duress in signing. Collins admitted 'the duress of facts'. The seven–member Cabinet was sharply divided. For acceptance were Griffith, Cosgrave and, because he had signed, Barton; de Valera, Brugha and Austin Stack, Minister for Home Affairs, were against it. Griffith and Collins, minimizing the duress under which they signed, said that, apart from the ultimatum, there was no moral obligation that prevented signing.

Austin Stack implored them: 'You have signed and undertaken to recommend the document in the Dáil. Well — recommend it. Your duty stops there. You are not supposed to throw all your influence in the scale . . . I believe if the Dáil rejects this we will be in a better position than we ever were, and England will have made only a trap for herself by her action. Will you do it?' Both Collins and Griffith refused.

That evening de Valera issued a statement to the Press saying that he could not recommend acceptance of the Agreement. It read:

A Chairde Gaedheal (Irishmen and friends),

You have seen in the public Press the text of the proposed Treaty with Great Britain.

The terms of this agreement are in violent conflict with the wishes of the majority of this nation as expressed freely in successive elections during the past three years.

I feel it my duty to inform you immediately that I cannot recommend the acceptance of this Treaty either to Dáil Éireann or to the country. In this attitude I am supported by the Ministers for

Home Affairs and Defence.

A public session of Dáil Éireann is being summoned for Wednesday next at 11 a.m. I ask the people to maintain during the interval the same discipline as heretofore. The members of the Cabinet, though divided in opinions, are prepared to carry on the public services as usual.

The army, as such, is, of course, not affected by the political situation and continues under the same order and control.

The greatest test of our people has come. Let us face it worthily, without bitterness and above all without recriminations. There is a definite constitutional way of resolving our political differences — let us not depart from it, and let the conduct of the Cabinet in this matter be an example to the whole nation.

This statement was a blunt answer to the enthusiastic reception the Agreement had received, especially in Britain. It must be set in this context: the day on which the Truce was signed the previous July was a most vital day for the Irish public. To most of them it looked as if peace had already arrived; that a great deal had already been gained. Men who had been on the run for years returned to their families. The signing of a Treaty was of much smaller emotional impact. Now the reality was the prospect of further war when peace had seemed secure. It is hardly surprising that many citizens rejected the idea instinctively, no matter what the cost to an ideal. This 'Peace at any price' feeling in a tired and bewildered people swayed many of them towards support of the Treaty. Nevertheless de Valera's view, though his repudiation of the Treaty and the realization that the insurgent movement was openly split shocked them, was supported by large numbers, both civil and military. But the newspapers could not now condemn what they had already welcomed — and what was, remember, for them a tremendous 'scoop'. They would hardly have supported de Valera anyway. The seven–day delay before the next Cabinet was disastrous to him. In that time public opinion, under pressure from the Church, the Press and vested interest pressure groups, hardened against him. The split that now came into the open had been latent for some time past, and was all but inevitable once the Truce was signed (see note at end of chapter).

It is clear, from the clash of personalities in the Cabinet alone and from individual public utterances, that at least an opposition would have emerged. No matter what agreement was signed other than the full Irish proposals, a splinter group was inevitable. Now Griffith was ready to lead a pro–Treaty party and de Valera one against. 'It was surely not asking too much of collective statesmanship to take precautions so that whatever else ensued there should be no Civil War.'[2] But there was a fatal inexorability about the progress of events between December 1921 and June 1922, when the Civil War began. On the day following de Valera's announcement Griffith issued this statement:

I have signed the Treaty of peace between Ireland and Britain.

I believe that this Treaty will lay the foundations of peace and friendship between the two nations.

What I have signed I will stand by, in the belief that the end of conflict of centuries is at hand.

That same day fifteen Irish bishops, individually, gave their support to the Treaty. The Supreme Council of the Irish Republican Brotherhood, a secret organization to which many IRA officers belonged, under the chairmanship of Collins, decided by a majority to support the Treaty and to inform its members accordingly. A meeting of the Dáil was called for 14 December. The schism was widening and two sets of opinions were hardening. Into the balance on the pro–Treaty side the full and enormous weight of the Church was added to that of the Press of two nations.

On 16 December the British Commons by a majority of 343 ratified the Treaty. The Lords followed suit with a majority of 119. There remained only Irish ratification.

Circumstances, at this stage, seem to have taken control of the men who created them. Bearing in mind the central fact mentioned above, i.e. that it is clear that an opposition, at least, would have emerged no matter what Treaty was signed, it appears that once the split was recognized for what it was, allegiance tended to revert to extreme points of view in contradiction of the facts. These facts were that (1) the Gairloch letter clearly states the terms of reference for a meeting as 'with a view to ascertaining how the association of Ireland with the community of nations known as the British Empire may best be reconciled with Irish national aspirations' (Lloyd George, 29 September 1921); (2) This implied some form of participation within the British Empire; (3) Any form of sovereign Republic outside this field provided no basis for discussions with Lloyd George; (4) Participation within the British Empire was not acceptable to several influential people, and their followers, in Ireland; (5) The inevitable outcome, therefore, of any conclusion reached on the basis of (1) was, at least, a constitutional opposition.

But when cleavage did materialize, passion, personal loyalties, jealousies, honest beliefs made the issue appear simply — which it was not — a matter of a Republic or Commonwealth.

For the meeting of the Dáil de Valera had prepared a re–draft of the Irish proposals. In this he hoped to present something which, rejecting the signed articles, they could accept, and which might also be acceptable to the British. He had no opportunity of presenting this document on 14 December, as the meeting reviewed the circumstances of signing only, but when, at a private session on 15 December, he did bring it forward, it had a poor reception, being opposed on the grounds that the signed articles were a *fait accompli;* de Valera then withdrew his proposal.

Speaking to the Dáil before it rose for Christmas, de Valera said: 'I am against this Treaty, not because I am a man of war, but a man of peace. We went out to effect reconciliation and we have brought back a thing which will not even reconcile our own people.'

Before Christmas of 1921, only a few days after the Treaty was signed: 'Party spirit for the first time split the Dáil into two factions violently antagonistic to each other. For the most part, those who opposed the Treaty would see no good in it, looking down from the height of the Republic, seeing it as degradation and sheer loss; while those who defended its terms'[3] — looked on them as giving Ireland a freedom it had not had in 700 years and as a means towards the end of the Republic.

Those who accepted the Treaty advocated it in the Dáil as an honourable settlement between nations, an entering into the Empire and becoming a Dominion by Ireland of her own free will — but in the face of an alternative of 'immediate and terrible war'. They pointed out that the Treaty gave Ireland full control of her economic affairs, her armies, her own flag. That acceptance of the Treaty at that time did not exclude the possibility of further advances towards complete independence . . . The 'stepping–stone' argument of Michael Collins who said: 'I signed it because I would not be one of those who commit the people to war without the Irish people committing themselves to war.' They had the freedom to advance towards independence and a Gaelic State, he said.

Counter–arguments by the Republicans were that what the Treaty conferred on the people of Ireland had been forced on them and fought against for generations. That for the first time in history the Irish people had voluntarily relinquished its independence and had become a satellite of Great Britain. The Treaty was a renunciation of the Republic proclaimed in 1916, established in 1919 and represented by the Dáil, they said, and that, in any event, the Dáil as an elected Republican administration, had no power to accept a Treaty denying existence of the Republic. The people, they argued, would have to accept or reject the Treaty themselves in an election.

Increasing partisanship and bitterness did not help towards an objective discussion on the Articles which had been signed. But as yet there was no appearance of war. There was, de Valera had said, 'a definite constitutional way of resolving' these political differences. But that way was not to be found. That Dáil session continued until 22 December with nothing concrete emerging.

Speaking for a large minority, who thought the Treaty wrong, but believed rejection of it would mean war; who did not know what to do and who, in large numbers remained neutral in the Civil War, Dr Patrick McCartan said: 'I see no glimmer of hope. We are presented with a *fait accompli* and asked to endorse it. I, as a Republican, will not endorse it, but I will not vote for chaos.'

In an eloquent and moving speech on 21 December Gavan Duffy defended the signing of the Treaty:

'The complaint is not that the alternative to our signing this particular Treaty was immediate war . . . the position was this, that if we, every one of us, did not sign and undertake to recommend, fresh hordes of savages would be let loose upon this country to trample and torture and terrify it, and whether the Cabinet, Dáil Éireann or the people of Ireland willed war or not, the iron heel would come down upon their heads with all the force which a last desperate effort at terrorism could impart to it. This is the complaint. We found ourselves faced with these alternatives, either to save the national dignity by unyielding principle, or to save the lives of the people by yielding to a *force majeure,* and that is why I stand where I do. We lost the Republic of Ireland in order to save the people of Ireland . . .'

This attitude was opposed by such deputies as Mrs Michael O'Callaghan, whose husband, the Mayor of Limerick, was murdered literally in her arms by British forces, who said: 'I cannot see what war has to do with it. If we had not a soldier or a gun in the IRA I would vote against it, Miss Mary MacSwiney, whose brother Terence had died on hunger strike the previous year, summed up the Republican attitude. 'I stand here,' she said, 'for all of the people, and the will of the people of Ireland is their freedom, which this so–called Treaty does not give them. The will of the people was expressed in 1918. The will of the people was expressed in the manifesto which sent every one of you here. And I ask any of you voting for this Treaty what chance you would have had if on the twenty–fourth of last May — (polling day) — you came out for Dominion Home Rule?'[4]

She said that the Treaty represented the life–long ideal of Griffith; that it might have satisfied Sinn Féin before it became Republican, but that 'half–measures are no longer possible, because on the twenty–first of January, 1919, this assembly, elected by the will of the sovereign people of Ireland, declared by the will of the people the Republican form of Government as the best for Ireland and cast off forever their allegiance to any foreigner'. She implored the Dáil to throw out the Treaty, not to commit 'the one unforgivable crime that has ever been committed by the representatives of the people of Ireland.'

Many of those who were still undecided looked to the Army Chief–of–Staff, Richard Mulcahy, for guidance, since it was the Army which would have to withstand a fresh campaign if it came. His position was clear: 'I, personally, see no alternative to the acceptance of this Treaty . . we have suffered a defeat,' he declared. His attitude was that acceptance was a matter of political and — possibly at a later date — military, expediency and not one of principles or ideals. On 22 December Michael Collins moved that the Dáil be adjourned until 3 January. This was agreed. Also agreed between the opposed factions in the Dáil was that there would be no speeches or 'canvassing' for public support by either side. But delay told against the anti–Treaty section. For while their political opponents in the Dáil honourably upheld their bargain, civic, commercial and industrial groups all over the country began a campaign in support of the Treaty and for peace at any price.

During the debates Miss Mary MacSwiney went to Griffith and said: 'Take out the oath and the Governor–General and we'll all be with you.' Not a word about Partition. The current belief was that there was no need to worry: the boundary clause would fix that. She also told Mulcahy that he would be putting the likes of her in jail, which idea he laughed to scorn.[5]

When the Dáil reassembled on 3 January at the National University in Dublin, it had before it the motion for acceptance of the Treaty and for the disestablishment of the Republic. When the Dáil rose on 22 December it is possible that a vote would have favoured de Valera. Eleven days later it was too late.

The public, of course, were edgy and receptive. They were tired of war, and terrified of a new one. Peace was a 'consummation devoutly to be wished', and the Press, with headlines such as 'Rejection and Chaos', 'Ratification or Ruin', exploited those feelings.

At the same time those who, during the struggle for independence, were pro-British, now, as groups or as individuals writing to the Press — in which they received generous space — supported the Treaty. Above all in the churches, always at Christmastide full to overflowing, Christmas sermons calling for peace were heard everywhere. The year 1921 closed in Ireland with a clamour for peace — at any price. Almost the entire middle–class supported the Treaty. The anti–Treaty faction, without the support of Church, Press or, in many cases, local bodies, lost ground heavily during the ten–day recess.

So far there had been no real attempt at analysing the Articles of Agreement which the delegates had brought back. In the Dáil discussion was concerned with why they had been signed — not with what had been signed.

'(An observer) will watch it (The Treaty) driving through the midst of the political leaders, and thence through every community, great or small, in Ireland, a deep penetrating wedge of resentment, alienation and suspicion; in such a way that from now on every motive and intention will be distorted, every act and gesture misconstrued.'[6]

This distortion of motives and principles on both sides was immediate, and prevented any real 'constitutional method' in dealing with ambivalent aspects of the Treaty. Both sides were agreed that acceptance of the Treaty and disestablishment of the Republic should be confirmed by the people in a general election. Agreement was reached between the factions concerning the outcome of the election, expected to favour the Treaty. This agreement came to nothing and the election was held with results favouring the Treaty. But it was conducted under such peculiar conditions that it is not clear whether it did or did not provide a mandate for the acceptance of the Treaty and the disestablishment of the Republic. The Dáil majority treated it as a valid mandate and set up a Provisional Government to put the terms of the Treaty into effect and to disestablish the Republic. The Republicans did not treat it as a valid mandate and repudiated the Provisional Government. The Provisional Government, in the interests of public order and because of pressure from Britain, made war on the Republicans who repudiated that authority.

This was not a revolt against authority in the accepted sense. Many men of sober conscience, who would not normally sympathize with revolutionaries, joined and actively supported the Republicans. Their reasons can be traced back to constitutional abuses on the part of the Government — which the Government vehemently and sincerely denied. Those Republicans who fought and who were outlawed by the Church were men who took arms in the conviction that 'the assault on the Republic, itself a lamentable sacrilege, was being conducted in a treacherous and unconstitutional form'.[7]

Yet the Government could say with sincerity: ' . . it was clear that the first native administration for a century and a half was being deliberately presented with an alternative of abdication or the employment of its armed forces against a section of its own people for the vindication of the right of the majority.'[8]

The single issue from the Dáil — maintenance or disestablishment of the Republic — was so obscured by the time it went before the public, that it is doubtful if the majority were aware of what they voted for. To them it was more likely a 'War or Peace' issue. The election took place in June and what happened between January and June will show why the simple issue became so obscured.

At the re–convening of 3 January, which lasted for five days and ended in a decisive vote, the 'stepping–stone' argument was forcibly put forward by pro–Treaty supporters. In reply Frank Fahy, later Cathaoirleach — speaker — in the Chamber, said: 'Had this instrument been submitted unsigned to Dáil Éireann I feel convinced it would have been rejected with an overwhelming majority. The signing of it does not make it more acceptable, but we must base our arguments and decisions on a *fait accompli*.'[9]

Fahy went on: 'But is not the declaration of the Republic also a *fait accompli*, or have we been playing at Republicanism?' Liam Mellows, to become one of the most tragic figures in the war of brothers, made a moving speech in which he said: 'There was no question of making a bargain over this thing, over the honour of Ireland, because I hold that the honour of Ireland is too sacred a thing to make a bargain over . . . The people are being stampeded,' he said, the fear of war which was the only alternative the people knew of 'is not the will of the people, it is the fear of the people'. He believed that unanimous rejection of the Treaty would put Ireland's case before the world in such a light that Britain dare not make war on the basis of rejection. 'Instead of discussing this Treaty here, we should be considering how we are going to maintain the Republic after that Treaty has been rejected and put on one side.'

The Army HQ was also split, seven members being against the Treaty and six in favour of it. The division extended right through the Army commands, and feeling on both sides ran high. Collins and de Valera both proposed plans which they hoped would bring unity, but these met with such opposition that neither compromise was adopted. De Valera's proposal was the Document Number 2 which was never presented to that Dáil.[10]

On 6 January de Valera offered to resign as President as the Cabinet was so sharply divided, but his followers protested strongly and he withdrew his resignation on condition that the motion to approve the Treaty be taken within twenty–four hours.

Cathal Brugha, in a long, passionate speech, said: 'I am against this Treaty because I know it does not bring peace. When they were in a strong position and England was so weak and had so many enemies — now more than ever — they were asked to do such a thing as this. Why, if instead of being so strong, their last cartridge had been fired, if their last shilling had been spent, if their last man were lying on the ground and his enemies howling around and their bayonets raised ready to plunge them into his body, that man, through the tradition handed down to him, if they asked: "Now will you come into our Empire?" would say, "No, I will not." '

Of the signing, he said: 'They have given certain undertakings to Lloyd George and his friends that when they signed they would recommend. Their undertakings went no further . . . I put it to the members of the Dáil that you should not allow yourselves to fall into the trap laid for Ireland by Lloyd George and into which your delegates fell.'

In reply to this, Griffith said he could not accept the invitation of the Minister for Defence (Brugha) to dishonour his signature and become immortalized in Irish history. He had signed this Treaty and the man or nation that dishonoured its signature was dishonoured forever.

'I believe,' he said, 'that I was doing right. I believe now I did right, and would do the same thing again.'

He said of the charges brought against the delegation: 'When they charge and insinuate that we went with a mandate to demand a Republic or nothing else they are maligning us. If we got that mandate we would finish in five minutes in Downing Street. At a meeting of the Dáil in August, President de Valera made a speech covering the ground on which they went there and saying, with reference to the form of Republican Government that they were not Republican doctrinaires as such, but were for Irish freedom and independence.

'We went to London, not as Republican doctrinaires, but looking for freedom and independence. If you think that what we brought back is not that, that is a legitimate ground for attack, but to attack us on the ground that we went to get a Republic and nothing else is false and maligning ground.'

Did the Treaty give away the interests of Ireland? he asked.

'I say no,' said Griffith, 'but I say it serves the interests of Ireland and I say that it is no more finality than that we are the final generation on the earth.'

Had they no duty, he asked, to the present generation? He said they had and it was the task of political leadership or statesmanship or whatever they liked to call it, to accept the weapons for the time and achieve the best results for the country by keeping the honour of the country safe, and if leadership did not do this it was not leadership.

'We have,' said Griffith, 'a duty to our country and our country is the living people of Ireland.

'Do your duty to your people, do your duty as far as your judgement goes, and do not allow yourselves to be led astray.

'Do not let your feelings tell you to do things you know you could not do, and do not save your faces at the expense of your countrymen's blood.

'. . . You have got to give the Irish people something substantial if you reject this Treaty. You have got to tell them where you are going to lead them, if you are going to lead them anywhere. And you have no objective! This is not sanity, politics or statesmanship. I take the voice of sanity, that this generation is Ireland and has got the right to live for itself, and that the future generation has to live for itself. The Treaty is the utmost Ireland can get.

'We have got to deal with people,' said Griffith, 'we have got to remember that they are our flesh and blood. We have got to remember that we were not sitting at a table playing chess with Mr Lloyd George.

81

Our countrymen and women and their lives and fortunes were what we were dealing with.'

Harry Boland, perhaps Collins's greatest friend — now on the other side of the House — said that in his opinion the Treaty denied the recognition of the Irish nation. He objected on principle and his chief objection was because he was asked to surrender the title of Irishman and accept the title of West Briton. The Treaty was the very negation of all that for which he fought, and it was the first time in the history of this country that a body of representative Irishmen had ever suggested that the sovereignty of their nation should be signed away.

De Valera said: 'Let no man say the Irish people have self–determined themselves within the British Empire as British subjects. The heart of the true Irish people is as Republican today as it was a month ago; as Republican today as it was on 14 December 1918; as Republican as it was on 21 January 1919; as Republican as it was in May 1921.'

He went on: 'The Republic of Ireland still exists; its sovereign parliament still exists and *the resolution recommending the ratification of a certain treaty is not a legal act.* That will not be completed until the Irish people have disestablished the Republic which they set up with their own will.'

During the debate Griffith said of de Valera's proposals for agreement — Document No. 2 — that the difference between them and the Treaty was only a quibble; to which Brugha replied: 'The difference between a draught of water and a draught of poison.' The rift between both sides was now deep and bitter. And it was widening.

On a majority vote of seven (sixty–four for, fifty–seven against) the Dáil recommended the people of Ireland to accept the Treaty. This meant suspension of the Republic for which the Dáil stood. The situation was complicated. The Dáil, as it was, represented the established Republic. The Treaty, however, did not recognize the Republic, only the Southern Parliament which had never sat and was still unrecognized in Ireland. The Dáil could not carry out the work of a Dominion Government. The vote in favour of the Treaty, therefore, left the administration in a constitutional dilemma. While remaining the Government of the Republic until a general election was held the Dáil had to agree to the summoning of a rival — and unrecognized — parliament, largely consisting of its own members, whose purpose was to put the Dáil out of existence. It had to agree to recognize one Government in Northern Ireland as well as its own rival in the south, both of which aimed to disestablish and subvert the Republic as soon as possible. Because the Dáil was elected by the people as the Government of the Republic it obviously could not, legally, accept a Treaty that would 'put the Republic out of business'. Hence the 'Provisional Government' — differing from the Republican Dáil only in name — had to be summoned. It was the bringing into existence — in fact it seems no more than legal fiction — of this 'Government', and its activities against the Republic, that stung Republicans to anger: The Provisional Government's actions were unconstitutional and an abrogation of the rights of the people, they said.

The Government attitude may be paraphrased: no matter what the people wanted two years ago when the Republic was established, they wanted the Treaty now — whether there had been an election to prove it or not. Griffith, satisfied that a majority of the people wanted to accept the Treaty, was prepared to suspend the Republic of which he was head in favour of a temporary Provisional Government, which would prepare the way for a Constitutional Twenty–Six Counties 'Free State' Government.

The anti–Treatyites were adamant about the position which could be altered only by a general election which would clearly show the will of the people. 'No executive that was not Republican could be formed from Dáil Éireann,' Miss MacSwiney pointed out.

De Valera and all his supporters left the House as a protest when Griffith, with a majority of two votes, was elected President; de Valera abstained from voting.

Griffith, who had been elected President of the Republic, replacing de Valera by vote on 9 January, prepared to hold a general election after the formation of a Provisional Government to discover whether the people wanted a Free State or a Republic. A new Dáil ministry of pro–Treaty members was formed.

When the Republican deputies returned to the House, de Valera said that when Griffith acted as President of the Republic they would not stand in his way, but when he functioned as head of another government — the Provisional — they could not give the government recognition.[11]

Even today, looking at the question with an impartiality that recognizes not only the disasters which followed the split, but the firm convictions and the mistakes of both sides, it is difficult to see from whom or from what source the Provisional Government's authority legally came. The only satisfactory answer is the dictum advanced to the author by Earnán de Blaghd (Ernest Blythe), a pro–Treaty Minister: that, in a crisis, those who have the power also have the authority.

The essential thing to remember about the road to Civil War is that those who found themselves on it were very often as confused about what was happening about them as is the casual observer today trying to establish the pattern of what did happen; indeed, for many on both sides, blind conviction, personal loyalties, the accident of geographic location at a precise moment, envy, friendship and similar locomotive emotions were decisive, and substituted for understanding and rationale.

For many more it was a question of what the oath which they had taken required of them. A considerable number, for example, took the pro–Treaty side not on the merits of the Treaty, but on the question of majority rule, not questioning the majority's right; many took the other side for precisely the same reason, questioning the majority's right scrupulously. And throughout the whole confused period, both sides were being continually nudged nearer Civil War by the shrewd statesmen of England who, alone, stood to benefit from such an outcome, morally if in no other way. For part of the immense value to England of her centuries old policy 'Divide and Conquer' is that, no matter what emerges, she can wear the snow–white mantle of Pilate, and say 'I told you so.'

Meanwhile, in Mellows's phrase, the Provisional Government was acting not from 'the will of the people, but for fear of the people'.

As far as the general public was concerned, the 'middle–class', the commercial and trades people and the professional class, by and large, supported the pro-Treatyites, but, and this is significant, in the name of 'law and order' — in other words to protect their own interests. Those who did feel genuinely concerned about the issues involved, found themselves as confused as those who were actively engaged.

The people wanted peace; above all they did not want war; they hoped to preserve and to extend the unexpected release from oppression that had come with the Truce a year earlier. Such was their outlook when the Treaty was signed. Who can blame them for being confused when it was immediately repudiated by the leader they most respected, de Valera? De Valera's personal influence, the logic and justice of his arguments, the belief in the Republic for which so much blood had been shed and hardship borne, won much sympathy for the anti–Treatyites. Nevertheless, as he himself acknowledged, an election at that time would have defeated them. Yet, perversely, while the anti–Treatyites fought the war so that it must be lost — and during the fighting sacrificed the support of many more of their followers thanks to general lack of civic consideration — the war was scarcely over when, in the face of incredible odds, the anti–Treatyites returned a huge poll at a general election. Why?

Because it seems that, though the people wanted peace, they did not like the price they had to pay for it; the aftermath of which was a feeling of guilt. In addition, particularly the very commercial trades and professional classes, hitherto so dependable, disliked some of the policies of the new Government. They now found that they had to bear the burden of rates and taxes retrospectively, a thing they had not foreseen and which struck them where they were most vulnerable, in the pocket.

The tragedy, which grew with cumulative force in six months, has been summed up: 'The people, in so far as they willed anything, willed the Treaty but they did not will Civil War. That became a private fight between two wings, and the anti–Treatyites turned it into a fight of the people against themselves by alienating the populace and arousing the enmity of the people . . .' thus a pro-Treaty officer[12]; and thus, not so dissimilarly de Valera himself:

Soldiers of the Republic, Legion of the Rearguard . . . The Republic can no longer be defended successfully by your arms . . . military victory must be allowed to rest for the moment with those who have destroyed the Republic . . . Much that you set out to accomplish is achieved. You have saved the nation's honour and kept open the road of independence. You have demonstrated in a way there is no mistaking that we are not a nation of willing bondslaves. Seven years of intense effort have exhausted our people. Their sacrifices and their sorrows have been many. If they have turned aside and have not given you that active support which alone could bring you victory in this last year, it is because they saw overwhelming forces against them and they are weary and need a rest . . . A little time and you will see them recover and rally again to the standard . . .

Note: But Civil War was made easy; firstly, the War of Independence, which was a successful military revolution, was a complete failure as a social revolution. When the Truce was signed the disparate elements which sank their differences of outlook to form the homogeneous Sinn Féin with a single dominant goal, national independence, began to look to their own interest and say 'what next? What kind of peace shall we have?'

Secondly, the mass of Irish opposition to Sinn Féin — Churches, Establishment, power-groups, vested interests, the Press, Home Rulers — were enabled to participate actively again in Irish politics without loss to themselves, once Sinn Féin split. Their support of the pro–Treaty element resulted in their out–numbering and swamping those who were actually Sinn Féin and Republican, but pro–Treaty.

Thirdly, Lloyd George was in political trouble in Britain. His Coalition Government was hanging together by a thread and by encouraging dissent and Civil War in Ireland he hoped to preserve support and strengthen his position in Britain, now seeing the first crack in the Empire. He was unsuccessful and fell to Bonar Law later that year.

[1] *Morning Post,* 7 December 1921. The other British newspapers were jubilant.
[2] Pakenham, *Peace by Ordeal,* p. 320.
[3] Dorothy Macardle, The Irish Republic, p.617.
[4] See Statements and Documents, p. 302 for Sinn Féin election manifesto.
[5] Mary MacSwiney was jailed by the Free State authorities from 9 November to mid–December 1922, during which time she went on hunger–strike.
[6] Pakenham, *Peace by Ordeal,* pp. 334 - 35.
[7] Pakenham, *Peace by Ordeal,* p. 335.
[8] Kevin O'Higgins, *The Civil War and the Events Which Led to It,* a pamphlet.
[9] The quotations used here and in the following pages are taken from the Dáil report of the proceedings.
[10] In it he introduced the famous 'External Association' idea, then condemned by his Irish opponents, but given serious thought by British Legislators and successfully used, subsequently, as a basis for India's relationship with the British Commonwealth, for the Cypriot agreement in 1959 and for the Association between Britain and South Africa as well as with several of the recently independent African and Asiatic nations.
[11] The Treaty oath and the Republican oath are given below:

'I ... do solemnly swear true faith and allegiance to the constitution of the Irish Free State as by law established and that I will be faithful to HM King George V, his heirs and successors by law, in virtue of the common citizenship of Ireland with Great Britain and her adherence to, and membership of, the group of nations forming the British Commonwealth of Nations.'

In 1919 every deputy, officer and clerk of the Dáil — and ultimately, every member of the Volunteers and the Irish Republican Brotherhood — took the following oath:

'I ... do solemnly swear that I do not and shall not yield a voluntary support to any pretended Government, authority or power within Ireland hostile and inimical thereto, and I do further swear that to the best of my knowledge and ability I will support and defend the Irish Republic and the Government of the Irish Republic, which is Dáil Éireann against all enemies, foreign or domestic, and I will bear true faith and allegiance to the same, and that I take this obligation freely without mental reservation or purpose of evasion, so help me God.'

[12] M. J. Costello.

4

THE ARMY AND THE IRB

The New Year began with a new Dáil, a new Republican Cabinet, a new Republican President (Arthur Griffith) co–existing with a Provisional Parliament contrariwise — pledged, on the one hand, to maintain the Republic, and, on the other, to break it up.

Every anti–Treatyite in the country looked with suspicion and distrust at the Executive. With five ministers of the Dáil Cabinet also ministers of the Provisional Cabinet, and with every member of the pro–Treaty Dáil also a member of the Provisional Government, this suspicion and distrust is hardly surprising, in spite of the assurance that it was still the 'Government of the Republic'.

'The maintenance of Dáil Éireann as the Irish Republic and the parade of loyalty to it, was, in fact, whether sincere or otherwise, the master stroke of pro–Treaty policy . . . The Dáil became, after 7 January, the matador's cloak; the quite impotent focus of loyalty and hope; the facade behind which the Provisional Government gathered the reins of control into its hands and massed its strength.

'In the heroic years the people had made this image in its own likeness; now, no one wanted to destroy it. If Dáil Éireann had been extinguished by the vote on the Treaty the issue would have been much more clear–cut.'[1]

National unity, that in the past had achieved much, was no longer there and differences were deep and of irreconcilable principle. When the parliamentary split spread to the people and to the army a serious situation arose. Control of that situation would lie with the most powerful body. A period of jockeying for position and power immediately began.

The Provisional Government went ahead ably and with the organizing skill and secrecy which old Sinn Féin had employed against the British — Michael Collins, master organizer, was Chairman of the Provisional Government and President of the Supreme Council of the IRB.

The Provisional Government made a promise to the people of a Constitution which would not be inconsistent with Republican aspirations. It was not explained how this was to be achieved without violating the terms of the Treaty.[2] When the terms of the Constitution — anathema to anti–Treatyites and not published until the morning of the election — were revealed there was no time for the public to pass judgement on them before voting.

The anti–Treaty group were slower to realize that the inevitable struggle for power was at hand and occupied themselves overmuch with legal and constitutional dialectic, now well on the way to being shouldered aside by more vigorous methods. Both sides, under–emphasizing the single issue, Free State or Republic, took to propaganda, over–exaggerating their own merits and, more so, their opponents' treachery. Unfortunately, the activities of individuals on each side provided the other with ample material for their campaign of vilification. Reason and logic appear to have gone out by the back door when the Treaty came in by the front.

Contrary to Provisional Government statements that the anti–Treaty party were in revolt against the wishes of the majority of the people, the other side held that it was the Executive of the Dáil — in the name of the Provisional Government —who were in revolt against the Legislature and Judiciary of the Dáil. Pro–Treaty supporters claimed that the anti–Treatyites were acting contrary to the wishes of the majority of the people. Subsequent events may tend to support this view but the fact remains that the Dáil, not the Provisional Government, was the Government of the Republic until the people said otherwise in an election.

But while maintaining their right to moral victory with this argument, and while their opponents prepared for victory at a more mundane and physical level (the temptation is to say practical, which would be incorrect), the anti–Treatyites neglected to make provision for possible civil war or for winning it. They seemed not only bound to lose such a war, they seemed determined to lose it. Their lack of foresight in not preparing for the defence of the Republic, militarily, politically or economically between January and June 1922, as their opponents did for the Free State, reduced their moral right to fight a civil war.

The Southern Parliament, summoned by Griffith on 14 January, sat for its one and only session, formally ratified the Treaty and established the Provisional Government. None of the anti–Treaty deputies attended.

Michael Collins was appointed Chairman of the Provisional Government, and to it on the same day, the British formally handed over control. Evacuation of British troops and Black and Tans from the Twenty–Six Counties of Southern Ireland was begun before the month was out. After the setting up of the Provisional Government the political battle waned; the pro–Treatyites had won. More and more, the issue became a military one. On the last day of that historic Dáil session in January, de Valera had expressed his concern about the Army.

Mulcahy, new Minister for Defence, reassured him: 'The Army will occupy the same position with regard to the Government of the Republic . . . as we have had to the present. If any assurance is required, the Army will remain the Army of the Irish Republic.'[3]

Griffith, convinced that civil war was inevitable, was anxious to get it over with as quickly as possible. Collins, however, was equally anxious to negotiate and would not succumb to the pressure of the other Cabinet ministers to get it over and done with quickly, so long as he still felt there was hope of a settlement.

Two years earlier, it will be remembered, the Army had put itself under the authority of the Dáil. Now the position of the Army was obscure. Both factions, though realizing that a split in the Army could lead to armed conflict, and viewing the prospect with horror, did their utmost to win Army support, with the effect of precipitating the very split they feared.

Collins's support of the Treaty, and acceptance of it by the IRB through his influence, were major factors in splitting the Army. It is significant that of the six officers in the GHQ staff who supported the Treaty, four were members of the Supreme Council of the IRB. Neither de Valera nor Brugha were members, though they had been. Liam Lynch, a member of the Supreme Council, opposed the Treaty, both for himself and for members of the IRB in his 1st Southern Division, the largest in the Army and about a quarter of the total strength.

The IRB was a compact and powerful secret organization with members in Sinn Féin, in the Army, in the Parliament and in the Cabinet.

Both the 1st, Liam Lynch, and the 2nd, Earnan O'Maille (Ernie O'Malley) Southern Divisions rejected the IRB order in support of the Treaty when it came. *O'Maille's Division went a step further by repudiating the authority of the Dáil and declaring itself independent, which it had the authority to do.*

All over the country during January and early February barracks were being handed over to the Army by evacuating British troops. Barracks and outposts were occupied, in some cases by pro–Treaty and in some cases by anti-Treaty troops. Minor clashes took place. A new police force, the Civic Guard, was recruited by the Government. They were a regular, paid police force intended to replace the RIC and the voluntary Republican police force from which they were recruited, each brigade and division being instructed to supply men for the purpose.

Detective headquarters were at ex–British CID headquarters at Oriel House, Westland Row, Dublin.

De Valera established, and became President of, a new political group called *Cumann na Poblachta*, the Republican Party. At the Sinn Féin Ard–Fheis (congress) the agreement that there would be no general election until *after* the proposed constitution of the Free State was presented to the people, was made. This, at the time, looked like a definite step forward. However, the Government refused to revise the 1918 electoral register before the election on the grounds that there was neither time nor personnel to do so.

Still jockeying, more successfully than the anti–Treatyites, the Provisional Government Cabinet was inclined to anticipate a mandate from the people in support of the Treaty, and assumed a licence to carry out some functions of an elected Free State Government. A body of troops, uniformed, equipped and paid by the Provisional Government, was established with headquarters at Beggar's Bush Barracks, Dublin, on 31 January. Recruited from IRA personnel, it continued to call itself the IRA in spite of raised eyebrows in the British Commons. It consisted of a small but expanding force of men loyal to pro–Treaty GHQ officers. It was the nucleus of the future Free State Army.

As they marched to their new headquarters, Michael Collins, Chairman of the Provisional Government, took the salute at a march past in Dublin. The raising of the Beggar's Bush force threw the whole question of Army allegiance into sharp focus. The Dublin Brigade, which had been something of a *corps d'élite* during the War of Independence, was not allowed to take over any of the evacuated British posts in its area. Maryborough (Portlaoise) barracks was the first occupied by the regular troops of the Beggar's Bush force, who, it should be emphasized, were at that time drawn from all units just as were the Civic Guard. Liaison officers in each brigade took over barracks in their area and in Cork, for example, it was regular troops who took over. What happened later, of course, was that these troops, drawn from the IRA, divided and fell back on old allegiances in one case, and expanded into a full, regular army giving its allegiance to the Provisional Government, in the other. Senior anti–Treaty officers had already agreed that, as the best means of taking control of the Army out of the hands of the Dáil and GHQ, the Army should revert to having its own Executive, and decided that an Army convention, for that purpose and to remove the Army from Dáil authority, should be held as soon as possible. Mulcahy, as Minister for Defence, was asked in early February to call a convention within two months to consider the following resolutions:

That the Army shall re–affirm its allegiance to the Irish Republic: That it shall be maintained as the Army of the Irish Republic under an Executive appointed by the convention: That the Army shall be under the complete control of the Executive, which shall draft a constitution for submission to a subsequent convention.

But Mulcahy instead suggested a meeting between himself and the 'Acting Military Committee of the IRA', of which Rory O'Connor was chairman. At that meeting agreement was reached and Mulcahy prepared to call a convention at which each division would be represented proportionate to its numerical strength. On that basis the anti–Treatyites calculated to have an overwhelming majority and hoped to preserve Army unity into the bargain. At the meeting Mulcahy repeated his assurance that the Army would remain the Army of the Republic. Another effort to preserve unity seemed fruitful. But the establishment of the Beggar's Bush force altered the arrangement.

Then, early in February, the 3rd Tipperary (anti–Treaty) Brigade under Denis Lacy raided a barracks in Clonmel which had been evacuated by British troops and was under police guard, and seized more than 300 rifles, 200,000 rounds of ammunition, two armoured cars, two armoured Lancia cars, ten ordinary Lancia cars and Crossley tenders and two other cars as well as seven machine–guns and hundreds of boxes of bombs. In Tipperary military hutments they got thirty–three rifles, two machine–guns and ammunition. The purpose of these raids was so that the material would not get into pro–Treaty hands. Whole brigades and divisions went pro– and anti–Treaty, and sometimes were divided within themselves. The IRA was now two armies. (Curiously, while the populace as a whole, confused as they were, were ready to accept the Treaty, the bulk of the Army rejected it. This, it has been argued, was because the soldiers had less to lose; more to gain.)

On the other hand, a responsible pro-Treaty source, whose estimate of the situation cannot be dismissed now as mere propaganda, says: 'Many of those who were violently anti–Treaty belonged to the post–Truce army, which had never seen action. They flocked in after the Truce and became more Republican than the Republicans themselves. The position in Limerick was average: and it clearly shows that, for example, the 2nd Southern was divided, roughly, on a fifty–fifty basis.'⁴ In February, passions boiled over in Limerick City which was included in the military area of O'Maille's 2nd Southern Division. Military positions in the city were to be handed over by the British to the IRA on 23 February. Both the Republicans and the Government realized that Limerick was a key position and neither side wanted the other to hold it. The Republicans, however, had the right of occupation.

But Commandant Liam Forde, OC of the mid–Limerick Brigade, over–reached himself on 18 February and played into Government hands by issuing the following statement:

'The aims of the head of the Army and of the GHO staff are now unquestionably to subvert the Republic and support the Provisional Government and make possible the establishment of the Irish Free State. We declare that we no longer recognize the authority of the present head of the Army, and renew our allegiance to the existing Irish Republic, confident we will have the support of all units of the IRA and of the loyal citizens of the Irish Republic.'

The Government reaction to this proclamation was to order Commandant Michael Brennan of Clare's 1st Western Division, known to be pro–Treaty, to move detachments into Limerick and take over positions evacuated by the British on the 23rd. This was the first time that pro–Treaty troops had been ordered into an anti–Treaty area to take over positions evacuated by the British troops, and it raised tension to breaking point. In addition pro–Treaty sympathizers in the mid–Limerick Brigade were organized under the Brigade Quartermaster, a Captain Hurley, and prepared to co–operate with the Western Division in taking over posts for the Provisional Government. But Hurley and his supporters were surrounded and arrested by anti–Treaty units which had converged in the east at the signs of trouble. They were all men of the 1st or 2nd Southern Divisions and were commanded by O'Maille. They occupied several public buildings and hotels in Limerick. The pro–Treaty troops of the Western Division, under Brennan and Commandant Slattery, occupied some evacuated British posts, while two fully armed battalions of British troops were still in occupation of others.

It was primarily the presence of Brennan's troops in Limerick that precipitated the crisis there. There were no large British garrison posts in Clare to be taken over and the Provisional Government had ordered Brennan's Clare troops to Limerick to take over the four barracks there — the New Barracks, the Ordnance, Strand and John's Castle — not, they claimed, because of Forde's statement, but on foot of an understanding that barracks were to be taken over by troops with active service. (Their interpretation of this understanding is another matter, of course; active–service troops were also available in Cork and in Tipperary.)

The situation was explosive, feelings ran high, and at any moment a trivial incident might have created an armed clash which would extend to the whole Army . . . the position threatened civil war. It was, Liam Lynch said . . . 'a disgrace to both sides.'[5]

O'Maille issued Slattery with an ultimatum to evacuate his position in Castle Barracks or be attacked. Only the refusal of Rory O'Connor and Liam Lynch, respectively Director of Engineering and OC 1st Southern Division, both his superiors, to support him and to provide him with explosives, nullified O'Maille's plan. De Valera appealed to Mulcahy to try to reach a solution. The Mayor of Limerick, Alderman Stephen O'Mara, approached Griffith. Finally, when rupture seemed inevitable, Liam Lynch and Oscar Traynor were asked by Mulcahy, Collins and O'Duffy to mediate, which they successfully did. A clash between about 700 men on either side had been avoided by a hairsbreadth — a clash that must, inevitably, have spread.

'It was a happy consummation for me to see about 700 armed troops on each side who were about to engage in mortal combat, eventually leave Limerick as comrades,' wrote Liam Lynch at the time.[6]

But the solution did not satisfy everyone concerned: Griffith in particular, who foresaw a longer and more bitter civil war with each postponement of its outbreak. There were three opinions in Government circles at this time. To the military leaders an armed clash was undesirable as it would undoubtedly send many volunteers to the anti–Treaty side. On the other hand Griffith and several of his Cabinet were anxious for the inevitable to happen as soon as possible, and there were those who hoped for a settlement. At a Cabinet meeting in early March when the Limerick crisis was at its height Griffith at last succeeded in persuading Collins of the need for immediate action. Collins, to whom Churchill had just written apropos the situation: 'Thank God you have got to manage it, not me', despairing of successful negotiations, had reluctantly agreed, when Mulcahy entered the room with the announcement that Lynch and Traynor had been successful in Limerick. Collins was delighted. It gave him an opportunity for further negotiations.

On 27 February, while the Limerick crisis was still unresolved, the Cabinet resolved to hold the Army convention. How far they were influenced in their decision by the Limerick incident is open to question. However, it began to look, if Limerick was settled, as if the Army might be saved and that the split would remain a political one. It was agreed that the convention would be held on Sunday, 26 March. A Council of four officers, two from each faction, was appointed, under Chief–of–Staff Eoin O'Duffy, to guarantee that the anti–Treaty position would not be prejudiced in the meantime.

[1]Florence O'Donoghue, *No Other Law,* p. 202.

[2]Richard Mulcahy, pro–Treaty leader, and retired head of the Fine Gael Party, says that such a promise was necessary in the circumstances, and was not without hope of realization. See Introduction, pp. 14 ff.

[3]This assurance, in the light of what happened next, may be what Mulcahy meant by 'finessing with honour'. (See footnote 2, Chapter 5.)

[4]Lt. Gen. M. J. Costello.

[5]Florence O'Donoghue, *No Other Law,* p. 206.

[6]A letter to the press on 27 April 1921, refuting charges by the Provisional Government that they had done everything for unity, while the other side had done everything possible to break it.

5

THE ARMING OF THE REPUBLIC

By 14 March delegates to the convention were selected in all brigades.
But on 15 March the Cabinet suddenly reversed its decision and banned
the convention. The Limerick crisis was past. Mulcahy, realizing that a
convention would show a large proportion of the Army to be anti–
Treaty, with consequent embarrassment to the Provisional Government,
had the convention prohibited by the Cabinet. Quite evidently the
Provisional Government could not view the prospect of a move to take
the only military force of the country from under its control with
anything but alarm. They feared, it was said, the setting up of a military
junta, although the matter in dispute was one of allegiance.

At all events a proclamation forbidding the convention was issued,
together with an order from Mulcahy stating that any Army officer
attending the convention would be, *ipso facto,* dismissed. This order, of
course, increased the likelihood of an Army split. The anti–Treaty
reaction had been telegraphed some time before when, at the time the
first approach was turned down, Rory O'Connor told O'Duffy that ' . . .
in view of the fact that you cannot see your way to call a convention of
the whole Army . . . a convention will be called by the signatories
referred to '. This was now done and the same date was announced, 26
March. The announcement was signed by fifty senior officers. At a
press conference O'Connor said: 'The holding of the convention means
we repudiate the Dáil'.[1] Every Army officer, whatever his views, was
invited to attend. 'We believe it is the only way to get unity,' said
O'Connor. He prepared to set up an Executive which would issue orders
to the IRA all over the country. He gave as the reason for holding the
convention just what the Provisional Government feared: that it would
make public that a majority of the Army was opposed to accepting the
Treaty. The convention was duly held on 26 March, with 211 delegates
present, representing, claimed the anti–Treatyites, about 80 per cent of
the Army — 95,000 men and more than 200 brigades.

The resolution, proposed originally by Mulcahy, was passed unanimously. A further convention was to be held on 9 April to draft an IRA Constitution. Until then an Executive of sixteen was elected with Liam Lynch as Chief–of–Staff and headquarters at Barry's Hotel, Gardiner's Row, Dublin, which Collins had so often used as HQ during the War of Independence. On 28 March, this Executive issued a statement declaring that the Minister for Defence and his Chief–of–Staff (Mulcahy and O'Duffy) no longer exercised any control over the Army, and demanding that recruiting for the Beggar's Bush force and for the Civic Guard should cease forthwith. The convention and its resolutions were minimized by the press and by the Provisional Government, which, of course, ignored the injunctions against recruiting. The day following the convention the machinery of the *Freeman's Journal* was wrecked in reprisal for an article attacking the convention.

At the 9 April convention — with 217 delegates — a new Army Constitution was formulated. The Constitution set out the aims of the Army, and placed the Army under the control of a sixteen–man executive. This was Liam Lynch (Chief–of–Staff), Rory O'Connor, Liam Mellows, Florence O'Donoghue, Joe McKelvey, Liam Deasy, Earnan O'Maille, Seán Moylan, Seán O'Hegarty, Séamus Robinson, Peadar O'Donnell, Joe O'Connor, Frank Barrett, Tom Maguire, P.J. Ruttledge, Stan Dardise and Tom Hales. The Provisional authorities were aware of what was happening. From the moment of the 'Banned Convention' on 26 March those participating were regarded as being actively mutinous and the representation at the convention was challenged by the Parliament as not expressing the feelings of a majority of the Army.

Liam Lynch wrote to his brother, Fr Thomas Lynch: 'If we can force the Treaty party to draw up a Republican Constitution we are A1 again. This I consider quite possible.' *(No Other Law* by F. O'Donoghue.)

The terms addressed by the new Executive of the Army stating the conditions under which they would agree to Army unity were, however, ignored by the Provisional Government. The new Executive itself was divided and lacking in any serious policy. Discussions frequently veered off military matters and became involved in social questions and theoretical economic systems. Decisions were taken and executed without reference to a common policy. The absence of political leadership or experienced guidance was amply evident. A proposal — rather playing into Mulcahy's hands it would seem — for a military *coup d'état* and subsequently military dictatorship was seriously discussed, but opposed by Liam Lynch and defeated. He at that time realized that whatever strength the Republic had lay in its democratic principles and foundation and in the hope that the Free State Constitution when it came would be one that the Republicans could accept. This promise was made, and was genuinely held, in an effort to hold off a clash. Meantime the Provisional Government grew more and more powerful.[2]

Arms were a crucial problem for the anti–Treatyites as, of course, none of those being handed over by the British to the pro–Treaty troops were available and they had to rely on what small supplies they could get, together with what they already had. The Beggar's Bush forces had, according to Churchill, been given 2000 rifles and considerable ammunition. But on 29 March men of the 1st Brigade (Cork City), 1st Southern Division, brought off a spectacular coup that helped arm the Republicans throughout the South. The story is a dramatic one.

Early in March a volunteer called de Lourey, employed at the British Admiralty HQ in Haulbowline Island,[3] reported to Brigade and Battalion Commandants Seán O'Hegarty and Michael Murphy that an Admiralty vessel, *Upnor*, was loaded with general war–like stores which were to be shipped from Haulbowline on an unspecified date in March in accordance with the general evacuation of British forces. The cargo of arms and ammunition was consigned to Woolwich Arsenal. He thought there might be an opportunity to pilfer some of the arms. The Brigade staff decided that there was an opportunity to get the entire cargo. At first the staff considered capturing the boat in Cobh (Queenstown), the mainland town opposite Haulbowline, and bringing it up–river thirteen miles to Cork City to be unloaded. The disadvantages of this scheme were obvious — the River Lee opposite Haulbowline was patrolled by British Admiralty vessels, and British troops — due to delay in evacuation plans which will be discussed later — were still in Cork Barracks.

The Brigade staff, Dan Donovan, Seán O'Donoghue, Michael Murphy and Seán O'Hegarty agreed to the alternative plan. The responsible officer in Cobh was summoned to a Brigade meeting in Cork City and was told to make arrangements to capture *Upnor* at sea. Brigade headquarters, he was told, would arrange the unloading and distribution of the arms. Details were to be worked out and he would be given further orders as soon as possible. Two days later the Cobh officer was told that Ballycotton, a small seaside resort and fishing village, about twenty miles from Cork, would be the unloading point. Arrangements were already in hand to transport the arms to prepared dumps inland. The Cobh officer promptly made his own arrangements, which included having a fast steam–launch in which to chase and capture *Upnor*. Days passed without further word. One week, two — three weeks. Vigilance relaxed a little. Then at 8.30 a.m. on 29 March word reached the Cobh officer that *Upnor* was due to sail at 9 a.m. and he discovered to his horror that the launch was not in Cobh. What probably happened was that its owners, who were not IRA Volunteers, finding no action on the way after more than three week's waiting, went off for a day's fishing. Money was scarce and unemployment was very high — Thomas Johnson, Labour M.P., established it at 112,000.[4] The Cobh officer tried for other suitable craft, but there was none.[5]

Meanwhile *Upnor* sailed on schedule and cleared the harbour. In Cork, the IRA, whose HQ was in the All–For–Ireland Club, Emmet Place, commandeered lorries and cars on the spot, drivers and owners included, when they received word that *Upnor* was to sail. In this operation 200 men were engaged. None of these 'conscripts' had much to eat that day as it was not possible to arrange suitable commissary facilities. Each commandeered car or lorry was in charge of one or more armed volunteers.

In all, seventy–seven lorries, six steam lorries, several private motor cars and — legend has it — the local steam roller, were pressed into service. Meanwhile *Upnor* sailed uninterruptedly on her way while the Cobh officer was still looking for a suitable vessel to chase her. By now, mid–morning, he had been joined by Donovan, who was in command, Murphy and O'Hegarty. Earlier, about the time *Upnor* sailed, the tug *Warrior* of Lloyd's, stationed in Cobh, arrived and tied up at the Deep Water Quay. It was decided to commandeer her. But when the Brigade officers with the local men went to take over the ship, they discovered that the Captain was ashore — no one knew where.

For several reasons the tug could not sail unless the Captain was aboard. For one thing, if he returned and found his ship missing, he'd rouse the Admiralty, and for another they needed an experienced navigator.

Leaving a boarding party behind. a systematic search of the town was begun. At last he was run to earth in a hotel in company with a noted local Unionist and both were arrested. Meanwhile, a master mariner had been pressed into service as skipper. *Upnor* now had several hours' start

98

— reports vary between four and six hours — and further delay was caused in getting up steam.

'None of us,' says Donovan, speaking of the Brigade officers, 'had been at sea before and we had more qualms about setting out on the ocean in this cockleshell, as it seemed to us, than we had over meeting the combined British Army and Navy.'

Navigating the harbour entrance, dominated by four massive forts, partly subterranean, there was an amusing incident in which the skipper, still a bit disgruntled, snatched the peaked cap from one of the Brigade officers and growled: 'Here, give me that. Did you ever see a skipper without a cap on? What'd they think?' he said, pointing to the gloomy forts and the snouts of the 9.2 inch guns eyeing them.

Clear of Roche's Point at the harbour entrance, a course was set for Waterford. They had half expected to see *Upnor* on rounding the point, but the sea was clear and calm. They hoped to pick her up on the Waterford course quickly. At this stage the anxious men of the IRA, who were crewing the vessel, were stoking so furiously that the crew, afraid that the boilers would burst, asked to be allowed stoke instead. After some hours sailing there was still no sign of *Upnor*. The skipper then plotted a new course for Portsmouth to intercept a direct line taken by *Upnor* which had been expected to hug the coast.

'What time will we catch her, do you think?' asked an IRA officer.

The skipper bent over a chart and pointed: 'I'll head her off just there. We can do three knots more than *Upnor*.' He drew a pencil through a triangle.

'I'll pick her up about 6.30,' he said.

With dusk approaching, Upnor was sighted at 6.30 about twenty miles off the coast with — a surprise — two armed escort tugs flanking her and slightly in advance, and, a further surprise, towing a sealed barge. *Warrior* steamed up at full speed. The men on the bridge waving official–looking envelopes hailed the captain and shouted to him that they had an important message for him from the Admiralty.[6]

Upnor hove to while the armed tugs sailed contentedly onwards. *Warrior* also hove to about 100 metres away and a small boat was lowered commanded by Murphy. In it were four volunteers armed with revolvers and a Thompson gun. A Lewis gun was trained on *Upnor* from the bridge of *Warrior*. With the boarding party was a fisherman, who was to skipper *Upnor* to Ballycotton on a course set in *Warrior*. A formidable undertaking for a tyro. *Upnor*, now towing a barge, was itself all of 700 tons. Complete surprise aided the volunteers, and the aghast reaction of *Upnor's* Captain, when he found himself looking down the barrel of a revolver, was a helpless: 'But you can't do this. This is piracy on the high seas.' By the time some of *Upnor's* crew had been transferred to *Warrior* under guard and both ships were ready to sail for Ballycotton, fifty miles away, it was dark: about 10 p.m. Michael Leahy, Brigade vice OC, had two pilots waiting outside Ballycotton harbour for the ships as they came in about 4 a.m. on 30 March.

The town itself had been sealed off by the men of the Brigade and the army of lorries was waiting under arc lights at the quayside. Unloading began at once. The disappointment was heavy when it was discovered that the barge, towed back with such care, held nothing but office furniture. The cargo of *Upnor* was different. Memories are not capable of pin–point accuracy after so many years, but the most conservative estimate of the yield to the IRA is 1500 rifles, fifty–five Lewis guns, six Maxim guns, three Vickers guns and 500,000 rounds of .303 ammunition, as well as 1000 each of revolvers and .455 automatic pistols with a comparable amount of ammunition, 3000 hand grenades and a quantity of rifle grenade throwers.

Until 10 a.m. the work of unloading the ship and loading the lorries went on until, as the last lorry climbed out of the town with its cargo, a grey shape — the destroyer *Heather* from Cobh — looking for the missing *Upnor*, steamed up to the harbour mouth and covered the town — too late. *Upnor* was empty and the Brigade with its precious spoils had vanished.

Together with 200 rifles and 10,000 rounds of ammunition landed at Waterford from Bremerhaven, brought in by a man called McGuinness, and the material and ammunition captured at Clonmel, the arms and ammunition taken from the *Upnor* represented the only additional equipment the Southern Division acquired before the Civil War broke out, except for odd captures or purchases in ones or twos.

At this time, March, the evacuation of Cork by the British military was suspended because of the disappearance of three British intelligence officers in Macroom, principal town of West Cork. This was an IRA stronghold — its very heart and core — and these officers had no business there in mufti during the Truce. They vanished, and the evacuation was halted. There were three principal barracks in and around Cork City at the time, Victoria (now Collins) Barracks, one of the biggest in the country, Elizabeth's Fort on the opposite side of the city, and the RA (Royal Artillery) Headquarters at Ballincollig, five miles west of the city. Negotiations were immediately opened between the British and the 1st Southern Division HQ.

Representing the IRA was Commandant Dan Donovan. Representing the Cork Infantry Brigade of the British forces was Brigade-Major Bernard Law Montgomery — later to achieve Field–Marshal rank, and distinction for his victory at El Alamein in 1942.

There was some little mystery surrounding the disappearance of the officers, who had lunched in a Macroom hotel, and left it about 4 p.m. or 4.30 p.m. They were never seen again. At 6 p.m. the town was raided by British military and Black and Tans who did considerable damage to people and property.

The close timing gave rise to great speculation. Next day Dan Donovan and two other Brigade officers met six British officers (including Major Montgomery) at Union Quay police barracks in Cork. Donovan and Montgomery were detailed to represent their respective forces.

The British wanted to search the area. But the IRA were adamant. Any searching to be done in their area they would do themselves. They assured the British officers that they knew nothing about the missing men. To which Montgomery said: 'As far as I am aware, if a tramp left Ballincollig the news of his arrival in Macroom would be heralded.'

Donovan agreed that this had been the case, but since the establishment of the Beggar's Bush force there was a change; people puzzled or divided in opinion were now more secretive. Montgomery persisted in requesting a personal search and Donovan in refusing it.

Montgomery, after weeks of negotiations and searching by the IRA proved fruitless, still insisted. 'Well,' said Donovan, 'since you are so insistent, but you may not take more than five vehicles, or if you do I cannot guarantee your safe return.' The convoy set off as arranged, reinforced with fourteen vehicles from Ballincollig. East of Macroom, the convoy was stopped by the IRA and refused permission to proceed since it was larger that had been agreed. Only the intervention of the local parish priest, Canon Treacy, and of Daniel (later Senator) Corkery, prevented bloodshed. The convoy returned to Cork and Donovan and Montgomery met the next day.

The Republicans told the British that they were satisfied the officers were not alive in the area. The British were, by now, satisfied that the

Republicans knew nothing of the disappearance of the three men. The evacuation of the Cork Barracks was re–commenced. Later, the bodies of the British officers were found and, when the British came to collect them, they seemed quite satisfied that the Republicans had not been responsible.[7]

During April the national situation deteriorated rapidly. Military allegiances had divided the Army all over the country, and the respective GHQs were in no position to exercise control over every one of their scattered supporters. Several armed clashes occurred. There were eight killed, forty–nine wounded. Tempers were rising and nerves were overstrained. Civil War, the spectre everyone had been closing their eyes to, now loomed unmistakably over the country.

[1]Which statement caused his political peers a lot of worry, as will be seen later.

[2]There can be little doubt that the material advantage was not overlooked, as seems clear enough from the speech of Mulcahy in which he said: 'It may be said that I was finessing with honour, but I was perfectly satisfied that the situation was not a military situation alone.' In addition, of course, and in fairness it must be emphasized that great efforts were made to secure such a Constitution, which was submitted to the British Cabinet in draft form. But Lloyd George's fear of the Collins/de Valera Pact proved, ironically, to be the catalyst which caused him to reject the Draft Irish Constitution and insist on a British interpretation. See Introduction.

[3] One of two part artificially-constructed islands built by Irish felons in Cork Harbour in the last century. One of the felons was John Mitchel, Irish patriot leader and later MP for Tipperary, editor of *United Irishman*. On one island is a fort for harbour defences, on the other naval administration buildings and HQ.

[4] This, of course, was due to conditions prevailing since the War of Independence when commercial life slowed almost to a standstill for lack of young men, from excessive restrictions and reprisals which included burning out local industries, especially co–operative creameries. It must be remembered that the figure relates to an almost all-male labour force.

[5]Liam Robinson, in the *Sunday Express* 17 May 1959, records Michael Murphy as saying that the IRA had arranged to seize the tug *Hellespont* for the pursuit of the *Upnor*. Donovan does not mention this vessel. Time has undoubtedly caused some of the details to be confused.

[6]The anti–Treatyites had also taken the precaution of stealing the Admiral's ensign from his home in Cobh and this was run up. The suggestion has been put forward that Lloyd George 'arranged' that the idea of capturing *Upnor* be planted in the minds of the anti–Treatyites with the object of encouraging Civil War by arming them to a limited extent.

[7]In a letter to the author Field Marshal Lord Montgomery acknowledged his service as Brigade-Major in Cork at the time, but, while acknowledging also that the IRA were not held responsible for the disappearance of the three officers, would not comment on, or otherwise indicate the reliability of, the commonly held view that they were murdered — possibly by mistake or mistaken identity — by the Black and Tans or Auxiliaries.

6

THE FIRST SHOTS

No longer able to ignore the prospect of a Civil War, both sides began a series of earnest moves towards reunification. Within the secret organization, the IRB, conferences took place at which Michael Collins and Liam Lynch, friends and comrades with deep mutual respect, sought time and again as leaders of their respective factions to find a solution.

A committee of IRB officers — three from each side — was formed on the suggestion of Florence O'Donoghue, Adjutant of the 1st Southern Division. They, in turn, proposed a joint committee from the divided Army, which could act in public. But all these meetings proved inconclusive. No satisfactory compromise could be reached. The terms of the Constitution were still undisclosed and efforts made by the pro–Treatyites to persuade the anti-Treatyites to accept the *status quo* until it was published were unavailing. Besides these efforts of the IRA, the civil and ecclesiastical authorities, with other military leaders, were sparing no effort to prevent the gulf widening.

On 13 April the Republican Army Executive, anxious to set up a permanent headquarters in Dublin, established themselves in the Four Courts, James Gandon's masterpiece and Dublin's high–domed judicial centre on the Liffey Quayside. The 1st and 2nd Battalions of the Dublin Brigade — a total of 120 men — garrisoned the building. Subsequently the Masonic Hall, the Ballast Office and Kilmainham jail were also occupied.

One of the first actions of the Four Courts HQ was to order the seizure of £50,000 from the Bank of Ireland, financial agents for the Provisional Government, on the grounds that the latter had not honoured their undertaking to pay traders throughout the country for goods — mostly foodstuffs — required by garrisons taking over from the British, when these garrisons were anti–Treaty. The money was wanted for that purpose. The Provisional Government, with some justification, made considerable capital of this event. Meanwhile, armed clashes continued throughout the country. Early in May anti–Treaty forces tried to drive pro–Treaty troops out of strategic Kilkenny City, and occupied Ormonde Castle — for two centuries the seat of the Butlers, Earls of Ormonde — two military barracks and the City Hall. Pro–Treaty troops of the now rapidly expanding new force were rushed from Dublin. More anti–Treatyites from the 2nd Southern Division in O'Maille's neighbouring Tipperary converged from the West. There was some firing, but no casualties. Both sides accepted an agreement made in Dublin which left positions to both sides in the city. The Dublin agreement was part of the constructive work done at the meeting between representative officers seeking unity. It seems to underline, however, that the most they were able to do was prevent the situation getting out of hand.

At this time the Hierarchy, sitting in Maynooth College, the major seminary in the country, solemnly condemned the anti–Treaty Executive and its attitude. This, though not unexpected, was a severe blow to the Republicans, most of them Catholics, whose faith and its observance were dear to them. Nevertheless they believed that they were right and the bishops and the Provisional Government wrong, and literally stuck to their guns.

'The forces accumulating towards a conflict seemed to be acquiring a momentum that would presently be too strong for any human effort to control.'[1]

In May, too, ten Army officers, five from each side — including Collins, but not Lynch, who had little confidence in further meetings — submitted proposals which they felt might provide a basis for unity.[2] The anti–Treatyites disclaimed knowledge of these proposals on the grounds that implicit in them was acceptance of the Treaty by both parties. Some idea of the anxiety and confusion at this time may be judged from the fact that when the anti–Treaty Executive issued its statement, three of its members already had their names on the signed proposals. In spite of the disclaimer the effort looked promising and on the day after publication Dáil Éireann, in session, admitted a deputation — a unique incident in parliamentary evolution — and permitted an outsider, Seán O'Hegarty, OC Cork No. 1 Brigade, to address the House from the floor.

'He called upon Dáil Éireann as the Supreme National authority to act promptly, to act with wisdom and courage, in endeavouring to find a solution which would save the country from Civil War.'[3]

The Dáil formed a committee of ten, under the chairmanship of Mrs Tom Clarke, widow of an executed signatory of the 1916 Proclamation of the Republic, for this purpose. Next day, 4 May, a four–day truce was agreed between the rival Army factions and when it expired a joint statement from the respective Chiefs–of–Staff, Eoin O'Duffy and Liam Lynch, continued it indefinitely.

But the results of these efforts were disappointing. Neither civil nor military committees, working independently, could find a basis for unity. However, out of a Dáil debate on the Committee reports came a request that de Valera and Collins re–examine the original proposal. For two days, 18 and 19 May, they did so and on 20 May the Collins/de Valera pact was announced.[4]

At last it seemed as if Civil War could be averted. The nation looked up in hope.

The pact, in essence, provided for a General Election to form a Coalition Government, in proportion to the pro– and anti–Treaty representation returned to the Dáil. Sinn Féin — the original undivided party — was to put forward a panel of candidates. From those elected would come the new Ministers, five pro–Treaty and four anti–Treaty, with Griffith as President; the Minister for Defence was to be approved by the Army Council — therefore likely anti–Treaty. It would be the third Dáil in succession to the first two and not the Provisional Government. If the Coalition failed, a new General Election on the Treaty issue was to be held as soon as possible.The Coalition proposal was also accepted by the anti–Treaty military leaders, who drew up an agreement with the Beggar's Bush leaders for joint control of a unified Army. But the British Government, uneasy since unity moves first looked promising, now became very alarmed. The prospect of political and military unity in the South of Ireland they found extremely unsatisfactory. The reactions in Westminster are best summed up in the following extracts from statements by some of the principal Unionist leaders. In Liverpool, that curious Irishman, Sir Henry Wilson, said on 25 May: ' . . . the surrender of the Provisional Government to de Valera, was 'one of the most pitiful, miserable and cowardly stories in history.' He said in Belfast next day: 'There is grave danger that the British Cabinet will come to the view that the pact between Mr Collins and Mr de Valera *does not* violate the Treaty.'

Churchill, in the Commons, reassured him: 'If the Republicans were to become members of the Government without signing that declaration (of allegiance), the Treaty is broken by that very fact, at that very moment, and the Imperial Government resumes such liberties of action, whether in regard to the resumption of powers which have been transferred or the re–occupation of territory, as we think appropriate to the gravity of the breach . . . In the event of a setting up of a Republic it would be the intention of the Government to take Dublin as one of the preliminary and essential steps for the military operations.'

Birkenhead made a speech in which he said that in no conceivable circumstances would they consent to the inclusion in an Irish Government of men who excluded themselves from the fullest obligations of the Treaty. He said: 'Should a crisis arise the resources of *civilization* are by no means exhausted — and England would be in a much stronger position to resume the inevitable bloody struggle.'

Such was the reaction in Britain, which Collins and Griffith soon had to face when summoned to London by Lloyd George. The reason for this apparently extreme British reflex is not hard to find. While the IRA was sharply — even bitterly — divided on all points of principle affecting the Treaty, there was one aspect of national defence on which they had a common policy at all times. This was in regard to the north. Even while the Limerick and Kilkenny crises threatened sudden Civil War, while military committees were meeting daily in desperate efforts to halt the momentum–gathering slide towards disaster, Lynch and Collins worked in unison on plans directed against the Northern Government.

Specially trained officers of the 1st Southern Division were drafted into the Six Counties to lead the less experienced Northerners. They were to continue the war in the North and plans for a general attack on the British and 'Special'[5] forces in the Six Counties were being drawn up by joint effort. Arms and equipment handed over to the Provisional Government were being passed to anti–Treatyites in exchange for a similar amount which went direct to the north. The purpose was, of course, to avoid a contretemps if weapons known to have been handed to the Provisional Governments were captured and identified. Lynch hoped that such activities would eventually lead to a united front in the south again. Collins's purpose is not so clear, except on the basis that he had complete faith in the 'stepping–stones' argument. In this connection it is significant that, about this time when speaking to an officer, Eamon Horan, then neutral, in Tralee, he said: 'Support me now and I guarantee you'll have a Republic in four years.'

The British Government were not totally aware of these activities, but they feared, with justification, that a united south meant a concerted attack on the north. This they were determined at all costs to prevent. Consequently, when news of the Pact reached them, Griffith and Collins were summoned to London for an explanation. There is the evidence of Churchill that Griffith did not approve of the Pact. Collins was embarrassed but defiant. Threats of re–occupation and war were renewed and the fact that fresh troops were in the north and plans for a naval blockade of the south were on the drawing–board, was added. England's fears are perhaps best summarized by the *Morning Post* which openly hoped to see the Provisional Government deal with the Republicans by force of arms. Otherwise they believed a conflict would break out in the north–east between Orangemen and Republicans which would mean the resurgence of pure Republicanism with a re–united rebel Ireland behind it. Under the shadow of the threats which this fear inspired, and while Griffith and Collins were in London, Ireland prepared for the election on 16 June — the election that became known as the Pact Election. The Coalition proposal — the Pact — began to draw more and more criticism from Government supporters and Darrell Figgis, a prominent member of the Sinn Féin Standing Committee, publicly attacked it in a speech on 25 May.

However, it still looked as if the Pact might be the means of securing Irish unity. Figgis was not over–popular with either side and Government leaders had not dishonoured the Pact. Collins had said that only enemies of Ireland were displeased with it. By early June the Draft Constitution of the new State was submitted to the British Cabinet for approval.

A word here about the Treaty framed with 'meticulous ambiguity',[6] and the kinds of Constitution which might honour it. The Treaty was capable of two clear interpretations, one so narrow that Lloyd George was able to 'sell' it to a Conservative and Imperialist Government, and one so wide that Michael Collins had been able to persuade half of Ireland that it gave a Republic in all but a name. In the belief that the widest possible Constitution in Ireland's favour would be forthcoming, with a united Government and a united Army behind it in support, the anti–Treatyites signed the Coalition Pact to avoid Civil War. In their turn, in the same spirit, the Irish Committee had drawn up a Constitution as favourable to Ireland as possible. Lloyd George and his Cabinet would not accept this. They altered the Draft Constitution and about the result the *Sunday Times* said: 'Instead of weakening the Treaty, as was generally expected in Ireland, it underwrites the Treaty, and underscores the Treaty in a most emphatic manner. The English victory is plain.'

Publication of the new Constitution, however, was postponed until the morning of polling day in Ireland. Even in the British House of Commons protests were heard that the Irish people were not to have the opportunity of approving their Constitution before voting. Then, in Cork on 14 June, two days before polling day, fresh from an interview with Lloyd George in London, Collins made a speech which was a repudiation of the Pact agreement.[7]

'After such a speech,' said the *Daily Mail,* 'the Pact can only be described as breaking up.'

On the morning of polling day the Constitution was published in Dublin. Obviously in most areas at any remove from the city it was never seen at all that day, and even those who did see it had no chance to digest it, or to discuss it, before voting. The result of the election was curious. The pro–Treaty party dropped eight seats to fifty–eight, the anti–Treatyites dropped twenty–two seats to thirty–six, Labour seventeen, Farmers seven, Unionists (Trinity College) four, Independents six. The general cloak–and–dagger atmosphere surrounding the progress of events from the Pact, through the Constitution discussion in London to the election on June 16, had produced an entirely new set of stresses and a situation far from clear, on top of one already highly complicated.

The anti–Treatyites claimed that the election — not so much in spite of their losses but because of the substantial gains by Labour, Farmers and Independents — was a clear manifestation of the people's desire for peace. The pro–Treaty party, however, consistent with their policy all along, took the result as a clear mandate for the Treaty. There was now no indication that a Coalition — which might yet prevent Civil War — was in the offing. De Valera optimistically expected a request for his nominees, but that request, not surprisingly, never came. The Provisional Government had tight hold of the reins.[8] The power they needed earlier was now in their hands. The Republicans had let it slip.

Events now moved swiftly and dramatically to a climax. The political situation, so carefully plotted towards improvement, was now worse than ever. The Army cleavage widened when the Constitution was published. The same Army delegates who proposed the measures for Army unity met on 18 June in convention to adopt those measures. As soon as the proposals were read there was a storm of protest. Distrust

108

and suspicion of the other faction, abated before the election and publication of the Constitution in an effort for peace, flamed higher than ever. Cathal Brugha and Liam Lynch, still hoping for the best, supported the motion. Tom Barry, a West Cork Column Commander at that time, proposed that, instead of discussing the measures any further, they should serve seventy–two hours notice of the ending of the Treaty to General Macready and resume war against any British forces remaining in the country. This proposal really put the cat among the pigeons. It was opposed vigorously by Lynch, Brugha and most of the delegates of the 1st Southern Division — to which Barry himself belonged — but was supported by twelve of the sixteen strong Army Executive. Barry and his supporters believed that such action would bring the pro–Treaty Army men in Beggar's Bush, and throughout the country, back in a united front with them against the common enemy. On a show of hands it looked as if the motion had been passed, but on a ballot it was defeated by 118 to 103.

The minority, however, did not abide by the decision of the ballot. They left the Convention, returned to the Four Courts and secured it against Brugha, Lynch and their followers, mostly belonging to the 1st Southern Division.[9] These established their HQ in the Clarence Hotel, not far from the Four Courts on the other side of the River Liffey. The situation would have been Gilbertian if it had not been so heavily invested with tragic undertones.

What happened next was unexpected, disastrous and at the same time precisely the weapon Lloyd George now needed to put the last ounce of pressure on Griffith and Collins. On 22 June Sir Henry Wilson, fanatical anti–Irishman, was shot dead in London by two London IRA men, Reginald Dunne and Joseph O'Sullivan. The order for Wilson's execution — murder it was claimed in Britain — has been traced to Collins, but whether he issued the order before or after the Truce is in doubt.[10] Lloyd George acted immediately. He insisted, in a letter to Collins, that the anti–Treatyites were responsible and that failure to take strong and prompt action against them would be considered a breach of Treaty. In the light of what happened a week later Collins's reply is more than significant. He made a statesman–like and dignified answer — which de Valera has called 'a very proper reply in the circumstances' — asking for Lloyd George's proof that the shooting had been the work of anti–Treatyite volunteers. Collins, of course, was well aware that it was not, but it is amply clear that he did not wish to misuse this knowledge and even bearded Lloyd George in his den in face of the reiterated threat of a breach of the Truce.

However, Lloyd George had another string to his bow. Macready was summoned to Downing Street and asked if he could capture the Four Courts at once. The same day a military conference on the same question took place in Dublin between Griffith and British officers. Back in Dublin on 24 June, Macready got orders to attack the Four Courts on the 25th. Next day, however, before the attack was launched the order was countermanded. Instead an ultimatum was sent out to the Provisional Government to do so. This ultimatum put the Provisional Government leaders in a dilemma. The new parliament was due to meet in five days' time on 30 June and a Coalition Cabinet set up. Now was the time to close the ranks once and for all in face of the common threat, but instead, the Provisional Government decided to form a government of its own, accept the British ultimatum and stamp out armed opposition once and for all.

This decision to attack the Four Courts was attributed to the arrest by the Four Courts men of General J. J. (Ginger) O'Connell of the Beggar's Bush forces, in reprisal for the arrest of a Republican officer, Leo Henderson, who had been captured while commandeering transport to take a column to the North, a project on which there had hitherto been agreement by both parties. That an attack on the Four Courts was pending was commonplace talk in Maryborough for weeks beforehand. Considerable shooting had been taking place, particularly in Dublin, for some time at several military posts of the pro–Treaty forces. The catalyst was the arrest of J. J. O'Connell, pro–Treaty authorities maintain. They support this claim with a list of attacks on their posts or on banks. At Tullamore, where the bank manager was shot, something like £75,000 was taken. The anti–Treatyites' case is that these monies, taken mainly from banks through which the Provisional Government negotiated, were to pay for equipment, salaries and food promised by the Government, but not forthcoming.

In many parts of the country small outposts of pro–Treaty troops were withdrawn two or three days before the Four Courts attack because of the increasing number of incidents and 'the likelihood of an outbreak'.

'There was great pressure from the public and from Griffith to restore public order,' says one source.[11] The excuses, for excuses there are bound to be, surrounding the actual attack, are so much brushwood.

The basic reason would seem to be, clearly, the British fear, rising progressively since the Pact, and culminating in the death of Wilson, of a united troublesome Ireland.

Pressure was brought to bear on Griffith — already more than half convinced that Civil War was on the way — to attack the Four Courts, and he succumbed without attempting arbitration or mediation — though both the Archbishop and Lord Mayor of Dublin were at hand for that purpose.

About 2 a.m. on the morning of 28 June the streets around the Four Courts were suddenly filled with troops and armoured vehicles, some of which were driven against the gates to block them. The garrison prepared for defence. Some of the men wanted to attack, but O'Connor was adamant that the other side should fire first. At 3.40 a.m. Commdt. Tom Ennis of the Government Forces sent in a note demanding the surrender of O'Connell and the vacation of the Four Courts before 4 a.m. It was rejected at seven minutes past four and the guns across the river acquired from the British troops still in Dublin and manned by Beggar's Bush troops, opened fire on the historic building. The Civil War had begun. Nobody is ever likely to know precisely what motives made Griffith and Collins agree to this attack. The sequence of events, in précis, suggests a possible motive.

The Republican Executive was split from 18 June, and the majority were with the more extreme revolutionary section in the Four Courts. The Provisional Government knew this. Collins and Griffith, the targets for British dissatisfaction over the Pact and the proposed Constitution and Coalition, became subject to extreme pressure when Wilson was killed. Collins's first reaction to the British demand to quash the Republicans on 23 June was to politely dig in his heels. He would not be the agent of Civil War. Then came Griffith's conference in Dublin with British military — Griffith viewed the Pact with suspicion and was anxious to get the clash, which he believed inevitable, over and done with.

Next came the British ultimatum. To Collins the position must have seemed: attack the Four Courts or be attacked by England. Civil War, deadly and prolonged or . . . but would Civil War be prolonged? Wasn't there a split in the ranks of the anti–Treatyites? In fact were not the leaders of the biggest fighting groups divorced from the Four Courts extremists? Hadn't they already withdrawn their support from the Four Courts, and wasn't there now little more than a local garrison to deal

111

with?

These questions must have crossed his mind. It may well be that in the answer to them seemed a solution to the difficulties of the Provisional Government. If all they were faced with was a small group of men in the Four Courts these might be easily and quickly subdued, and after that it would be plain sailing. Not really Civil War at all, merely suppression of a small body of recalcitrants who didn't support the Provisional Government, the Pact or the majority of their own comrades. It may well have seemed an opportune moment to secure peace at very little cost.

But what Collins and the Provisional Government did not know was that the rift between the Four Courts and the Clarence Hotel was all but healed. During the ten days of Republican chaos following the split on 18 June each party had come to realize its dependence on the other in this moment of crisis, and full Executive meetings were still being held in the Four Courts, attended by officers from the Clarence Hotel HQ. Liam Lynch left the Four Courts only a few hours before it was attacked. Civil War was certain if either anti-Treaty HQ was attacked — but did Collins and Griffith know this? There is no clear-cut answer. If they did it is reasonable to assume that they became, under pressure, blinded to the facts by the possibilities of a quick victory.[12]

[1]Dorothy Macardle, *The Irish Republic*, p. 702.
[2]See Statements and Documents p. 331 for full text.
[3]Florence O'Donoghue, *No Other Law* p. 238.
[4]See Statements and Documents for short text of Pact, p. 332.
[5]A, B and C Specials, the 49,000 strong force who were largely responsible for the systematic terrorism against Nationalists and Catholics in the north in 1920–22, in which time 23,000 people were driven from their homes, 700 were killed and 1500–2000 wounded.
[6]Frank Gallagher, *King and Constitution,* a pamphlet.
[7]The Pact, remember, provided for a Sinn Féin panel of candidates from both factions to go forward together. Voting was to be by Proportional Representation so that the second and third votes of each elector might well go to the opposite faction. Collins asked the people of Cork to vote pro-Treaty only.
[8]It is interesting to note that the Provisional Government did not have an overall majority. Supported by the Unionists, they would have had — with a margin of two. They were unquestionably the strongest party in the south after the election. The Republicans say that, because of the last minute repudiation of the Pact, the Government party confused the issue, and that, first and foremost, the issue was not the Treaty, but a constructive coalition. In any event the pro-Treaty party would probably have topped the poll. The results of the election did not become known until June 24 — four days before hostilities began.

⁹This left the Four Courts, with few active troops, immediately available. Most of the senior officers, with the exception of O'Malley, were not unit commanders. Rory O'Connor was Director of Engineering, Liam Mellows, Director of Training. Whereas the 1st Southern Division was by far the best and biggest single fighting machine in the ranks of the IRA and had the ablest and best-trained officers. O'Malley, in his *On Another Man's Wound*, remarks on this difference between the Corkmen and his own easygoing Tipperary and Limerick troops. Tom Barry, as 1st Division officer, did not go to the Four Courts with those who supported his motion, but was captured later trying to fight his way in to join them when the Four Courts was attacked.

¹⁰In a private conversation with the author in 1987, shortly before his death, Seán MacBride said that he was satisified the order was issued by Collins and that he was 'well aware of it.' MacBride, although a member of the Four Courts Garrison, was working for Collins on the joint Arms-for-the-North-Plan, and — sad comment that it is on the roller-coasting events — met him on the night before the Four Courts was attacked.

¹¹Col. Patrick Paul.

¹²It is emphasized that this interpretation is conjecture which is open to contradiction. But the possibility of the Provisional Government ignoring significant information because they did not believe it or for whatever reason is no more difficult to accept than the fact that the anti-Treatyites in the Four Courts knew for more than twelve hours beforehand that they were going to be attacked and yet they did nothing about it, or disbelieved it. Certainly Lynch, who left the Four Courts a short while before the attack, either did not know about it or did not believe it would happen. (See Introduction to previous edition.)

PART TWO

THE CIVIL WAR

Chronology of Battles in Campaign

	from	*to*
Dublin	28 June	5 July 1922
Blessington	2 July	7 July 1922
Limerick	2 July	20 July 1922
Waterford	28 June	21 July 1922
Tipperary	9 July	30 July 1922
Carrick-on-Suir	28 July	2 August 1922
Clonmel	8 August	10 August 1922
Wexford		
The West	June and July	1922
Midlands		
Dublin	6 July	5 August 1922
Dundalk	28 June	15 August 1922
Kilmallock	21 July	5 August 1922
Tralee	2 August	6 August 1922
Cork	28 July	12 August 1922
Collins (Beal na mBlath)		22 August 1922
Munster		July, August, September 1922
Kerry		Autumn 1922 - Winter 1923

7

DUBLIN IN ARMS

In spite of the congregation of events since January; in spite of the external withdrawal by both sides from the common centre that had once united them; in spite of indications and warnings — several of them in blood — that only an isolated spark was needed to cause the explosion; in spite of the accumulation of evidence showing that power governing the march of events had passed from the collective mind to the collective muscle, neither side was fully prepared for civil war when it struck.

The Provisional Government, expecting only local resistance, were not prepared for it; the divided anti–Treatyites, with neither government nor unified military leadership, were taken by surprise — and the people had closed their minds to the thought of further bloodshed and had pinned their hopes on the Pact, the election and peace under native government. Consequently when the shooting began in Dublin on that dull June morning, it had immediate and unforeseen reactions — (and how often had the course of history turned on a similar chance?) — that laid down the pattern which the Civil War was to assume.

If the anti–Treatyites outside the Four Courts were horrified at the attack on their comrades within, the Provisional Government though anticipating that Oscar Traynor, OC of the Dublin Brigade, might occupy positions in O'Connell Street and Parnell Square, were shocked when anti–Treaty officers in the Clarence Hotel at once returned to their comrades in the Four Courts. Liam Lynch resumed the post of Chief-of-Staff which he had relinquished at the 'split' convention ten days before.

Many citizens, with Lloyd George's threats still fresh in their minds, jumped to the conclusion that British warships were shelling the city. The attitude of the British Cabinet is best summed up in Birkenhead's earlier remark: 'War by the Irish on the Irish is the kind of political development which I observe with great pleasure.'

In the dismal pre-dawn a drizzle blurred the yellow lights on the tramway standards on 28 June 1922. Dublin was grey and troubled in the half-light through which, not much earlier, the tramp of men marching through the streets of the worried city had dragged the curious from uneasy sleep. The columns tramped, two long files of Irish soldiers in green uniform, fully equipped for war, on either side of the streets. No one seemed to know where they were going, save that they headed northwards from their barracks in Beggar's Bush in the south side of the city, as they were swallowed up in the mist beyond the glowing lights with nothing but the tramp of feet hanging in the streets. Behind them lumbered — grim emblems of mercy — scarlet crossed ambulances, stretchers empty and folded. It was a dirty morning and the first blackbird had welcomed it doubtfully when the field guns opened up. Daylight comes quickly out of the sky in midsummer and by half past four a knot of spectators — who were to become an increasing menace, especially to themselves, during the eight-day battle for Dublin — were already gathered on O'Connell Bridge looking up-river to where the bronze dome of the beleaguered Four Courts towered fifty feet above the surrounding buildings.

The troops attacking the Four Courts were under Commandant Tom Ennis, but the artillery was in charge of Commandant General Emmet Dalton who had two batteries handed over to him by General Macready. Anti-Treaty sources maintain that they were crewed — or, at all events, officered — by Royal Artillery personnel. The pro-Treatyites denied this, though it is true that the gunners had been in the British Army.

Within the Four Courts was a total of about 180 men, under the command of Commandant Patrick O'Brien, and the twelve members of the Army Executive, which included Rory O'Connor, Earnan O'Maille, Liam Mellows, and Joe McKelvey. The latter issued a proclamation,[1] and de Valera issued a public statement in which he said: 'At the bidding of the English, Irishmen are today shooting down in the streets of our capital brother-Irishmen—old comrades in arms . . . '. He then reported to his old battalion of the Dublin Brigade, the third, and was attached to HQ Staff in the Hammam Hotel.

Traynor occupied positions in the centre of Dublin — not dissimilar to those taken by the Volunteers in the 1916 Rising — which made a great triangle, one corner of which was Moran's Hotel, Talbot Street; another the famous landmark — Nelson Pillar; and the third, Barry's Hotel in Parnell Square. Other strategic positions in the city were also occupied, but this triangle was the principal anti-Treaty area. Streets approaching these positions were mined.

The relative strengths of the opposing forces at this time were in sharp contrast. Some authorities estimate the total strength of the pro-Treaty forces at about 7000. This is probably an underestimate. Double that figure would be more probable; but the anti-Treaty forces outnumbered them by at least four-to-one, and the odds may have been greater. (A surprising number of the IRA were neutral, thus accounting for the discrepancy between the total for the combined armies and the much larger total represented at earlier conventions.) However, in Dublin, the pro-Treaty troops were in superior numbers and they had larger supplies of arms and equipment.

Traynor hoped to bring up reinforcements from the country to take the pro-Treaty troops in the rear, believing that opposition would be slight, and easy to deal with. But the commanding officers, many of them in the Clarence Hotel, had first to return to their units and mobilize them. A great deal of confusion occurred and in what followed, the anti-Treatyites forfeited the chance of possible victory.

For three days the Four Courts was shelled by artillery, with rifles and machine-guns making sure that there was no withdrawal by the garrison. A hospital, under the direction of Nurse Geraldine O'Donnell, was established in the building to care for the wounded. Soon the field guns were surrounded by hundreds of empty brass shell cases, some of them still smoking. Bullet holes and dents marred the steel surfaces of the gun shields. Dead and wounded were taken to hospital. On Wednesday morning the streets were packed with sensation mongers. Rumours flew: Rory O'Connor had been killed — the Dublin Brigade was mobilizing for the Republic[2] — armies were converging on the city; yet the ordinary life of Dublin seemed to go on as usual. In spite of the continuous booming of the field guns and the rattle of rifles and machine-gun fire, the restaurants and cafés were full of men and women in summer dress. By that evening the mood of the city had changed. Shops, unexpectedly, had their shutters up. The crowds in the streets were thinner, more serious. More buildings had been seized by both sides, and snipers' bullets electrified the air from the rooftops. Armoured cars crashed through the open street, Vickers guns searching for a target, or chattering at one they had found.

As it became clear that the Four Courts could not hold out indefinitely, the anti-Treatyites dug themselves in deeper in the heart of

119

the city, and more clashes took place between the opposing forces. Sudden bursts of firing and the streets seemed to duck with a fearful shudder. Then they were empty. Steadily the hospitals began to fill. By Thursday virtually every city shop was shut. Communications with the rest of the country were at a standstill. Even the trams were deserted, idle and forlorn, motionless on their own tracks.

In the Four Courts the situation was bad. Communications throughout the building were haphazard and dangerous because of the streams of bullets which poured into it. On Friday morning — 30 June, the day on which the Coalition Government and Cabinet should have met — the Four Courts caught fire. Smoke from the burning building billowed up and mingled with the drifting smoke from the guns. The Dublin Fire Brigade was summoned by Brigadier O'Daly of the Government forces, but when he arrived, he refused the fire chief's request to cease firing while the fire was dealt with, saying: 'Ireland is more important than the fire at the Four Courts.'

The flames had a strong hold on the northern side of the building and the firemen, courageously, attempted to deal with something quite beyond their control. They were given every assistance possible under the circumstances by the men inside and O'Daly was prevailed upon to cease fire. However, it was no use. The building was doomed. The firemen finally withdrew, two of their number wounded. By now the attackers had fought their way into part of the buildings and grenades were being used freely. Some of the Four Courts garrison were dead and several wounded. Flames, as well as the enemy, were closing in. A dispatch was sent to Traynor, who replied:

> I have gone into the whole position re your situation, and have studied the same very carefully, and I have come to the following conclusion: to help me carry on the fight outside you must surrender forthwith. I would be unable to fight my way through to you even at terrific sacrifice. I am expecting reinforcements at any moment.
>
> If the Republic is to be saved your surrender is a necessity.
>
> As senior officer outside I take it that I am entitled to order you to make a move which places me in a better military position. This order must be carried out without discussion. I take full responsibility.

Most of the building was now in the hands of the pro-Treaty forces and the garrison was fighting desperately to hold on when this order arrived. About midday the attacking troops made a sortie into the 'no-man's land' part of the building between them and the anti-Treatyites. As they did so an ear-splitting explosion shook Dublin. Compared with it the sound of the field-guns was the merest murmur. Windows for a mile around were shattered, houses shook and the sky was darkened by a cloud of debris as the Four Courts was engulfed in smoke and flames. More than fifty of the attackers were wounded in this explosion and many were killed. What caused it? Mines, say pro-Treaty supporters; exploding magazines say the anti-Treaty men. On the whole it is most likely to have been the anti-Treaty magazine in the cellars of the building fortuitously exploding in the fire, as the explosion was so enormous. An eye witness says:[3]

> I was standing where I could clearly see the burning building, in a place where two men had been shot and killed not long before. As I watched a terrible explosion shook us and part of the roof seemed to lift in the air.
>
> Black as ink, shot up, 400 feet into the sky, a giant column of writhing smoke and dust, not more than fifty feet in diameter at the base. It spread into a mushroom some 200 feet up and glared in the sun with lurid reds and browns, through which could be seen thousands of white snowflakes, dipping, sidling, curtsying, circling, floating as snowflakes do. But the shower was not falling, it was rising.
>
> Higher it rose, and higher. All around us as we stood, 300 yards away, the bricks and mortar of the great explosion were dropping like hail, but the great white snowstorm eddied ever upwards till, at the height of 600 feet it drifted . . .

The account ends with these curious and thought-provoking words:

> A freakish eddy drifted one of the great flakes to my feet. I picked it up. It was the last sheet of an order made by the Probate Judge! *'And the Judge doth order that the cost of all the parties shall be costs in the cause.'*

The following correspondence is illustrative:[4]

Statement by GHQ (Government):
    Those who were in the hall of the Four Courts at the time of the explosion are well aware that it was a mine that exploded, and that it

was connected.

Other connected mines have since been removed from the Four Courts.

Our men were in the hall when the explosion took place. At that time the fire had not reached that part of the building. No shells came near that part of the building while our men were there.

Other traps were laid with the intention of slaughtering our troops, after their occupation of the building, but this was the only one which succeeded. One of these traps was a mine concealed by a typewriter cover.

In a letter dated 29 June, addressed OCV, Mr. Oscar Traynor, a leader of the Irregulars, wrote: 'Congratulations on getting down your mine. If you have no more of these let me know.'

Mr Ernest O'Malley assured Brigadier-General O'Daly that the mine was exploded by Irregulars in the Four Courts. He also expressed regret that the casualties among the troops were not greater.

The following letter was sent to the Secretary of Dáil Éireann by the Secretary of the Irish Labour Party:

July 4th, 1922

The Secretary,
Dáil Éireann,

A Chara,

In view of the published statements as to the cause of the explosion at the Four Courts, I think it is necessary to convey to you the following information:

In the course of the interviews which I and my colleagues were permitted to hold at Mountjoy with the leaders of the Executive forces we were positively assured that no mine was fired by the garrison. The explosion arose from the ignition of two tons of explosive material, either by shells or by flames, from petrol stores which had become alight.

I think that justice demands that this denial by the Executive leaders should be made public, and I, therefore, propose to send a copy of this letter to the Press.

Yours faithfully,
Thomas Johnson,
Secretary.

This letter drew the following public reply from the pro-Treaty authorities:

Government Buildings, Merrion Sq.,
Dublin, 4th July, 1922.
Mr Thos. Johnson, TD

A Chara,

I am directed to acknowledge your letter of this date. I am to remind you that you asked and obtained the privilege of visiting the military prisoners at Mountjoy Prison for a particular purpose.

The Government feel that you have abused that privilege by taking advantage of it for another purpose — namely, the circulation of a statement taken from the prisoners. Such action is wholly inconsistent with ordinary prison discipline.

I am to point out, however, that the abuse is aggravated by the fact that the statement you propose to publish, which is a belated denial that the prisoners perpetrated a cowardly act of exploding a mine under their victors shortly before surrendering, cannot be accepted as disposing of the charge, as it is in direct conflict with the information before the Government and as to the reliability of which the Government is satisfied — Mise le meas,

Colm O'Murchadha,
Secretary, Dáil Éireann

However, one way or the other, it is clear that the explosion took place before the surrender so that the moral issue is, in any case, slight. At 3.30 p.m. the garrison threw their arms into the flames and surrendered to Ennis's troops. Rory O'Connor had been slightly wounded. The men — about 140 of them now — were lined up and marched to Mountjoy Prison. On the way six — including Earnan O'Maille — escaped. The Four Courts — one of the finest buildings in a city of notable architecture — was a smouldering ruin, bullet-torn and disembowelled by fire and shell. The Records office, with its precious contents dating back to 1174, had disappeared. Having inspected the ruins General Eoin O'Duffy, Chief-of Staff of the pro-Treaty forces, announced that the 'revolt' was all but over so far as Dublin was concerned, and that the provinces showed no signs of following the example put before them.

On both counts he was mistaken. In what was immediately to follow Dublin's O'Connell Street — one of the finest thoroughfares in all Europe — was, for the second time in six years, to be reduced to rubble.

When the firing around the isolated Four Courts stopped on Friday, ominous silence settled over the city. Movement and shopping were confined to the suburbs and supplies of provisions were in unusual demand. By Saturday morning, 1 July, the city was like a patient ready for a major operation without anaesthetic. On Saturday afternoon came the first clash between the opposing forces; an armour-plated lorry of pro-Treaty soldiers was fired on from Moran's Hotel. More fighting flared up as the pro-Treaty forces tightened their cordon around the anti-Treaty positions and the latter threw out flanking parties to such places as the Corporation workshops in Stanley Street and Arnott's of Henry Street, where they had a machine-gun post on the roof tower.

On the same day the Provisional Parliament, convened in place of the Coalition Cabinet, was prorogued to 15 July.

On Sunday morning, the church bells mingled curiously with the snap and whine of rifle and bullet as snipers did their deadly work. Pedestrians and motor traffic were sparse, or forbidden altogether. At noon an anti-Treaty position at Harcourt Terrace/Adelaide Road was attacked and fell: the 'Swan' public house was also attacked, and by mid-afternoon firing was more or less continuous on the entire anti-Treaty position. Pro-Treaty troops took the initiative and moved into buildings in Lower O'Connell Street. The evening saw the attack develop and field guns in Beresford Place began to pound Moran's Hotel. Armoured cars and lorries nosed in, seeking fire-positions. The last battle for Dublin was about to begin.

Five days had passed since the attack on the Four Courts. Where were the reinforcements the anti-Treatyites so confidently expected?

Leaving aside, for the moment, the question of the 1st Southern Division, so far away in Cork and Kerry, what of anti-Treaty forces nearer at hand? Nearest to Dublin were the counties of Wicklow and Kildare. They are quite different geographically: Wicklow largely mountainous, with deep, wooded valleys in the north and west and rolling farmland sloping southwards to the coast. Kildare, on the other hand, is the flattest county in Ireland where, in ten miles, the greatest eminence is often a hump-backed railway or canal bridge. Plain and bog combine to produce this billiard-table effect, which, as it is well timbered, is not unattractive. From this area were expected to come the anti-Treaty reinforcements so urgently needed in Dublin by Traynor.

The South Dublin Brigade, which included Wicklow units from Bray and elsewhere under the command of Commandant Andrew McDonnell, received Traynor's mobilization order on the day the Four Courts fell. On the same day Commandant Paddy Brennan of the Mid-Kildare Brigade received similar orders. They were to mobilize in a place called Blessington in Wicklow, about eighteen miles from Dublin, and there meet troops of O'Maille's already advancing from Tipperary under Commandant Michael Sheehan.

In all there would be about 500 men available for the advance on Dublin from Blessington. But Blessington was attacked before the advance could be organized. Consequently, when Traynor found himself encircled on Sunday, 2 July with no sign of the expected reinforcements forthcoming, he was forced to change his plans.

'He arranged that the anti-Treatyites should try, simply, to evacuate their posts, leaving a small garrison to carry on resistance as long as possible . . . On Sunday, by his orders, part of the garrison went out with a white flag and surrendered. De Valera, Stack, Brugha and other leaders remained.'[5]

The explanation of how the anti-Treatyites got themselves into such straits, particularly as they commanded the loyalty of a far greater number of troops in the country, is simple enough. The pro-Treaty organization, though numerically weak, was a strong, compact, confident unit, with political and military leadership in harness, and with a clear, active chain of command in both spheres, and they had the men at hand to carry out their orders. They had four distinct advantages: a clear policy, a common purpose, united leadership and action and public support. It was precisely this lack of policy, purpose and political (and irresolute military) leadership which then bedevilled the anti-Treatyites and did so for months to come.[6] They lost the initiative, and the pro-Treatyites never afterwards let it slip out of their hands — except for small temporary set-backs — until the Civil War was won.

When the Four Courts was attacked there was no active political leadership to which the anti-Treaty forces of the Army could give allegiance. Consequently there was nothing except the Army round which the anti-Treaty supporters could rally, and the Army Executive, most of it in the Four Courts, was ill-fitted to lead a military campaign — as became increasingly evident — much less to give the all-embracing progressive, confident leadership which a people with an ideal have a right to expect. The Dáil itself was the instrument of Republican leadership, but it had been put aside by the Provisional Government. Theoretically — and according to the Provisional Government and the national Press — de Valera and Brugha were the leaders, military and political, of the Republican movement, but in fact they were no more than leaders of the anti-Treaty group in the Dáil.

It is important to establish that de Valera, in particular, remained fully conscious of the 1919 Republic and of its Dáil, to which he had taken oath, and neither set up a 'factional' government to represent anti-Treaty sentiment nor took decisive part in the military leadership. On the contrary, he opposed anti-Treaty military tactics. Many believe, while his arguments for not setting up a Government of his own are always impeccably judicial, if not judicious, that the Republic might have benefited from the dictum of the Government — those with the power have the authority in a crisis.

The anti-Treaty centre which did materialize was purely military — and as a result dictatorial — in character. Anti-Treaty lack of foresight in neglecting to provide against possible Civil War now cost them dear. A shadow Cabinet, a military council, an operational plan held in readiness against such circumstances, would have cost them little. So when Traynor found himself surrounded in Dublin on 2 July 1922 by his former friends and comrades, there were no reinforcements ready to support him.

On the day that Traynor began evacuating his positions a conference of the Irish Women's International League and several other women's organizations sent the following resolution to Griffith:

> That we, as Irishwomen, viewing with horror the present fratricidal strife, call upon the Provisional Government to take immediate action by summoning forthwith the newly elected Dáil before any further military operations be attempted. This we demand in the interests of Democratic Government.

Griffith sent the following reply:

> Mrs Despard, President, Irish Women's International League, Dublin.

> Madam,
> I have received the resolution handed in by you here this afternoon, urging on behalf of your association and others the

immediate summoning of the Irish Parliament.

The Parliament was summoned, as you are no doubt aware, for yesterday, the 1st instant, but before that date the authority of the Government and the sovereignty of Parliament were challenged by an irresponsible group, which, in defiance of the people's will, expressly declared, attempted by seizure of persons, property, and menace of arms, to arrogate to itself authority over the lives, liberties, and properties of the citizens, by whom it had been repudiated.

No Government would submit to such challenge without being guilty of betrayal of the people's fundamental right. The Government had, therefore, met the forces of despotism and disorder with the forces of the Democratic nation, and is determined to re–establish the security of life, liberty, and property within its territory.

For obvious reasons it is impossible for Parliament to meet in the present circumstances, it has, therefore, been prorogued until the 15th instant in order to ensure that it will be physically possible to meet, discuss, and decide freely, as in all civilized countries.

Mise le meas,

Art Ó Griobhtha (Arthur Griffith),
President, Dáil Éireann

The anti-Treatyites held positions in Harcourt Terrace and in Great Denmark Street, nearly two miles apart as the crow flies. In between they held buildings which commanded nearly every important thoroughfare in the city, with headquarters in the Hammam Hotel in O'Connell Street. The attack on this position began on Sunday about half past three in the afternoon. The pro-Treaty ring, extending from Amiens Street through Seville Place and up the Tolka River to Phibsborough, began to tighten and a heavy gun mounted on a flat truck was manoeuvred into position between Amiens Street Station and the Customs House — where Busarus, the Dublin bus terminal, now stands — for the attack on Moran's Hotel. After about four hours exchange, during which the hotel was reduced to a shell by gunfire, the hotel garrison surrendered — on Traynor's instructions.

A spontaneous, encouraging paragraph appeared in the *Irish Times* on Monday morning — on the same page as a pro-Treaty notice announcing complete censorship of all publications bought or sold in the country. (It is significant that the last tributes in the pro-Treaty press to anti-Treaty valour or chivalry appear in this paragraph.)

> Although many non-combatants have been hit, both sides are carrying on the war in the most scrupulous fashion and non-combatants are respected and left unmolested in an astonishingly generous way.
>
> But in no case that has come under my observation since the fighting started has either side deliberately broken the most exacting courtesy of war, and if in any cases shots have been fired at the Red Cross Services, I am convinced that it was through the inevitable mistakes which must occur when fighting is going on in a crowded mass of streets . . .
>
> [Again:] . . . remarkable thing was the way in which the firing from both sides ceased when the ambulances appeared, only to be continued furiously when the ambulance workers got through the danger zone.

Such public tribute to these observances of the 'courtesies' of war was deemed hurtful propaganda by pro-Treaty censors. Very soon these same newspapers had the anti-Treatyites firing, deliberately, at ambulances and Red Cross men and, generally, using dum-dum ammunition. On the other hand the *Cork Examiner* and the *Cork Constitution,* principal organs of anti-Treaty influence and censored by them since hostilities began, never attributed chivalry to their opponents at all and from the beginning, had them using dum-dums, ex– Black and Tans, and firing on Red Cross men and ambulances.

On Monday de Valera, Stack, Traynor and several other anti-Treaty leaders left the ring of steel around them, passing, to their own astonishment, through the cordons unrecognized due, one imagines, to the unexpectedness of the move. They left behind them Cathal Brugha with — according to Macardle — seventeen men, to continue the fight as long as possible before surrendering. Pro-Treaty accounts maintain that there was a larger garrison left behind, but this is difficult to verify as no one source agrees with another. On Monday, too, pro-Treaty troops closed in on O'Connell Street from three directions; north, north-west and south, capturing buildings as they advanced. In preparation for the prisoners they expected to take, Diarmuid O hEigceartaigh, Secretary of the Provisional Government, was appointed military governor of Mountjoy Prison with the rank of commandant.

During the attack on Brugha's little garrison, defending Upper O'Connell Street, the war, as usual, provided its ironies and grim humour. Killed in the attack was a Private Kelly of the pro-Treaty shock troops, the Dublin Guards, a Kerryman who had, just before the war began, applied for transfer to the 1st Southern Division, now wholly anti-Treaty. An anti-Treaty armoured car called 'Mutineer' was captured, pressed into service by its captors, and re-named 'Ex-mutineer'. By noon on Monday, Parnell Square, Talbot Street, Earl Street and the western side of O'Connell Street were all in pro-Treaty hands. After a brief lull the attack resumed and continued without respite all that evening and into Tuesday. By mid-morning on Tuesday, Gardiner Street, Marlborough Street and the east side of O'Connell Street, were a shambles. Glass, débris and the shattered remnants of fallen buildings littered the streets.

Smoke hangs over the whole area and suddenly it is shot with flame. The entire east side of O'Connell Street bursts into burning life. The attackers advance further on the last position held by Brugha, hurling petrol before them from the armoured cars in an attempt to drive out the defenders. The whole street is full of the dull roar of the fire, loud above even the clatter of machine-guns and the boom of artillery.[7]

Right and left the buildings that had been the noble hotels of Dublin lay in flaming ruins. The east side of O'Connell Street was rubble, as the west side had been six years before, in 1916. More than fifty buildings were in ruins. Brugha was called on to surrender. From the rubble he gave this reply: 'Nil aon chuimhneamh agam ar a leitheid do dheanamh; I have no such intention.' Bit by bit, step by step, the garrison was driven back, the flames and the opposing troops advanced, one in front of the other. Somehow a dispatch rider from Traynor — Mr Seán M. Glynn, then acting Brigade Intelligence Officer, the same who guided de Valera, Traynor and Stack to the safety of a house in Upper Mount Street the previous day — reached Brugha with an order to surrender. Brugha refused this also, although the building he occupied was now on fire.

That night an attempt was made to finish the battle, but the men in the Hammam still held out. Inside the building at this stage were, in fact, Brugha, seventeen men and two nurses under the direction of chief anti-Treaty nurse, Miss Linda Kearns. Civilians in the area had already been evacuated to Marlborough Street Model schools and the pro-Treatyites had provided them with provisions. They were in charge of a

Fr O'Reilly. At 2 a.m. on Wednesday morning the final attack began when three armoured cars charged up O'Connell Street, firing as they came, and bombs and petrol were lobbed into the staggering building. All morning the attack continued. By daylight the building seemed utterly untenable, nothing but blackened ruins all round it and itself a smoking pyre. Again the dispatch rider managed to make his way through, this time with a peremptory order from Traynor to surrender immediately, only to fall wounded in a laneway behind the Hammam. He was taken to the Mater Hospital.

The defenders held out until evening. At last Brugha called them together and ordered them to surrender before the blazing building collapsed on them. Twice he had to order his reluctant men to leave the building before they would do so. Then they shook hands with him and plunged through the flames to capture. Behind, with Brugha, stayed Nurse Kearns and Dr J. P. Brennan.[8]

Brugha was, in that instant, standing alone on the funeral pyre, as it were, of his ideals. Suddenly he appeared in the doorway of the crumbling building, a revolver in his hand. Was it loaded? Nobody knows for certain, but Dr Brennan maintains that it was not. If it was unloaded, the question is, why did Brugha have it in his hand? What is certain is that he started forward, in spite of appeals to halt, towards the ring of troops surrounding him who fired at his legs to wound him. He immediately fell, his femoral artery cut. Dr Brennan ran to his assistance. He was driven to the Mater Hospital, Nurse Kearns holding the severed artery in her fingers. Two days later he was dead. The first of the giants had fallen. Before the Civil War ended four more would fall also, together with many who followed them or fought against them.

Brugha, like de Valera, was an old 1916 veteran commander. In that they differed a good deal from the great majority of their comrades during the war of Independence, most of whom were younger — too young to have fought in 1916. Yet de Valera was only thirty-nine at this time. Collins, though in the GPO in 1916, did not blossom as a leader until later. He was thirty-one in 1922. Most of the military leaders were in their early or mid-twenties. Brugha, very much an elder statesman of the Sinn Féin movement, was forty-eight when he died.

'He was,' says an anti-Treaty veteran and comrade, 'the bravest man I ever knew.'[9] William Cosgrave, political enemy, personal friend, said that he walked into death-traps with a jest. He was a Dubliner and a company director in the firm he helped to found. In 1916 he was second-in-command to Eamonn Ceannt (who was later executed) in the South Dublin Union where, sitting before a barricade in a pool of his own blood four yards square, riddled with seventeen bullets and bomb splinters, he held off, with his parabellum and Mills bombs, for two hours, an entire British company in attack.

Friend and foe alike believed him to be doomed to die of his wounds and he was spared from execution with the other 1916 leaders. But he did not die. It was of this episode in the south Dublin Union that Cosgrave, then one of Brugha's lieutenants, said: 'He was as full of fight when he lay with his life ebbing out of him as going into the fray.'

Brugha lived to propose the establishment of the Republic in 1919 and to become its acting President and, subsequently, Minister for Defence in the Sinn Féin Cabinet. With his death the overture to the Civil War came to a finish in victory for the triumphant pro-Treatyites. Meanwhile the stage was being set for the main campaign which was now certain to follow.

On the day that Brugha was captured the Provisional Government issued a national call to arms. Recruiting for five Dublin battalions was opened at five city centres and local commanders were authorized to accept recruits through the country. Service was to be for a period of six months (or, presumably, the duration). The response to this call to arms was fantastic and, on the first day of recruitment, queues formed outside the centres and recruiting officers were unable to deal with the number of applicants. There were several reasons for this.

1. Large-scale unemployed in the country, reaching 150,000.
2. Ex-British soldiers were anxious and willing to continue a way of life to which they had grown accustomed.
3. The general refusal — ill-advised, many people hold — of the anti-Treatyites to accept ex-British army men into their ranks. 'Hundreds of ex-British Army men offered their services to the Republicans in Cork and elsewhere, but they would not be taken.'[10]
4. The natural enthusiasm of youth for adventure coupled with the equally natural desire to show that they could emulate the exploits of the IRA men who had achieved heroic stature — much against their will — after the War of Independence and during the Truce.
5. Idealistic motives.

Dublin had seen the beginning. Banks were closed, workers were added to the unemployed, homes were destroyed, streets laid waste, rail, social and postal services were cut or suspended, looters shot, food was scarce — but it was only a foretaste that had already cost £6,000,000. The fighting in Dublin had lasted eight days. More than sixty people were dead and over 300 had been wounded. The city centre was in ruins.[11]

[1]For texts see Statements and Documents, p. 327. Both Dorothy Macardle and Florence O'Donoghue say that this proclamation was issued with the added signatures of Liam Lynch, Liam Deasy and Peadar O'Donnell, but a copy of the proclamation in the author's possession does not contain these names.

[2]Macardle says that Commandant Seán Dowling's 4th Battalion remained neutral except for Dowling himself. But Dowling emphatically denies this and says his battalion bore the brunt of the fighting in Dublin; Dalton maintained that the bulk of the Dublin Brigade was pro-Treaty. This appears to have been the case and the confusion probably arises through faulty definition, i.e. the anti-Treatyites might not consider Beggar's Bush members of the Dublin Brigade as Dublin Brigade members at all. This source also maintains that Dalton only got twenty rounds for each field gun, but Macready makes it clear that he gave Dalton much more H.E. shells, and, when they were all gone, fifty shrapnel shells as a stop-gap until further supplies arrived from Carrickfergus or England.

[3]Irish Times, 1 July 1922.

[4]Daily Press, 5 July 1922.

[5] Dorothy Macardle, The Irish Republic, p. 753.

[6]Traynor, for example, had, all along, been opposed to the occupation of buildings in the city because the Government had artillery at its disposal and he had not. He had, in fact, gone to the Four Courts on the night before it was attacked, and advised the members of the Executive there to evacuate the building. He was unable 'to convince them.' (Florence O'Donoghue, No Other Law, p. 259)

It is also known that the Four Courts garrison knew of the impending attack nearly twelve hours beforehand, and yet did nothing about it. Furthermore it was largely true that for the entire course of the Civil War, little or no fighting took place in pro-Treaty areas other than Dublin, i.e. Clare, Meath, Kilkenny, etc.

[7] Contemporary account.

[8]Dublin County Coroner 1923.

[9]Seán Neeson.

[10]James Dunne. This statement of Dunne's is contradicted by other authorities and by the fact that several prominent anti-Treaty officers were ex-British soldiers; Tom Barry, the most notable. It is not improbable, however, that recently discharged British soldiers were considered with a certain lack of enthusiasm by the anti-Treatyites when they offered their services.

[11]The unemployment problem was a pressing urban problem, not so serious in rural areas. There had been no emigration for years, firstly because it was not favoured by the English authorities and then because it was not favoured by the Irish. Had it not been for Civil War there would very likely have been a great exodus after the Treaty anyway. As it was, this was postponed until post-Civil War.

8

BALTINGLASS AND BLESSINGTON

The reinforcements Traynor was waiting for were still in Blessington on 2 July, the day he gave up hope of their arrival. In Blessington O'Maille took charge and decided to defend the area and straddle the route to the south.[1] O'Maille had escaped with Seán Lemass[2] from Jameson's Distillery where the Four Courts prisoners were taken en route to Mountjoy. Liam Mellows would have escaped with them, but he had not finished shaving at the time and when he was ready the opportunity was gone.

O'Maille and Lemass made straight for Baltinglass where they were later joined by Paddy O'Brien, Four Courts OC, who had been wounded and escaped from hospital. The first troops to arrive in Blessington were the men of the South Dublin Brigade under Commandant Andrew McDonnell, who began moving in on the day of the Four Courts attack. They numbered 150-200 and they were waiting for Sheehan and his men from Tipperary to join them.

Due to the general chaos the mobilization order was slower in reaching Kildare than it had been reaching Wicklow. When it did get there, the men were unprepared. All their arms, except for large stocks of explosives, a few revolvers and seven rifles, had been given to Beggar's Bush for shipment to the North[3] and replacements had not come through. With about forty men active they had to postpone going to Blessington until they were armed. They proposed to attack Rathangan police barracks, garrisoned by thirty-five pro-Treaty troops, and capture the equipment there. The seven rifle-men were placed in two groups, one of four and one of three, which alternately raked the lower story of the building.

Under this cover the OC reached the wall of the barracks and lobbed grenade after grenade into it, driving the defenders up to the first floor. The cover party raised their aim and pinned the enemy there until the grenadier fired the building with incendiary bombs. Then the

133

garrison surrendered. The attackers armed themselves with twenty-two captured rifles and several thousand rounds of ammunition. A proposed attack on the near-by barracks of Robertstown, garrisoned by forty men, was thwarted when the garrison withdrew.

Units of the 6th Battalion of the Kildare Brigade were already at Blessington while O'Maille had gone south to Bunclody in Wexford to supervise the withdrawal of anti-Treatyites from Enniscorthy in a strongly pro-Treaty county. In Blessington an ex-British officer was anxious for quick offensive action before pro-Treaty troops grouped to attack, but he had no authority. Advance parties were sent out to villages and strong-points all over the area to prepare a defensive position. The 6th Kildare Brigade men went to Ballymore-Eustace, a small village in Kildare west of Blessington, commanding the Naas approach and the main road from Dublin. They were later reinforced with some of Sheehan's Tipperarymen. About thirty men occupied the village of Tullow. When Blessington was occupied, the men of the Kildare Brigade held a line extending from Kilteel, near Blessington, to Coolcarrigan, near the Meath border, cutting the main Curragh-Dublin road. Brittas, Crooksling and Kilbride were also occupied to give warning of a flank attack. The anti-Treaty position, concentrated in the Blessington vicinity, was now extended along the Dublin-Tullow road from Crooksling to Baltinglass.

The road-link between Dublin and the Curragh was vulnerable at Naas, only seven miles to the west, but O'Maille, when he returned from Wexford, was not anxious for offensive action in this direction.

O'Maille realized that the Blessington position could not be defended for long against a concerted attack. He decided, therefore, to fight a delaying action for as long as possible in order to give time for complete mobilization and re-grouping behind him. This tactic, it is claimed, delayed the Pro-Treaty advance south by over a week — but his losses in men were considerable: about 150 captured, killed or wounded. Pro-Treaty sources contradict its success.

At all events over Saturday, 1 July 1922, Sunday, Monday and Tuesday the anti-Treaty troops took up their positions. From Bray, Rathfarnham, South Dublin, Wicklow, Kildare and Tipperary they moved in. There was little excitement. By Tuesday strong points were manned and the triangle Blessington, Brittas, Kilbride was occupied. In Blessington the garrison blocked and mined the roads, machine-guns — usually Lewis — poked their drain-pipe muzzles to guard every approach, most of the houses were sand-bagged or had loop-holed steel shutters clamped in position. The Ulster Bank was General HQ. The Bank of Ireland was also occupied. A hospital was established in a dairy with a full staff of doctors and nurses. Most of the civilian population had already gone — many of them to join the throngs of refugees leaving by boat for England, or for the south and supposed safety. For those who remained a civilian committee was established to deal with any difficulties that might arise and it co-operated with the military in controlling the town. Food, with the exception of bread, was plentiful.

Meanwhile pro-Treaty HQ lost no time and as early as Saturday and Sunday — 1 and 2 July — had begun a drive on the south Dublin mountains, clearing the way as they advanced towards Blessington. By Monday, divided into three main bodies, they were converging on a twenty-mile-long front. South and east of the anti-Treatyites, through Carlow and Wicklow town, Commandant Bishop advanced with units of the Curragh Brigade between the anti-Treatyites and the coast. From the north Commandant Heaslip and the Dublin Guards were sweeping the mountains eastwards towards the coast and from the west Commandant McNulty had the unenviable job of closing in on the town over the Wicklow mountains. In all about 500 troops were involved. The weather was broken and miserable. Although small clashes took place as the net grew tighter, the first serious fighting occurred about 6 a.m. on Tuesday at Ballymore-Eustace between Bishop's men and those of Sheehan. The pro-Treaty troops, with armoured cars and infantry support, advanced and in the first exchanges their commander on the spot, Commandant Dineen, was seriously wounded. Finally the anti-Treatyites fell back on Brittas fighting, almost in hand-to-hand encounters, through encircling troops to do so. One of them later discovered that his brother, on the opposite side, had been killed in the battle — perhaps by a bullet from his own rifle. Their father had fought in 1916 with the heroes of Mount Street.

Immediately the village was cleared of the enemy Commandant Bishop established his HQ in Ballymore-Eustace and continued his advance on Blessington during the next two days, Wednesday and Thursday. Late on Thursday night his troops were within half a mile of the town. At that point the advance was halted to wait for artillery and armour before pressing home the attack. In the advance from Carlow, Ballytor, Monasterevan, and Ballymore-Eustace had been taken, and

135

with them some fifty prisoners.

Bishop's position was carefully chosen. His right flank lay along the King River, which joins the Liffey about a mile and a half south of Blessington, flowing from the south. His left flank lay along a low ridge running parallel with the tram line a mile or so west of Blessington, while his centre was on the road between Blessington and Poulaphouca. Meanwhile, Heaslip's men, coming southwards from Dublin, ran into their first serious opposition at Crooksling and Brittas.

A two-hour battle took place at Brittas before the anti-Treatyites pulled back to Baltinglass; and another collision occurred near Kilbride before, leaving prisoners, dead and wounded behind, the anti-Treatyites pulled back. The same pattern was followed at Crooksling. By Friday the vast majority of the anti-Treaty forces had been pushed back to Blessington and the town itself was ready for siege. Approaches were well-defended with road blocks and mines. Tension was at a height and the men were prepared to fight as long as possible.

But one of the groups most recently fallen back on the town brought news that altered the whole picture for O'Maille and caused him to improvise a second plan. Dublin Brigade and Battalion Commandants Andrew McDonnell and Gerry Boland had been captured at Crosschapel on the Slate Quarries Road between Kilteel and Hempstown.

It happened like this: the anti-Treatyites were dug in at a farmhouse barricaded with tram-tracks against armoured-car attack. They were forced after severe fighting to withdraw to Blessington. The pro-Treaty troops had just occupied the buildings, when three cars with McDonnell and Boland and some of their men drew up to inspect the post, not discovering it was in enemy hands until too late. They were taken to Tallaght.

When he heard this news O'Maille decided to evacuate Blessington as soon as possible — if possible. In this he had, it would seem, more luck than he deserved; he was already three-quarters way to being a sitting duck because he chose to wait to be attacked.

McNulty, coming across the mountains, had found his forces too small for the task they were expected to do and sent back for reinforcements. This delayed him and it was early on Saturday morning before his troops negotiated the rough country and closed the ring around Blessington. Meanwhile the artillery and armour had come up. Battle-scarred guns, with the slogan 'The Four Courts' still painted on them, were ready and trained on the town.

Escape for the anti-Treatyites seemed impossible. Baltinglass is surrounded by hills and the approaches to it span the Liffey and the King rivers. The bridges across them were held by the pro-Treaty troops. But, as McNulty closed in on the town about 5 a.m. on Saturday, a heavy mountain mist closed in on him. It was the opportunity O'Maille had been longing for. Leaving behind him fifteen men with ample ammunition, he left on the west side of the town with about 800 men.

No sooner was he on the way than the attack began and the fifteen-man rearguard replied to it with a will. In the confusion O'Maille and his men slipped through McNulty's lines, turned east towards Kilbride and so south. The Kildare men continued to march westward, fighting as they went, and reached their bases safely.

The action at Baltinglass lasted for four and a half hours and when Commandant Bishop entered the town at 10 a.m. on Saturday morning he was surprised and chagrined to find only fifteen men with little ammunition left, facing him. They were taken prisoners.

The official pro-Treaty notice of the affair, which was issued on the following Monday, underlines their fears of an attack on Naas and the Curragh:

The National troops operating from South Dublin and the Curragh within the past few days almost completed an encircling movement around the Brittas, Blessington and Kilbride areas, to which large numbers of Irregulars[4] had retired. The entire operation, which concluded this morning, has been successful, and over 100 prisoners, including the leaders — A. MacDonnell and G. Boland — were captured, with most of their arms and ammunition. The others dispersed south-eastwards into the mountains. The enveloping movement was carried out on a front of fifteen to twenty miles, almost complete encirclement being brought about by troops, many of whom were only in training, and fresh from other strenuous operations.

There were several casualties among the troops and those wounded included Commandant Dineen. Some volunteers were killed early in the operation. Documents captured on the Irregulars showed that their objective was to retire to Naas, and cut off communications between the Curragh and Dublin. All danger to these communications is now removed by the success of this operation.

¹He picked bad terrain for his purpose. Undoubtedly he lay between the two main southbound arteries — the road-rail link with Cork and Limerick and that with Wexford/ Waterford — but he was cut off from both by formidable natural barriers, while he himself occupied a position with doubtful means of escape — and to the rear. James Dunne says it was possible at this time to capture and hold the more vital area of Naas, Newbridge, Kildare — and the Curragh — and that sympathizers among the pro-Treaty troops in the Curragh were ready to help.

²Minister in Fianna Fáil governments 1932-66. Became Taoiseach (Premier) 1919, when de Valera was elected President; retired 1966.

³In accordance with the plan outlined in Part 1, Chapter 6.

⁴Irregulars: the name by which the pro-Treatyites always referred to the anti-Treatyites, just as the anti-Treatyites called pro-Treatyites 'Free State Troops' or 'Staters' long before the Free State came into being.

9

THE BATTLE FOR LIMERICK

When the Four Courts was attacked the anti-Treaty command was divided physically and in outlook. Of the 180 men in the Four Courts about 100 were garrison troops. The rest were officers in Dublin for the Convention and twelve members of the Army Executive. O'Maille was the only senior field commander among them. Of about 120 men in the Clarence Hotel after the Convention, a majority had returned to their units. Lynch, who represented most of the anti-Treaty fighting units, had been Chief-of-Staff of the Executive up to the time of the internal split on 18 June when he resigned. During the interval between 18 June and the attack on the Four Courts rapprochement was almost complete between the two anti-Treaty elements, but there had been no final agreement.

The essential difference between them was that the men in the Four Courts believed war, civil or against Britain, inevitable. They were anxious to strike the first blow against Britain and thereby, they argued, force a new national unity to emerge in the face of the old common enemy. The men in the Clarence felt that national unity might yet be achieved politically through the proposed coalition Cabinet due to be set up on 30 June. The attack on the Four Courts on 28 June resolved their differences.

Lynch set off for Cork at once. On the way to Dublin's Kingsbridge station he was arrested by pro-Treaty troops in charge of Liam Tobin and taken before O'Duffy, who allowed him to go; further evidence, it would appear, in support of the theory that the pro-Treatyites believed that they had only the Four Courts to deal with. On that basis it would have been impolitic to antagonize the men of the 1st Southern Division by detaining Lynch and his Second-in-Command, Liam Deasy who was with him.[1]

Lynch and his senior staff officers, Deasy and Seán Moylan,[2] arrived in Mallow, Co. Cork, on 29 June. Next day Lynch issued a statement announcing his resumption of the office of Chief-of-Staff of the Republic with military command of the south and west. The assistant Chief-of-Staff, O'Maille, was given command of the Dublin and northern areas. Lynch appealed to his troops to maintain discipline and not to interfere with the civilian population unless absolutely necessary. On the same day he moved his HQ to Limerick. Formation of a policy was his most vital concern; and without one little could be achieved. Anti-Treaty forces held large areas all over the country and there were active units even where they were in a minority; yet, so far, the pro-Treatyites had every advantage except in actual numbers, and that balance was easily redressed (as the recruiting campaign was to show). The pro-Treatyites were prepared, they had policy and control of the public purse, unlimited supplies and a firm grip of civil and military affairs, as well as the major share of public support.

Lynch's first step was to eliminate possible danger from within his area and on 1 July the only two pro-Treaty posts in the First Division territory, Skibbereen in Cork and Listowel in Kerry, were attacked. Listowel surrendered the same day and Skibbereen was captured on July 4th.

Liam Deasy, now Divisional O.C., reached agreement with Commandant-General Donncada Hannigan, OC of the pro-Treaty forces in Limerick city and county. Hannigan's troops, surrounded in Ashford barracks, were allowed to withdraw with their arms. Lynch now had complete control of Munster from Limerick city in the west, through Clonmel, to Waterford city in the east. Lynch formed a new staff and set up his H.Q. in New Barracks, Limerick, and his troops occupied the Strand, Castle and Ordnance barracks as well. Hannigan was occupying the Customs House, the Jail, the Courthouse, William Street Barracks and Cruise's Hotel. Commandant-General Michael Brennan of Clare was still in Limerick under Hannigan's command and his troops were part of the garrison. When Lynch arrived in Limerick the Mayor, Alderman S. M. O'Mara, arranged a meeting with Hannigan and the tentative agreement already established by Deasy was hardened into something more concrete. On 4 July the following proclamation was published:[3]

AGREED

that:

1. Commdt.–General Hannigan will not at any time attack the

Executive forces; Executive forces will not attack Commdt.–General Hannigan's forces;

2. Executive forces will not occupy any post in the East Limerick Brigade area;

3. Both sides only to occupy their normal number of posts in Limerick city;

4. There be no movement of armed troops in Limerick city or in East Limerick Brigade area, except by liaison agreement;

5. Commdt.-General Hannigan withdraws any of his troops drafted into the city since Saturday (July 1st);

6. Executive communications to be maintained between 1st, 2nd and 3rd Southern Divisional H.Q. and Limerick city;

7. This agreement holds during the period of fighting between Executive forces and Beggar's Bush or until both sides of the Army find a solution to the problem;

8. We agree to these conditions in the practical certainly that natural peace and unity will eventuate from our efforts, and we guarantee to use every means in our power to get this peace;

9. This agreement to be put into effect by 12 o'clock midnight, tonight.

This agreement was obviously far too one-sided to last for very long — in fact it lasted less than twenty-four hours.

Paragraph seven, in effect, immobilized Hannigan and Brennan and left Lynch free to fight. Paragraph five permitted Lynch to keep what forces he had in the city while it committed Hannigan to withdrawing whatever troops he had brought in during the previous four days. Obviously the pro-Treaty leaders were not going to sanction an agreement which immobilized their forces in Limerick city, much less agree to weakening of their military strength there. What blinded Hannigan to these considerations it is hard to say.[4] Next day, however, Commandant-General D.A. McManus, an ex-British officer of field rank and assistant Director of Training pre-Truce, was sent hot-foot from Dublin to readjust the pro-Treaty position. He sent the following despatch to Lynch:

This is to inform you that I arrived here from Dublin with definite instructions as to military operations in this area. Before coming into this area I made arrangements for certain positions to be taken up immediately. On arriving here I discovered that Commdt.-General Brennan and Commdt.-General Hannigan had been discussing terms of agreement with you for some days past. I have definite instructions that no such agreement if signed could be admitted by GHQ and these officers had no authority whatever to enter into such an agreement. I hear that another meeting between these officers and yourselves had been arranged for 8 a.m. today. I have instructed them that this meeting is not to take place and they are to have no further communication with you on this matter. I herewith reserve full liberty of action and I have made certain dispositions to protect my posts in the city and their communications.

D.A. Mac Maghnusa, Commdt. Gen.[5]

In spite of this document the officers commanding the respective forces met on the morning of Friday 7 July. The result of this meeting was the following interesting document:

We agree in the interests of a united Ireland and to save our country from utter destruction to call a meeting of Divisional Commandants representing the 1st and 2nd Southern Divisions and the 1st Western Division of the Executive Forces Irish Republican Army and the Divisional Commandants representing the 4th Southern Division and the 1st Western Division and the Mid–Western Command (Commandant-General Seán MacEoin) of the Dáil Forces Irish Republican Army. The meeting to be held as soon as Seán MacEoin can be got into this area. The forces now opposed to one another in Limerick City end for all time this fratricidal strife in view of the meeting of the Divisional Commandants in Limerick. And as a guarantee of good faith towards a permanent agreement the Divisional Council of the Western Division Dáil Forces IRA (Brennan) agree to hand in their resignations if agreement is not reached at the meeting of the Divisional Commandants. The agreement as regards the resignations of the Divisional Councils to be signed by Saturday evening. The buildings to be occupied by the Dáil Forces Irish Republican Army are the Custom House, the Jail, the Courthouse, Cruise's Hotel and William Street Barracks. No troops in Limerick City to appear in public with arms except by liaison arrangement. A truce now exists between Executive Forces Irish Republican Army and the 1st Western Division and the 4th

Southern Division Dáil Forces Irish Republican Army until the conference ends between the Divisional Commandants. All outposts to be withdrawn to the agreed centres by six o'clock Friday evening, 7th July 1922. The agreement takes effect from the moment it is signed, 1.30 a.m., 7th July 1922.

Liam Lynch, Chief–of–Staff Executive Forces.

Donncada O hAnnaogain, Commdt.-Gen., 4th Southern Division.

M. Brennan, Commdt.-Gen., commanding 1st Western Division.[6]

The same day McManus wrote to Lynch

I have just returned here to find that Commandant-Gen. Hannigan and Commandant-Gen Brennan have entered into a signed agreement with you. While absolutely disapproving of this agreement, in order to try and avoid a conflict all over the country, I am willing to allow this matter to go ahead on condition that there is no change in the military position here. I cannot agree to interference with our present strong military position. While I have great hopes that peace will result from this agreement, I have no power to change the whole military position here, either on my own authority, or on that of any local commander. I agree strongly that negotiations would have the best results at this stage and I am willing to forgo using the advantage I have gained in the military position for an attempt at getting national agreement.

D.A. McManus, Commandant-Gen.

However, at 5.30 p.m. that evening pro-Treaty troops from the William Street Barracks opened fire on the anti-Treatyites in the Ordnance Barracks. The battle for Limerick was on and the murmur of agreement was lost in the clatter of gunfire.

Lynch's purpose in these Limerick negotiations is far from clear. Undoubtedly he wanted peace, but the war was already ten days old on 7 July; the Four Courts, Dublin Centre, Blessington and Brittas had fallen. The latter two were under attack as early as 4 July, when the first agreement was reached. Lynch, like Collins, but for different reasons, may have hoped the Civil War would be confined in and about Dublin. Yet, paradoxically, by remaining in Limerick he may have done the very thing that prevented this.

Had he commandeered every available means of transport on 1 July and marched on Dublin, the outcome might have been altogether

143

different. 'If the Republicans had concentrated on Dublin and on finishing the fight there, instead of consolidating themselves in the south, the end might very well have been different. There is every likelihood that if they had come up from the south during the ten days of fighting in Dublin to reinforce the Dublin Brigades that the Government Forces would have been contained and, eventually, beaten in the capital.'[7] Why did he not do this instead of going to Limerick? There are four major possibilities:

1. He did not want to leave strong pro-Treaty forces under Hannigan and Brennan which might attack him from behind and/ or take control or Munster while he marched on Dublin, in his rear.
2. He intended to march as soon as these pro-Treaty troops had been immobilized in accordance with the 4 July agreement.
3. He thought it wiser to strengthen Munster behind the Limerick-Waterford line and wait for that to be attacked rather than stake everything on an offensive one way or the other.
4. He couldn't do it.

Whatever his private attitude to the first, and with the second ruled out as circumstances developed in Limerick, the third course was the one he adopted. The plan — the 'Republic of Munster' as it was lightly called — is attributed to de Valera, but this is unlikely in view of the fact that he did not join anti-Treaty HQ until it moved to Clonmel on 11 July and then only as assistant to Seán Moylan, Director of Operations. South and south–west of this line from the city of Limerick in the west, bordered on the north by the long Shannon estuary, to the city of Waterford in the east flanked by the River Suir, was the only large block of territory held exclusively by the anti-Treatyites. Northwards, on the west coast, in Galway, Connemara, Mayo and parts of Sligo, there were other strong anti-Treatyite areas, but Brennan's forces in Clare lay like a wedge between them and the Munster stronghold. The defence of Munster seemed to be the only plan that the anti-Treatyites considered. It should surely have been a *coup d'etat* or nothing. However, the people had not yet withdrawn their sympathy; on the contrary, the Four Courts revived it where it had flagged and the hope of widespread public support may have inspired the anti-Treaty policy of waiting and defence which was, inevitably, to crumble piecemeal.

The pro-Treatyites were in no great hurry. Although, mistakenly, they did not foresee a protracted campaign they were not anxious to commit themselves with inadequate forces. Recruiting since it began on 5 July had been at the rate of almost 1000 men a day and it continued until there was an army of about 60,000 men in the field. It was early recognized that the principal theatre of war was going to be in the south and to that all other commitments were subordinated. Strength was massed for an attack on both flanks of the anti-Treaty position in Munster in an unhurried and professional manner. The capture of Limerick would drive deeper and strengthen the wedge between the anti-Treatyites in Munster and those in the west, and it would open a gateway to the counties of Cork and Kerry, where the anti-Treaty spirit was most powerful.

The fighting in Limerick was not typical of most of the bigger Civil War battles in that there was no artillery in action until 19 July. After the first exchanges it settled down to raids, sorties and attacks on enemy positions with neither side gaining any decisive advantage.

One woman refugee who remained until she saw the artillery coming in, told a newspaper correspondent in Nenagh, where, with thousands like her, she fled for safety, that she travelled all night with her two children to get away. She had not been able to sleep for ten successive nights because of the continuous gunfire and explosions and, after that time, food was desperately scarce, almost to the point of famine. The pro-Treatyites in Dublin despatched some food to relieve the distress where they had control, and the anti-Treatyites did what they could to ease the hardship, but the necessity of feeding two armies complicated already overtaxed supplies. Profiteering by some shopkeepers was inevitable and was dealt with severely by the military authorities on both sides.

On Wednesday, 12 July, pro-Treaty troops captured an outpost and thirteen men in the city. On the following day an anti-Treaty attack gave them the Munster Tavern in Lane Street. At that time Lieutenant Frank Teeling, captured by the British and condemned to death, but who had escaped before the Truce, was wounded. Again the pro-Treaty forces attacked up Lane Street with armoured cars and carried the assault through the barricades to the walls of the Ordnance Barracks, but failed to mine them. In this attack they re-captured the Munster Tavern. They were being reinforced daily.

Commandant Dan Donovan (who negotiated with Montgomery) was anxious to attack these reinforcements coming south through Nenagh and Roscrea, but was not allowed to do so because of the weakening it meant of the anti-Treaty positions. Commandant Peter Kearney of the 3rd (West) Cork Brigade made a successful attack at a place called Cahirconlish and held a position there until recalled to Limerick.

After a week's fighting the Republican HQ was moved to Clonmel. Limerick was clearly too vulnerable, but the demoralizing effect of a war–policy — if it may be so–called — so clearly wanting in aggressiveness needed a strong antidote which was not found in the shifting about of HQ.

No army, it has been said, acting purely on the defensive can hope to succeed, as the morale of the troops inevitably suffers and the initiative passing to the opposite side amounts to an increase of 50 per cent in their forces in the field.

Commandant-General Tom Barry[8] says: 'Some of our leaders (military) were a joke in a revolutionary movement,' while an officer of the East Cork Brigade says:[9] 'At no time did I see a plan of attack. We never took over proper control of communications. There was a complete absence of organized military efficiency.' How much this lack was due to want of political government is open to speculation, but it is obvious that the absence of a civic authority contributed largely to this lack of military efficiency. Under these circumstances the fall of Limerick to the pro-Treaty forces was only a matter of time. Meanwhile the hardship became greater every day. In Mungret College, for example, two priests and five lay brothers cared for more than 500 women and children. Casualties were high among them already and there was very little food.

On 13 July a pro-Treaty Army-council, consisting of Michael Collins, Commander-in-Chief; Richard Mulcahy, Chief-of-Staff and Minister for Defence; Eoin O'Duffy, Asst. COS, had been set up. Several other military appointments were made including those of Fionan Lynch as Deputy OC South West, Commandant-General; Kevin O'Higgins,[10] assistant AG, Commandant-General; Joseph McGrath,[11] Director of Intelligence, Major General; Diarmuid Ó hEigceartaigh (recently appointed Governor of Mountjoy), General Staff Officer, Commandant-General. This move surprised the country as it came without warning and appeared to be, though it was not, a military junta. In fact it closely resembled what the pro-Treatyites themselves said they most feared from their opponents.

Parliament was prorogued again as it was now evident that the war was to continue indefinitely. The decision, however, was sharply criticized by the Labour Party which called a peace meeting in Dublin's Mansion House on 20 July, but with little success. At the same time the Republican Courts, which had successfully operated since 1918, were suspended in favour of the old, British-established judiciary, now in Irish hands. 'The justification for continuing a system, in so large a measure irregular and unlawful, had now disappeared' said the official notice of the suspension.

Because of the Government refusal to recognize a writ of habeas corpus from these courts on behalf of Count Plunkett's son, a prisoner in Mountjoy, Gavan Duffy, Minister for Foreign Affairs, resigned from the Cabinet of the Dáil: 'On July 25th it was determined to abolish the Supreme Court and its judges rather than meet a writ of habeas corpus made on behalf of one of the military prisoners in Mountjoy . . . This is an attack on the first principles of our freedom and democracy . . . '

It became a test-case on the part of the anti-Treaty leaders concerning the attitude of the pro-Treaty party to the Dáil legislature and a warrant was issued by Judge Crowley for the arrest of Richard Mulcahy and the Governor of Mountjoy. The warrant was, of course, ignored and the authority behind it declared suspended. Presently Judge Crowley was himself arrested and imprisoned by the pro-Treaty authorities.

Tuesday, 18 July, was the day anti-Treaty Waterford was attacked by Commandant Prout in the east. On the same day anti-Treaty positions in Limerick city, now overflowing with fresh pro-Treaty troops and with artillery close behind, were also attacked. Civilians had been asked by Mayor O'Mara to evacuate the districts of Coney Street, Edward Street, Colooney Street and places near New, Strand and Castle Barracks — all held by the anti-Treatyites — because of the great danger. Thus was the artillery heralded.

East of William Street the city was in pro-Treaty hands while the anti-Treatyites held Upper O'Connell Street, adjoining areas and the docks; the YMCA building in Percy Square, Cecil Street, the Post Office and the Telephone Exchange. Many of the buildings were connected by tunnels.

The realization that the fall of Limerick opened the way for a thrust into Kerry and North Cork stiffened the anti-Treaty defenders. On Saturday pro-Treaty troops attacked the Strand Barracks and King John's Castle near Thomond Gate with armoured cars, machine-gun fire and grenade and mortar action. The attack was continued on Sunday and

147

by Saturday evening part of the barracks was on fire.

On Tuesday, 18 July, a general assault on all anti-Treaty positions was made and street-fighting occurred. Casualties on the pro-Treaty side for that day were over forty and these were accommodated in St. John's Hospital, Barrington's Hospital, the County Infirmary and the Union Hospital. On Wednesday, the arrival of the artillery, as was to be so often the case, heralded the end of anti-Treaty occupation of the city. The shelling of Strand Barracks began. Before it started, a messenger was sent to the defenders giving them five minutes to surrender. Two nurses from the Red Cross Hospital beside the barracks brought the reply from the OC of the garrison saying he would not surrender while he had ammunition. The nurses then returned to the hospital and the guns opened fire from Arthur's Quay. For some hours they shelled the building, finally breaching the four-foot thick walls. The gun was then moved to the back of the barracks and fire concentrated there and the rear breached.

The action had taken all day and by 8 p.m., when the walls at the back were breached, a twelve-man storming party led by Captain Con O'Halloran raced through the gap, hurling grenades before them and firing as they went. Even as that party raced into the anti-Treaty stronghold, a counter-attack by anti-Treaty forces from O'Connell Street came up against the pro-Treaty besiegers. The object of this counter-attack was to relieve those in Strand Barracks, but it was beaten off, as heavy machine-guns on the northern bank of the Shannon enfiladed the anti-Treatyites while they crossed the ends of Thomas and William Streets, making it impossible to press home their attack. Meanwhile the storming party in the barracks were meeting with fierce opposition in the blazing building and Captain O'Halloran fell wounded in the chest from a sub-machine-gun burst. The bulk of the garrison succeeded in escaping, allegedly through the hospital next door, and the remainder were taken prisoner.

Elsewhere the anti-Treatyites, making full use of their fire-power from smaller weapons, destroyed or occupied a number of pro-Treaty positions on Wednesday and Thursday. O'Mara's bacon factory was the scene of a bitter battle when pro-Treaty forces tried to take it without artillery, and there were many casualties on both sides.

Castle Barracks was next to be attacked by the artillery. It was this attack, maintain the anti-Treatyites, that damaged nearby historic King John's Castle. But the pro-Treaty forces insist that the anti-Treatyites themselves fired the building. However that may be, the barracks was soon blazing and the troops holding it evacuated. At midnight shells fired the Ordnance Barracks in Musgrave Street and soon afterwards other anti-Treaty strongholds blazed also. Undoubtedly many, if not all of them, were burnt by the withdrawing troops.

William Street, where houses across from each other were held by opposing troops, was the scene of a day-long battle which lasted right up to the anti-Treaty withdrawal from the city after midnight on Thursday.

They evacuated along the Ballinacurra road under cover of machine-gun fire from a rearguard. The main body fanned out to the south-west and blocked roads with trees and mines, and blew bridges as they went. They dug in at Bruree and Kilmallock where they successfully delayed the pro-Treaty advance to the south for over two weeks.

---

[1] A full account of Lynch's journey and the controversial aspects of it is given in O'Donoghue's *No Other Law*, pp. 258 *et seq*.

[2] Seán Moylan, late Fianna Fáil Minister for Agriculture, died in office, 1957.

[3] *Daily Press*, 5 July 1922.

[4] O'Donoghue's *No Other Law*, p. 262, says: 'This represents something of what was in the minds of the officers like Lynch and Hannigan. . . . Both still hoped that by limiting the area of conflict some solution of the whole Army problem would be found and were prepared to use every means in their power to secure peace.' It was a vain and, one is inclined to think, unrealistic hope — which may explain Lynch's curious decision to remain in the south rather than advance on Dublin. How Hannigan and Brennan overlooked the reaction of their superiors and of their Government remains a mystery. One of the conditions Hannigan agreed to, in clause 6, was that Lynch could communicate with 3rd Southern Division headquarters in Birr. Hannigan informed Nenagh (pro-Treaty) headquarters of this agreement, as communications would be via Nenagh area to Birr, and was told, in effect, to go to hell.

[5] *Daily Press* of the period.

[6] O'Donoghue, *No Other Law*, p.264

[7] Florence O'Donoghue, Army Executive Member during the 'cold war', neutral during the Civil War, in a conversation with the author. According to Liam Deasy 'Lynch hoped that his old friendship with Brennan and Hannigan would enable a united South (as a last hope) to talk to the Free State GHQ and stop the war.' In a note to the author.

[8] Captured trying to get into the Four Courts during the attack, escaped in September 1922, from then on Director of Operations in succession to Moylan and de Valera. By far the most outstanding anti-Treaty military leader.

[9] The late Seamus Fitzgerald.

[10] Minister in Fine Gael Governments, assassinated in office 1927.

[11] Founder and director Irish Hospitals' Sweepstake.

10

THE ASSAULT ON WATERFORD

Pro-Treaty troops, though numerically smaller at this stage than their opponents, were mobile and well armed. When the war began they held the key positions for launching assaults on the anti-Treaty-held areas — namely Nenagh against Limerick, Athlone against the Midlands and north-west and Kilkenny against the south-east. They had the support of the Press, with its great influence, they were paid and could pay for supplies, their 'Government' had authority and power which they used and which claimed that 'Possession is nine points of the law' and were supported by a majority of the people in this claim. Finally they had the full and unstinted support of the Irish Hierarchy, who added to that support specific condemnation of the anti-Treatyites. The moral licence thus bestowed on the pro-Treatyites and their troops and denied to the anti-Treatyites cannot be overestimated. Pro-Treaty troops almost, but not quite, became Crusaders. The anti-Treatyites, while not infidels, were quite definitely generic heretics.

Kilkenny, with ten main roads radiating from it like the spokes of a wheel, was the key to the pro-Treaty attack on the Waterford City. Here the pro-Treaty forces assembled as the anti-Treatyites withdrew to the south, and moved out cautiously, consolidating as they did so.

By mid-July the anti-Treaty military position became suddenly and dramatically clear. Except for parts of the west and most of Munster, the principal military posts in the country were in the hands of the pro-Treaty forces. Lack of heavy equipment hampered the anti-Treatyites and should have made them all the more reluctant to fight pitched battles along fixed lines, which was a type of fighting that they had no training for; moreover it lost them the initiative and forced them on the defensive. But they manned the 'line' of 'The Munster Republic' and waited.

From Kilkenny the pro-Treatyites made the second main thrust against the anti-Treaty line. They hoped to roll it up as far as Clonmel, where they would join with troops moving south from the strong triangle, Thurles, Cashel, Roscrea. Opposing them in Waterford were local anti-Treaty units and a small contingent from Kerry,[1] principally Tralee, all under the command of 'Pax' Whelan, the Brigadier in the area.

The anti-Treatyites in Waterford were content to sit in the city waiting to be attacked without attempting to form the most elementary perimeter on the heights dominating the city on the northern bank of the River Suir — from which direction the attack was bound to come.

'There was,' says Colonel Patrick Paul,[2] 'no need of maps. We had all the local knowledge we needed at our fingertips — and if we had not we had the men who did have it.' The anti-Treatyites, on the other hand, though they had all the local knowledge they could require, made little use of it. They should, for any hope of success, have been entirely self-contained, with outstanding leadership and a tightly-knit chain-of-command; continuous supplies of food, ammunition and transport, none of which prerequisite facilities they had. When, in the crisis, they took up the threads of military administration, they completely overlooked those of civil administration and it was this in the long run, which led to their downfall. If they had wooed public support instead of flouting it, the outcome of the war might well have been affected.

During the 1798 Rising against the British oppression the Protestant leaders had a very full and comprehensive system of civic committees planned to carry on public administration.

Nor were anti-Treaty lines of communication given the attention they demanded. Commanders were instructed from HQ to operate within their own territories and this, intentionally or otherwise, was interpreted as an order to operate without the intricate and continuous communications essential in modern warfare, with the result that anti-Treaty operations were directed largely at the whim and convenience of local commanders without reference to any overall plan.

The pro-Treaty War Council of Collins, Mulcahy and O'Duffy planned their campaign with detail. In general its aim was to capture the enemy forces or annihilate resistance.

Throughout July responsible bodies in the country repeatedly called for the meeting of the Dáil which had been summoned for 30 June, but which was twice prorogued because of the attack on the Four Courts, and 'in the hope that no further prorogation may be necessary that the parliament may meet free from the threat of arms'. But there was no response from those in power.

They hoped to end the war quickly and it looked as if their hopes were to be fulfilled. Three of the most important anti-Treaty military leaders (two of them, Rory O'Connor and Liam Mellows, political figures of the utmost significance) were captured. The third was Joe McKelvey.[3] Cathal Brugha, one of the great architects and advocates of the Republic, was dead. All this within a week. At a blow the pro-Treatyites had struck severely at the brains and nerve-centre of anti-Treaty militarism. Arms, ammunition, transport, money — or credit — men and benedictions were all readily available to pro-Treaty forces ... All, or nearly all, were denied their opponents. The policy of the pro-Treatyites was to finish the war quickly with as little bloodshed as possible. But it was to prove a bitter and long campaign of nearly twelve months before Cease Fire.

In Waterford, just before it was attacked, hotels, boarding-houses, and barracks were seized and occupied, and stores commandeered. The approaches to the city were enfiladed, mined and blocked. City transport, telecommunications and the ships in the harbour came under military control. Ballybricken jail, in the heart of the Redmondite district,[4] was heavily defended in case of internal trouble. It was later destroyed by shellfire and arson. The northern approaches to the city were mined and barricaded and defence posts established in 'strategic' positions while the defenders awaited attack. But the preparations, particularly in retrospect, appear to have been indecisive and were certainly inadequate.

The full story of the battle for Waterford began the previous May when twenty-six-years-old Brigadier Patrick Paul, who, in the War of Independence, had been Brigadier in east Waterford and who later supported the Treaty, was sent down from Dublin to take command of the Waterford area. He arrived alone and was promptly arrested by his former Second-in-Command and friend, then OC of the anti-Treatyites in east Waterford. In protest Paul went on hunger-strike and, after ten days of hunger strike and three of thirst, was moved to the county infirmary for medical attention. There was an armed guard on the hospital while he was there. After a day or so in hospital, and with some nourishment inside him, Paul began to think about escaping. Two girls of Cumann na mBan,[5] supporters of the Treaty, went to the Convent of the Sisters of Charity where they were, with the approval of Monsignor Kearney, Dean of Waterford, provided with complete nuns' outfits. In

152

these they came to visit the hospital and made their way to Paul's room. Once inside, the door was locked and he changed clothing with one of the girls. Then, with the other 'nun' as companion and with his hand on a smuggled .45 at his waist, the 'visiting sister' came out into the corridor.

'We had to pass the guards,' said Paul. 'I was very slow and weak and had to move carefully in my nun's shoes. Luckily I am small and they fitted me all right. I had everything, Rosary Beads, belt and all, but I kept my hand on my revolver.' Outside a car was waiting and sympathetic men of his old brigade were posted to cover the hospital entrance in case of trouble. 'When we had the guard at the main entrance to pass I thought we'd never make it,' said Colonel Paul. 'The door in front of us was shut and we would have to knock for him to open it. I was sure of detection.' Steadily the two 'nuns' approached down the large echoing corridor that must have seemed interminable, with the door at the end like the passageway between some Scylla and Charybdis — danger on every side. Then, as they approached, the door began slowly to open as if of its own volition. Wider and wider until the 'nuns' could see the blue square of the sunlit sky, bright at the end of the corridor. In the gap stood a well-armed young sentry. He had seen them approaching through a peep-hole.

'This is it,' thought Paul. 'He's on to us.' The dark figure of the sentinel stood silhouetted against the freedom beyond, one hand resting on his revolver, the other holding his rifle steadily. As the 'nuns' approached he stood to one side. Paul waited for the challenge. His hand tightened on his revolver. Then the sentry spoke. 'Good evening, Mother,' he said.

'God bless you, my child,' stammered Paul, with genuine feeling, stepped past him and walked towards the car fifty yards away. Once in the car, he sat back as it raced for New Ross and safety. There he spent the night and, next day, was moved to the pro-Treaty stronghold of Kilkenny where he convalesced. During his convalescence the Civil War began. OC the 2nd Southern Division of pro-Treaty troops comprising most of the counties of Waterford, Wexford, Kilkenny and part of Tipperary was Commandant John T. Prout, who had served with the US Army during the first world war. Prout's first objective was Waterford. As assistant he appointed the officer in command of Waterford area, Brigadier Paul, and asked him to submit a plan for taking the city. Paul, who had also seen service in the 1914-18 war, submitted three plans, as follows:

(1) To attack quickly and directly with armoured cars and lorries and capture the vital — and only — bridgehead in the city linking it with the Kilkenny shore, before the anti-Treatyites raised the cantilever bridge;

(2) To come in on the enemy's flank where the wide River Suir estuary to the east bordered the territory he controlled, crossing the river before it turned south at right angles, east of the town. Little resistance was expected from such an attack, as the anti-Treatyites had nowhere to fall back on except westward towards Cork;

(3) To cross the River Suir up-river on the defenders' left flank and attack the city from the west.

The first plan was ruled out as the anti-Treatyites had warning of the pro-Treaty troop concentrations in Kilkenny and, without further ado, raised the bridge — as Paul himself had done about a year previously in the War of Independence in an attack on the British — nor were sufficient armoured cars available with which to make the swift thrust. The third plan was risky because it meant exposing the attacker's right flank to the full weight of a possible attack from the anti-Treaty hinterland, with the further risk of a battle on two fronts with the river in between. The second plan was the one adopted. It was decided to cross the river east of the city by night and make an assault on it from the other side. The one fear the troop commanders had was of an attack from the Carrick-on-Suir direction on their right flank, which would have meant altering the direction of their own thrust, by-passing Waterford for the time being. This fear was well justified, as will be seen, although, curiously, the pro-Treaty troops never realized just how close the danger of attack came.[6] At this time, of the four principal cities in the south, only Dublin (which was, to a large extent, the key to the whole situation), was in pro-Treaty hands. Pro-Treaty troops — of which there were about 400 involved according to Colonel Paul — advanced in battle formation over open ground towards Waterford, meeting with little or no opposition. As they approached the heights dominating the city from the northern shore, where one would have expected a strong anti-Treaty perimeter facing the other way, some scattered shots from a few snipers was the only opposition offered. As they closed on 'Mount Misery'[7] the attackers came under fire from the city, and took cover on the reverse slope of the hill. On 18 July at 6.45

154

p.m. the firing began. The anti-Treatyites held an advance strongpoint on Bilberry Rock in the Suir and between it and the 'Mount Misery' cliffs occurred the first serious exchanges. The firing continued heavily until after 10 p.m. The following morning the first ranging shell from the pro-Treaty artillery screamed into the city, and after that the barrage lasted all day. Pro-Treaty troops opposing the Waterford and Kerry men in the city were composed, principally, of men from Kilkenny with a strong sprinkling of Tipperary and Waterford men.

The strength of the artillery used by the attackers has been greatly overestimated by the defenders, only one gun, an eighteen-pounder, in fact being used.[8] It was firing at first from the reverse slope of the hill in an indirect shoot, but a few shots were sufficient to show that this was likely to cause considerable damage to private property. On Paul's suggestion the gun was moved to the crest of the hill — into the line of fire — and over open sights firing commenced on the Infantry Barracks, the Jail and the Cavalry Barracks, which were in a straight line behind each other from the point of aim, at 1,200 to 2,300 yards range. Prout himself laid the first aim and the shell hit the boundary wall of the jail. From then on a rain of shells was directed at the three targets so that each was kept under fire and offered no refuge to the garrisons from the other two strong points.

'Our object', says Paul, 'was to break their morale. They had no experience of shellfire and the effects of high-explosives on men who had never known them can be imagined. Once their morale was gone, our objective was nearly gained.' The pro-Treaty gunners had the advantage of being up over the city and could see into it quite clearly. Their targets were prominent and distinctive and visibility was excellent. Paul, because of his local knowledge, was directing the shelling, and ironically enough, one near-miss hit his own house, which bordered on the Infirmary Barracks, while his mother was in it. The motto of the city — 'Urbs Intacta' — proved to be more hopeful than accurate once the attack got under way.

The field gun had point blank range and was only harassed from time to time by machine-gun and rifle fire from the city where the defenders were dug in in the barracks and in heavily barricaded buildings: Breen's Hotel, J. H. S. Phelan's Stores, Hall's Stores, Hearne & Co., The Munster Express office, the Grenville Hotel, the Adelphi Hotel, the Post Office and Reginald's Tower.[9] They set up a hospital in the Imperial Hotel. The attack on the anti-Treaty right flank was launched under

155

cover of darkness on Thursday, 20 July. The attackers were under the command of Captain Ned O'Brien, a local man, old IRA man and journalist on the staff of the *Waterford News*, who was later killed on patrol in the city. They crossed the river at Giles' Quay, about a mile outside the city. The defenders were taken completely by surprise. No fighting, other than that involved in the capture of some anti-Treatyites in a motor car, is recorded. The entire anti-Treaty garrison might have been asleep. There was no protection on that flank at all and the attackers crept in unchallenged. They had orders to by-pass any outposts they might come across and capture a strong position which could command the river, from where they could give the main body of their troops covering fire in a general attack. There was such a position in the block of buildings on the corner of the quays and the Mall, which included the Adelphi and Imperial Hotels and the County Club. Through the connivance of a Unionist called Dobbyn they had the key to the back door of the club. They crept through the apparently sleeping city and knocked on the door, which was also bolted. The sentry, at that hour, was expecting his relief and he opened the door, saying: 'It's about time you came.' Only to be told 'Put up your hands.' The attackers posted machine-guns in the club, covering the approaches to the hotels.

On the same day an attack against the weak pro-Treaty right flank was to have been mounted by Clonmel anti-Treatyites under Commandant General Denis Lacy, but, once again, their plans backfired. 'They had no central command,' said Paul, 'and didn't know what was happening, even in their own lines. They didn't know where our fellows were. There was terrible confusion.' The anti-Treaty plan was to attack the pro-Treaty forces from the rear so that they would have to face about and be caught between two fires, leaving them open to a thrust from the west. Three columns of about 150 men all told were to take part. There was a column each of Cork, Tipperary and Kilkenny men under the overall command of Lacy of the South Tipperary Brigade. The columns were under Jim Hurley, Cork, Michael Sheehan, Tipperary, Andrew Kennedy, Kilkenny. There was a reserve of about 100 men under Commandant Dan Breen[10] about ten miles north-east of the rendezvous at Mullinavat, itself seven miles north of Waterford City. This force was to protect Hurley's men, who were to engage Prout from the rear, at the same time keeping the right flank clear for fresh troops from Clonmel which would strike decisively at Prout's flank.

Sheehan and Kennedy were to lie farther back and hold the Mullinavat area, preventing pro-Treaty reinforcements from Kilkenny doing to their own forces what they proposed to do to Prout. The success of the operation depended on surprise. For this reason it was essential that no large body of anti-Treatyite troops should be known to be in the vicinity of Waterford City.[11]

But Sheehan's enthusiasm overcame his good judgement — and his orders — and he precipitately attacked a pro-Treaty supply column of little importance as it passed through Mullinavat.

Almost simultaneously anti-Treaty leaders learned of the successful pro-Treaty crossing at Giles' Quay. Incorrectly, they assumed that this was the result of Sheehan's attack and that Prout, suddenly realizing the danger to his rear, had crossed the river because of the Mullinavat action. They also believed that concealment was no longer possible and withdrew to Carrick-on-Suir, twenty miles north-east of Waterford, systematically destroying bridges and blocking roads as they went. Their conclusions were wrong, as it turned out. The pro-Treaty forces considered the action at Mullinavat to be only the effort of a small local force. The anti-Treaty plan of attack might well have succeeded. However the crossing of the river had been planned by Paul in Kilkenny and to ensure total surprise and possible success the anti-Treaty attack should have been mounted at least twenty-four hours earlier.

Lacy, now commanding in Carrick-on-Suir, was given the following orders on which he based, first his offensive, and then the defence of Carrick:

Operations order No. 1, Field HQ, 2nd Southern Division, to the Brigadier in command, Carrick-on-Suir:

1. To hem in the enemy in Waterford from the north side, co-operating with the 1st Southern Division which is to hem him in on the south side;
2. To interrupt enemy communications between New Ross and Waterford in every possible way;
3. To interrupt communications between Kilkenny and Waterford at Mullinavat;
4. To maintain Carrick-on-Suir as a reserve base for transport and communications and to take every precaution to prevent the town from being captured.

157

With Lacy's men withdrawn to their base there was now no threat to Prout's rear and he continued to press the city as hard as he could. He moved his men down from the heights of 'Mount Misery' and occupied the district known as Ferrybank on the northern shores of the river. Between this position and the anti-Treaty position across the 250 yards of the river a continuous fire was maintained. Prout also brought down his field-gun and used it at point blank range to dislodge the enemy from the Post Office, where he had a strong machine-gun post. More of his troops crossed the river to the city where street fighting occurred. The pro-Treaty troops established themselves in the outskirts and during this exchange the first civilian casualty of the fighting was killed. He was William Long who lived at Bath Street. It is not known by which side he was killed.

On Thursday, with the pro-Treaty troops flanking them in south east, and the artillery fire still continuing, the anti-Treatyites abandoned the Cavalry and Infantry Barracks, both of them, by this time, in flames. Each side accused the other of causing these fires. The pro-Treatyites said that the anti-Treatyites deliberately set fire to the barracks before they evacuated them, while the anti-Treatyites alleged that the fires, together with fires in Hall's and Breen's and the Post Office, which was completely destroyed, were caused by incendiary shells fired into the city. 'Incendiary shells' said Paul, 'were not used. The only shells used were H.E. and shrapnel.' Red-hot shell splinters may have caused some fires, but the general anti-Treaty policy of firing barracks was very likely the source of most of the fires in Waterford.

A Kilmeaden witness described the city at the time as: 'Looking like an erupting slag-heap. A great pall of smoke, visible for many miles, hung over it and was lit from time to time by dull tongues of flame shooting up through it.' Into these flaming barracks raced looters, men, women and children, running figures etched in black against the flaming buildings. Beds, bedding, kitchen utensils, food, bathroom equipment, doors — even the horses and carts to carry the stuff away — were stolen. One small boy, his face blackened with soot and ashes, is reported to have been seen, crying with desperate frustration as he tugged and tugged at a zinc bath full of pots and pans, stuck in a doorway. A man came to his assistance, freed the bath, and then made off with it.

On Thursday evening the magazine in the Infantry Barracks exploded. By now the artillery fire and the steady advance of the pro-

Treaty troops had forced the anti-Treaty forces back into one corner of the city. Anti-Treaty bulletins announced that their troops were 'falling back in good order, due to the intensive artillery barrage, but were forming columns outside the city and continuing to fight from there.'

These were the Kerrymen — and Corkmen — of the 1st Southern Division; their withdrawal from Waterford could hardly be called orderly. 'We had the experience of finding dinners steaming in the plates left behind as they made off to the west,' said Paul. ''Twas like a nest after a hen leaving it — still hot. They were gone like fair Billy-oh!'

With the capture of the Grenville Hotel, anti-Treaty HQ, and of Captain Jerry Cronin, who was left by Whelan to command the city, the end was virtually in sight. By Friday, 21 July, the anti-Treatyites were concentrated in and around Ballybricken Jail. In the capture of this final bastion an unknown and unsung sergeant of the attacking troops plays a prominent and heroic part. In order to breach the walls of the jail, Prout decided to set up the field gun on the Ferrybank railway bridge. But the site came under heavy fire from the anti-Treaty positions and every time men came out to dig in the trail, one of them was shot. After this had happened several times, the unknown sergeant leaped to his feet with a Lewis gun held in both hands, and feet straddled to take the shock, stood in the centre of the bridge covering the digging party with short bursts until he himself fell riddled with bullets from the jail. But his job was done. The trail was set and within seconds eighteen-pounder shells breached the jail and forced the defenders to come out and surrender or die in the stricken building. With their surrender the Battle of Waterford was over and the anti-Treaty line in the south-east was turned. It was soon to be rolled up as well.

---

[1] Colonel Paul maintains that there were also Cork troops opposing him and thinks they were members of the University College Cork Students' company of the Cork No.1 Brigade.

[2] Pro-Treaty brigadier in Waterford; retired as Colonel in the Defence Forces.

[3] With Dick Barrett they were executed — virtually as 'war criminals' — on 8 December 1922. See Chapter 25, Part III.

[4] The Redmondite Home Rule Party at Westminster had disappeared after the landslide of the 1918 election.

[5] The women's semi-military organization which stood in relation to the IRA during the War of Independence as the women's auxiliary forces did to the defence forces during 1939-46. It split, like the IRA on the Treaty, but the majority were anti-Treaty.

159

⁶ Colonel Paul was surprised to learn of anti-Treaty moves in this direction — given later in this chapter.

⁷ The River Suir at Waterford is about 250 yards wide with the city stretching back from the south bank. It is dominated by the cliffs of 'Mount Misery' which overlook the city from across the river and the main railway terminal which nestles below them. The bridge links the city with the station and the road to Kilkenny.

⁸ Anti-Treatyites claimed that a full battery of four pieces was in action.

⁹ The tenth-century historic building in the Mall built by Sidric, a Norse invader. Now a civic museum.

¹⁰ Fianna Fáil deputy since 1933; autobiography, *My Fight for Irish Freedom*.

¹¹ Preliminary plans were successful. Though they feared such a move, Colonel Paul knew nothing of the threat to the pro-Treaty rear until informed of it by the author. Many of the comments made by Colonel Paul have, not unnaturally, been challenged by anti-Treaty sources.

11

BEGINNING TO CRUMBLE

With both Limerick and Waterford in Government hands all hope of defending the 'Republic of Munster' disappeared. True, the advance south was held at Kilmallock, but the left flank of the anti-Treaty line had been pushed back from the Shannon, opening the way westward between the mountains and the sea, to Cork. On 15 July anti-Treaty HQ was again moved, this time to Fermoy, in County Cork. The pro-Treaty pincers closed on the 'line' where it still held from Tipperary town to Carrick-on-Suir, with Clonmel in the centre.

There was now no possibility that the anti-Treatyites could gain victory by force of arms alone, so quickly had the situation developed in pro-Treaty favour. However, their military leaders did not contemplate conceding the struggle. But, a vigorous protest in arms against the disestablishment of the Republic having been made, de Valera favoured ending hostilities at this time. He did not, however, have the power to bring this about. Lack of political authority within the anti-Treaty organization had placed leadership of the movement entirely in the hands of soldiers, determined to go on fighting, over whom de Valera had no control. Furthermore, the only alternative to carrying on the war at this time was acceptance of pro-Treaty demands for unconditional and absolute surrender which anti-Treaty militarists considered dishonourable.

The pro-Treaty authorities believed that the war was nearly over. Cautious statements to this effect were issued and jubilation was loud — but premature. The war lasted another ten months with increasing bitterness.

While the extreme flanks of the line were being attacked by the pro-Treaty pincers an attempt to capture Thurles and the flanking town of Golden was made by the anti-Treatyites in order to protect Tipperary. It resulted in minor disasters for them in both towns. Two columns of the 1st Southern Division were to make the attack on Thurles, one a Cork column, the other from Kerry. There was a Tipperary column from the 2nd Southern in support. Lacy was in command of the operation. The attackers concentrated on a small village, Littleton, on Sunday 16 July, coming in from three directions.

It is commonly believed nowadays that pro-Treaty troops during the Civil War were all uniformed and that their opponents were not. This is far from true, and was particularly untrue of the fighting at this stage. On the pro-Treaty side, there were far more men out of uniform than in it and many anti-Treatyites, especially officers, wore the same green uniform as that with which the pro-Treaty troops were being issued. Friend was often indistinguishable from foe, which led the Kerry column of anti-Treaty troops at Mary Willie's near Littleton to allow itself to be surrounded and captured by troops thought to be friendly. It was immediately after this incident that their HQ was moved to Fermoy.

The attack on Golden did not take place for nearly two weeks after the Thurles débâcle and was then made only in the face of a direct threat, by troops advancing through Golden from Thurles, to the Tipperary-Cashel-Clonmel salient. The pro-Treaty troops, consisting largely of local volunteers from Thurles, Templemore and Goulds Cross with a stiffening of Dublin Guards, advanced from Goulds Cross through Dundrum and occupied Golden midway on the main road linking anti-Treaty centres Tipperary and Cashel (which had been evacuated by the anti-Treatyites as early as July 1st but was re-occupied at the personal request of de Valera).

The Cashel OC decided to attack the pro-Treaty troops in Golden before they attacked him. The attack was to be from three sides; west, south and the OC himself coming in from Cashel in the east. However, synchronization was bad and — before the others arrived — one party with an advanced armoured car foolishly opened the attack. Surprise at first lent success, but luck deserted the attackers when the car broke down on the bridge leading to the town, rammed the parapet, blocked the road and became the target of defensive machine-gun fire effectively screening the way into the town. Directing these machine-guns was a Sergeant-Major Lemon who had been warned of the impending attack some hours earlier when anti-Treaty mine-layers were spotted.

The anti-Treaty advance party withdrew under covering fire, abandoning the armoured car, but the covering party, about twenty-six men, were all captured or killed. The OC, coming up from Cashel. marched into pro-Treaty positions just as the Kerrymen had done at

Mary Willie's, but managed to escape with some of his men, himself by throwing his revolver in the face of the officer who called on him to surrender.

The time was about 5 a.m. and fresh pro-Treaty troops coming in from Thurles quickly decided the issue. The defence of Golden had been in the hands of Commandant Jerry Ryan, a local officer of the pro-Treaty forces, who decided to press home his advantage and attack Tipperary town the next day, Saturday, 29 July. The anti-Treatyites in Tipperary were commanded by Vice-Brigadier Patrick 'Big Paddy' Dalton.[1] As it happened he had an uneasy command area, restless long before the pro-Treaty troops marched to the attack at five o'clock on that Saturday afternoon. Apart from the unco-ordinated militarism of the anti-Treatyites who gave little heed to the needs of the civilians, the populace was subjected to curious and peremptory treatment from a group of self-styled Communists who endeavoured to take over the administration of the local co-operatives. These 'Communists' were mostly irresponsible and disaffected individuals, as great a danger to each other as to the community, who sought to establish 'Workers' Councils' under the Red Flag. They received scant support from the farmers, but when they took over the creameries of Messrs Cleeve Bros., and issued cheques which had no credit, at the same time stirring up the unemployed to violence, the farmers appealed to the anti-Treatyites and shots were exchanged before partial order was restored. The anti-Treatyites were satisfied with partial order and neither then, nor at any other time, did they worry much about civic affairs.

Commanding the units of the Dublin Guards in the attack was Commandant Patrick O'Connor, who expressly asked O'Duffy, GOC, to be allowed to take the town without artillery in order to spare the civilian population as much danger as possible. The battle, according to the official pro-Treaty notice released on 31 July, lasted eighteen hours — anti-Treaty sources make it twenty-six. At all events the town changed hands in a day of bitter fighting. There were about 500 pro-Treaty troops employed under the joint commands of O'Connor and Ryan. After the defeat of the anti-Treatyites at Golden, the pro-Treaty troops pressed on towards Tipperary by two roads, converging on the town from the north and north-east. The first defence was a strong position at a place called Rosanna House on a hillside about a mile outside the town and covering these approaches. The defenders withdrew to the town. Within the town Dalton had made what defensive dispositions he could, but his forces were small — less than 100 men — and reinforcements were not anticipated.

Approaches to the town and the principal streets were mined and fortified according to the usual procedure. Barricades blocked the streets and many of the most prominent buildings were sandbagged and defended. The Abbey School, Carroll's Hotel, Dobbyn's Hotel and the Infantry Barracks were all occupied, Spital Street being particularly barricaded. At five o'clock the attack began. Ryan's men closed in from the north and attracted anti-Treaty fire while O'Connor made an assault on Spital Street, his men fighting their way into the gas company's offices and, after a two-hour battle which developed into a hand-to-hand exchange with grenades and rifle-butts, finally into the house of Mr Carew, which was an anti-Treaty strongpoint. A simultaneous attack by some of Ryan's forces made slower progress and it was the early hours of the morning before his troops reached the Abbey grounds, where they immediately came under heavy fire from Carroll's Hotel. Between these two positions a duel began which was inconclusive until the anti-Treatyites in Carroll's were ordered to withdraw with the rest of the town garrison. Pro-Treaty troops which had stormed Meeling Street were caught in a sudden fire from Benn's Hotel, Heaphy's and O'Callaghan's and were driven back the way they had come. An anti-Treaty outpost on Bridge Street corner then opened up on the attackers in Meeling Street, catching them in the cross-fire. This outpost became the rallying centre for the anti-Treatyites as they were driven from house to house, from street to street, until finally the fighting at Bridge Street became the fiercest in the town.

When Ryan made an encircling movement westward towards Bansha the anti-Treatyites decided to evacuate the town and withdrew into the wilderness of the Glen of Aherlow from where they continued to fight. By five o'clock on Sunday afternoon the town was in pro-Treaty hands and the anti-Treaty line, as well as being turned at both ends, was smashed through in the centre. Clonmel was cut off from the main anti-Treaty area, now Cork and Kerry. Casualties in this were fantastically light with an overall total, including prisoners, of about forty — less than eight per cent of the total committed. The figure illustrates the truth of what veterans still say: 'There was no heart in the fighting at that time.'

'North and mid-Tipperary are already under the control of the Government forces,' said O'Duffy in Tipperary two days after it was

164

captured, 'and with the capture of the town a deep wedge has been driven into South Tipperary.' Apart from the capture of Limerick and Waterford, it was the most significant operation yet against the anti-Treaty line. Besides isolating Clonmel, it broadened the front against Cork and opened the Kilmallock flank. Cashel, of course, was untenable by the anti-Treatyites with three sides occupied by enemy forces, and was evacuated on Monday, incidentally withdrawing the most advanced of the remaining peripheral Clonmel defences.

The value of the capture of Tipperary was two-fold because it enabled the pro-Treaty troops to encircle the mass of the Silvermines and Slievefelim mountains, where the anti-Treatyites of the area were certain to concentrate sooner or later. The great drawback of such concentration and of guerilla warfare in general is the problem of supplies and this explains why the anti-Treatyites held on to towns and villages as long as possible and also why most of the battles were in and around towns and villages.

But these are extremely vulnerable to artillery, as the anti-Treatyites were to find out in each city, town and village they tried to hold. They had no artillery themselves and against it they had no effective defence. When warfare is moved out into open country then organized transport, supply services and communications are vital, in all of which the anti-Treatyites were conspicuously lacking. Withdrawal to a mountain fortress, which was the familiar tactic adopted against the British, depends on having support from the civilian population, otherwise the supply problem becomes acute. The anti-Treatyites did not have sufficient civilian support.

The hostility of the populace was a determining factor in the fight against the British. It played an equally decisive part in the anti-Treaty collapse in the Civil War. The pro-Treaty troops had, in large, the benefit of the people's sympathy and help. The troops entering Tipperary received a great welcome from the population who had resented the anti-Treaty rule, especially as Cleeve's factory had been fired by the anti-Treatyites before they left the town and the watermain blown up to prevent the fire being put out.

Finally the problem of manpower was now becoming a major one with the anti-Treatyites. Although commanders were ordered to arrange for regular reliefs for their men, in practice it was frequently the same men who were in operation from the beginning of the war until the Cease Fire. Flocks of new recruits enabled the pro-Treatyites to have

165

fresh troops whenever or wherever they were wanted. Their opponents also suffered from desertion, sometimes, as in Kilkenny, of considerable magnitude. And, as the pro-Treaty troops advanced into anti-Treaty areas, hundreds of arrests were made and known or suspected anti-Treatyites were rounded up, reducing the potential fighting strength at their disposal.[2]

[1] Killed in action at Donohill, Tipperary, on 26 October 1922.

[2] The proclamation of the Irish Bishops, issued about this time, was a further handicap for the anti-Treaty leaders as its most debilitating result, in their eyes, became the number of soldiers who followed the hierarchical prescription and returned to their homes; the remainder, of course, to a greater or lesser degree, suffered from feelings of serious moral doubt.

12

IN CARRICK-ON-SUIR

Carrick-on-Suir stood in relation to Waterford as Tipperary town did to Limerick. The pro-Treatyites' advance from Waterford against Clonmel could not proceed to the west as long as Carrick-on Suir was in anti-Treaty Hands. Tipperary was captured on 30 July and on the following day the battle for Carrick-on-Suir began. Lacy had been ordered to hold Carrick as a reserve base from which offensives against the enemy in Wexford, Waterford and Kilkenny could be launched. He had three columns of Tipperary men under Commandants Michael Sheehan, Andrew Kennedy and Jack Kileen; a local company under the ex-Charleville battalion Vice OC Denis O'Driscoll, a small Cork column with those of Dan Breen — Kilmoganny (directly north, ten miles away) — and Dorney Regan (Cashel about twenty miles north-west) — in support; a total of about 500 men. The Waterford men between Portlaw and Kilmacthomas to the south and south-east, according to anti-Treaty reports at the time, were 'not inclined to do anything'.[1] A further support column was later drafted into Carrick from Templemore in north Tipperary and it now became, to all intents and purposes, the extreme right flank of the wavering line. At this time de Valera, Robinson the Divisional OC, Lacy and unit commanders were using the Carrick workhouse as local HQ from where de Valera operated.

But, behind the lines, it was the old story. The attitude of the soldiers towards the civil population was far from helpful. Food and supplies had, of necessity, to be seized on requisition and there was occasional looting — though (as in Mullinahone, where Cork troops looted some shopkeepers and Lacy, in a rage, ordered the goods returned at the point of a gun) it was severely dealt with when discovered. Civilians were commandeered for the manual labour of road-blocking, entrenching and so on. The result was inevitable. More and more people supported the 'new Government' and many of the civilians behind the anti-Treaty lines were Republicans under duress: not surprisingly since, in the face of the anti-Treaty policy of defence and withdrawal, it was only a matter of time before the 'Republic' became militarily ineffective. As the pro-Treaty forces advanced to town after town, they were overwhelmed with eager recruits — 'Local Volunteers' — who advanced with them against their anti-Treaty former military authorities.

At this time there was little heart in the fighting, anti-Treatyites still vaguely hoped for a sudden reversal of policy by their opponents and a joint attack on the British still in Ireland and the pro-Treatyites felt that the war would be over in a matter of weeks and that they would then be free to implement the Free State policy to the full. Both attitudes were based on the assumption that the principles of their opponents were false and, therefore, easily malleable faced with the truth.

In Carrick-on-Suir food was running short by 28 July; business was almost at a standstill and communications, though open, were unsatisfactory with outlying areas and HQ at Clonmel and Fermoy. While Prout's troops massed in Waterford and Mullinavat, the Carrick defences were prepared. A line of defence from Cregg, on the Kilkenny road, to Three Bridges on the Waterford road about three miles east of the town was strengthened. A general order was sent out to all local commanders in the anti-Treaty army saying that when roads, railways, bridges and so on were destroyed no provision was being made to prevent them being quickly repaired by advancing enemy troops; the order said that such destruction must aim at being permanent. This order did little to endear the anti-Treatyites to the hearts of the farmers and tradesmen who used these same roads and bridges in the ordinary commerce of their everyday lives. Even though Munster was the seat of Republicanism, the civil population there was rapidly losing patience with the anti-Treatyites.

Because of the anti-Treaty war effort, commerce in the province — and also in the west where the second anti-Treaty stronghold lay — was at a standstill, and communications with the rest of the country were almost entirely cut off. The anti-Treaty troops were living off the populace, no plans for co-operation between military and civilians existed and it was becoming increasingly evident that the present anti-Treaty war policy could end only in defeat. When, in October, the anti-Treatyites formed a 'Government' of their own it was far too late to rally the support of the populace to it. The truism that it is a people and not their army who make a cause democratic was ignored behind the anti-Treaty lines. Efforts to improve matters were limited and largely confined to orders, such as this, issued from 2nd Southern Division HQ in mid-July, which illustrates the alarm felt by some responsible individuals at the turn of events: 'Officers must constantly keep in mind the fact that we *do* want the people with us, and that they deserve to be treated properly by us. Our behaviour towards them should and will be guided if we remember that we are real soldiers — *not* of the Black and Tan type.'[2]

Ironically it is true that although the Provisional Government swept to authority on a reversal of this same truism, they had three important assets that the anti-Treatyites had not:

(1) Power.
(2) A political policy which the people accepted.
(3) The moral and material support of banks, churches, population at large — plus the 'encouragement' of Great Britain.

The anti-Treatyites alienated many Republican supporters, most of those who were neutral, and squabbled among themselves. As we shall see there were significant differences of opinion, not only between the political and military leaders but between the military leaders themselves.

At the end of July Madame Markievicz, Erskine Childers — anti-Treaty Director of Publicity — and Dr Kathleen Lynn were in Carrick with de Valera. Two days later Cashel and Cahir had fallen and Harry Boland, Collins's greatest friend, was shot and fatally wounded by pro-Treaty troops in the Grand Hotel in Skerries, County Dublin, where he was staying with another anti-Treaty officer, Joe Griffith. He died in St Vincent's Hospital on 1 August. The effect on Collins was that it hardened his purpose to end the war quickly as nothing else had.[3]

On Monday, 31 July, Prout sent an advance party from Mullinavat through Rochestown and Piltown — from which village the anti-Treatyites had just pulled out — and so to Castletown, coming westward. The route they took was through difficult, hilly country until they hit low land at Raheen and Jamestown, about two miles north-east of Piltown. Near Piltown they had their first clash with the enemy, who was holding an advanced position in wooded country between Piltown and the River Suir.

While the advance was held up here on Tuesday, 1 August, troops moved up from Waterford via Kilmacow to Mullinavat to join Prout's main body. The same day the advance began in earnest towards Carrick, twelve miles south-west. At Bessborough demesne near Piltown the column had to leave the road and, because of obstructions, travel through the estate. (A local legend has grown up around de Valera in Piltown where he and Seamus Robinson spent some time preparing for the attack, to the effect that he gave away his rifle rather than use it against fellow Irishmen.) By the evening of 1 August, the main body of Prout's troops had made contact with their advance guard beyond Piltown who were engaging the anti-Treatyites with rifles and machine-guns.

They were lucky not to be attacked in the rear. They had foolishly bypassed Fiddown bridge, held at both ends — it is a very long double bridge connecting an island with the mainland on either bank — by forty-four anti-Treatyites under Denis O'Driscoll, CO of Carrick. He and his men, with a Vickers machine-gun, were behind the pro-Treaty troops. Ready to attack that night, O'Driscoll inexplicably received orders not to do so: nor was he ordered to attack on the following day when his intervention might have been decisive. He was not told of the withdrawal from Carrick, three miles west of him, until after it had been effected. His subsequent dry comment on the line to be held was : 'It warped in the sun.'

On Wednesday, 2 August, a field gun was brought up and the wood where the anti-Treatyites were dug in, near Killonery House, was riddled with shrapnel. When this had done its work and forced the anti-Treatyites back through the wood to their line along the Lingaun River, that line was attacked in force along the whole front.

But about 3 p.m. the anti-Treatyites made an assault across the river at Cregg, hoping to turn the pro-Treaty right flank. With Dan Breen holding the country behind them this might have been possible, but with the advance of Commandant McCarthy southwards on Carrick from Callan through Mullinahone, Ninemilehouse, Kilmoganny and Windgap, Breen had withdrawn from the Kilmoganny area towards Kilsheelin between Carrick and Clonmel. The anti-Treaty assault was supported by covering fire from Tinvane House, owned by Mr Edward Dowley, which was anti-Treaty Field HQ. It came in for a good deal of attention from the pro-Treaty field gun and, in the face of point blank shrapnel fire over open sights supported by heavy machine-gun fire, the attack was broken. At this point had O'Driscoll's men, still on Fiddown Bridge, been called into action they would have caught the pro-Treaty troops in low ground with little cover and between two lines of fire and

170

they might have been forced to withdraw. Whether the anti-Treatyites could have followed up any such withdrawal to their own advantage is another question. As it was once the anti-Treaty assault was broken, there was only sporadic fighting during the night and on the following day the advance guard of the successful troops entered Carrick from which the anti-Treatyites had withdrawn under cover of darkness. All bridges in the town were blown and there was no water supply. Business was at a standstill, and several premises to this day bear the marks of battle on their walls. Anti-Treaty snipers were active long after the town had fallen; but the pro-Treaty road to Clonmel was now open.

[1] Captured documents published in the daily Press, 21/22 September 1922, and in *Sgeal Catha Luimnuighe*.

[2] This order has an unknown source, but in sentiment and because of its place and time of origin, might very well have been issued by de Valera. O'Donoghue says: 'It is far more likely to have been written by Con Moloney.'

[3] Earnan de Blaghd.

13

THE TAKING OF CLONMEL

After the capture of Carrick-on-Suir, Tipperary and, in the southwest, Tralee,[1] pro-Treaty forces paused to draw breath before delivering what were expected to be two-fisted knock-out blows, delivered simultaneously at opposite ends of the Munster stronghold. The targets were Clonmel and Cork City, the principal centres still held by anti-Treatyites.

A speedy victory was, at this stage, confidently anticipated by pro-Treaty supporters. The troops moving south were young and cheerful and lighthearted in this 'summer campaign'. In every town they occupied or captured they were welcomed as heroes and deliverers by an enthusiastic populace who were welcoming, together with the troops, the new impetus which they hoped would be given to trade from resumed contact with Dublin and the rest of Ireland. Head offices in Dublin sent, in the wake of the onward-rolling Government armies, frantic demands for information. Telegraphs and telephones were at a premium in towns that had changed hands. Anxious friends and relatives who had been without news for weeks waited uneasily — and hundreds of youths who could not wait for the wheels of commerce to start turning again to return to their old jobs, flocked to join the victorious forces; they were attested in the field and thrown immediately into combat, armed but not uniformed, to become what General W. R. E. Murphy[2] called 'some of the most valuable of our troops'.

But as they were driven from one stronghold after another, the retreating anti-Treatyites became grimmer and more determined. Unfortunately for themselves this effort and determination were largely wasted in haphazard military action which was an absurd and inadequate defence of high principles and ideals. During the legal and political battle for the Republic, between January and 28 June, virtually no steps to defend the Republican ideal had been taken at a military level. Hence the position that the anti-Treatyites found themselves in in

172

early August. In a review of the situation on 8 August O'Duffy said: 'We control Limerick, the Midlands and the east; we are attacking Cork and Kerry and we have established a strong outpost at Newport in Tipperary and extended the Pallas-Oola line to Tipperary town — and Limerick Junction, a most important point . . . with the possible exception of Clonmel the Irregulars now hold no post in Tipperary, though they still continue to harass the civilian population in a few quarters.'

The same day — Tuesday — pro-Treaty troops moved out of Carrick-on-Suir for an assault on Clonmel and, when it was captured three days later, Tipperary was entirely in pro-Treaty hands.

From then on, for the anti-Treatyites (there were simultaneous landings at their rear in Cork and Kerry) it became a guerilla war against a now thoroughly established enemy. Moreover they were burdened with another severe handicap; in pursuance of the May Pastoral letter of the Irish Hierarchy, they were being denounced from various pulpits throughout the country and, in some cases, prisoners, so long as they swore allegiance to the Republic, were denied access to the Holy Sacraments or to the rites of the Church. Formal excommunication was pronounced by the Bishops in a pastoral letter in October. This involved, of course, only the ordinary and the secular clergy in each diocese, and excommunicated anti-Treatyites were frequently and promptly absolved by the monks and the friars of religious orders outside the jurisdiction of the Bishops.

In Clonmel the anti-Treaty garrison had time to become thoroughly organized. One of the leading commercial distribution centres in the South of Ireland, it had large supplies of clothing and foodstuffs available, and liberal use was made of these stores. Payment was by promissory note, or by cash, £20,000 being appropriated for the purpose from the local banks. What transport was in the town had been commandeered and an estimated 100,000 gallons of petrol was in the town. A good deal of preparation was given to defence and Lacy, Robinson, Breen and de Valera were busy in the vicinity. De Valera had asked to be left in Clonmel when HQ was moved to Fermoy. Robinson was GOC of the 2nd Southern Division ever since O Maille was appointed assistant Chief of Staff and GOC Eastern and Northern Command and de Valera felt that the principal burden of holding the ill-fated anti-Treaty line was going to fall on Robinson's men and that they would need whatever moral and physical support he could give.

173

De Valera did not always see eye to eye with the anti-Treaty commanders, but, while his political influence was still considerable, his military authority was limited to that of his appointment — that of assistant Director of Operations to Seán Moylan — and, at most, he could make suggestions on policy — which were not always well received.

But he was active in preparing the defences of Clonmel and there is an eye-witness account of his inspecting the defences of Kilcash Castle and studying the terrain through binoculars and with the aid of a map. Strong points were established well outside the town, facing Carrick and Callen in Kilkenny. The by now customary barricades and shutters were given a final inspection; business was at a stand-still; the town and all that were in it waited.

The columns that left Carrick on Tuesday, 8 August did not advance by the heavily defended main road, but north via Ballyneale and Ballypatrick, into country which had been isolated since the war began. It is a heavily wooded and picturesque district, but heavy rain which had fallen earlier made the going slow and unpleasant, and there was a drizzle falling. First shots were exchanged at Kilcash Castle, inspected by de Valera not long before, but it had already been decided by the anti-Treatyites to evacuate Clonmel after a delayed defence to avoid street-fighting and the danger of civilian casualties. The attacking column advanced in its usual formation — advance guard, horse and motor transport, and a rearguard some distance behind. Between Kilcash and Ballypatrick they captured two anti-Treatyites driving a staff car of the *Freeman's Journal* which they themselves had captured, together with its occupants, only that morning. The prisoners were released and the erstwhile guards became prisoners themselves.

Along the romantic valley of Sliabh na mBan, the breast-like mountain demurely veiled in a thin mist, the troops advanced towards Ballypatrick at the foot of the mountain. Here one of the main engagements of the day took place. It was presaged by an incident which underlines the pathos and bewilderment of the period. Led by Commandants Carew and McCarthy, two parties of the advance guard, made a flanking movement towards Ballynockan Wood behind the village. Their troops — local volunteers — were not in uniform. As they moved into the fields they noticed a party holding a trench behind a fence. They challenged the party and got the reply:

'Who are you?'

Two of the pro-Treaty volunteers crossed the field to interrogate them and it was only then that they identified the others as anti-Treatyites. One of the two volunteers was particularly friendly with one of the anti-Treatyites and, after a short discussion, they shook hands and it was agreed that the pro-Treaty volunteers would be allowed to return to their own line before firing commenced. As one of them was crossing the last bank to rejoin his unit the shout came from behind:

'Are you Republicans?'

'Yes, but we are not diehards,' was the reply. Immediately both sides opened up with machine-guns and rifle fire. This incident was the signal for an outbreak of heavy firing all along the line of the wood — which was strongly defended by the anti-Treatyites — and similar incidents were repeated more than once,

A large body of pro-Treaty troops coming up on the right were mistaken by the anti-Treatyites for Commandant Tom Bellew's men, or other friendly troops, and were greeted with: 'Kerry No. 1 . . . Up Kerry' and so on, to which they replied with rapid fire.

After a lengthy battle the anti-Treatyites retired towards Ormonde Lodge under cover of the wood, but heavy firing continued until nightfall. Just before that, several shells were fired into the wood by the attackers, the gun-flashes and explosions lighting up, fitfully and threateningly, the crouching twilight. The pro-Treatyites retired for the night as far as the estate of Mr. Constable at Ballyglasheen House, capturing an anti-Treaty doctor on the way. The anti-Treatyites withdrew to Kilmore and Powerstown where they intended to make a last stand before Clonmel. It was while they were withdrawing that the doctor was captured. Next day the advance was continued around the base of Sliabh na mBan. Preparations by the anti-Treatyites for the evacuation of the town were complete and the military and police barracks were fired. A great cloud of smoke, visible for many miles, hung over the town.

At Redmondstown the advancing troops were pinned down for a while by an anti-Treaty position on a hill south between them and the railway line. This naturally fortified position was supported by men in a bohereen in front of and parallel to the railway line, and from these two positions, and between them, machine-guns controlled the approaches to the town. In addition, several snipers' posts gave the defenders a wide field of fire. An advance by the pro-Treatyites on a wide front could not be attempted without heavy losses. For over an hour the advance was

175

halted and an attempted flanking movement repelled. But finally a column under Commandant Tommy Ryan inched its way forward under cover of the railway line, until it reached the outskirts of the town. A second flanking movement forced the anti-Treaty main body back on the town leaving only one or two snipers, with Lewis guns and rifles, to hold off the attack. Shelling had been taking its effect on the defenders for about two hours and now the extreme range of these guns was used to shell them as they retired from the town on the other side of the Suir 9000 yards away.

The advance was a stop-and-go, stop-and-go affair as post after hidden post opened fire on the pro-Treaty troops, and each had to be cleared before the advance continued. The main body of anti-Treatyites had withdrawn and the columns which had fought under Lacy's command since the beginning of hostilities were now sent back to their own areas as Active Service Units. The only column left in Clonmel on Wednesday evening was the 5th Battalion column, which acted as a rearguard. Between 6 and 7 p.m. it was decided by many of the officers on the pro-Treaty staff that Clonmel would not fall that night, so determined was the column's defence. But the advance guard made a sudden charge with Prout in personal command and cleared the approaches. The attackers then came into the town in three columns. That under Ryan which came along the railway line was met by an anti-Treaty armoured car at King Street and held for a time. A second column, under McCarthy, came in by Horse Pasture Road and the third, under Prout, came in along Kilsheelin Street where they were attacked by the anti-Treaty rearguard. During the last battle for the town the anti-Treaty armoured car, dashing to reinforce point after point, capsized under fire and the occupants, carrying their machine-gun, were lucky to get away with their lives. During this action the men of the anti-Treaty rearguard left the town over Gashouse Bridge and as the pro-Treaty troops came up the Mall one Jim Nugent held them there with machine-gun fire while about seventy of his comrades withdrew. The effect of his fire is indicated by an eye-witness:

'Suddenly the machine-gun rattled; bullets pierced the air with sharp vicious hisses and chips of stone flew from the road all around us. All of us dived for cover and I lay huddled in a ditch, but all the time with an uneasy feeling that my body had enlarged to such an extent as to expose me to every bullet that sang by.'

It was midnight or after it when the troops marched into the town,

176

past the blazing barracks and under heavy smoke clouds, which in turn lay under dull rainclouds that had drenched the men continuously since they left Carrick-on-Suir two days before. Their welcome was encouraging. The townspeople thronged the streets to greet the troops. Only a few quiet faces — or a few absent ones — were witness to the fact that the anti-Treatyites also had friends and relatives in the town. It was Wednesday night — Thursday morning, 9 and 10 August. Clonmel was in pro-Treaty hands. Cork was being attacked from the front at Kilmallock and in the rear from the sea, so was Kenmare. Tralee was now, also, in Government hands. On 11 August, Liam Lynch and his staff walked out of their headquarters in Fermoy barracks, leaving it blazing behind them, and took to the mountains.

'[He was] once more the leader of a guerilla army without barracks or bases, stores or supplies,' wrote O'Donoghue in *No Other Law*. He might well have added, without Government. The main anti-Treatyite forces were now concentrated between the rivers Lee and Blackwater, north and south, and between the Clonmel-Youghal line and the Tralee-Kenmare line, east and west.

[1] See Chapter 18.
[2] Later Chief Commissioner of the Garda Siochana, the Civic Guard (police force).

14

WEXFORD — THE WEST — THE MIDLANDS

Outside Munster the most significant area recognized as being clearly Republican was that which included the western counties of Sligo, Mayo, Galway — the district known as Connemara — and Leitrim. This compact area might have offered formidable resistance to the pro-Treaty forces sent against it but for the fact that local leadership was, again, inadequate, lacking national guidance. There were, besides, anti-Treaty pockets all over the country. When the news of the Four Courts spread from Dublin most local anti-Treaty commanders looked to their *defences* and waited to be attacked. Where they did not do this of their own initiative they were ordered to do so by GHQ, which also instructed many units to adopt guerilla tactics early in July.

Immediately after the Four Courts fell, O'Maille, after his escape from Jameson's distillery, made his way to Blessington and from there to Bunclody in County Wexford. A glance at the map will show that with Munster in anti-Treaty hands and strong anti-Treaty forces in Wicklow, Wexford was a vital link between the two — providing a jumping-off place for any proposed advance north through New Ross and Enniscorthy. O'Maille may well have hoped for a line curving, unbroken, from Wexford to Waterford and so to Limerick. However, there was strong pro-Treaty feeling among the IRA in Wexford and south Wicklow. Key town in the county was Enniscorthy. Whoever controlled Enniscorthy controlled the county and the principal roads through it. At the outbreak of hostilities in Dublin, Enniscorthy was occupied by elements of both sides, the pro-Treaty troops under Staff-Captain Séan Gallagher in the old police barracks, Abbey Quay, and in the castle which they commandeered from the owner, Mr Henry Roche, establishing a machine-gun post on top. The anti-Treatyites were men of Michael Sheehan's column from Tipperary who had occupied the Courthouse, the Portsmouth Arms Hotel, the Technical School and St Mary's Protestant church, in the belfry of which they set up a machine-gun post dominating the town. On Sunday, 2 July, they delivered an ultimatum to Gallagher demanding surrender. He refused and the ensuing battle, lasting for three days, was comparatively heavy in casualties, a total of six being killed and eighteen wounded.

Most of the fighting, with machine-guns and rifles, was at a fair distance. Business, as usual, came to an abrupt standstill and there was a noticeable flow of refugees from the town. An assault with bombs, grenades and machine-guns dislodged the pro-Treaty troops on Wednesday. Unsuccessful negotiations had already been attempted by the local clergy. The anti-Treatyites captured twenty-eight rifles, two Lewis guns, several shotguns, revolvers and grenades; and a considerable quantity of ammunition. At the same time as the fighting began at Enniscorthy, Ferns was attacked by some of O'Maille's troops and, after two days, the pro-Treaty troops surrendered.

The situation soon went into reverse, however. When, on Friday, 7 July, a strong force of pro-Treaty troops from Dublin approached Enniscorthy, the anti-Treatyites withdrew after firing the Courthouse. Ferns was taken after a brief exchange. Thereafter anti-Treaty activities in Wexford were confined to guerilla tactics.

At this time, about the middle of July, two things of importance occurred. The first was the realization by the pro-Treatyites that they had a full-scale Civil War on their hands, as the following communiqué from O'Duffy shows: 'Personal liberty is at an end . . . The whole economic life of the country is threatened. The safety and future welfare of the nation depend upon the power of the Irregulars being broken. It is the duty of all to stand solidly together to establish that the will of the people shall prevail. A peace built upon a compromise with forces that have behaved as the Irregulars have behaved would be a peace too costly for the Irish nation.'

The other important occurrence was the prorogation of the Dáil, again because of the realization that Civil War was nation-wide. The official announcement, issued on 12 July, is a remarkable piece of skilled propaganda:[1]

The armed conspiracy to defy and override the authority of the Irish people is being defeated in open warfare . . . and is resorting to brigandage . . . in a last effort to frustrate and reverse the national policy approved by Dáil Éireann and endorsed by the electorate. The soldiers now being sniped and ambushed are the servants of the people. Injury to these soldiers is, therefore, an attack on the people.

It is the first duty and the firm intention of the Government to assert the authority of the people and re-establish in every county full security for the individual and the free working of the economic life of the nation.

Were the armed groups who are taking upon themselves to make unnatural war upon the Irish people to be permitted to remain under arms for any length of time, the country would be faced with economic ruin and famine, as well as the return of the British Army and the re-establishment of alien authority. It is not by discussion, but by action, that such calamities can be averted. Parliament will stand prorogued for a further period of fourteen days . . .

The document was signed by the entire Cabinet of the Provisional Government.

Meanwhile towns and counties continued to fall to their army. In Nenagh the situation was typical of many areas where pro-Treaty forces were strong. The brigade OC was William Houlihan. He appointed an officer, James Nolan, as OC of the police in Nenagh after the Truce and Nolan occupied the old RIC barracks. On the outbreak of hostilities Nolan declared for the anti-Treaty cause with a minority of the troops in and about Nenagh behind him. But there was no open breach until a pro-Treaty officer, Terence Byrne, was shot and killed in the local hotel on 1 July (it is maintained that he was shot in the back). Houlihan immediately arrested Nolan, but he was later released by two sympathetic officers. With his followers he left town, but returned some time later with a mine intending to blow up the barracks of which he had lately been OC. Instead he blew himself to bits and shattered the windows of the entire street. There was a good deal of haphazard shooting for the next few days until, on 8 July, the last anti-Treatyites were forced to withdraw.

In Laois there were several minor engagements before the county finally surrendered to pro-Treaty control. The capture of Abbeyleix Courthouse and other anti-Treaty strongholds early in July weakened resistance in the county. In a clash at Cappard, nine miles north of Portlaoise, Colonel-Commandant P.A. Mulcahy,[2] brother of Richard Mulcahy, was wounded in the hip. The anti-Treatyites were holding Cappard House, in which the original of the Treaty of Limerick between Ireland and England in 1691 was supposed to be preserved.

180

Later they were forced to surrender in another engagement in which two pro-Treaty soldiers, McCurtain and Collins, were killed.

With the Midland towns in pro-Treaty hands, the east and centre of the country provided a relatively secure area for attacks south and west. In Galway City a situation similar to that in Limerick was reached. The city roughly marked the boundary between south Galway, which was largely pro-Treaty, and Connemara, north and west Galway, which was anti-Treaty. In the city units of both forces had establishments. Strong anti-Treaty areas in the periphery all around the city, except in the immediate south, isolated it from the rest of the pro-Treaty controlled country. The pro-Treaty troops of the 1st Western Division of Clare occupied the County Jail, the Courthouse, the Railway Hotel and Renmore Barracks just outside the city. The anti-Treatyites, under Commandant Kilkelly, occupied Eglington Street Barracks and several other posts in the city.

Between them the rival commanders reached a tentative truce, but the anti-Treatyites soon decided to evacuate the city and on Saturday, 1 July pulled out, burning the posts they had occupied behind them. They retreated into the mountainous countryside, cutting communications, barricading and trenching roads, and pulling up railway lines as they went. Looting in the isolated city, where supplies were dangerously low, reached such a pitch that next day an 11 p.m.-5 a.m. curfew was imposed. On Monday, while the thick smoke from the many fires (with which the fire-brigade was totally unable to cope) still hung above the city, Kilkelly launched an attack on Renmore Barracks as a preliminary to taking the town. Fighting was sporadic and confined to the Renmore area until Friday, when a lively engagement took place in the centre of the city, at Abbey Street. After a two-hour battle in and around the Bohermore district, the anti-Treatyites retreated westward, leaving some dead and wounded behind. Pro-Treaty casualties were light, several wounded and one killed. The pro-Treaty troops managed to beat a plan to encircle them in this engagement and turned the tables on the attackers. The city was now in pro-Treaty hands but was almost completely surrounded by anti-Treatyites.

The food situation was serious. In some areas notices threatening 'profiteers' appeared and some foodstuffs were unobtainable. Bread supplies were only maintained thanks to the efforts of Dr Walsh of the University College who provided liquid yeast, and those of his assistant, Dr Dillon, who acted as food controller in the city.

181

In Connemara also the food situation was acute and the area was completely isolated by 16 July. Flour was unobtainable in Clifden, principal town in the area, as early as 8 July. Food supplies normally came in by rail and road, but roads were blocked and bridges blown up. Arrangements were considered to send in supplies by boat.

Back in Galway, once the city was in their hands, the pro-Treaty troops decided to push out into the surrounding county, clearing it as they went, to join up with MacEoin's troops advancing from the Midlands. By Monday, 17 July, they were on the move towards Gort with eight armoured lorries and, in the area made famous by Lady Gregory in her plays, where the Gort-Ennis railway runs east of Kinvara, they surprised a column of anti-Treatyites and a running battle ensued over rough country. Most of the fighting was at ranges in excess of 400 yards and the anti-Treatyites retreated when they found themselves being attacked from two sides by the pro-Treatyites who had spilt into two forces, one of which used the transport to flank the enemy. It was unfortunate for the anti-Treatyites that their commander was captured at Craughwell next morning. By the end of July the anti-Treatyites in County Galway, sandwiched between two hostile forces, were leaving the towns altogether and burning installations as they went. In Oughterard only a small garrison remained to patrol the town and maintain civic order, while the remainder flocked to the surrounding high country. In most towns public services, as elsewhere, were at a standstill and, because of the blockade, Connemara faced the threat of a typhus epidemic. Old age pensions and public assistance money were not available and the people suffered in consequence, which gave birth to resentment against the anti-Treatyites even in this predominantly anti-Treaty area. Guerilla bands of anti-Treatyites, acting on their own initiative, had not yet been properly organized and hundreds of the troops hid their arms and returned home to wait for re-organization. Meantime, their local commander, Kilkelly — a member of the Galway County Council — had been captured and by the beginning of August the entire county was well in pro-Treaty hands, so far as the towns were concerned.

In Sligo the pattern was not quite similar, though the result was the same. At the beginning of July the town was sharply divided, the anti-Treatyites in the police station faced the pro-Treaty troops in the Courthouse, across Albert Street. The pro-Treaty unit decided to attack and succeeded in taking the police station with only a few casualties and one civilian killed. The barracks was fired and destroyed. Thereafter there was an uneasy truce for ten days. Then the anti-Treatyites carried out a successful attack at Rockwood, near Colooney, in which they captured the town and its garrison and along with the latter, an armoured lorry and an armoured car, complete with Vickers gun. Returning hot-foot to Sligo the anti-Treaty OC, Devins, established himself in the town, occupying buildings commanding the pro-Treaty positions. On the flat roof of the Ulster Bank he placed a couple of Lewis guns.The Hibernian Bank was fortified as was the Harp and the Shamrock Hotel, which became the anti-Treaty HQ. In front of the hotel, he put the armoured car commanding the Courthouse and the approaches to it across the river. Next day the following ultimatum was sent to pro-Treaty troops:

July 14, 1922.
    You are hereby commanded to surrender unconditionally the positions held by your troops before 6.30 p.m. this evening in the name of the Republic. Please reply in writing per bearer.
                    Séamus Devins, Commdt.
                    O C 1st Brigade, Western Division,
                    Executive Forces.

The pro-Treaty commander paraded his men and read the ultimatum to them, saying at the same time that he was sent there to hold the garrison. His men cheered and said that they would not surrender. He sent the following reply:

Being the National Army, with a mandate from the Irish people, I as OC and my men, shall never surrender our barracks unconditionally. I would wish you to distinctly understand that we hold these positions for the Irish people and for the Republic when they so will it.

Shortly after this Fr J. B. Mulligan, a Catholic curate from St Mary's parish church, arrived at pro-Treaty HQ with a message to say that if they released their anti-Treaty prisoners the anti-Treatyites would then make terms. They refused. Fr Mulligan again returned to say that if the prisoners were not released within ten minutes the Courthouse would be attacked. Again they refused. Before the attack could begin the

Bishop of Elphin, the Most Reverand Dr Coyne, arrived from his sickbed and asked the pro-Treatyites to surrender in the interests of peace. Their OC replied that his instructions were to hold the position for the 'Government' and he could not surrender. Then a remarkable thing occurred. The Bishop, holding that the pro-Treatyites were right, entered the building saying that he would remain with the garrison to the last. However, at the request of the Bishop, an exchange of prisoners was agreed to, the exchange to take place in front of the Courthouse.

The anti-Treaty OC replied that he had no prisoners, whereupon the pro-Treaty OC is reported to have said: 'Come on and fight.' This, of course, was just what the anti-Treatyites could not do now. With the Bishop in the Courthouse an attack was out of the question. No surer method of utterly damning the anti-Treaty cause could have been found than such an attack on the Courthouse with the sick Bishop inside. Had the prelate been killed or injured, there would have been a public outcry which must surely have ended the anti-Treaty cause there and then. How the pro-Treatyites would use such an occurrence to their advantage may well be imagined. Even if the Bishop were not injured in such an attack, the risk to the anti-Treaty cause would have been far greater than the attack, however successful, would have warranted. The two commanders realized this all too clearly and it is hard to believe that the Bishop himself did not realize it. His action, indeed, won for the pro-Treatyites a significant bloodless victory. Both garrisons 'stood-to' during the night, but on Saturday morning the anti-Treatyites withdrew, no doubt in disgust, northwards towards Bundoran.

At Drumcliffe they turned sharply east and on Sunday morning at 3 a.m. attacked the pro-Treaty garrison at Manorhamilton, but with little success. Subsequently activity in Sligo during July and early August was slight and was confined to raids and guerilla actions.

In Roscommon and Mayo the pattern was identical. The anti-Treatyites, unprepared for war, without policy or central leadership, demoralized and without even civilian support, retreated in confusion as the well-controlled tentacles of the pro-Treaty military machine reached towards them. In Roscommon there was a brief and spectacular encounter in the county town, Boyle, in which Brigadier-General Michael Dockery of the pro-Treaty forces was killed.

In Mayo, there were many Republican sympathizers, but here, as elsewhere, the anti-Treaty soldiers effectively alienated a civilian population largely as Republican in outlook as themselves. The renowned Foxford Woollen Mills, which employed more than 300 people, were forced to close. Families suffered and people began to look eastwards towards the areas in pro-Treaty hands, as to a kind of promised land. They waited for 'deliverance' or 'liberation' as it would undoubtedly be called today. The curious thing is that this did not make them any less Republican as the results of the 1924 General Election — after the war — show. But they saw no future for the hunted military anti-Treatyites who were bringing them to starvation. Unfortunately, the alternative meant abandoning the Republic — but many civilians at the time held that rejection of the anti-Treaty military system and abandonment of the Republic were two quite different things.

When the push on Mayo began the capture of the towns was undramatic and routine. The pro-Treaty troops, coming in from Roscommon on a good road, halted at Claremorris in the south county where they effectively blocked any attempts by anti-Treatyites north of them to link up with Galway and waited to attack the large town of Castlebar fifty miles north-west of them until they learned that reinforcements had landed by sea at Westport, eleven miles west of Castlebar, now ringed. Their troops then made a forced march to Castlebar by night, clearing the road as they went, until they arrived at French Hill — so called from the fact that it was here that the French allies of Ireland in 1798 defeated the Redcoats in a rout that has come to be known as 'the Races of Castlebar' — three miles from the town. Castlebar was occupied without incident on 25 July. Ballina in the north of the county was taken on the 28th. Thus did the pro-Treatyites occupy the stronghold of the west. Only in Donegal, where it might have been least expected, was there further serious resistance.

The bulk of the Donegal IRA supported the Treaty. They were attached to the 2nd Northern Division commanded by Commandant-General Charles Daly, a Kerryman of twenty-six, who had been sent up to organize the area.[3] He was anti-Treaty. The terrain was difficult, consisting, except for the extreme south, of precipitous mountain ranges separating thinly populated villages, and with an irregular and deeply indented coastline. It was these valley 'pockets' that made it possible for Daly and a few anti-Treatyites to hold out for a time. But in groups of between twenty and forty anti-Treatyites were rounded up and captured after several running fights had taken place. Daly, with Derry Brigadier Seán Larkin, and two of his lieutenants from Kerry,

185

Daniel Enright and Timothy O'Sullivan, was imprisoned in Drumboe Castle. There they were shot by firing squad on 14 March 1923 eight months after their capture and eight weeks before the war ended.

[1] Press of the period.
[2] Major-General P. A. Mulcahy, Chief of Staff, Defence Forces 1957.
[3] The IRA in Donegal were, in fact, within the 1st Northern Division Area commanded by Commandant-General Joseph Sweeney. The 2nd Northern Division territory was in what later became Six County territory. But, as a majority of the Donegal troops became anti-Treaty, while most of the remainder of Sweeney's troops went pro-Treaty, they came under Daly's command for operational purposes.

THE ISOLATION OF DUBLIN

When the Beggar's Bush force was established in January it attracted three types: those who whole-heartedly supported the Treaty and followed Michael Collins's lead: ex-soldiers who saw in it the nucleus of a professional army and mercenary soldiers of fortune who knew no other way of making a living. All three types produce leaders. In the development of a new army the first type is found either at the top or bottom of the chain of command, the professional and the mercenary, capable, experienced and formidable, in between. Thus the pro-Treaty officers combined the brilliance of amateurs gifted in guerilla warfare, the professional knowledge of officers who had field command and experience in the British Army — and the ruthless efficiency of the mercenary.

The anti-Treatyites with few exceptions, had to rely solely on the guerilla 'amateur', gifted or otherwise, who had fought the British. The bulk of the anti-Treaty personnel was made up of mixed guerilla troops, those of the pro-Treaty forces, once recruiting started, were raw troops except for those who had seen British Army service and who, quite frequently, became NCOs.

The anti-Treatyites were faced with an entirely new kind of warfare. Not the hit-and-run ambush of War of Independence days, with the friendly people to conceal them, but a 'regular' war of masses of men, tactical advantage and to some extent, strategy, all of which had to be handled on a nationally integrated scale. The situation was entirely foreign to them and they had neither the means nor the experience to cope with it. The best they could achieve was a totally unsuitable application of the guerilla principle they had perfected. Moreover their army was organized on a purely voluntary basis in which officers had been chosen by vote prior to hostilities.

In France in 1940 the French Supreme Allied Command pinned its faith to the Maginot Line and a left-flank wheel through Belgium and Holland to stop a German thrust expected through the Low Countries.

The blitzkrieg crashed through the Ardennes[1] with seven armoured divisions, motorized infantry and artillery, and rolled up the Allied line to the sea. The German High Command believed that tanks could thrust far and fast into the hinterland of an enemy and that motorized infantry could hold the ground thus won. It seems a commonplace idea today. In 1939 it was one of genius. The French High Command had, with the experience of the long-drawn-out struggle between fixed positions of 1914-18 behind them, pinned their faith to a defensive line of impregnability — the Maginot Line.

The anti-Treatyites adopted a similar attitude in 1922 — even if an actual comparison seems very far-fetched. Their line was far less impregnable and, by the end of July, the pro-Treaty assault — in this case the thrust was with artillery and not with tanks, though some were in action — had rolled up the line from both ends. Nor was there any need for the pro-Treaty forces, as has been seen, to expend useful fighting troops in holding conquered territory. There was no hostile population to face, quite the contrary.

Anti-Treaty reverses were so general towards the end of July that it was realized that an offensive of some sort was urgently necessary in order to restore public confidences and maintain the morale of the troops. Two, to some extent complementary to one another, were planned. One was the capture of Baldonnel aerodrome, ten miles from Dublin, together with the military aircraft there. There was a proposal that Leinster House, seat of the Provisional Government, should then be bombed from the air — according to Dunne. Mr Patrick Mullaney, then the local Kildare Brigadier, maintains that this is incorrect and that the proposal was to bomb Beggar's Bush Barracks, other barrracks and the Curragh military encampment, and that fires were lighted on the nights on which the attack was to take place (it was twice postponed) as a guide to the aircraft.

The second plan, which was originally intended to take place at about the same time, was the isolation of Dublin from the rest of the country by blowing up or cutting all road, rail or water bridges and lines of communication a few miles outside the city.

The plan to capture Baldonnel came from Mullaney, who, incidentally, was not aware that it was hoped to carry out both operations at more or less the same time, as maintained by Dunne and other sources. Since he was captured on 29 June and did not escape until 20 August — fifteen days after the attempted isolation of

188

Dublin — his account may be accepted as being accurate.

He was captured, together with Domhnall O Buachalla (later to become Governor-General) and Michael O'Neill, on the day after the Four Courts was attacked. They were kept in Kilcock and Lucan for about three weeks, after which he was transferred to the Curragh internment camp while the other two were sent to Dundalk. They were released when Aiken captured Dundalk on 14 August (Chapter 16). Mullaney escaped on 20 August by cutting the bars of the dining hall window with a couple of hacksaws made from two bread knives hit edge to edge to create serration. The reason for his capture was that, during the latter part of the Truce — round about Easter — he captured arms, trucks and stores from the Meath Divisional HQ at Dunboyne, which was pro-Treaty. Mullaney and his men had earlier, in accordance with the IRA agreement, handed their weapons over for use in the North and had not been given any in exchange. Hence the attack, planned by Mullaney and Andrew Cooney — and hence Mullaney's subsequent arrest on the outbreak of hostilities.

After his escape it took about a month to build up a force sufficient to contemplate the attack on Baldonnel.

The aerodrome, a few miles inside the Dublin county border, was within striking distance of his territory. He had made certain arrangements before proposing the plan to GHQ and had made contact with a number of men of the pro-Treaty garrison who were sympathetic. There were, however, thirty officers, including pilots, who would have to be overcome. He was confident that this would not prove difficult. He would provide twenty-two fully armed men. James Fore of Clondalkin was to provide another fifteen and — according to Dunne — Dunne was to provide a further forty men who were unarmed. About 100, also unarmed, were to come from Dublin. The purpose of these men being unarmed was to carry off the stores and equipment they expected to capture. Two pilots were available for the bombing attacks should they materialize.

Twice the action was planned and twice it had to be cancelled because the Dublin men were unable to rendezvous. Dunne says 'Tod' Andrews[2] arrived from Dublin to take charge, but there were only seven men with him. He decided to call it off.

Mullaney says that Andrews was in charge of organization and Seán Dowling was in charge of the Dublin contingent. He does not know why the Dublin men failed to turn up, but without their aid the

189

plan had to be cancelled on the second night as well, which was a week later. The Kildare men were fiercely enthusiastic about the offensive and there is no doubt that if it had succeeded as planned, it would have had considerable effects.

However, with aerial bombing in the state it then was, had the attempt been made to bomb Leinster House, the likelihood is that the building would have escaped serious damage and the surrounding residential areas would have been plastered, making angrier an already thoroughly angered population. When the plan was cancelled on the second occasion, Mullaney launched a diversionary attack on a pro-Treaty post at Lucan to ensure the safe return to Dublin of those who had come from there. When, on 2 or 3 December, his column (operating in what was almost exclusively pro-Treaty territory) was surrounded between Maynooth, Leixlip and Celbridge, a running fight of several hours took place in the area during which, says Mullaney, 'Casualties on both sides were not small.'

Mullaney adds: 'With the requisite number of men and the co-operation from inside which I had, the plan to capture Baldonnel was easy. But Dublin got two opportunities to supply the men and failed. I felt bitter about this as it meant subsequently the execution of some of those men who left Baldonnel and joined me.'

The other plan, if successful, would also have had considerable morale-boosting value. Fate, however, took a hand.

The Intelligence officer of the South Dublin Brigade was captured by pro-Treaty troops under Colonel Hugo McNeill[3] two days before the isolation of Dublin plan went into operation. He had the entire battle plan on him at the time, and the password to be used.[4] Consequently, when the anti-Treatyites closed in on the roads, bridges and railway lines, they found units of the pro-Treaty forces in ambush and prepared with the password and countersign waiting for them. Upwards of 200 prisoners were taken. The attack was scheduled to take place on Saturday, 15 August.

This elaborate plan to isolate Dublin — which turned out to be such a débacle — had been approved by GHQ in Fermoy who had gone to the extent of sending men from Cork to Liverpool and thence to Dublin to take part in it. These men were mostly engineers and explosives experts, who were to supervise the destruction of the bridges, roads, and railways. The plan was the subject of scathing pro-Treaty comment:[5]

The coup . . . was designed to isolate Dublin . . . If they had succeeded the chief bridges leading north, south and west from Dublin would have been destroyed. Main roads would have been made impassable. All railway communications would have been interrupted. The isolation of the capital would have threatened starvation to a core of Irish counties. Dublin is the chief distributing centre for the Provinces of Leinster and Connacht. The midlands, the west and large areas in the south would have been deprived of all imported food supplies . . .

There is some truth here, but it is highly exaggerated in the interests of swaying public opinion. Dublin was, and is, the chief distributing centre for Leinster and Connacht, but it was not the only distributing centre. There were several ports in both provinces which were open centres of commerce at this time. Traffic could have operated through many ports in the country even if Dublin were isolated. As it turned out, however, this boldly-conceived plan failed and must have had as great a demoralizing effect on the anti-Treatyites as a victory would have been a morale-booster.

At Glencullen, near the Dublin-Wicklow border, two groups of anti-Treatyites were captured during this round-up by the alerted pro-Treatyites. The first group was an outpost of four men and the second consisted of five officers in a car. One of them was Commandant Noel Lemass who later escaped, was recaptured after the Cease Fire, and was killed in the Dublin mountains. He was a brother of Seán Lemass.

In general the pro-Treaty troops moved into position silently in lorries and armoured cars, coasted into position several hours before the anti-Treaty zero hour. The anti-Treatyites were captured with the minimum of trouble. On the south side of the city they were captured as far away as Enniskerry, and on the north at Finglas, Cabra, Blanchardstown, Donnycarney; at Fairview, close to the city, forty-two anti-Treatyites were captured without a struggle.

As the capture became general and the anti-Treatyites realized what was happening they tried to counter-attack in the city and firing began about 3 a.m. all over Dublin. It lasted all night long and pro-Treaty posts at Finglas, Phibsborough, Drumcondra and Harcourt Street received particular attention. Mountjoy Jail was the object of a concerted attack — in an attempt to release prisoners — but it was not successful. There was a number of civilian as well as military casualties who were treated in the city hospitals. The offensive had failed. Its possible success and its effect on the course of the war are conjectural. But it is unlikely that it would have had a decisive or even lasting effect.

[1] Curiously it had first been planned — OKH original plan yellow — through the Low Countries, at a time when French High Command feared it might come through the Ardennes. The German plan was altered at the suggestion of Von Manstein and of Rommel at about the time the French plan was switched. The Ardennes was thought to be impregnable.

[2] The late C. S. Andrews.

[3] Later Lieutenant-General Hugo McNeill of the Defence Forces.

[4] It was: 'Any good hotels about?' The reply was: 'Yes, what about the Hammam?'

[5] Contemporary daily Press.

16

AIKEN'S DILEMMA

The situation in which the 4th Northern Division — Armagh, West and South Down and Louth — found itself when the split occurred is a good example of what happened to many men concerned for the future of their country. The division was commanded by Commandant-General Frank Aiken[1] who did not attend or send representatives to the banned Army Convention in March. He decided to remain neutral in the split and remain under the Dáil Ministry for Defence. With the establishment of the Northern 'Quisling' Government, he moved his divisional HQ to Dundalk and occupied the barracks there with about 300 men. When the Four Courts was attacked he succeeded in keeping the peace between the pro- and anti-Treaty elements in his command, and still remained neutral: but, as a precaution, he dumped the bulk of the division's armaments. On 3 July, a week after the attack on the Four Courts, he wrote to Mulcahy:

> . . . there is an opportunity of framing a new constitution that would make the Treaty acceptable to everyone as an honourable breathing space in our fight for independence. Boil down all this wrangling and fighting, and however great the tactical mistakes of the anti-Treatyites may have been, you have the simple national abhorrence of swearing allegiance to a foreign king and allowing part of the Nation to be ruled by people who have sworn loyalty to that king. . .
>
> Are you prepared to carry on a war with your own people to enforce that oath of allegiance to England, while you have a splendid opportunity of uniting the whole Nation to fight against it with success?
>
> Are you prepared to smash the National strength to force these men who helped greatly to build up that strength, to take the oath which they feel they cannot honourably take?

He told Mulcahy that he would fight on neither side because the fight would 'only ruin the country without gaining any ground for the Republic'.

He went to Limerick to try to persuade Liam Lynch to stop fighting, but returned to Dundalk without success. There he found his troops under orders from pro-Treaty HQ to attack anti-Treatyites in the area. A meeting of his officers on 14 July agreed that, unless the Provisional Government gave the anti-Treaty parties, civil and military, a constitutional way of carrying on for the Republic, such as withdrawing the oath for admission to Parliament, they would give them no support, moral or material. This decision was in accordance with his earlier stand.

In the early hours of 16 July, Aiken was awakened to find a revolver at his head, his unarmed men prisoners, and men of the pro-Treaty 5th Northern Division in possession of the town. Dundalk and its garrison of 4th Northern Division volunteers had been bloodlessly — or almost bloodlessly — captured. Two of Aiken's men, Campbell and Quigley, were shot trying to escape. Pro-Treaty troops had slipped into town by the Monaghan road at 4.30 a.m. The Anne Street barracks garrison, seeing they were surrounded, attempted to escape through the 'Demesne' — then a big stretch of land extending from the back of Main Street to the Railway line — and it was at this time that the two casualties occurred. Campbell was killed instantly by a shot in the neck which blew off his right arm. Quigley was shot in the arm which had to be amputated; he died later. One result of the capture of the town was that the 'B' Specials, whom Aiken had captured in the North, were released and returned to the Six Counties where their comrades still pursued their reign of terror.

Aiken wrote to Mulcahy from prison pointing out that the Civil War was being 'waged by eight Irishmen without a mandate from the people and without consulting the representatives of the people, to force Irishmen to take an oath of allegiance to a foreign king'. During the days between 16 July and 27 July there were intermittent attacks on the pro-Treaty positions in the town. On 27 July anti-Treatyites from outside breached the wall of the prison and Aiken, with about 100 of his men, escaped.

The coup was well-planned. About 200 men of the 4th Northern Division infiltrated the town. Shortly after 7 p.m. a strong group of them reached the prison wall undetected, and mined it. When the mine exploded, every window in the district was shattered — and the jail was breached. Through this breach poured the prisoners, who had been warned and were waiting. Immediately after the explosion the pro-Treaty posts in the town were attacked. Streets were blocked — an old railway engine being used in one instance, at Quay Street — and in the general mêlée the prisoners made good their escape. Two days later, Aiken issued a statement to the public which appeared only in the anti-Treaty controlled press. In it he made the following points:

1. Dundalk is HQ of the 4th Northern Division and the 300 troops stationed there on 16 July were neutral and had, up till then, recognized the authority of the Dáil Minister of Defence, but were unwilling to fire on Republican soldiers.

2. When he received the order to attack the IRA Commandant-General Aiken concealed the arms of his division and went to Dublin with his staff to see the Minister and place his views before him. He was told to return to Dundalk and prepare a full memorandum. He told the Minister (Mulcahy) of the concealment of the division's arms.

3, Having written the memorandum, on the night of 15/16 July, he went to bed. He was awakened to find the barracks seized by the Government troops and himself and his men prisoners.

4. Parole was given him, during which he saw Mulcahy and demanded his men's release with the full truth published lest the honour of the IRA be smirched by the bloodless capture of 300 men, said by the Government to be on active service. Mulcahy said the prisoners would be released if they signed an undertaking to recognize the Government. This was refused, but he (Aiken) was given a guarantee of prisoner-of-war treatment.

5. Back in Dundalk, he learned that his officers were imprisoned as criminals. He himself was placed in custody when he again asked to see Mulcahy.

6. He appealed to his men not to join the Government Army as long as the oath was in the Constitution.

Two days later a further statement by him included the following:

195

An Officer who had been reduced for inefficiency and some men under arrest for drunkenness opened the gates of the military barracks on 16 July and so — a brilliant victory for the National [*sic*] Army. 300 Irregulars arrested. Not a shot fired. 'General Mulcahy', said Aiken, 'when taxed said he did not know how the attack was made or who was to be attacked.'

Aiken concluded:
The best thing for the country's sake is to put your trust in God and keep your powder dry — and make sure you don't lose it.
Bail ó Dhia orraibh uilig,[2]
Frank Aiken.

He wrote an appeal to IRA volunteers serving with pro-Treaty forces to 'down-tools'. The onus of stopping the fight rests on you, he said, 'while you attack the men who can never accept the oath, you are in the wrong and must be met'. The exhortation to his men to preserve their powder was timely for, on 14 August he launched an assault against Dundalk, recaptured the barracks, and released the remainder of his men, together with many prisoners captured during the attempted isolation of Dublin on 5 August.

The anti-Treatyites infiltrated the town in the early hours of the morning and mined the military barracks in several places. About 4 a.m. a pro-Treaty sentry, suspicious of a noise he had heard, called out the guard. The duty officer investigated and found a cable outside the main gate. As he went to cut it he was wounded by machine-gun fire and, simultaneously, the mines were exploded. They were at the gate to Point Road, the hospital, the officers' quarters, the HQ office block, the orderly office and guardroom, and in billets in the barracks. Two others at the officers' mess and main gate failed to explode. An enormous amount of explosive was used.

There were about 300 pro-Treaty troops in the barracks at the time. All the officers were put out of action by the explosions, one was killed, seven were seriously wounded and one was buried in debris. The sentry at Point Road gate was killed and the gate destroyed. The mines in the billet killed one and severely wounded many. The orderly office explosion stunned the guard, immobilizing them. Two sentries at the main gate were shot dead. The sentry at the transport sheds was knocked out by the force of the explosions: he recovered within a minute, picked up his rifle to fire at the attackers, but was cut down by machine-gun fire and badly wounded. Within a short time the entire barracks had changed hands again and the pro-Treaty troops were, in their turn, prisoners. The other barracks in the town surrendered quickly.

When the mine at the main gate, which had failed to explode, was being dismantled, it exploded, killing the anti-Treaty officer, a man named McKenna, in charge of the party. The prisoners were confined to the jail where they were guarded by boys of Fianna Éireann — the revolutionary boy scout movement founded by Countess Markievicz in 1915. A considerable amount of equipment — about 400 rifles, machine-guns, grenades, ammunition and at least one eighteen pounder — was captured.[3] The field gun was put out of action. Whether the anti-Treatyites would have been well-advised to keep it or not is an open question. It is likely that the lack of anyone capable of handling it, as much as the difficulties of transport and of ammunition, deterred them.

Released anti-Treatyite prisoners from other units were given food and arms and ordered to return to their commands. They included two Kildare men and they marched together with about sixty men in their joint command, for four days and nights from Dunleer, just outside Dundalk, when the town was evacuated by the anti-Treatyites three days after the attack as two pro-Treaty divisions under General Hogan and Colonel McNeill closed in from the south and west. (During this operation an aircraft was used, for the first time offensively, in the campaign. It attacked the barracks on Wednesday morning at low level and had considerable effect on the morale of the anti-Treatyites, before they drove it off with machine-gun fire.)

The two groups of anti-Treatyites separated at a place called Skreen and very shortly afterwards each was in trouble, only a mile or so apart. Crossing a main road one party was surprised by a couple of armoured cars. A third of the men were on one side of the road and the OC was with the remainder on the other. The smaller group, about ten men, dashed for high ground under a hail of bullets, while the OC withdrew to what cover was to be had in the middle of a field. 'We couldn't stick our heads up,' he said, 'the cars kept patrolling the road in opposite directions. That was bad enough but a plane (possibly the one which had attacked Dundalk) came over and directed them. We just had to wait for darkness and hope for the best.' Eventually they made their escape at nightfall.

The other party was not so lucky. In their position half-way up a hill they were attacked, says an eye-witness, by two full companies of

Dublin Guards who advanced downhill on them, breaking from timber cover. The OC leaped to his feet with his nine comrades and charged the guards, uphill, driving them back; they took cover in a new position and for four hours, held out until their ammunition — 500 rounds — was down to seven rounds and the wood was burned off their rifles in places. Finally, deaf, with swollen hands and jammed rifles, they surrendered. It is said that the pro-Treaty OC personally shook each man's hand and congratulated them on the fight they had put up. 'It was the best fight I ever saw,' he said.

Two further things of significance happened in Dundalk at this time. On Sunday, 30 July, the Rev. Fr. McKean read a letter from Cardinal Logue, which said:

'I don't know what Dundalk is coming to or how it will end. It must have a rare supply of desperate rascals and robbers. I am deliberating whether I should not go up on Sunday and put the whole place under excommunication, *as I had to do in this parish of Carlingford*. That would not affect the desperate characters who fear neither God nor man, but it might deter some people who have a rag of conscience left, from co-operating with, or aiding and abetting them. They are bringing a respectable Catholic town into disgrace.'

This was a few days after the escape of Aiken, since when the town had been, more or less, under continuous fire. The second important thing took place on the day after the anti-Treaty re-capture of the town when the following notice was put up in the market square:

Óglaigh na hÉireann, HQ 4th Northern Division, Dundalk.
14th August, 1922.
To the people of the Divisional area:

In previous statements issued to you we have pointed out our position fully and directed your attention to the fact that we have always been out for unity of the Army and honourable peace for Irishmen.

We feel confident that your views are the same as our own, but we regret that you did not make them publicly known. Had this been done the casualties of today's struggle on both sides, which we heartily deplore, might have been avoided.

We believe you still have a chance to achieve both your and our desires, and we invite you to *A Public meeting in the Market Square tomorrow* (Tuesday at 1 p.m. sharp.)

198

At which the following resolutions will be proposed:

That the people of this area demand an immediate truce and that the Dáil[4] be summoned at once in order —1) to re-affirm, the sovereignty of the Irish people and arrange an honourable peace among all parties, or —2) If this is not possible, to dissolve the Third Dáil —[the coalition parliament would have represented the Third Dáil had it met and parliament convened] — and hold a new election, at which the issue shall be the present Constitution, which means a dishonourable peace with England, unrest and Civil War in Ireland — or a mandate from the Irish people to maintain the independence of the sovereign Irish Nation at all hazards. Officers 4th Northern Division.

The meeting was held and the resolution was passed amid mixed booing and cheering, some of the former from the pro-Treaty prisoners in the jail.

---

[1] Cabinet Minister in every Fianna Fáil Government until 1973. Represented Ireland at the United Nations.There were considerable differences between Commandan. General Dan Hogan and Eoin O'Duffy on the one hand, and Aiken on the other. The 4th Brigade of the 4th Northern Division was an independent Brigade and was re-grouped within Aiken's command just prior to hostilities. An officer of the 4th Brigade says that when Aiken moved his HQ to Dundalk he was uncommitted, but that when Hogan and O'Duffy tried to take control of his troops while he was in Limerick, he reacted against this, and was subsequently attacked.

[2] The blessing of God on all of you.

[3] The word 'considerable' is used in relation to the amount of war material employed in the Civil War and captured from time to time.

[4] The assembly elected on 16 June is meant.

17

THE FOURTEEN-DAY BATTLE

Waterford and Limerick fell on 21 July. A glance at a map will indicate the position. All the principal towns and the connecting roads between the two cities, and in the immediate hinterland, were in the hands of pro-Treaty forces under the command of Eoin O'Duffy. An assault on Cork by the back door — the sea — was planned, but meanwhile troops under Paddy O'Connor, Jerry Ryan and Liam Hayes, elated with their successes in Tipperary and in Limerick, jumped the gun on the planners and fought their way towards Cork from the north.

The chief rallying points in Munster apart from Cork, i.e. Waterford, Limerick and Clonmel which also dominated the approaches to the province, were in pro-Treaty hands. The cities were ports and through them flowed the commerce of several counties; from them radiated roads penetrating the anti-Treaty positions. On them depended the livelihood of many people behind the anti-Treaty line; in them the pro-Treatyites build up troops, supplies and headquarter base depots for the final assault. The anti-Treatyites prepared for this assault in the east by planning the abortive counter-attack on Waterford, and in the west by the defence of the Kilmallock triangle.

This triangle was an area in south Limerick just across the north Cork border and a little east of Kerry border. It was contained by the towns of Bruff, Bruree and Kilmallock and the battle for this area, which lasted from Sunday 23 July until Saturday 5 August, was the most prolonged, and possibly the most decisive, of the whole field campaign. It is an area of rich farmland, broken by rising hillocks — the first outcrops of the Ballyhoura Mountains rising twelve hundred feet some five miles due south of Kilmallock. Bruff and Bruree flank Kilmallock respectively six miles to the north-east and four miles west, and the position was a natural one for the anti-Treatyites to try to hold when they abandoned Limerick. It is the first large town between Limerick and the Cork border, dominating the approaches to Cork from the north and giving some cover to part of Kerry also. Furthermore it is the most important road junction in south Limerick, seven major roads branching from it: the main Cork-Dublin railway line passes a quarter of a mile south of the town towards Limerick Junction fifteen miles to the east, which is between Kilmallock and Tipperary.

The area was occupied by veteran, disciplined soldiers from the War of Independence, some of whom had been fighting in Limerick earlier. But many were fresh troops up from the south and west. Behind them, in Cork and Kerry, lay the bulk of their forces, and their supply lines and communications could not easily be cut. Liam Deasy (Divisional OC), Seán Moylan, (Director-of-Operations), Moss Twomey (General-Staff-Officer) and Liam Lynch (Chief-of-Staff and Commander-in-Chief) had a grasp of the situation not elsewhere — with the exception of Dundalk — evident in the anti-Treaty side.

The vicious to-and-fro battle, with now one side victorious, now the other, began insignificantly as the pursuing troops fought southwards out of Limerick and were checked near Kilmallock on Sunday, 23 July. These pro-Treaty soldiers had had little rest since Limerick fell to their guns two days before. The demands made on officers by soldiers and civilians alike were heavy, and the officers in turn kept their men moving as quickly as possible on the heels of the retreating anti-Treatyites. The weather was poor, wind and driving rain making progress slow, reducing visibility to a minimum and turning the, for the most part, unsurfaced roads into avenues of mud and large brown pools. Pools and mud, however, were the least of the obstacles that confronted them. Mines and trees blocked the roads at intervals, and clearing them took time.

The country is here a chequerboard of small fields, high hedges and a multitude of natural obstacles offering plenty of cover to attackers. But in order to make proper use of this cover the attack should be well co-ordinated, with all the troops in close contact to achieve full deployment unobserved. Careful scouting and close contact are vital. Raw troops, such as these pro-Treatyites — lucky if they had a week's training — were handicapped, the terrain offering better assistance to the defenders who, knowing the country, could counter-attack to effect. However, the pro-Treaty troops assembled in Limerick for the advance, a grey-haired priest standing with uplifted hand between the dripping, silent columns of men, giving them General Absolution. The convoys moved on slowly, the heavy armoured lorries making little more speed than the winding lines of infantry plodding on either side of the roads, indifferent to the mud that splashed them.

Finally, the rain still falling, they came within a mile or so of the enemy positions. The order to fall out was given. It was Sunday night, 23 July 1922 — wet and miserable. Oblivious of mud and rain, under the everdripping trees, the men sank down for what rest they could get. They had been fighting and marching non-stop for over a week. Their anti-Treaty enemies — out there somewhere in the wet darkness — were in no better condition.

There was a sudden burst of firing away to the left. A couple of Verey lights soared upwards, haloed in a nimbus of rain, suffusing the countryside beneath in a hard light. Simultaneously two explosions rocked the night.

At Ballycullane Cross, about a mile north of Kilmallock on the road to Bruff, an anti-Treaty armoured car of the 1st Cork Brigade supported by men of the 5th Cork Brigade, encountered the advance guard of the pro-Treatyites, capturing men and ammunition and probably accounting for the action mentioned above and heard by the pro-Treaty troops under Commandant Tim Flood. Shortly afterwards, in the early hours of Monday morning, an engagement took place at Thomastown south of Kilmallock and between it and Charleville, the details of which are described by Frank O'Connor, an anti-Treaty eye-witness,[1] in the *Cork Examiner* of July 1922.

Together with two companions and the car in which they were travelling he was captured between Charleville and Kilmallock by troops trying to encircle the latter town. The prisoners were taken to a farmhouse at Thomastown. Here the attackers bivouacked for the night, keeping their prisoners with them. In the morning, as they were being taken to lorries in the yard for transportation to Limerick, there was a sudden shout of 'Boys, we're surrounded,' and the entire party retired to the farmhouse under heavy fire from the surrounding anti-Treatyites, who had an armoured car with them.

'We were ordered to lie on the ground,' said O'Connor, 'and the Free State soldiers lay on top of us returning the fire . . . ' When the officer in charge of the pro-Treaty troops was shot through the mouth and put out of action, and the Sergeant, Denis O'Mahoney of Blarney Street, Cork, was killed, the pro-Treaty soldiers abandoned their hopeless position and surrendered.

The same day the anti-Treatyites counter-attacked Bruff, which was being used as a pro-Treaty dispersal point, captured it and established a field hospital just outside the town. One assumes from this that it was their intention to counter-attack in strength towards Limerick, but memories are now unreliable on this point.

Meanwhile Flood's troops were on the move again, but by mid-afternoon on that Monday they were in difficulties. They were advancing along a sunken road with high hedges on either side about a quarter of a mile south of the railway line, somewhere near a place called Pouldragoon Bridge as near as can be established — when the officer on point, about fifty yards in advance, found himself face to face with a manned barricade. Firing two shots from his revolver he doubled back, signalling to the troops to take cover as he did so.

'Then' in the words, of an eye-witness with the pro-Treatyites, 'the ball began. It was about 3.30 p.m. and I was belly-down in a ditch the men stretched all around me. We had no field of fire as the hedges were too thick to see through and the bullets whizzing through them rendered any attempt to extend very hazardous. We were remarkably like rats in the proverbial cage.'[2]

Twenty minutes later, however, a section succeeded in breaking off to the left through a gap in the rear, and, bit by bit, the pro-Treaty troops managed to withdraw under fire. The eye-witness noticed four soldiers crouched at the bottom of a bank waiting an opportunity to fire and had time to hope that the anti-Treaty machine-gunners didn't see them bunched together, before a burst tore through them, killing three and fatally wounding the fourth. 'Any minute,' he said, 'I expected them on top of us.'

The battle lasted for several hours and then, bit by bit, the pro-Treaty troops managed to withdraw under fire. Two hours later, at an advanced dressing station, the wounded were being treated.

The column had established the whereabouts of the anti-Treaty defences, although losses in men and arms had been severe. Next day, Tuesday, a Red Cross party went through the anti-Treaty lines with an ambulance and a cart under a flag of truce to bring in the dead. 'We were received with courtesy by the well-armed and well-disciplined men and, on our undertaking that the three men with the cart were unarmed, we were allowed to come forward. One of them conducted us to where they had laid out the bodies with their Rosary beads in their hands,' remembers a veteran of the battle. Anti-Treaty sources claimed a total of seventy-six men, seventy-six rifles, machine-guns and ammunition captured during the two days. Prisoners were taken to Buttevant, County Cork, barracks.

The pro-Treatyites decided that Bruree must be captured before Kilmallock could be attacked, and it was taken on Sunday, 30 July. A statement issued by O'Duffy that day said: 'I am well pleased with the progress made by the troops in the command. The best fighting material the Irregulars can muster is ranged against us. Having concentrated all their forces from Munster on the Kilmallock frontier, they have the advantage in quantity . . .'[3]

'I consider the capture of Bruree today of much strategic value, making Kilmallock untenable. Kilmallock is now covered on three sides by our troops and its fall is, I believe, inevitable.'

The battle had been a fierce affair. Diversionary and holding attacks were launched at Bulgaden, east of Kilmallock, and at Ballygubba Cross, between Kilmallock and Bruree, to contain anti-Treaty troops which might have hastened to the relief of Bruree. Bruff, which had again changed hands, was used as the spingboard from which to launch the attack. Bruree is a small town in a saucer shaped depression surrounded by little hills, flanked on the east by the Croom-Charleville railway and on the west of the swift-flowing River Maigue, both running south to north. The weather, in contrast to the previous week, was dry as the attacking troops, covered in dust, passed through Bruff, taking with them a machine-gun carrier called 'Danny Boy' and a field gun.

Major-General Murphy was to lead the main attack while a 'shock' attack by the Dublin Guards under Flood (whose brother Frank had been hanged by the British in the War of Independence) were to attack the town and deliver a knock-out blow from the south-east, via Ballygubba Cross, while Murphy made his frontal assault with artillery and armoured cars from the north-east. Surprise was essential as Bruree was believed to be strongly defended. The diversionary attacks were successful in holding troops which might have caught the Bruree attackers in the rear, and the anti-Treatyites in the town were surprised and caught in a cross fire from the attackers. After a stubborn defence the anti-Treatyites withdrew from the town as artillery came up to open fire on their last cover-party which was holding a bridge with a Lewis gun.

An amusing side-light on the grim business — and one which may have helped the anti-Treatyites withdraw — is the fact that when a hole had been made in a field for the trail of the eighteen-pounder and a shell had been rammed home ready for firing, a herd of cattle wandered across the line of fire, bare feet from the brass muzzle of the gun. The gunners had to leave their weapon and drive the cows away before they could open fire. By 11 p.m. after less than five hours fighting the town was in pro-Treaty hands and the troops were parading triumphantly in the streets of the town.

This capture of Bruree was immediately taken as an indication that Kilmallock, flanked now both in Bruff and Bruree, would be evacuated.[4] By Tuesday reports were more cautious. More than a thousand men were estimated by the pro-Treatyites to be in Kilmallock, men described by O'Duffy himself as 'the best fighting material the Irregulars can muster' . . . Minor clashes indicated that, far from preparing to evacuate Kilmallock, the anti-Treatyites were jockeying for position around it. Patrickswell — fifteen miles north of Bruree — was attacked and captured by them at 2 a.m. on 2 August and preceded by only a few hours a large-scale counter-attack on Bruree, both of which were part of an overall plan to re-establish anti-Treaty dominance in the area: a plan which failed for lack of weapons and man-power and because of the seaborne landings in Kerry behind the anti-Treatyites, which had much more than a tactical effect on the defenders at Kilmallock, as will be seen.

Patrickswell straddles the direct lines of communication between Bruree and Limerick and the town provided an effective 'screen' behind which to attack Bruree. The attack on Bruree was not, as pro-Treaty sources alleged, planned by Erskine Childers. Liam Deasy was in command of the area and Seán Moylan was responsible for operations. For this attack they had three armoured cars, a large number of machine-guns, rifle grenades and the only mortar — 'Lizzie' —in anti-Treaty possession. Bruree was held by Flood and his Dublin Guards with HQ in the Railway Hotel, covering the bridge and the main road from Kilmallock, and strong points at Bruree Lodge on the Charleville Road and in the schoolhouse which controlled the road from Newcastlewest.

The anti-Treaty plan was for an armoured car to attack each of these positions. Between them the three armoured cars had ten machine-guns. The first intimation the pro-Treaty troops had that they were being attacked was when the sentry on the railway bridge saw the armoured cars emerge from the darkness and the mist round the bend in front of him. He was called on to surrender, but refused to do so, and dived for cover instead, firing as he did so. Assault troops which had been in the cars leaped out and a concentrated fire was turned on the hotel, which was riddled, the light bricks not being strong enough to stop the bullets. Inside the pro-Treaty OC managed to keep his men together and they withheld their fire until one of the men from an armoured car tried to force a window and was killed by a burst from a Thompson gun. The OC then evacuated his men via the back of the building, getting cover from a Lewis gunner in a water tower which he gained from the roof of the hotel. There are contradictory stories of what happened to this man. Anti-Treaty sources say that the OC of a Cork brigade fired through the loophole in the water tower and killed the machine-gunner. The story from a war correspondent — who did not arrive until much later — attached to the pro-Treatyites is much more exciting but much less likely to be true.

He says that a burst from a Thompson gun came through the loophole. One bullet cut the Lewis gunner's coat, another was deflected by his cartridge-belt, two more ripped his clothing, one pierced his hand, his machine-gun was put out of action . . . and he escaped down a water pipe.

Meanwhile, the second armoured car had charged through the town, rammed the door of the school and captured the twenty-five defenders under a Sergeant-Major. The town OC for the pro-Treatyites in the interval took up a position in the mill which he was able to hold and ordered his men to bake bread in preparation for a lengthy siege, but by this time reinforcements had been summoned and were on their way from Bruff under Generals Galvin and Hogan. These reinforcements were sporadically attacked en route but the anti-Treaty forces retired from Bruree without attempting a serious engagement with the approaching reinforcements.

Meanwhile, what of the third armoured car with which they had attacked? There is a rather extraordinary incident connected with it. One of the pro-Treaty 'Whippet' Rolls-Royce armoured cars with Hogan in it entered Bruree with, behind it, a very mountain of an armoured car with a huge domed roof and an enormous span. Two Lewis guns and three Thompsons bristled from its sides. Round the bend and into the town swung the Whippet. But the second car halted about 100 yards behind, concealed from view. For precious moments the huge war-chariot stayed still, until some pro-Treaty officers spotted it and, realizing that it was anti-Treaty, sounded the alarm. The car moved slowly off towards Kilmallock. But it had been seen by the Whippet which gave chase. Whether by accident or by design, it was led into a trap for, round the bend was not one, but all three anti-Treaty armoured cars which immediately opened fire. The Whippet returned the fire but, after a few bursts, its Vickers gun stopped and it had to retire.

Anti-Treaty sources explain this fantastic incident by a laconic official announcement that in Bruree the crew of an armoured car were about to attack a pro-Treaty armoured car, but the engine failed and the crew jumped out and saved the car by pushing it to a hill under fire.

This attack on Bruree was the beginning and the end of an anti-Treaty offensive. The following is an attempt to summarize the position:

1. Except for isolated incohesive, or abortive actions — Limerick, Nenagh, Galway, the isolation of Dublin, Kilmallock, etc. — the anti-Treatyites had adopted a defensive attitude from the beginning leaving the initiative almost entirely with the pro-Treatyites;

2. The anti-Treaty 'line', such as it was, was broken irrevocably;

3. Anti-Treaty communications were, and had been, chaotic. No offensive could be co-ordinated to any central authority and plans were limited to local effort as a result. Furthermore, it was impossible for their troops to move with safety by day in most areas;

4. Although doubt has been cast on this point, it seems certain that possession of artillery by the pro-Treatyites was decisive in breaking formal anti-Treaty resistance;

5. An offensive was unlikely by the anti-Treatyites at this stage because of lack of war materials and transport, limited supplies of food and money and no means of obtaining credit except by forced levies;

6. Lack of civilian co-operation; lack of adequate intelligence;

7. Lack of a Government providing a concrete visible centre round which Republican civilian supporters might rally;

8. The pro-Treatyites had the power and support their opponents lacked;

9. Although the leadership on the pro-Treaty side was not necessarily superior to that on the other side they did possess many material and moral advantages: equipment, reserves, freedom of movement, civic support, an Army chain of command lacked by their

opponents, the backing of the commercial circles as the forces of law and order and the support of the bishops;

10. In August pro-Treaty troops under Major-General Patrick O'Daly landed at Fenit, seven miles from Tralee, behind the anti-Treaty line, while the Tralee anti-Treaty brigade was fighting at Kilmallock.

This last factor not only made any attempt at an anti-Treaty offensive impossible, but caused a drastic change of plan with regard to the defence of Kilmallock.

When the local offensive against Bruree and Patrickswell petered out after twenty-four hours of fighting on Thursday, pro-Treaty troops were again ready to attack Kilmallock, around which they held a semi-circular position stretching from Bruree, through Dromin, by Bulgaden to Riversfield House.

The attack began on Friday and was accompanied by a simultaneous thrust from Patrickswell towards Adare and Kerry. This westward movement was under the command of Brigadier Slattery while Murphy, who had been a Lieutenant-Colonel in the British Army, was in command of the attack on Kilmallock. More than 2000 troops with armoured car and artillery support are estimated to have taken part in the attack.

The Dublin Guards under Flood advanced from Bruree to Knocksouna Hill, covering the anti-Treaty line of retreat to Charleville, while the Limerick and Kerry men of the pro-Treaty forces pushed down the centre on the town itself.

The troops at Riversfield House remained there to cover a possible retreat to Buttevant. The artillery was first used from a hill outside Dromin about three and a half miles from Kilmallock and was trained on Kilmallock Hill, a defended position half a mile outside the town. Small arms fire was spasmodic and no serious clashes took place until about 10 a.m. when Kilmallock was well in sight of the advancing troops. They were held up for a time by a position on Quarry Hill, but a few rounds of shrapnel from the field gun, all direct hits, silenced the post and the hill was occupied by the attackers. Kilmallock Hill, where there was a similar post, had suffered the same fate. Fatal casualties among the anti-Treatyites in these two positions are estimated as being very high. But General Liam Deasy contradicts this report.

Murphy brought up his infantry after a lively battle on the southern fringes of the town, and occupied both hills. No further advance was made on Friday as, with the example of Bruree only two days behind him, Murphy first wanted to consolidate his position all along the line. What he did not know was that the bulk of the anti-Treaty defenders had succeeded in withdrawing — past Flood on Knocksouna Hill — before the first assault was launched. The stray outposts on the hills and in the town itself were a screen behind which the evacuation took place. Their job had been to fight a rearguard action while the remainder of the garrison withdrew.

The reason for this sudden change of plans was the Tralee landings by O'Daly. A large proportion of the Kilmallock garrison was made up of men of the Kerry Brigades who were ordered to return to Kerry and fight in their own localities.

Kilmallock was the last of the large, deliberately planned, field actions and it had now become a delaying rearguard action, covering the withdrawal of these troops. The rearguard action was fought with great courage and determination by the men of the Cork Brigades who volunteered to stay behind to cover the retreat to Charleville. Kilmallock was occupied by Murphy's troops at 4 p.m. on Saturday, 5 August, at about the time that the anti-Treaty plan to isolate Dublin was being defeated at the other end of the battlefield.

[1] Michael O'Donovan, who was to become the famous short-story writer and novelist, Frank O'Connor.
[2] *Irish Times* reporter.
[3] By no means certain at this juncture.
[4] Especially by Sgeal Catha Luimnuighe, a contemporary Government propaganda paper.

18

THE 'INVASION OF KERRY'

By the beginning of August the cities of Dublin, Waterford, Limerick and Galway and the towns of Carrick-on-Suir, Tipperary, Castlebar, Ballina, Dundalk, Wexford, and Sligo, all of which had been anti-Treaty strongholds, Dublin excepted, were in pro-Treaty hands. The anti-Treatyites were hemmed in in the twin counties of Cork and Kerry and, on 2 August, this stronghold of anti-Treatyism was attacked from the sea. The target was the Kerry capital, Tralee.

North Cork, Kerry and South Limerick includes some of the richest and most prolific land in Europe — if not in the world — the tail-end of the so-called Golden Vale which stretches eastwards for another fifty miles into Tipperary and to the borders of Leix-Kilkenny. This 'Golden Vale' is green and fertile undulating country drained by broad, stately salmon rivers. What hills there are, are low, green and cultivated. Tralee marks the very toe of this valley, and this toe is poking into country in the most violent contrast. For, where the Golden Vale ends to the north of Tralee, the mountains of south Kerry and west Cork begin, rearing themselves up out of the surrounding countryside like the battlements — almost desert-bare in places — of some gigantic fortress: battlements which they were to become, as south Kerry and west Cork became the last fortress of anti-Treaty resistance.

In capturing Tralee the pro-Treatyites gained entrance to the anti-Treaty rear and anti-Treaty troops committed at Kilmallock were drawn off to engage the attacking force which was the thin wedge which was to cleave the lowland north from the highland south-west of what remained of the 'Republic of Munster'. When the anti-Treaty resistance at Kilmallock wavered, staggered and was finally withdrawn, the whole of the open, fertile lowland was clear and virtually defenceless before attack from pro-Treaty forces, which came in conjunction with the Tralee landings.

The landing at Fenit — the port of Tralee — by the Dublin Guards under O'Daly met with some local resistance, but the landings were a surprise and the bulk of the Tralee Kerry No. 1 Brigade commanded by Humphrey Murphy was busy at Kilmallock under the command of Vice-Brigadier J. J. Sheehy. A Tralee family had been on a picnic near Fenit when the landing took place. Hurriedly packing their hamper into the pony and trap that brought them, they set off for Tralee at a gallop bringing the 'bad word' with them. The official pro-Treaty report of the landing and the capture of Tralee, which was issued on Saturday 5 August, is somewhat sparing of the facts.[1]

We landed at Fenit on Wednesday morning. Fire was opened on us from the coastguard station and from the other posts along the beach. Our troops landed successfully and rushed the village. We suffered two casualties, Volunteer Shiels and Volunteer Sieman being wounded in the dash. We captured one prisoner here. The Irregulars retreated before our fire and were closely pursued by the men of the Dublin Guards. We overtook them at Spa where after a bitter engagement, the Irregulars were again forced to retreat, leaving behind them one dead, one wounded and six prisoners. Our losses were Volunteer Byrne killed and Lieutenant Martin Nolan wounded. We divided forces at Spa. Commandant McGuinness and Vice-Commandant Dempsey, with one party, pushed on towards Tralee. Captain McLean with another party, advanced along the coast road to enter the town at Boherbee. At the industrial school, just outside the town, we again came under the fire of the Irregulars, but, after a few minutes, they retreated here. The railway gates at Pembroke Street were heavily chained and barred, but the troops smashed through and Pembroke Street was taken by assault. Vice-Commandant Dempsey advanced around the town and occupied the workhouse, linking up with Captain McLean's party on the south. Commandant McGuinness advanced into the town from Boherbee.

The first of our troops entered Tralee at 1.30 p.m. by Pembroke Street. They rushed Rock Street from this point and it immediately fell into our hands. At the same time Commandant Dempsey encircled the town, while Commandant McGuinness, forcing his way by Boherbee, took possession of the Staff Barracks. A fierce engagement lasting over an hour took place here. A large body of Irregulars evacuated Ballymullen Barracks and set fire to the building before they left. But a large portion of the building was

211

saved by the troops. The police barracks in Church Street was also set on fire by the Irregulars before they left. The town was completely in our hands at 8 p.m. During the assault at Rock Street one soldier was wounded. The Red Cross men immediately started to his assistance, carrying two large Red Cross flags and stretchers. Fire was opened on them from the police barracks and Volunteer Harding was shot dead and Volunteer Fleming wounded, both dead and wounded falling across the stretcher they were carrying. This cowardly act was witnessed by a number of townspeople, who were loud in their condemnation of such a despicable act. At Fenit we discovered that the Irregulars had the landing pier mined. A prisoner taken by us here was got to remove the mines on our orders. We subsequently found two mines, one at each side of the pier, both of which had failed to explode.

This document is a good example of the bulletins that were issued from time to time, and of the more successful kind of propaganda weapon used by the pro-Treatyites. The inference is that Tralee was captured after a heavy engagement in which the anti-Treatyites were routed. The anti-Treaty version is very different and appears more reliable in this instance. Because of Kilmallock there was little more than a handful of anti-Treaty troops at Fenit and Tralee. The fighting on the road between the towns was brief and bloody. Only one or two anti-Treatyites were available to occupy each defensive position and today a procession of little white crosses along the roadside marks the places where they died trying to halt the pro-Treaty forces. An anti-Treaty official report issued in Cork city on 6 August said: 'The Free State troops advanced to Kilfenora with an armoured car from Fenit via the Scrahan Road, Spard and on the Strand Road to Tralee. They met with opposition from Republicans ensconced in the middle of Rock Street, killing twelve and wounding thirty.'[2]

This casualty list, like the even more impressive pro-Treaty one which refers to anti-Treaty losses, is probably an exaggeration, as is the phrase 'Republicans ensconced in Rock Street.' The late Mr Johnnie Connors, TD, was dug in on his own near a dairy in Rock Street with a Lewis gun and fired on the pro-Treaty forces as soon as they came in on one side of the town. Mr Charlie Daly of Clash, Tralee — cousin of his namesake, OC 2nd Northern Division, captured in Donegal — went out on the other. He was making for the local anti-Treaty HQ at Currane

212

seven miles away on the Killarney Road. At a place called 'the Mile Height' outside Tralee a car pulled up beside him. In it were Brigade OC Humphrey Murphy and two or three other officers. Daly reported that the pro-Treaty troops were entering Tralee.

'Have they reached the barracks yet?' asked Murphy.

'No,' said Daly, 'Connors is holding them up at Rock Street.'

'Come on then, we'll make it,' said Murphy, 'we want to burn the barracks before they get there,'

The car turned west across country and the four men in it entered and set fire to the barracks before it fell into pro-Treaty hands. Such was 'the large body of troops' referred to in the pro-Treaty report. Only token resistance was offered in the town and by nightfall it was occupied by O'Daly's men. But there was one notable incident before the final capture. This was a miniature 'armoured battle' which took place in the Moyderwell suburb between two anti-Treaty and two pro-Treaty armoured cars. For more than an hour these four-wheeled-ironclads manoeuvred around each other, firing as they did so, through the streets of Tralee on the dull, wet and windy night that was 2 August 1922. None of the cars became a permanent casualty and, surprisingly, not one was captured, but all four were punctured and some casualties may have been inflicted on the occupants. The anti-Treaty cars withdrew under orders when the last anti-Treaty soldier left the town.

An account of the taking of Tralee issued on July 7 is worthwhile recording in the light of what is now known. It reads:

'Advancing upon Tralee . . . in three columns which carefully avoided the main roads they (the pro-Treatyites) again surprised the Irregulars and after some of the most stubborn fighting in the war captured the town. The National Troops claim to have killed seventy-five Irregulars; the deaths of thirty seem fairly certain. Brigadier Daly's troops now needed a rest and reinforcements before they could venture more. As it was, the Irregulars outnumbered and surrounded them, barring the road from Fenit to Tralee . . . Colonel-Commandant Hogan set out with reinforcements (from Listowel) . . . and, in spite of the enemy being in considerable strength, the two forces combined to take Castleisland and Farranfore.'

A witness, one of the anti-Treaty Kerry No 1 Brigade soldiers, who had fought at Waterford and at Kilmallock says: 'There were hardly seventy-five men in all north Kerry at the time, let alone in Tralee, to be killed. There was no question of surrounding or out-numbering the Free

State troops even when Kerry No. 1 came back from Kilmallock.'³

Simultaneously with the landing at Fenit a general sweep through the rich lowlands of north Kerry was launched. On 3 August troops under Colonel-Commandant Hogan crossed the Shannon estuary at Tarbert, a small village in the extreme north-west of Kerry, which was occupied without trouble. From here Hogan drove south-west to capture Listowel. 'At Ballylongford,' said an official report, 'the troops captured six prisoners,' While this was happening in north Kerry, Brigadier James Slattery was making a concerted sweep through Limerick and mid-Kerry. From Patrickswell he drove down on the picturesque model village of Adare, where he overcame determined resistance — very heavy machine-gun fire pinned his men down beyond the blown bridge until he brought up a field gun behind an armoured car, shelled the village and then swept on to Newcastlewest and Rathkeale.

Rathkeale capitulated easily as soon as the first artillery shells began to fall, but at Newcastlewest the anti-Treatyites held on as long as possible against the artillery and armoured cars — one of which is credited with pushing forward against the retreating anti-Treatyites and killing or wounding more than twenty men.

When the Tralee anti-Treaty brigade did return from Kilmallock with about eighty men it assembled at HQ in Currane a few miles north of Farranfore. That was on Saturday night, 5 August. An attack was planned to take place on Sunday night against Farranfore with Humphrey Murphy in charge. The details have been given by Mr Charlie Daly, who was one of the scouts.

> The attack was planned for that night and myself and another man were to scout along the road into Farranfore across the railway bridge. We crept up on each side of the road in our stockinged feet as far as the bridge and saw some of the enemy on it. We went back and reported to the OC and were told to go ahead again and open fire on them, shooting them if possible. I knew one of the lads. He was a neighbour of my own from Castleisland and I wasn't happy about the orders we got. We went on again — we had our boots off all the time — and got within a few feet of the bridge, but they were gone . . . I was delighted . . .

Daly and his companion scout pressed on into the village without seeing any of the enemy. They finally came to a corner on which there was a shop owned by Daly's aunt. Here, one on either side of the road, they looked up and down the village — 'Like a couple of rats reconnoitering a pantry' — but did not notice two soldiers in a deep doorway opposite. These soldiers ran down the village without firing and Daly and his companion were able to get off a few shots before doubling back to their own men.

As they raced back a machine-gun opened up, tearing chunks from the road all round them and they had to dive for the ditch. Meanwhile, Humphrey Murphy and his men were waiting for word from another anti-Treaty column who were on the road from Firies to Farranfore and who were to attack simultaneously, but no word came and, with the machine-guns still rattling and the town alerted, he called off his attack. Ironically, the man with the despatch from the second column was later located waiting at the wrong spot with his report. From this time onwards action in north Kerry was limited to similar guerilla attacks by anti-Treatyites against established pro-Treaty posts.

[1] Daily Press, 5 August 1922.
[2] The phraseology is at fault, giving the impression that casualties were among the anti-Treaty defenders whereas what is meant is that they were inflicted by the defenders on the pro-Treaty attackers.
[3] Con Casey of Tralee, sometime Editor of The Kerryman.

19

THE END OF 'THE MUNSTER REPUBLIC'

Cork city was the capital of 'The Munster Republic' and when Waterford and Limerick were taken by the pro-Treaty forces the city was open to attack by land or by sea. The anti-Treatyites did control the inner Cork Harbour, but British-manned forts and warships controlled Cobh Harbour. The city became, in the minds of soldiers on both sides, a last ditch, not at all in accordance with the existing situation or with subsequent events. The position of the citizens of Cork, for example, was far from being that of a populace preparing for a siege, though there was some hardship. (Cork Regatta, it is rather amusing to learn, was held as usual on 26 July irrespective of impediments such as war, siege, and civil disruption.) Cork has a tradition of civic leadership going back beyond the reign of Elizabeth I, when it won the title 'Rebel Cork' because Florence McCarthy Mór shut the gates against her Reformation armies,[1] the only city in the country to do so. It is an important centre of Government institutions and public services with a powerful Chamber of Commerce. It was therefore an easier matter for responsible citizens to take over the reins of order and effect some sort of civil authority than it was in smaller and more volatile communities. In fact Cork gives an accurate picture of the unhappy relationship that existed generally between the civilian population and the anti-Treaty administration, during the Civil War. A caustic remark, not infrequently heard nowadays, says that there are far more old Republicans now than there were active ones during the Civil War.

Such remarks underline the predicament in which a large section of the people — many of them Republican in outlook — found themselves. They had suffered four years of war and terror under the Black and Tans; physically, morally and spiritually they were exhausted; they had been offered a degree of independence better than ever offered to the nation — an offer which (but for Partition) would ten years before have been hailed enthusiastically. A majority of citizens were in favour of accepting that degree of independence and now they were being asked to support a militarized Republic — which was steadily bringing the wheels of trade and commerce to a standstill.

Furthermore, it looked as if pro-Treaty policy would bring about an economic blockade of the south; unemployment, already disproportionately high before the war began, rose rapidly in Munster as workers and office staffs were dismissed from their employment with production and distribution coming to a standstill.[2] The people were subjected to the pressure of the Churches, the Provisional Government and the national Press and, as sources of employment shrivelled locally, they heard of boom conditions in Dublin and in other pro-Treaty -held areas; heard of revival of trade in places — Waterford and Limerick for example — that had changed hands; heard not only of revival, but often of expansion due to military contracts.

As commerce and economic life came to a halt many Republican sympathizers longed for peace and many more became actively pro-Treaty. For the pro-Treaty supporters — of whom, in Cork city, there was an influential section — the situation was simple and clear-cut. Whenever possible they refused to co-operate with anti-Treatyites; when that was not possible, they co-operated to the minimum degree. At all times they were contemptuous, openly 'waiting for liberation'.

But the anti-Treatyites in Cork did not have to contend with raids and attacks such as occurred nightly all over Dublin. Opposition was entirely political and came principally from the bourgeois element, the merchants and professional classes. An attempt to collect income tax from the city merchants was successfully met with stubborn resistance. A loss of £1,000,000 in the butter trade as a direct result of the disruption in trading was estimated and farmers were pressing the creameries for payment, which could not always be made. Butter dumping by some creamery managers was alleged, with a resultant drop in prices, and supply in the city was much greater than demand. About 40 per cent — 30,000 — of the city's population was calculated to be unemployed and food supplies were running short. Stores needed by the anti-Treatyites from traders were being paid for with £100,000 Customs and Excise revenue seized from the Customs House when the merchants refused to pay the income tax. The banks were beginning to run short of ready money and had, in fact, been ordered by their head offices to close down as part of the economic attack on the south, and because of moneys seized from their offices by the anti-Treatyites.

With reference to the attempt to collect income tax a pro-Treaty announcement on 10 August said,[3] 'A crisis of the most grave character has arisen in Cork and the entire closing down of the city is threatened.' The demand notes for this income tax were as follows:

Irish Republican Army, Cork No. 1 Brigade, Civil Administration Dept., Inland Revenue Offices.

August 1, 1922.

It appears that Income Tax amounting to £ .... is payable by your firm for the year 1921-1922. You are hereby ordered to pay this sum in full to the collector of Customs and Excise, Cork, within three days of the date hereof. If the whole or any part of this tax already is paid, please furnish the receipt.

Officer I/C Civil Administration.

This demand note came as a bombshell to the tax-payers, especially to the directors of large firms, and a joint meeting of the Cork Incorporated Chamber of Commerce and Shipping, the Cork Chamber of Commerce and the Cork Employers' Federation, Ltd. was held. The law adviser to the latter, Mr Maurice Healy, MP, advised against paying the tax except to the Provisional Government and all the firms agreed and decided that any victimization would mean that they would take the drastic steps of closing all industrial and trading operations and discharging all hands. The Lord Mayor, Alderman D. O'Callaghan, was asked to convey the decision to the military authorities. A curious sequel took place on the following Friday when Healy was arrested and deported to England.

Preparation for the defence of the city took a more ordered course than elsewhere. A factory with suitable equipment had been taken over and was being used to manufacture munitions. Chemicals and explosive ingredients could be seen in the streets by the lorryload. Munitions were also made in the laboratory of the Crawford Municipal Technical Institute.

But other vital war materials were necessary, yet there was no money with which to buy them as the following story illustrates: Ford's factory, which employed about 2000 men — many of whom were active anti-Treatyites — on two separate occasions made a successful stand against the demands of the anti-Treatyites. The first was in late July when the military told the factory manager that they wanted pig-iron. The manager — an American — agreed to show them where it was, asked how much they wanted, and was told, all he had. The manager replied: 'Very well, but if you do take it all, you'll have to take the 2000 men working here as well.'

Moreover, when goods were seized, even under requisition, it angered the bulk of the populace who believed (a) that the requisition orders were worthless, and (b) that the anti-Treatyites were in the wrong and would be defeated. For all the time they had been sitting on one committee or council after another trying to avert what seemed to many a relentlessly oncoming Civil War, the anti-Treatyites never appear to have asked themselves the question: 'What if Civil War does come?' They had no shadow cabinet in preparation; there was no Republican war loan raised. The war was fought on the anti-Treaty side for five months on the sole authority of the Army Executive, with little money and with no Government authority functioning behind it. If the anti-Treatyites had prepared for all eventualities, a warlike as well as a constitutional solution to the situation, had raised money during the 'cold war' and prepared a civil as well as a military governing authority (paradoxically, although they prepared for a constitutional settlement, when hostilities broke out there was only military leadership available to them), then they might have recruited enough public support to alter the course of the war.

On 24 July Cork Harbour Board, which included sympathizers from both sides, passed and forwarded to the Provisional Government a resolution calling for a meeting of the Dáil with every TD pro- and anti-Treaty present to find a solution to the problem. Nothing more was heard of it. Two days later an anti-Treaty manifesto to the people of Ireland, outlining the reasons for their stand, occupied two columns in the Cork newspapers. It was signed by George Noble, Count Plunkett, and by Seán T. O'Ceallaigh.[4] Now the leading citizens joined in a determined effort to make peace, calling themselves the People's Rights Association. The first step was to contact Lynch. That done and a reply received from him, they communicated directly to Collins, enclosing Lynch's message with their own memorandum, which asked Collins to reply in time for a public meeting in Cork on 5 August. It was signed Michael Ó Cuill and dated 1 August.[5]

It was decided immediately to communicate to Mr Michael Collins the following reply received from General Liam Lynch, Chief of Staff, Fermoy:

'I wish to inform you that when the Provisional Government cease their attack on us, defensive action on our part can cease.

'If the Second Dáil, which is the Government of the Republic, or any other elected Assembly, carry on such Government, I see no difficulty as to the allegiance of the Army.'

It was further decided to put the following queries to Mr Michael Collins, and to request an immediate and explicit answer to lay before a public meeting summoned for Saturday:

'1. Do you agree to arrange for such a cessation of hostilities as General Liam Lynch intimates he is prepared to accept?

'2. Do you agree to call forthwith a meeting of the Second Dáil, to be followed by a meeting of the Third Dáil, as previously arranged, and to allow the sovereign assembly of the people to decide on the necessity or policy of a bitter and prolonged Civil War?

Collins sent the following reply, dated 4 August:

Michael Ó Cuill, Runaidhe, People's Rights Association, Cork.

Your memorandum dated August 1 addressed to me, has been delivered to me by Mr T. P. Dowdall, who was accompanied by Fr Duggan.

With reference to the reply received from Liam Lynch, described by you as 'General, Chief of Staff, Fermoy' — with reference also to the two categorical questions you ask me:

. . . presumably your communication was meant to be addressed to the Government.

So far as the Army is concerned, I am merely obeying the orders of my Government, and all the General Staff and soldiers of the Army are merely carrying out the instructions given in accordance with such orders.

The Government has made it fully clear that its desire is to secure obedience of proper authority. When an expression of such obedience comes from the Irregular leaders, I take it that there will no longer be any necessity for armed conflict. When the Irregulars — leaders and men — see fit to obey the wishes of the people, as expressed through their elected representatives . . . there will be no longer need for hostilities.

It will, I have no doubt, have been observed by your body that the Government, in connection with the prisoners taken in the recent conflict and still being taken, have merely asked the following form to be signed:

'I promise that I will not use arms against the Parliament elected by the Irish people, or the Government for the time being responsible to that Parliament, and that I will not support, in any way, such action. Nor will I interfere with the property or the persons of others.'

From the fact that most of the prisoners have refused to sign this form it can only be inferred that they mean to take up arms again against the Government of the Irish people. If this is the spirit which animates Liam Lynch then I am sure your body will agree that it is very little good endeavouring to talk about terms.

It is the first duty of a Government to secure its citizens in the exercise of their rights, and until this is done, until there is peace, security, and the free exercise of opinion, I do not see how the Government can rest without failing in this elementary duty . . .

In conclusion, I can only re-state what I said in my letter of 23 July — namely, that there is not a single member among your body who is more heartily anxious to see representative Government prevail in this country than I am . . . The issue is now very clear.The choice is definitely between the return of the British and the Irregulars sending in their arms to the people's Government, to be held in trust for the people. It should not be difficult for the people's representatives to say which action they counsel.

> Micheál Ó Coilean, General,
> Commander-in-Chief.

The acting chairman (Griffith) of the Government, replied on the same date:

A chara, the Commander-in-Chief, General Michael Collins, has forwarded to us your communication of August 1.

In reply to your two categorical questions we have to inform you:

1. The Irregulars' actions are wrongly described as defensive. The existence of an armed body which claims independent authority and commits outrage on persons and property cannot be tolerated;
2. The functions of the Second Dáil came to an end on 30 June. The meeting which was to have taken place on that date would have been purely formal, for the purpose of bringing its

business to a conclusion. The sovereign assembly of Ireland is now the Parliament elected on June last, whose authority the Irregulars have flouted.

The present military action undertaken by the Government is necessary to enforce obedience to Parliament: It will cease only when that obedience is un-equivocally given. There must be no misunderstanding of what that obedience connotes.

It means the surrender into the national army of all war materials.

It means the restoration without exception of all seized property and money.

It means that particulars must be furnished about bridges, railways, which are or have been mined or rendered otherwise unsafe.

The general tone of your letter, including as it does such terms as 'General Liam Lynch, Chief of Staff' and calling the Government's action to secure obedience to law ' a bitter and prolonged Civil War' is such that we might take serious exception to it. Realizing, however, that you may have been acting under duress, as was applied to the *Cork Examiner*, we are willing to overlook it.

We can assure you that we are as anxious for peace in Ireland as are the members of your body. But that peace must be firmly established on the basis of the supremacy of the elected Government of the Irish people — Is mise.

Acting Chairman.

The Government Publicity Department made the following comments, which skilfully manipulated the facts in accordance with circumstances as seen pro-Treaty wise:

The Irregulars now hold in subjection a large part of Munster . . . Mr Lynch proposes that the elected Parliament of Ireland should leave all the power of Government in that area —   including summary power over the lives and property of the citizens — in the hands of men possessing no authority but the fact that they are armed. He demands in addition that the Dáil elected in June should abrogate its sovereignty, ignore the *mandate it received* and base its policy entirely on the lines dictated by Mr Lynch and his association, in *utter disregard of the will of the Irish people.* Finally he proposes that the irregular bands now waging war upon the people should be constituted into an army paid by the Irish people; that that army should be the master and not the servant of the people, and that the Government created by the people should be allowed to function only in so far as it obeyed the orders of that army.

The desire to ignore the decision given by the Irish people in the June elections accounts for the stress laid upon a further meeting of the Second Dáil. That body ceased to be a representative body the moment that the result of the election was declared. It was to have met on June 30 for purely formal reasons. It now possesses no authority whatever . . .

It is as well here to reiterate that the terms of reference for the June election specifically excluded the Treaty issue. It is also well to note that it is the pro-Treaty publicity — i.e. propaganda — department that makes so much of the election and so little of the meeting of the Second Dáil which should have taken place on 30 June to form a Coalition Cabinet in accordance with the Pact and which completely ignores Lynch's phrase — 'or any other elected assembly'.

In Cork at the beginning of August a water shortage threatened to become serious and it was rationed. Supplies of food, in the event of a siege, were not expected to last more than three weeks. One by one as the days passed, the city's larger drapery and provision stores closed. Unemployment rose and new voices were heard in support of pro-Treatyites as it did so. On 2 August, a Wednesday, a meeting of the women electors of Cork under the chairmanship of Mrs Leader proposed a motion for a Cease Fire, which was seconded by Mrs Thompson.

Then, on the night of 8 August, a mysterious dark ship steamed up the River Lee with the tide between 11 p.m. and midnight. It was a sultry summer night and nobody on shore knew who she was, or where she had come from, or what was her purpose. But that ship heralded a stop-press notice two days later which read:

'National troops have landed in Youghal, Union Hall and Passage West, in Cork.'

In spite of the landings which had already taken place in Kerry, the anti-Treatyites were taken by surprise which barely seems credible in view of the local circumstances. Cork Harbour and its approaches were dominated by five great forts — three of them subterranean — Carlisle, Camden, Temple-Breedy, Spike Island and Haulbowline Island, Headquarters of the Royal Navy in Ireland.[6] These bases were held by

223

British Forces in accordance with the Treaty and British military and naval intelligence were reasonably informed of local anti-Treaty dispositions. They in turn, it was believed by the anti-Treatyites, passed whatever information they considered fit on to the pro-Treatyites.

The precautions which the anti-Treatyites took against a surprise landing at Cobh were based on the assumption that British intelligence were co-operating with the pro-Treatyites and were the inspiration of the local Commander, Captain Michael Burke, who laid no mines at all. This, he claims, confused Naval Intelligence which advised against a landing at Cobh as it was not known where the supposed minefields were.[7] Passage West, though mined, was considered to be too far up-river — seven miles from the harbour mouth, and seven from Cork city, i.e. half way between the two — for an enemy ship to reach in safety and carry out a successful disembarkation. Nevertheless it was here that the landing took place, thanks to the foresight of a local officer, Commandant F. J. O'Friel, orderly officer on board the first pro-Treaty troopship to approach the harbour.

The landing was made by troops from Dublin who embarked under the command of Generals Emmet Dalton and Tom Ennis, at the North Wall, Dublin, on Monday 7 August, in *Arvonia* of the London and North Western Railway Co., and in *Lady Wicklow,* of the British and Irish Steam Packet Co. Commandant O'Friel said: 'I was told by General Dalton when he appointed me orderly officer on the ship, that we were bound for Ford's wharf, Cork. However, when the pilot boarded us at Roche's Point he informed the General that the river was blocked just above Passage and General Dalton then decided we would land at Cobh. I pointed out to him that Cobh was an island and that a few machine-guns at Belvelly would make it impossible for us to advance beyond that point. He asked me where I would suggest making a landing. I replied that the only place I could see was Passage. He replied: "Right, you will take twenty men and land there".'

When the ship first appeared in the harbour to lie off hilly Cobh, glittering like a string of precious stones by night, none of the anti-Treatyites ashore could identify her. The Cobh OC was alerted and he ordered out a small boat to investigate. This boat, however, was unable to make contact with the ship, according to the OC's account.[8] 'We had the ship under observation from about 11 p.m., ' he said 'and when our boat was unable to make contact, I ordered out the patrols.' The patrols were three cars with machine-guns mounted on them which followed the ship on the road running parallel to the river to Rushbrook. Here a warning shot was fired — perhaps that heard by Fynes — but there was no reply. The ship still nosed silently on with the three cars dogging it along the bank, Lewis guns trained on her. At Carrigaloe, opposite Passage West, the ship anchored and remained mysteriously silent. The Cobh OC ordered one of his guns to fire a burst across her bows. Before the staccato echoes had died away there came an answering burst, but the anti-Treaty OC was not able to discover whether it came from the ship or from his comrades on the far shore. He decided to report the presence of a strange ship in the river to Brigade HQ in Cork and made for the nearest telephone, at Fota, a few miles further on. He told the OC Michael Murphy, that he was afraid he might have fired on a civilian ship. The answer was at once reassuring and disastrous.

'You have not,' he was told. 'It's the enemy, They landed in Passage ten minutes ago and in Youghal and Union Hall earlier.'

Commandant O'Friel's account of the landing is as follows: 'When the ship tied up I took the party of twenty picked men from the company under my command and we landed behind Dock Terrace. We captured the mill and the Police Barracks and scouted the Glenbrook side of the village. Whilst our party did this, General Tom Ennis and party did likewise at the Cork end of Passage.' Fyne's version is slightly different, but only in detail. The general picture is that the anti-Treatyites at Passage were taken by surprise, but managed to detonate a few mines, making it difficult for *Arvonia* to come alongside. As the pro-Treaty forces landed they came under fire from the Coastguard station and the schoolhouse, but there were few casualties in the subsequent exchange, only one proving fatal. In about an hour the village had changed hands. Across the river in Cobh, Rushbrook and Carrigloe the anti-Treatyites tried to organize an attack, but it was of little use. A general warning to all shipping was issued by the British Admiralty not to use Cork Harbour because of cross-river firing. This exchange lasted until Thursday when Cork was evacuated and local anti-Treaty officers were ordered to disband their men. ('The order was given,' says one of them, 'that the men should return to their own unit areas and await instruction. I dismissed a couple of hundred and two weeks later was asked to re-group them again into active service units.'[9]) And it was on Thursday that *Lady Wicklow* arrived with pro-Treaty reinforcements. On the same day the anti-Treatyites sank the Glasgow steamer *Gorilla* as an additional barrier in the river channel.

When the news of the landing first reached the city there was literally 'consternation in the camp'. Most of the available troops had to be rushed to unprepared positions at Rochestown, between the city and Passage. Their object, it was now decided, was to hold the enemy long enough to allow the destruction of the barracks and bridges of the city.

There are confusing accounts of the advance from Passage. Some sources say it began on Wednesday, others on Thursday; the alternative dates have also been given for the battle of Rochestown, which was a determined effort by the troops mentioned above to hold the pro-Treaty advance as long as possible. It is probable that the battle actually took place on Wednesday, 9th August.

O'Friel says: 'Two parties left Passage with armoured cars and a field gun to advance on the city. Some time in the afternoon a soldier returned with the first fatal casualty and told us that General Ennis, Commandants Kilcoyne and Conlon's troops were in a bad way. Leaving a small guard on ship, we mustered all possible troops and, led by General Dalton, started for Rochestown. We arrived there without incident'.

The battle which brought them racing to Rochestown was heralded when the anti-Treatyites blew Rochestown railway bridge on the Cork Crosshaven line — now defunct — to prevent the pro-Treaty forces going direct to Cork by railway. Near the railway station the first clashes took place. The defenders were holding high, wooded ground near the monastery and the hills (which extend southward for three miles towards Crosshaven) covering every approach to Cork from Passage. These hills rise almost directly from the shoreside of broad Lough Mahon. The woods near the monastery run north to south and form an excellent defensive line against forces attacking Cork, and the anti-Treatyites took what advantage they could of it in the time at their disposal.

The battle continued in this area all day and pro-Treaty troops were not able to make any progress towards the city. A string of strong defensive positions at O'Grady's house and the crossroads near the monastery through Oldcourt (owned at the time by Sir Henry O'Shea) and Ballincurrig, held the troops advancing from the railway station. Unable to penetrate to the west these troops under General Dalton split into two groups, one heading southwards into the hills, and the other doubling back towards the coast, in an attempt to close a pincer movement on the enemy. O'Friel says: 'I advanced up Monastery Road

226

to Dr Lynch's house where I met a platoon of Commandant Conlon's company at the crossroads. After a short interval Conlon returned and told me he had been very heavily engaged and that we would have to clear high ground towards Douglas to get his men back from their present position. We advanced up the road with twelve men and two machine-guns and were successful in gaining our point, after encountering very heavy machine-gun fire.'

About 3 p.m. the jaws of the pincers began to close and the biggest engagement of the entire battle took place on a narrow front of about a mile between Ballincummins Cross and Doctor's Cross. An anti-Treaty armoured car was very active. Of this armoured car Fynes says: 'It was a coal lorry with armoured plating all round it and was put out of action and captured in a running fight with "The Manager" — a pro-Treaty car. It took two men to steer it and it travelled with the second battalion, Dublin Brigade, from Rochestown to Cork and on to Fermoy, Tallow, Cappoquin, where it was left when the battalion moved to Bantry and West Cork.'

Casualties are reported to have been considerable. There were several hand-to-hand combats in which soldiers on both sides showed much bravery. One example has been recorded: that of a pro-Treaty NCO named Michael Collins — a relation of the Commander-in-Chief — who succeeded in approaching anti-Treaty machine-gunner at Rochestown unnoticed, but, as he tried to use his automatic pistol, it jammed. He then attacked the machine-gunner bare-handed and grabbed the weapon, but the gunner was able to turn it on his enemy and fired a burst point-blank at him as Collins held the gun barrel. Miraculously the NCO was not killed, but he was wounded terribly in the groin.

By dusk relative quiet, interrupted by intermittent bursts of firing when patrols clashed, had settled down over the area. During the night the anti-Treatyites retired to Douglas village. Meanwhile on the northern bank, across the river — which is two miles broad at this point — the anti-Treatyites had been holding Fota House near Cobh Junction, the seat of Lord Barrymore. The demesne, which is a peninsula, two miles by one, connected to the mainland by a narrow strip of land, had been heavily trenched and barricaded as it commanded an extensive stretch of the river.

The defence of Cork had been based, largely, on the assumption that any attack would come by land from the north. The rolling up of the

Waterford-Limerick line and the concentration of forces, of both sides, on the Kilmallock front had encouraged this notion. The pro-Treatyites did nothing to discourage it. On the contrary, they ordered diversionary attacks well to the north of the city, which had the desired effect of employing the bulk of the anti-Treaty forces over a broad front to prevent what was never intended — a break through from the north. Not long before the landing, for example, anti-Treaty troops from the Cobh area had been sent to Kilmallock.

When the surprise attack did come from the sea the anti-Treatyites decided to abandon the city rather than submit the civilians to the trials of a defence. It was a speedy evacuation. 'Cork city was burning before the battle of Rochestown commenced and could be seen from Doctor's Cross,' says Fynes. An anti-Treaty intelligence officer who walked from Crosshaven, a seaside resort fourteen miles from the city, found Cork empty of troops when he got there and the barracks burning. An officer of the Cork No. 1 Brigade was seen alone on one of the empty city streets behind a machine-gun waiting for the incoming pro-Treaty troops. Union Quay Barracks, anti-Treaty HQ, was systematically stripped and files and maps were removed. A fleet of cars and lorries waited outside as the troops assembled for evacuation. On the South Mall huge, silent crowds looked on. Together, almost, the city barracks — Victoria, now Collins Barracks, one of the largest military barracks in Ireland and reputed to have had the largest square in the British Isles — Union Quay and Tuckey Street were all fired; so were Elizabeth's Fort, the Bridewell and Shandon Street Barracks. There was a spirited attempt by the Cork ex-Servicemen's Association to interfere with the preparations for withdrawal, but it was speedily dealt with. Considerable looting took place before the barracks were destroyed.

As Thursday evening wore on, the anti-Treatyites, some of them straight from the firing line, retreated westward on foot and in every conceivable kind of vehicle. The old Muskerry railway was commandeered, as was the Western tram service; cars, motor-cycles and bicycles were used; troops, tired and weary from fighting, came in at the eastern side of the city looking forward to food and rest, only to march straight through and out the other side without stopping. Attempts were made to blow up several city bridges, particularly Parnell Bridge, but it was only slightly damaged. The cantilevered Brian Boru and Clontarf Bridges were opened and some machinery removed.

When everything possible to delay pursuit had been done, the last of the anti-Treatyites left Cork a bare hour before pro-Treaty troops under Ennis marched in. Meanwhile, an aeroplane had circled the city, apparently scouting, and disappeared again without incident.

It was a bright sunny evening such as fills Cork with a particular loveliness at that time of year, but when General Ennis drove in, in 'The Manager', to be welcomed by the people, a low black pall of smoke from the burning barracks hung over the city hills hiding the sun shining behind Gurranabraher. An hour after the troops had marched in many of them were seeking billets. Already the dead and wounded were being brought to their native towns for burial. The anti-Treatyites, where possible, had taken all their wounded with them, but several intelligence officers remained behind to gather information.

One of these owed his subsequent arrest to the friendly action of a local TD Barry Egan. Mr Egan (some six months later) was travelling through Cork with a pro-Treaty intelligence officer called Scott when he saluted a pedestrian.

'Who's that?' asked the intelligence officer.

'Oh, that's so-and-so,' replied Egan, 'don't you know him?'

'Know him!' he roared, 'I've been looking for him for months.'[10]

The following proclamation was issued by the pro-Treaty authorities in Cork on Saturday, 12 August:

PROCLAMATION

The National troops have entered the City of Cork in order to restore and preserve the rights and liberties of the citizens. They have no desire to interfere unnecessarily with the normal civilian activities of the community. It is for the Citizens of Cork to organize and administer their own affairs. The National forces, so far as is consistent with their military duties, will assist and co-operate with the Civilian representatives.

All arms, munitions, equipment and uniforms in possession of civilians must be immediately delivered to the Military Authorities. Also all stolen property, by whomsoever held, including unlawfully commandeered motor cars and illegally seized money, must be forthwith handed to the police or military authorities.

Civilians are expected in their own interests to co-operate with the military by returning information concerning sniping positions, ambushes, road mines and plans for destroying property.

Signed
J. E. Dalton, Major-General.

Some of the anti-Treatyites objected to the policy of burning the city barracks. Commandant-General Tom Barry said: 'I was very much against burning the barracks. It was a mistake. Instead of keeping them (the pro-Treaty forces) in one place where we could get at them easily, it meant they were scattered in ten or twelve different places round about.'

The evacuation of Cork meant that from now on the anti-Treatyites were forced to operate from temporary headquarters. They moved west by general consent even when the order to do so was not specific. The nature of the country in west Cork and Kerry made successful guerilla action possible. Mr J. J. Rice, at that time Commandant of Kerry No. 2 Brigade, says of events subsequent to the landings: 'The positions myself and Ted Sullivan[11] took up we could have held forever. It would have taken the whole Free State Army twenty years to dig us out.'

Now, more than ever, anti-Treatyites were dependent on the hard core of civilian supporters who had remained faithful to their cause, badly shrunken though the core might be, and it was to be found in west Cork and Kerry where, in contrast to the remainder of the country, the bulk of the civilian population was openly anti-Treaty. It was here, therefore, after the barracks of Cork had been evacuated and burned that the anti-Treatyites concentrated.

In Cork, General Dalton, with HQ in the Imperial Hotel, was visited by the Most Rev. Dr Cohalan, Bishop of Cork, who welcomed the pro-Treaty troops to the city. On the same day the following notice was published:

Cork Unemployed Central Committee: To the Citizens of Cork.

As unemployment benefits have been stopped for some time past owing to unsettled conditions, the above committee are in a position to announce that the benefits will be almost immediately restored; that Fords and other works and industries will be encouraged by the army authorities; that all classes of pensions will be paid as usual, as soon as the essential communications can be restored.

In the way of a temporary relief to meet the present distress, £200 will be immediately handed to the St Vincent de Paul Society to

230

relieve very acute cases, pending representations being made for relief on a large scale, in view of the conditions in Cork.

The same day Dalton saw the city bank managers collectively and ordered them to re-open their banks. Thus ended the economic blockade of the south.

Then, unnoticed, one of the most significant events of the period — and one which might have had far-reaching effects — occurred: de Valera, feeling that there had been enough bloodshed and that the Republican ideal had been sufficiently well defended in the face of the attack against it and with little prospect of final victory, at this time recommended that the anti-Treaty troops lay down their arms. Lynch, however, would not hear of the suggestion.

These events took place on, or close to, Saturday 12 August 1922, and on that day, in Dublin, Arthur Griffith, President of the Provisional Government and of the Second Dáil, died.

[1] According to John George McCarthy, who wrote an interesting history of the city published about 1878. Another source says that the title was acquired when Perkin Warbeck, pretender to the English throne, was 'crowned' King in Christ Church, in 1493.

[2] It is certain that co-operation between anti-Treatyites and the merchants would have given the pro-Treatyites cause for much greater alarm. Furthermore, opinion among Provisional Government leaders was divided on the question of economic blockade of the south. Conditions in Cork had much the appearance of a deliberate blockade, but this was as much due to individual action by the banks and private firms with headquarters in Dublin as to any action by the pro-Treaty authorities. Because of high unemployment those in favour of a blockade argued that it would cripple the anti-Treaty war-effort through idleness, famine and lack of resources that much quicker, while those opposed to the blockade emphasized the (very real) danger of anarchy and Communism.

[3] Sceal Catha Luimnuighe.

[4] Late President of Ireland after two terms of office.

[5] Correspondence from *Cork Examiner* and *Cork Constitution* of the period.

[6] They were handed over to Mr de Valera's Government in 1938 together with other naval and military installations around the coast.

[7] This is supported by Seamus Fitzgerald, D. Litt., who was Burke's immediate superior in the Cork No. 1 Brigade. 'The landings at Passage West took place there,' says General M. J. Costello, 'because there were a number of troops from the locality on board. Commandant Peter Conlon of Longford led the attack.'

[8] J. J. Fynes, who was on board *Arvonia*, contradicts this and says that the ship was challenged by a tender. The captain replied 'Passengers from Liverpool'. But a soldier fired a shot and this brought fire all the way up to Passage. But there is no verification of this version. Burke says he did not open fire until the ship was near Passage West, nor does O'Friel, who was on board *Arvonia*, agree.

[9] Seamus Fitzgerald.

[10] The officer — the author's father — was arrested in his flat that evening by a pro-Treaty officer. Seán (Neeson) had some despatches on him at the time but succeeded in hiding them while his bedroom was searched. After his arrest he sent a coded message to the Cumann-na-mBan girl he later married (Geraldine Sullivan), and she found and delivered the despatches to the anti-Treatyites.

[11] OC West Cork Brigade.

20

MICHAEL COLLINS

When Cork was captured there was no central rallying point from which the anti-Treatyites could direct military affairs. Throughout Munster they made for the mountains; westward in Cork to the chains there, to the Comeraghs of Waterford, the Galtees of Tipperary and the MacGillycuddys of Kerry: columns of men there made preparation for a guerilla war. To men like Lynch, surrender of the Republican ideal, for which he was in arms, was unthinkable.

Yet there were some who, like de Valera, still hoped that an early and honourable settlement might be reached. The Republican ideal had been defended in arms. The anti-Treatyites were now demonstrably defeated in arms and out of favour with the people. Continued force could not improve the situation. Peace and 'Constitutional means' might do so. If such was the attitude of some of the anti-Treaty leaders, it was also the attitude of some of those on the other side, among them Michael Collins. Together, Collins and de Valera might have worked out a solution, as they so nearly did three months earlier in the unjustly derided Pact. Fate, however, intervened in a manner which proved disastrous in many ways, which may well have prolonged the war for nine months, and which was certainly the cause of mounting bitterness and vengeance.

On 22 August 1922, a small mobile column of pro-Treaty soldiers was ambushed between 8.30 p.m. and 9.30 p.m. at a place in West Cork called Beal na mBlath — the Gap of the Blossoms. In that action General Michael Collins, the thirty-one-year-old Commander-in-Chief of the pro-Treaty forces, was killed. (See the author's *Michael Collins*.)

Ten days beforehand, when Arthur Griffith died in Dublin, leaving the young Commander-in-Chief heir to the leadership of the pro-Treatyites, Collins said: 'There seems to be a malignant fate dogging the fortunes of Ireland, for at every critical period in her story the man whom the country trusted and followed is taken from it. It was so with Thomas Davis and Parnell, and now Arthur Griffith.' It was so also with Michael Collins, whom the country trusted and followed more than any man since Parnell.

By 20 August the situation in Munster was extremely satisfactory so far as the pro-Treatyites were concerned. One by one the anti-Treaty towns had collapsed and been captured by Generals Dalton, Ennis, O'Duffy, Slattery, Murphy and O'Daly. Dalton and Ennis had, in the previous week, made a drive into Collins's own country (west and south-west Cork) and captured Skibbereen and Clonakilty. On the eve of his departure south to review the situation at first hand, Collins heard that Bandon had been captured that day. The same evening he was involved in a motor accident at Dun Laoghaire (then Kingstown), an ill-omen which he characteristically ignored. Next day he set out on his tour which was to include the recently-captured west Cork areas. 'I'll hardly be shot in my own county,' was the comment of the Clonakilty man. On Sunday he travelled to Limerick and that night on to Cork city. Two days later he was dead.

It took something over a week after the fall of Cork city on 11 August before anti-Treaty re-organization at brigade and division level could be attempted to meet the new situation. Units were operating without the benefit of general day-to-day orders from HQ and the resulting lack of liaison produced considerable confusion — particularly in regard to exchange of information — which now results in contradictions and differences of opinion concerning events which led up to the ambush in which Collins was killed, especially concerning a significant meeting in Ballyvourney about that time.[1]

Whether, then, as the result of the confusion mentioned in the note or not; whether as a general order, or as the policy of local commanders, anti-Treaty forces all over Munster reverted to the guerilla tactics they had employed against the British, and used them against pro-Treaty units after Cork fell. On Monday, 21 August, O'Duffy, was ambushed three times during a tour of Cork and Kerry. A large ambush took place at Liscarroll (on the Cork-Limerick border) in which Commandant Cregan was killed, while Collins was actually on the route; at Ninemilehouse, near Clonmel, Colonel Frank Thornton was wounded in an ambush, the only man to survive it.[2] The ambush at Beal na mBlath was on Tuesday. Six attacks on senior officers in three days.

It is commonly believed that the ambush in which Collins was killed was an accident of war and was due to the prevailing lack of anti-Treaty military cohesion as much as to any other single factor. It has been argued that if it were known to the ambushers that Collins was in the column it would not have been ambushed. This is not so. The ambush at Beal na mBlath was planned for ten hours before it took place. It was directed against one particular column and Michael Collins was known to be travelling in it.

The ambush in which Collins was killed, was planned, laid and manned by senior officers, including the brigade staff of Cork No. 3 Brigade, officers from the five brigade battalions and some divisional officers. A meeting of brigade and division officers had been called for Beal na mBlath for Tuesday, 22 August. The purpose of the meeting was to determine future brigade policy (and possibly seek a means of ending the conflict). Some of the officers stayed at John Long's house at Beal na mBlath cross on the night of the 21st and a sentry, Dinny Long — no relation — was on duty all night. The meeting was to be held at Mrs Murray's house a few hundred yards from the crossroads. Naturally the officers did not expect Collins to pass through Beal na mBlath that morning, but that is just what happened.

Dalton travelled with Collins on the tour of inspection and gives an account of the ambush. The convoy, consisting of a motor-cycle escort, a tender of eighteen soldiers, a Lancia car containing himself, Collins and two drivers, and an armoured car, drove into the ambush on Tuesday, 22 August.

> We had reached a part of the road commanded by hills on all sides . . .we had just turned a wide corner when a sudden and heavy fusillade of machine-gun and rifle fire swept the road in front of us and behind us, shattering the windscreen of our car. I shouted to the driver 'Drive like hell' but the Commander-in-Chief said: 'Stop. Jump out and we'll fight them.' We took what cover we could behind the little mudbank on our left. It seemed that the greatest volume of fire was coming from our left-hand side. The armoured car now backed up and opened heavy machine-gun fire at the hidden ambush . . . .

It was the Crossley tender, in charge of Commandant O'Connell, which received the first shot. The road had been barricaded by an old cart, which the occupants of the tender promptly removed. After a few minutes firing ceased and the ambushers concentrated their fire on Collins and the other men who had occupied the touring car. General Collins and I were lying within arms' length of each other. Captain Dolan was several yards farther down the road. We opened rapid fire at our seldom visible enemies. About fifty or sixty yards farther on, round the bend, we could hear that our machine-gunners and rifle-men were also heavily engaged. We continued to fight for about twenty minutes without casualty when a lull in the attack became noticeable. General Collins now jumped to his feet and walked over behind the armoured car to obtain a better view of the enemy's position. Suddenly I heard him shout: 'Come on, boys, there they are.' When next I turned round the Commander-in-Chief had left the car position and run about fifteen yards back up the road. Here he dropped into a prone position and opened up on our retreating enemies.

Moments later, Dalton, O'Connell and Dolan found their chief lying motionless, gripping his rifle, across which his head rested. There was a gaping wound at the base of the skull behind the right ear.[3] The firing continued while Dalton said an Act of Contrition into the dying man's ear and while the body was dragged to cover. As they were getting into the car the second casualty, motor-cyclist Lieutenant Smith, was shot in the neck, but he remained on his feet and helped until the party was ready to leave for Cork.

In his book Taylor says:[4] 'The Republicans didn't know Collins was in the vicinity, say the Republicans . . . Approximately forty men formed the ambushing party . . . the ambushing party were drinking heavily in a tavern . . . the ambushing column had pulled out of position and only a few of the rearguard party were with them . . . '

These four statements are not in accordance with the facts: (1) The anti-Treatyites did know Collins was in the area; the ambush was planned to surprise his party. (2) Twenty to twenty-five men were in the ambush party. (3) Nobody in the ambushing party was drinking, let alone heavily. (4) It was not a column that conducted the ambush.

It was a fine, clear autumn morning. The meeting was due to start early. About 9 a.m. the sentry, Long, removed his bandolier and left his rifle down and went for a 'breather'. While he was on the road outside he saw a motor-cyclist approaching and following it came a Crossley tender, a Lancia car and an armoured car. This column stopped and asked to be directed to the road to Bandon. Long directed them through

Newcestown. He recognized Michael Collins in the open tourer. The council meeting had already started in Mrs Murray's house when he reported the incident. The meeting decided that Collins's party had come from Macroom and that there was a reasonable chance that he would return by the same route. It was decided to lay an ambush for the party about 800 yards from the cross. Accordingly, the officers took up a position on the southern side of the road, which was barricaded with a cart. It was a fine, sunny day, and the party lay in ambush all through it until twilight when tea was brought to them from Murrays' while they stayed in position. At length it was decided that the column must have returned by another route and that the main body of the ambush party should return to Murrays and continue the meeting, leaving a small squad of four men behind to cover removal of the barricade.

The main party had just reached the cross when firing broke out from the ambush position. The rear-guard had been about to leave their position, having moved the barricade to the roadside, when the motor-cyclist appeared. The men on the road dived for cover while those still in position fired at the oncoming column, principally in order to warn the unsuspecting main body on the roadway of the approach of this mobile column in their rear. As soon as the firing began, the main body of anti-Treatyites dived for cover on the northern side of the road hoping to work back and get the enemy in a cross-fire. They had no machine-guns in action that day.

The pro-Treaty machine-guns — that in the armoured car and those in the tender — immediately opened a tremendous fire on the attackers. 'They mowed the place down with fire: raking the section for the better part of half an hour,' said Commandant Peter Kearney, who was one of the ambush party. 'Our rearguard didn't stick their heads up much, you may be sure.' The action continued for some time, during which dusk closed in rapidly enough to see the flashes of gun-fire. 'Apart from the heavy fire on our positions, the dusk alone made it virtually impossible to get off an aimed shot,' said Kearney. This would have been about 9 p.m. or a little after it.[5]

Meanwhile, the main body of the ambush party moved up the northern hill and tried to get in position for a flank attack, but by the time they succeeded in doing so dusk had fallen and the firing had stopped. Taylor (*op.cit.*) refers to the last shot which is alleged to have killed Collins, but both Dalton and Kearney deny this. The last shots in the action were fired by the pro-Treaty forces. 'Four or five men with rifles pinned down by machine-guns were not in a position to dictate action,' said Kearney. Dalton points out that his troops maintained covering fire until they were under way with Collins's body. The column then moved off eastwards towards Crookstown and Aherla. The anti-Treatyites did not then know that Collins had been killed. They went back to Murrays and continued the interrupted meeting which went on until Volunteer Seán Ó Galbhín of Crookstown arrived with the news that Collins was dead.

Taking all the factors into consideration, the extent of the firing, darkness, the distance and evident surprise (on both sides) as well as the description and location of the wound, it is likely that it was a ricochet. (See Neeson, *Michael Collins*.)

Another popular legend has it that when Collins stopped at Long's to ask the way, de Valera was upstairs looking down at him from a window. It is an attractive story without an atom of truth in it. De Valera did pass through the cross within minutes of Collins but he had no connection with the meeting there or with the ambush.

Collins's death was announced to the pro-Treaty forces by the following exhortation from the Chief-of-Staff:

> *To the men of the army*. Stand calmly by your posts. Bend bravely and undaunted to your work. Let no act of cruel reprisal blemish your bright honour.
>
> Every dark hour that Michael Collins met since 1916 seemed but to steel that bright strength of his and temper his gay bravery.
>
> To each of you falls his unfinished work. No darkness in the hour; no loss of comrades will daunt you at it.
>
> Ireland: the Army serves — strengthened by its sorrow.
>
> R. Ua Maolcatha (R. Mulcahy). Chief-of-Staff.

The most important point affecting the subsequent course of the Civil War in connection with the Beal na mBlath ambush is that Collins himself hoped for an early Cease Fire and intended to 'concentrate my efforts in endeavouring to end hostilities'. That was the last thing he said to his brother, Sean Collins, at Clonakilty on the day he was killed. He had already instructed Thornton to contact Lynch to that end. Indeed he was en route to a vital meeting in Cork with neutral and enemy officers when ambushed.[6]

In an article discussing Taylor's *Michael Collins* in the *National Observer* in December 1958, General Seán MacEoin, TD, says that the purpose of Collins's visit to Cork was to establish contact with anti-Treaty officers who had been members of the IRB at the time of the split in the Dáil. He says that the IRB's decision to support the Treaty had not been correctly reported in the Munster area due to the disobedience of Liam Lynch, and that Collins was to contact these officers and apprise them of the true situation. This is unlikely. The officers had a full six months in which to become 'aware of the true situation' to their own satisfaction before hostilities began, and it is improbable that Collins can have believed that such an approach would have had more effect in August, after nearly two months of war, than it had earlier.

Collins and Mulcahy had several times been in Cork at conferences with these officers during the 'Cold War' period — one notable meeting was at Mallow — and every opportunity had presented itself to correct any false impression Lynch might have given. Furthermore, Lynch was in Dublin when the IRB officers of 1st Southern Division rejected the motion to support the Treaty. The officers who rejected the IRB's decision were responsible men who were well able to reach an independent decision. Finally, it must be borne in mind that Lynch did not actively support the extreme militant anti-Treatyites in the Four Courts until after they were fired on in June. He was ready to compromise, subject to seeing the new Constitution up to the time it was published (16 June 1922) and subsequently pinned his fading hopes on the unlikely possibility that the Provisional Government would summon a Coalition parliament. It is reasonable to assume that Collins's purpose in trying to make contact (in August) with responsible anti-Treaty officers was that which he mentioned to his brother Seán: 'To concentrate on endeavouring to end hostilities.'

In the same article General MacEoin released for publication for the first time a significant memorandum from Lynch to Deasy:

Irish Republican Army. Field General Headquarters, 28th August, 1922, Dept. C/S. 'To C/O 1st Southern Division. A Chara (My friend),

1 Yours of the 24th inst. reporting attack on the enemy at Beal na mBlath to hand yesterday.
2 Considering you were aware of the fact that the convoy contained an armoured car, it is surprising you had not laid mines to get this.[7]
4 Nothing could bring home more forcefully the awful

239

unfortunate National situation at present than the fact that it has become necessary for Irishmen, and former comrades, to shoot such men as Michael Collins, who rendered such splendid service to the Republic in the late war against England. It is to be hoped our present enemies will realize the folly of trying to crush the Republic before it is too late. Mise le Meas, Liam Lynch C/S.

General MacEoin quotes this as an example of documents which have not been released to writers and historians on the period and criticizes those who, like himself, have such documents and do not make them available. He also says that the document clearly shows where the responsibility for Collins's death lies.

Responsibility is an unfair word in the context since Collins died in war territory and in battle, but the memorandum could be construed to prove that Collins was killed at Beal na mBlath in an ambush deliberately planned for that purpose. The third paragraph of the memorandum proves that, beyond doubt, the anti-Treatyites knew what the formation they were ambushing consisted of before it was ambushed and Long knew who was in it.

[1] The following information has been supplied by an officer who was at the meeting:
It is that on the same weekend that Collins travelled south a meeting took place at Ballyvourney, County Cork, twenty miles west of Beal na mBlath, which was attended by anti-Treaty officers, including de Valera. According to this source de Valera was told that Collins was known to be on his way to Cork and that all units had been alerted to ambush his convoy. The road between Cork and Cobh, known to be on his schedule, was mined. De Valera was told that Collins might not leave Cork alive, and he is said to have replied: 'I know and I am sorry for it. He is a big man and might negotiate. If things fell into the hands of lesser men there is no telling what might happen.' This has been contradicted on the grounds that (a) the Ballyvourney meeting, if held, took place subsequently to 22 August 1922; (b) if de Valera made such a statement, he made it (or a version of it) after Collins had been killed; (c) the first intimation anti-Treaty officers had that Collins was in the south was on the morning of the ambush, and (d) the suggestion that a general order to anti-Treaty forces to ambush Collins's convoy was issued is 'completely unfounded'. Obviously there was (and is) confusion here, probably due to lack of liaison at the time. It seems incredible that the fact that Collins was south on Sunday did not reach anti-Treaty responsible officers *at all* until the morning he was killed. There was no secret of his general movements (*vide* note 2). De Valera confirmed to the author his attendance at the Ballyvourney meeting.
[2] This officer had been instructed by Collins to try to contact Lynch or Deasy to arrange a meeting with Collins with a view to ending hostilities. He was on this mission when he was ambushed. He had already seen Dan Breen on the same errand. Breen referred him to his superior officers.
[3] Dr Oliver St John Gogarty, who later saw the wound, said it was caused by a

ricochet. It has never been established — in spite of many rumours to the contrary — what calibre bullet caused the fatal wound. Gogarty, who had no love of the anti-Treatyites and who had experience of treating troops wounded in the First World War, was decided on the point of it being a ricochet. A great deal of nonsense has been written about Collins's death — including tales of apocryphal 'last' shots — all of which have clouded the point that he was killed at a crucial stage, while seeking to negotiate.

[4] Rex Taylor, *Michael Collins*, (Hutchinson 1958).

[5] Lighting-up time in Cork for the period 23 August is now given as 9.44 p.m. but, of course, this refers to new — or summer — time, which was not in use in west Cork in 1922. There was a Vickers gun in the armoured car in operation as well as at least one Lewis gun in the tender. Troops were using Thompson guns which would have been mistaken for machine-guns by the men on the hill. The Vickers gun stopped at one stage and it is the belief of many authorities that Collins, who was lying with his back to the armoured car and between it and the enemy, was killed by an accidentally-discharged round as the gunner, McPeake, tried to clear the gun. Shortly after this McPeake deserted, taking the armoured car — 'Slievenamon' — with him. For this he is alleged incorrectly by Taylor (*op. cit.*) to have received £500. The situation after the death of Collins may be likened to that which arose during the American Civil War when Lincoln was killed. Jefferson Davis, who had insisted on recognition of the Confederacy at tentative peace talks a few weeks earlier, realized that things had fallen into the hands of lesser men and that (particularly after Lee's surrender at Appomattox) a settlement imposed by the North would inevitably be coloured by a desire for vengeance. Consequently he crossed the Mississippi with General Magruder in an effort to prolong the struggle from Texas. (There was some justification in his fears because politicians in Washington did attempt to cancel some of the more generous terms imposed by Grant, who insisted on their observance.)

[6] Mr John L. Sullivan of Skibbereen, who met Collins as he left his brother's house en route for Beal na mBlath, says that Collins emphasized: 'I'm going back to settle this thing.'

Tom Barry in his notable account of the War of Independence, *Guerilla Days in Ireland,* records how, when the news of Collins's death reached Kilmainham Jail in which he was a prisoner: 'I looked down on the extraordinary spectacle of about a thousand kneeling Republican prisoners spontaneously reciting the Rosary aloud for the repose of the soul of the dead Michael Collins, President of the Free State Executive Council, and Commander-in-Chief of the Free State Forces . . . '

There is a great deal of hearsay evidence in support of the belief that Collins was determined to achieve peace without delay. The lengths to which he was prepared to go in this direction can only be conjectured, but there is considerable credence given to the following:

(a) He was sympathetic to anti-Treaty views (b) he (not always in accord with the views held by his fellow Cabinet members; *vide* Limerick) would put certain proposals to the leaders of both sides, and (c) he would use every means in his power to see that these proposals were carried out. So far as is known no copy of these proposals survives. What action he might have taken is speculation. But the use of the IRB as a vehicle for a Republican *coup de main* is not impossible.

[7] The reason that mines were not laid is additional proof that a column was not involved and that the ambush was the spontaneous product of the circumstances. Brigade and divisional officers at a conference were not equipped for ambushing and therefore did not have mines with them.

21

THE MUNSTER TOWNS

One by one the small towns in Munster were occupied by pro-Treaty troops. Sometimes the towns changed hands again, but from mid-August onward the whole character of the war altered. Such anti-Treaty successes as occurred were local and the result of guerilla tactics, seldom of central planning. But guerilla tactics, which had startling success against the foreign army of occupation, were useless against a domestic army of local troops, supported by the public and powerful Government. By mid-August the feeling, which had been growing for some time, that the war was over, was general and welcome. The Press prophesied complete victory within a few days. But it was a false prophecy, and the resulting disappointment, no doubt, accounted in some measure for the bitterness that developed in the next few weeks. A contemporary summary of the situation is full of confidence in a speedy victory for the pro-Treatyites. The effect of the Press's jingoism on the public (but more particularly on troops, fed with such optimistic ballyhoo as the war continued and with it raid after raid, ambush after ambush, death after death) was to produce exasperation, becoming callousness in the public and vengeful bitterness in the military, particularly after the death of Collins.

It took a few weeks for the nature of the new phase of the war to become apparent. Anti-Treaty commanders had been ordered to dismiss their men to their homes after the evacuation of the areas they were defending. This gave the final blow to a communications system rickety at its best. When the decision was taken to continue the war as long as possible, fighting as guerillas and 'underground', the task of bringing the men together in strength was hopeless and even guerilla war had to be conducted on a somewhat limited scale. But 'no guerilla war can be effective unless it is wholeheartedly supported by the people of the country. Without that support it is only a question of time before proper garrisons in the towns and proper mobile columns on the roads render the existence of guerillas impossible' wrote a correspondent at the time.

When these tactics became general, old War of Independence bogies were revived in new colours. As when the responsibility for destroying Mallow bridge — an important junction twenty miles from Cork city — was apportioned by a pro-Treaty source; it is a tragic example of the hounding of an individual, but not without its humorous side. It said: '. . . the destruction of Mallow railway bridge by Mr Childers aided by engineers from Krupps . . . ' Lloyd George's old standby, 'a German plot', rearing its head in the Civil War.

Accounts of ambushes, many being no more than unconfirmed reports by excited soldiers, were heard of in every county several times a day. In Dublin one week saw an average of fourteen such incidents reported each day. But these were minor affairs. Major actions were launched either as large-scale ambushes or as attacks on towns newly captured by the pro-Treatyites. An official summary of the position in the south on 15 September says: 'The most notable feature of the operations during the last ten days has been the offensive spirit shown by the Irregulars who have successfully attacked Abbeyfeale, Kenmare and Tarbert and have made heavy, but unsuccessful, attacks on Newmarket and Macroom.'

In east Limerick and north Kerry the report estimated that about 300 anti-Treatyites were active; 200 more were said to be in and about Castleisland and another 200 on the Mullaghreirk mountains with Seán Moylan. 'By far the most dangerous and important concentration is in the south-west slopes of the Derrynasaggart mountains. Here are the two villages of Ballyvourney and Ballymakeera and five or six hundred Irregulars and many of the most prominent leaders. Here a few days ago Mr de Valera signed his name in the visitor's book of the Irish College; here is published a daily broadsheet of Irregular propaganda, styled a southern edition of *Poblacht na hEireann*. Here was initiated the attack on Macroom, and from here started the troops which took Kenmare . . . the next month should see some of the most fatal, though not the most dramatic fighting of the war.'

Three days after this, on 18 September, eight members of the pro-Treaty forces, including Commandant Thomas Keogh and Captain Dan O'Brien, were killed in a mine explosion at a place called Carrigaphonea near Macroom. A booby-trap is said to have been placed under a mine on a bridge so that the mine exploded when lifted.

In Waterford the pro-Treatyites were less harassed. The pro-Treaty Brigadier met with little opposition when he broke out of the city and drove westward, clearing the country as he advanced, after recruiting and regrouping without hurry. First he took Tramore — without difficulty — to secure his left flank. 'The day I made my thrust out,' he says, 'the enemy occupied Whitefield, Butlerstown Castle, Dunhill and Annestown. The weather was ideal for our purpose, heavy fog and drizzle. We moved out in two main columns. At the same time a column moved westward along the coast from Tramore. Our first objective was Butlerstown Castle.' According to him it was captured without a shot being fired. His men advanced in battle-order and got through the anti-Treaty sentries in the fog and were actually on top of the castle towers, dominating the building with machine-guns, before the enemy realized it. 'Once the hinge at Butlerstown went,' he says, 'with our columns all round them and with no proper intelligence or control, they broke up and cleared out as best they could.'

He confirms that the only serious opposition in Waterford County came from anti-Treaty units from Cork and Kerry, but that even these showed little inclination for determined action. 'After Butlerstown we regrouped in the county and reorganized for the next push. When you leave them (the enemy) for a while it keeps them guessing, and we didn't want to overreach ourselves. Time was on our side. We practised a scheme of manoeuvre — a movement of columns that confused the anti-Treatyites and kept them guessing. I was particularly pleased at this time (mid-August) because casualties were negligible. We had a tremendous advantage over the Cork and Kerry columns opposed to us, as we knew every lane and road in the county and every gap in the Comeraghs. It was made easy for me. It is also a great advantage to know your opposite number and I knew the anti-Treaty commanders thoroughly. Our next objectives were Kilmacthomas and Dungarvan, which we took without opposition on the same day, 23 August.'

Some estimate of the respective measure of support given to pro-Treaty and anti-Treaty forces by the general public may be gleaned from the following address of welcome which was presented to the pro-Treaty commander when he entered Dungarvan:

To the commandant in charge of the National forces in Dungarvan:

Gallant Sir, on behalf of the people of Dungarvan (Borough) we extend to you a hearty céad mile fáilte (hundred thousand welcomes), which would be much more expressive were it not for the gloom cast upon our people by the lamented death of the *brightest gem in the diadem of our dark Rosaleen.*

In his great name we greet you, and we pray that the God of our destinies may protect you and those who serve you until Ireland enters upon freedom.

Signed — Michael Brunswick, CUDC, John Moore, Michael J. Casey, John F. Foley, Maurice Griffin, Thomas Ó Fataig (Chairman and members of the Urban District Council).

In Kerry at the opposite end of the anti-Treaty area Kenmare town was attacked and captured by the pro-Treatyites. It offers a good example of what happened in a number of Munster towns. By 15 August most of the north Kerry towns were in pro-Treaty hands. South Kerry, with its mountainy fingers reaching out into the Atlantic was a more difficult problem. On that date the attack began to spread southwards into the mountains.

An official report reads:[1] 'On Friday morning an expedition was sent from Limerick City to Kenmare under Brigadier Thomas O'Connor, Commmandant, Kerry No. 2 Brigade. A number of local leaders including the local Irregular battalion OC were made prisoners.' O'Connor had been an officer of Kerry No. 2 Brigade, which divided during the 'Cold War', and, with a small number of men, he joined the pro-Treatyites. The remainder, under Brigadier Humphrey Murphy — later transferred to Kerry No. 1 at Tralee because of command difficulties — supported the anti-Treatyites. At the time of the attack on Kenmare the brigade was under the command of anti-Treaty Brigadier J. J. Rice, a Kenmare man who was not captured in the attack. The troops who took Kenmare embarked from Limerick under the overall command of Major-General McManus (the same who refused to treat with Lynch in June), with O'Connor to lead the attack.

They travelled in two ships, *Margaret* of about 600 tons with a Thames pleasure boat — *Mermaid* — in tow. The troops on board were excited and gave vent to their exuberance by firing into the air as they left Limerick. The farther down the coast the two vessels travelled, the rougher the going became, *Mermaid* with her shallow draught, in particular, making heavy weather of it on tow, and the high spirits of the men rapidly gave way to seasickness. Twice the towrope broke and finally it was decided to cast off and let *Mermaid* proceed under her own steam.

Down past Brandon Head, the Seven Heads, the Blaskets; past Bray Head and Valentia Island and the remote, mysterious Skelligs Rocks with their ancient ruins, went the troopships, until they entered the mouth of the Kenmare River at dawn on 11 August. O'Connor and a few scouts were put ashore at Coongar Harbour and they brought back word that there were thirty men in Lacken Coastguard station — which had earlier featured in an incident with a British warship. Accordingly it was decided to land troops at once. In point of fact there were not thirty anti-Treatyites in all Kenmare at the time as the local fighting-men were employed elsewhere, similar to the situation at Tralee.

As the first boat of the landing party drew near the beach, it was challenged and warned to come no nearer or it would be fired on. The boats then returned to *Margaret* for reinforcements and then all landed without incident. Before the disembarkation was complete columns of smoke could be seen rising from Lacken Coastguard station which the small anti-Treaty garrison had fired and abandoned. The pro-Treatyites decided to continue up-river by boat and most of the troops were taken on board again, a smaller party being detailed to advance overland. About 5 p.m. both parties drew near Kenmare — those on board ship just in time to see the anti-Treatyites march out of the town in good order. These men who captured Kenmare were men of the 1st Northern Division from Donegal.

From a new base in the mountains, Rice strengthened his position and planned a counter-attack. On 9 September he struck as part of a general anti-Treaty drive in the area. There are several versions of the attack, as usual; two contradictory ones from pro-Treaty sources, both differing in substance from what did in fact happen. All accounts agree, however, that O'Connor was killed in the action. Pro-Treaty sources believe that the anti-Treatyites attacked in the strength of some hundreds, outnumbering the defenders. The prisoners were marched over the mountains to Kilgarvan and there set free — 'because their captors had little food for themselves' — according to a pro-Treaty account. The account continues: 'The first break in the defence was in the successful rushing of outposts by the Irregulars, leaving them to concentrate in the banks. The Nationals were in charge of Brigadier O'Connor of Kenmare. He was at home when the attack opened and was unable to join his troops. He was shot in his own house . . . A piquant incident in connection with the fall of the town is that a food ship arrived there on Friday. Local labour refused to unload it without an increase in remuneration. The first thing the Irregulars did was to commandeer labour and unload the vessel.'

The contradictions between this and the paragraph relating to the reason for the release of the prisoners is too obvious for comment. Anti-Treaty sources say that the men who refused to unload the ship did so because they were Republicans who knew the attack was coming and wanted to keep the food for the anti-Treatyites. The official anti-Treaty version of the attack is most likely to be accurate, if only because it was given recently when time had helped to increase objectivity. It was given by Mr J. J. Rice, who was in charge.

During the early hours of September he and his men converged on Kenmare.

'Altogether there were about seventy men, of whom twenty never saw action because they were on outpost duty,' said Rice. 'During the night we infiltrated the town and opened the attack about 7 a.m.' One section of his men bypassed the town and came in from the west while he attacked from the east. The pro-Treaty troops were holding the National Bank, the Workhouse and the Library on the corner of Henry Street and the main street. The anti-Treatyites worked through from building to building until they were in position opposite the pro-Treaty strongholds. 'We were in before they knew it,' said Rice.

The battle lasted well into the afternoon. Brigadier O'Connor was shot in his house as he attempted to fight his way out and join his troops. In the end chivalry won the day in an unusual manner. Rice had a Lewis gun covering the pro-Treaty position in the Bank, from which another machine-gun kept up a heavy defensive fire. He was crouching beside his machine-gunner when they saw a group of women hurrying across the street several hundred yards away. Immediately the machine-gunner raised the butt of his weapon, gripping it with his left hand to fire.

Rice, seeing what he was about, knocked the gunner's arm with a blow and asked him why he was going to fire on women. 'Damn it,' said the gunner, 'didn't you see the leggings under their skirts?' He fired only one shot and it went over the heads of the 'women'. But it killed the enemy machine-gunner in the Bank. He was the only man in the garrison able to handle the weapon. With the Bank captured, the rest of the town soon fell to Rice's men. More than 200 rifles, two

247

machine-guns, and 'wagons of ammunition' were captured. It was nearly Christmas before Kenmare again changed hands.

[1] Released to the Press on 14 August 1922.

22

GUERILLA TACTICS

When the anti-Treatyites adopted guerilla tactics they at once acknowledged that they were beaten in the field, but that they would not stop fighting for their ideal. Although the towns were in the hands of the pro-Treatyites it became difficult for their troops to move outside without being ambushed. A systematic and continuous campaign of ambushes directed against their supply lines and communications became the principal weapon of anti-Treaty resistance. It was their misfortune that attacks, on railways in particular (which later resulted in the introduction of several armoured trains in an endeavour to protect the lines), further turned the anger of the general public against themselves.

Documents captured in Cork by pro-Treaty troops give an outline of the pattern for guerilla fighting. The ideal column was to consist of thirty-five men, including engineers, signallers, and machine-gunners, sub-divided into squads of five men and a leader, who would keep in close contact, and the war was to be carried on by all the methods used against the British. The difficulty and importance of communications were stressed in these documents. To appreciate the problems involved it is necessary to know something of the topography.

The rivers and mountain chains run east and west, dividing the area into long swathes like a freshly-cut cornfield. The Slievemish Mountains on the Dingle Peninsula, the Mullaghreirk Mountains of west Cork to north Cork's Ballyhoura Hills separate the plain of Limerick from a general depression extending from Killarney, on the west, over a low saddle in the hills to the valley of the River Blackwater, where are situated the towns of Millstreet, Kanturk, Mallow and Fermoy. Communication between the two low-lying districts is by two passes. The first is between the Mullaghreirk and Ballyhoura Hills from Charleville to Mallow, the second through a narrow gap in the Ballyhoura Hills themselves, from Galbally, through Mitchelstown, to

Fermoy. A second main chain of mountains extends south of the Blackwater valley; the MacGillycuddy Reeks, the Derrynasaggart Mountains and the Nagles Mountains north of Cork city. South again of the Lee valley runs another line of hills separating this valley from that of the River Bandon, where Dunmanway and Bandon lie. In these areas the pro-Treaty troops held all the towns and valleys and had a somewhat precarious tenure of the connecting passes.

The anti-Treatyites held the hills and continually harassed communications through the passes. Their headquarters were near the gloomy and ill-omened Lough Guitane, close to Killarney. Lynch was still in command, but had his HQ farther east, in the Glen of Aherlow in Tipperary. Shaw, who had been visiting Ireland at this time, made the common error of attributing the guerilla campaign to de Valera and Childers. He wrote:

> Mr de Valera and Mr Childers have attempted the first alternative (to subdue the country by armed force and coerce it to become an independent little Republic, whether it likes it or not) but, having no war chest and apparently no programme beyond calling Ireland a Republic, they have been forced to tell their troops on pay day that they must live on their country, which means, in practice, that the leaders are to be Republicans contending for a principle and their troops are to be brigands. This is an impossible situation.

Shaw's arguments may not have been flawless, but his conclusion is not altogether without substance. The situation was impossible. On 11 September 1922,[1] de Valera is reported as saying that he was still opposed to the Treaty in its present form, but that he was sure that satisfactory revision could be obtained, and without such revision, he said, there would be violent political agitation and turmoil in Ireland for many years to come. He summed up the Civil War: 'No one gains by the war, all lose by it.' But, in spite of his opposition to a continuance of hostilities, continue they did.

The limited successes of localized guerilla tactics seem to have blinded anti-Treaty commanders to the fact that they were merely local actions, that the Provisional Government now had control of the country at large, that they had power and national support: the anti-Treatyites could not win. The refusal to face this fact; the continuance of the war, and the bitterness that was the outcome of the ambushes — where 'victorious' pro-Treaty soldiers heard of their comrades surprised and shot or blown up when, logically, fighting should have ceased — brought about a new and ruthless campaign of terrorism in parts of the country and produced a policy of the iron heel and mailed fist on the part of the pro-Treaty authorities, who determined to stamp these guerillas out once and for all.

The life of a guerilla is hard; in winter almost insupportable. He is driven, sooner or later, to seek refuge in farmhouses, in villages, or in towns, where his security depends entirely on the support of the local inhabitants. The three cardinal points necessary for him are popular support, local knowledge and goodly supplies — and these are sufficient only where the enemy forces are operating in a hostile country, strange to them. With this in mind considerable reorganization of method was developed by the pro-Treatyites to deal with the anti-Treaty guerillas. They had to be cut off from all towns where they might find succour which, consequently, had to be garrisoned, immobilizing large bodies of troops. Intelligence services were brought to a high pitch, and special units were equipped for special duties. The procedure became something like a fox hunt, with, in all too many cases, a like end to the chase and a consequent demoralization among some of the troops involved.

Nowhere did this fearful aspect of the war become more apparent than in Kerry, though it manifested itself everywhere. But Kerry, where the anti-Treatyites concentrated and struck back, offers a hideous cameo of what went on all over the country. Here, in the autumn and winter of 1922-3 the password might have been 'And no quarter.' The idealism that had burst into the great flame known as Sinn Fein now turned upon itself in hatred and vengeance.

Recall de Valera's words on the death of Collins: 'He is a big man and if things fall into the hands of lesser men anything might happen.' It was a prophetic observation. Things did fall into the hands of lesser men on both sides.

Collins's personality dominated the Provisional Cabinet when he was alive. When Griffith died he had, for ten days, what amounted to unlimited power in the unswerving allegiance of the Cabinet and their unquestioning faith in him and in what he was doing. His declared policy was speedy victory, no compromise with the enemy and complete surrender, yet he was not ruthless in pursuit of this policy. Almost his last words of significance were of the efforts he intended to make to bring about peace. He never lived to make peace and the mantle of leadership fell on the shoulders of others. They were the heirs of Collins's policy. The policy was not their brain-child, it was that of their hero-leader; accordingly they followed it more rigidly and ruthlessly than he might have done and without a corresponding willingness to adapt to changing circumstances.

While the war in the field had, to some extent, been fought with a degree of recognition of mutual rights, this disappeared altogether with the end of the 'summer campaign' and the beginning of the guerilla war. One can understand that soldiers, having fought through a campaign — short though it may have been — having run the ordinary risks of war and having beaten their opponents, looked forward to peace and the fruits of that victory. When, instead, they were attacked and ambushed by guerillas who faded away when one's comrades were dead and mutilated from bullets, bombs and booby-traps, a natural hatred of the men who gave a bullet in the back as the price of victory is understandable. It did not take much to turn individual rancours into mass vengeance.

Dislike of the war became channelled — by propaganda, official war policy and successive pieces of calculated legislature — into hatred of the anti-Treatyites as the cause of the war, and this was interpreted as an official imprimatur for the personalized 'mass vengeance' feeling mentioned above. General lack of discipline contributed to the excesses which occurred on a scale too widespread to have been isolated incidents. The fact that the troops were raw and that discipline was, understandably, lax does not excuse depravity, be it that of an organized mob or a controlled body. The troops in Kerry were from Dublin and the North of Ireland — the 27th Battalion in Tralee, the 6th in Killarney, the 9th in Cahirciveen, the 17th in Kenmare, the 19th in Castleisland.

The dangers inherent in a situation in which the pro-Treatyites assumed absolute powers were stressed by Labour members Thomas Johnson and Cathal O'Shannon at a meeting of the Provisional Parliament in September, at which a new president was to be elected. Cosgrave was proposed for the office by Mulcahy. Before the motion Johnson addressed the House.

He said that there had been a decision before the last meeting of the Dáil (the Sinn Féin Dáil which met before the attack on the Four Courts) to have conferences between ministerial members and the opposition and between army leaders on both sides and that it might have been presumed that the results of these conferences would have gone before the House before any action was taken by the Government of the day. But, he said all the public knew as a result of these conferences — which they were assured had taken place — was Civil War. All they knew was that a few days after the conferences (when members of one party had been in fraternal relations with members of the other) the guns began to speak — three days before the announced meeting of the Dáil.

He said when the Government said it was doing what was necessary in the best interests of the country, it did not indicate who were the best judges of what was necessary . . .

He asked to know, officially and authoritatively, what the intentions of the Government were (a) in regard to the people's assembly and (b) in regard to the conduct of war. He was satisfied that a way to peace might be found if the country accepted the present situation as something short of their rightful aims. His colleague, O'Shannon, wanted to know if the new executive was going to conduct war operations or peace operations . . .

Cosgrave replied: 'We are willing to come to a peaceful understanding with those in arms, but it must be on a definite basis. We want peace with England on the terms of the Treaty and we will not tolerate any armed interference with that peace.'[2]

Johnson brought up the matter of torture and murders and said that certain ranks and officers in the Army were carrying out their work in a manner which was entirely indefensible. O'Higgins denied this and said that the first and most important consideration at that time was to vindicate the authority of the parliament.

The anti-Treaty change of tactics in August made it extremely difficult for the pro-Treatyites to strike effectively at them. So long as the anti-Treatyites held fixed positions the superior equipment and experienced command of the pro-Treaty forces enabled them to rout their enemies, but, while they suffered all the hazards of guerilla fighters — lack of food, clothing, rest, equipment, housing, physical and psychological ailments, including a skin disease known as 'Republican Itch' and what is now termed battle fatigue — the anti-Treatyites were more accustomed to this type of warfare and applied themselves to it with new energy.

A report on the difficulties of getting them out of their main retreat in the mountains stretching from the Dingle peninsula to Millstreet, says: 'The task of routing them from the region will be a formidable one. It may be that methods other than those already adopted elsewhere in

253

similar circumstances may suggest themselves, thereby rendering the work less difficult and guaranteeing, perhaps, a greater measure of success.' The writer could hardly have anticipated the 'methods' that would 'suggest themselves'.[3]

As a beginning, a strong force of reinforcements, together with transport, armoured cars and artillery, was drafted into the area. General Murphy was given command of the Kerry and West Cork area and he immediately set to work to organize the troops under him. A very large proportion of the population of Kerry was openly in favour of the anti-Treatyites and their fighting troops — of whom there were three brigades and some from outside — had much more support than elsewhere. The more important towns were occupied by the pro-Treatyites, but enemy columns could move among the hills with impunity. A shipload of petrol was even run into Tralee and unloaded by the anti-Treatyites while an attack on Tralee barracks pinned the pro-Treaty troops down. The general atmosphere produced mounting intransigence, determination and bitterness on both sides. From this time onwards the position in Kerry deteriorated. The war became a hunt. Sometimes prisoners were not taken. When they were taken they were liable to summary execution, torture or death without the formality of trial. Fellow feeling was quenched in bitterness to the extent that old comrades tortured and shot one another in cold blood, but what worsened it was the official blind-eye and even condonation.

In the spring of 1923 brutality reached a climax, early in March, after an anti-Treaty mine killed a Free State officer, who is alleged to have been notorious for torturing prisoners.[4] On 7 March nine anti-Treaty prisoners, one of them with a broken arm, another with a broken wrist, and one, John Daly, unable to walk from spinal injuries, were taken by lorry to Ballyseedy Cross about two miles from Tralee. The hands of each prisoner were tied behind him. Each was tied by the arms and legs to the man beside him. A rope was passed completely round the nine men so that they stood in a ring facing outwards. In the centre of the ring was a landmine . . . The soldiers who tied them took cover and exploded the mine. The remains of the prisoners killed were flung far and wide, bits of bodies hung from trees in the wood that bordered the roadside. By some explosive freak, one man, Stephen Fuller, instead of being blown to bits was blown into a ditch. He escaped across fields and ran until he reached the home of Charlie Daly, where he took refuge.

The soldiers, thinking all the prisoners had been killed, put the remains of the eight men into nine coffins. The official explanation of these deaths was that the men were killed by mines attached to barricades set up by the anti-Treatyites which they had been clearing. But for Fuller's escape this story might have been credited. Several of the men had been 'interrogated' in Tralee barracks by officers armed with hammers before the murders, hence the broken limbs.

On the same day five prisoners, after similar beatings and deprivations, were taken to Countess Bridge in Killarney where there was a low barricade of stones. They were ordered to move the stones and throw them inside the fence. The soldiers took cover. The prisoners saw them cock their rifles, and, thinking they were to be shot at, ran to the barricade and jumped over it. Suddenly the soldiers scattered for cover. 'My God,' cried one of the prisoners — Coffey — 'It's a trap.' He bent to look for a wire. Instantly there was an explosion. Just as at Ballyseedy — and at roughly the same time — a mine was exploded and, as at Ballyseedy, a prisoner was blown clear by a freak blast. Coffey looked up after the explosion to see some of his companions still alive. Bomb after bomb was thrown at them. Coffey and another prisoner, Jeremiah Donoghue, ran and machine-gun bullets splintered the wall beside them. Coffey was hit in the leg, but he stumbled on. Donoghue crumpled and lay still. A military tailor who had warned the prisoners of their impending fate talked about it in his cups in Killarney. When he returned to barracks an officer shot him dead.

At Cahirciveen on 12 March five prisoners were killed in the same way, but this time precautions were taken that there would be no escape. Each prisoner was shot in the legs before the explosion. A pro-Treaty officer, Lieutenant McCarthy, resigned and published an account of what had happened, including a description of this shooting.

The funerals of the victims created such violent feeling in Kerry that the pro-Treaty authorities felt further precaution necessary. The following order was issued on 21 March: 'Prisoners who are in military custody in the Kerry command shall be interred by the troops in the area in which the death has taken place.'

¹Manchester Evening News
²While this first parliamentary session since the Civil War began was in progress, a serious postal strike threatened further paralysis of the already distressed communications.

³For a detailed account of what was to happen see *Tragedies of Kerry* by Dorothy Macardle.

⁴Dorothy Macardle: *Tragedies of Kerry, The Irish Republic*. An anti-Treaty statement said: 'A trigger mine was laid at Knocknagoshel for a member of the Free State Army, Lieutenant O'Connor, who had made a habit of torturing Republican prisoners in Castleisland. On Tuesday a party of Free State troops, including Lieutenant O'Connor, proceeded to the place. Two captains, O'Connor and two privates were killed.' An overall figure for fatal casualties is hard to estimate. Close to 600 men of the pro-Treaty forces were killed during July and August 1922 alone. The fatal casualties on the anti-Treaty side for the same period must have been even higher. For the entire period of the war a very rough estimate would put overall fatal casualties at under 4000 men, 300 a month approximately.

23

THE END OF A PHASE

Largely as a result of what happened in Kerry, particularly at this time, Colonel Fred Henry of the pro-Treaty forces was appointed Provost Marshal, and part of his function was to investigate allegations of ill-treatment of prisoners, torturings, shootings and group murders. In justice it must be said that the anti-Treatyites did not, so far as is known, ill-treat or torture their prisoners. They seldom — except as at Charleville and Cork where they had facilities to do so — kept prisoners, but turned them loose after extracting a (futile) promise from them to discontinue fighting.

Executions carried out as policy by the pro-Treaty authorities were met by counter-reprisals, shootings and burnings; in one such case, that of the home of a TD Seán McGarry, the house was burned while one of his children was still in it, in spite, it is said, of appeals to have the child rescued. The child was burned to death. The executions had the effect of fomenting hatred and bitterness on both sides. A result was that every time an execution was reported it was assumed to be punitive, whether in fact it was or not. Moral or political considerations apart, the execution policy had the effect of encouraging excesses in some of the pro-Treaty troops when dealing with captured enemy. General lack of law and order confused matters still further. In the main the anti-Treatyites tried to do the impossible, fight a civil war as a gentleman's war; the pragmatists, of course, not only took the wind from the sails of the Don Quixotes' windmills, but proclaimed the Don Quixotes as heretics and murderers who must be exterminated.

The claims by the pro- against the anti-Treatyites were given some weight by the civic chaos the war brought about. Unscrupulous men on both sides were given the opportunity, in the name of a high principle, to exploit the public and its property in their own interests. The list of bank robberies, burglaries, taking by force of arms, etc. at this time is formidable. The culprit had only to fly to the hills or barracks and declare for one cause or another to be relatively safe. Bandits appeared from nowhere; sometimes they were members of one or other of the armies, more often they were not of either, but the anti-Treatyites were always held responsible by the Press and public opinion — a notion cheerfully fostered by the pro-Treatyites. Yet when a bank was robbed by a pro-Treaty officer — as happened in Kerry — and he was executed by his own authorities for it, the matter passed almost unnoticed.

In July was published an alleged memorandum from Mulcahy to a divisional commander telling him that several officers in Dublin, including an officer on guard at Oriel House, were convicted bankrobbers and deserters from other units. The pro-Treaty army, which mushroomed from 12,000 to 60,000 men in a few weeks, attracted some who were not angels. The vast proportion of recruits were not and had not been members of Sinn Féin or of the old IRA, and lacked the 'vision splendid' and the ideals and personal discipline that distinguished their enemies.

Nevertheless a general — and telling — charge made against the anti-Treatyites at the time was that they wanted to bring back the British. It was given weight by the capture of such documents as this:

Headquarters, Army No. 1 Brigade, July 19, 1922.
Ref, No A/8. To OC 8th Battalion (North Kerry).

With regard to the E.D.J. I understand Ryan of Kilrush who has large shares in her is, and always had been friendly to us and that another merchant named Glynn, who is not friendly, has two boats — the *Corunna* and the *Turk*.

Will you arrange with the bearer that if the E.D.J. is not of any great use to us that she be returned as soon as possible and make arrangements that one of the others are to be taken. With regard to the Free State who are trying to get across, or those of the workhouse around who are active in your area; you will see that they are immediately rounded up and sent here (Tralee) under escort and I will get them sent to Fermoy (then still in anti-Treaty hands) which is now a detention camp for Free State prisoners. If that Triumph bike is not running have it sent here immediately. Have any information transferred to us through Listowel as soon as possible.

If an English destroyer or sloop comes within rifle range of your shore, snipe it and, if possible, have rifle grenades dropped on deck. Possibly they may shell the cost or try a landing, the very thing we want them to do. Then we will have the old enemy back and that will

258

clear the whole aspect of the present war.

A. O Murchada (Humphrey Murphy)
O.C. Kerry No. 1 Brigade.

The pro-Treaty propaganda machine fell on such documents with great glee and announced: 'The objective of the Irregulars is defined at last. They are fighting to bring back the British.'[1] The implication, though absurd, was permissible due to the ambiguity of the last paragraph of Murphy's document, curiously echoed in a similar document — by Aylward of Kilkenny — captured about the same time.

What the phrases conveyed to their rightful recipients was the commonly held anti-Treaty hope that if the British were provoked into an attack it would rouse public opinion and military tempers to a pitch where national unity and purpose would again be secured in the face of a common injury, and Sinn Féin emerge re-united. It was Tom Barry's old formula of 18 June. It is only just to point out that Birkenhead, speaking in the House of Lords in July 1923, said that the British Government would not have been able to crush a united Irish Volunteer Force with less than 200,000 men, and it would not have been possible for them to put into Ireland enough troops to overcome an undivided Sinn Féin. Thus the irony of the Civil War, that the pro-Treatyites agreed to the Treaty only from the fear that rejection would mean 'immediate and terrible war'; yet, in implementing it, brought a more terrible war. The anti-Treatyites felt that if war must come, it should be waged by a united Ireland against an unfavourable Treaty, instead of by one body of Irishmen against another so that an unfavourable Treaty might operate.

Whether Britain would have gone to war or not is problematical. Lloyd George threatened it, Birkenhead said: 'Parliament would not have granted the money and the country would not have given the volunteers.' Winston Churchill — at time the most ardent advocate of a war policy — remained silent on the subject which he might have clarified, though he was approached by the author and others. (*But see Introduction to this edition.*)

On 6 August the first significant steps in the official campaign of elimination against the guerillas were taken when an official notice of 'offences against humanity . . . which the civilian world calls war crimes . . . all who are concerned in such war crimes are hereby warned that no application by them for the privileges and treatment given to other prisoners will be entertained'. This rule came to be adopted against the bulk of anti-Treaty prisoners taken from then onwards.

Much of the bitterness can be traced to personal animosity. When, in the early months of 1922, hundreds of barracks were taken over by local battalions of the IRA, officers were appointed to command each barracks. For each one so appointed several were disappointed. It is no reflection on them to say that they were human beings, not angels. Minds, already confused on the Treaty issue, drifted almost unconsciously to one side or the other. It is helpful in trying to understand the tragedy of the Civil War to consider the youth of those who, in the main, guided it. Most were in their mid-twenties, some, like Collins and Lynch, were thirty; a few, like de Valera and Cosgrave, were forty. 'All were young and inexperienced and not at all as tough as older men would be.'[2]

It seems clear, for example, that those who accepted the Treaty and 'Stepping-stone' basis were, in fact, much closer in spirit to the anti-Treatyites than they were to those who formed the overwhelming bulk of their supporters, and who accepted the Treaty and welcomed dominion status. This close affinity between the main parties and the personal issues involved, added fuel to what was already a highly combustible situation and contributed to the Four Courts débâcle, of which Dr Seamus Fitzgerald says: 'If a Constitutional Assembly had met on Saturday[3] it would have solved the Four Courts problem.'

The final phase of this part of the Civil War was the meeting of the Provisional Parliament on 9 September at which Cosgrave, who was to become the first President of the Free State, said, in his statement of policy:

It is my intention to implement this Treaty as sanctioned by vote of the Dáil and the electorate *in so far as it was free to express an opinion;* to enact the Constitution (not yet framed); to assert the authority and supremacy of the parliament; to support and assist the national army in asserting the people's rights; to ask parliament, if necessary, *for such powers as may be deemed essential for the purpose of restoring order.*

Perhaps those who seek a symbol will find it in the fact that almost the first act of this newly constituted Irish Parliament was the expulsion from the House of Mr Laurence Ginnell, an anti-Treatyite, and the only one of de Valera's political supporters to attend the meeting held in Leinster House, in spite of persistent rumours of a proposed *coup de théâtre*.

This provisional parliament sat for five days. In that time Cosgrave was elected president, having made the above statement of policy. Mulcahy made a similar statement referring to purely military matters, in which occurred his injudicious 'Finessing with honour' phrase. During that week it was made perfectly clear to those, who, ostrich-like, preferred to consider the Civil War as 'local disturbances', that such was not the official attitude. In the King's Bench Division, before the Lord Chief Justice, Mr Justice Dodd and Mr Justice Gordon, in a case against the military governor of Wellington Barracks and the King (of England), on writ of *habeas corpus* for a Mr Seán Beaumont and an Englishman, Mr White, who were arrested and imprisoned without charge or trial, it was established that a 'State of war existed in Ireland, and that Martial Law prevailed'. The applications were dismissed.

The following letter (*Irish Times*, 30 September) must have helped to harden anti-Treaty minds against any embryonic doubts they may have felt about the self-evident results of their military leaders' policy:

Sir

. . . We need more honest speaking in Ireland . . . The present outbreak of civil war may be traced to the evictions by the Free State Government of the Republicans from the Four Courts. Under the circumstances the Provisional Government had no alternative. Two opposing Governments cannot exist in the same country. But we must go farther back to explain our present troubles. They began with the seizing of the General Post Office and other buildings by armed men in 1916. The then existing Government of Ireland (British) had likewise no alternative but to evict insurgents. And so the trouble commenced . . .

. . . When men are desperately in earnest they will not surrender their own reason and conscience to any external authority. There is only one way of dealing with them — you must appeal to their reason and conscience.

Under the Free State Ireland will have more freedom than she could ever have under a nominal Republic, for she will have the friendship of Great Britain and of the British Empire and Commonwealth; whereas if she insisted on complete separation she would have to face their hostility, with all its serious consequences. If the Government of Ireland under the Treaty fails, the alternative is not a

Republic, but the return of government by the Imperial Government. A Free State Government must govern or abdicate. If it fails the British must take up the reins again. A Republic is ruled out. We must face facts. The Republican struggle may ruin Ireland. It cannot gain its end.

On these grounds, I would appeal to the reason and consciences of Republicans to throw in their lot with the majority of their fellow countrymen. In doing this they will be doing the best possible for Ireland under the circumstances. No man can do more than this.

Yours, etc., Dudley Fletcher, Coolbanagher Rectory, Portarlington.[4]

This respected clergyman was expressing a wish sincerely felt, but his exhortation, while given, no doubt, with the best possible intention, is notable for the fact that it does not say why 'a Republic is ruled out'. It was no more than sugar-coating the bitter pill to the militant and non-militant anti-Treatyites, now facing the third, final and most ferocious phase of the struggle.

[1] Official Government announcement 4 August 1922.
[2] Florence O'Donoghue, private conversation.
[3] The Four Courts was attacked on Wednesday morning at 4 a.m., 28 June; the Dáil was to meet for the first time, since the election of 16 June, on 30 June, to elect a coalition Cabinet in accordance with the Pact. That Dáil never met.
[4] Fletcher was a man of no significance, politically or otherwise, who had a passion for writing to the *Irish Times,* at that time an organ of Protestant and Unionist outlook, on matters of public interest. But his letter is, nevertheless, a reasonably accurate expression of the feeling of many of the public at large.

Part Three

THE GUERILLA WAR

24

DE VALERA AND THE ARMY

In September the entire character of the conflict underwent a change. Though guerilla warfare by the anti-Treatyites became general, now, for the first time since hostilities began, they also became politically active. The thrice-prorogued parliament met on 9 September, but before that a meeting, far more significant and dramatic, took place in secret. On 6 September, de Valera met Mulcahy in Dublin to discuss the war situation and to find, if possible, a means of bringing it to an end.

The meeting was arranged by Monsignor John Rogers, an Irish priest of the San Francisco diocese. But the meeting proved fruitless, Mulcahy insisting on surrender by the anti-Treatyites while de Valera was unable to persuade him to revert to the conditions of the Pact. De Valera resumed the role of hunted and Mulcahy that of hunter. A letter to 'C. O'M.' (Dr Conn Ó Murchadh, Dáil Deputy for South Dublin) written by de Valera on the day of the meeting with Mulcahy, throws a penetrating light on his attitude at this time.

> Yours received. As regards the Dáil, the following suggestion had been made — that it be proclaimed in advance by the Army as an illegal assembly, inasmuch as it is summoned by the illegal junta called the 'Provisional Government', and inasmuch as the Second Dáil, which is the legitimate Parliament and Government of the country, had not been dissolved.
>
> This is much more positive and much better than mere abstention of the Republican members, and if we are to be consistent at all it is the attitude we should adopt. We will be at sixes and sevens with one another, I think, if any other policy is adopted. I favour it accordingly. I do not know whether anything which may happen at *tonight's interview* will change my mind in the matter . . . E. de V.

This letter was dated 6 September. Next day he wrote again after his

265

meeting with Mulcahy, and the letter clearly shows how that meeting altered and hardened his attitude.

> Personal: A Chara. Attached you may read for the party. You will note a change in my decision — I feel this course is the one that will make most rapidly for peace. Could you have a copy made of this letter and send it to me? I put the carbon in the wrong way. I cursed, naturally! I hope our two guards got back alright last night. I was anxious about them when I left. Tell ED [possibly Eamonn Donnelly] that he is to tell Rogers to call tomorrow to the office, that I left word last night that I was writing him a letter. Nothing came of last night's meeting. There is nothing to be gained by my seeing Golden[1] and I met him in Cork. Get proposals put on paper. I'd like to see S. O'Keefe for a press interview. If you get in touch with him I'll see how it can be arranged. Ask him to send me along 'Leading questions' ... E de V.

He enclosed a document with this letter which will be referred to later. On 9 September Parliament — called the New Dáil[2] — met for the first time since the war started. It should have been a National Assembly based on the Pact Election of June which would form a Coalition Cabinet, in fact it was no more than the original Provisional Government and, finally, did what that body set out to do; namely, set up the Irish Free State — Saorstát Éireann — and frame the Constitution of that State.

The anti-Treaty position became clearer immediately this Dáil met. They considered the pro-Treaty assembly unconstitutional and felt that they were now justified in taking positive political steps to preserve the administration elected in January. Until the new parliament convened de Valera felt himself unable to take such steps. He had not dishonoured the terms of the Pact and it was still possible — although highly improbable, particularly after the death of Collins — that the pro-Treatyites might yet agree to a Coalition on its terms. Not until he met Mulcahy was de Valera satisfied that this was out of the question.

Satisfied of the pro-Treaty decision to repudiate the Pact, de Valera was particularly anxious that Séan O'Mahony, Sinn Féin deputy for Fermanagh, one of the Northern Six Counties, should attend the assembly. Refusal to allow him — as a representative of Fermanagh — to take his seat would be clear evidence of a violation of the Pact and

266

would show that the assembly was not Dáil Éireann. It is, of course a jurist's point. But it did not arise, as O'Mahony decided not to attend. Laurence Ginnell, who was ejected, had tabled several motions, including a vote of censure of the deputies 'who did illegally usurp authority as a Government and establish themselves as military dictators' and 'did illegally, at the bidding of a foreign government, begin a civil war and are steadily over throwing Dáil Éireann and substituting their own government'.

Mulcahy proposed Cosgrave as president of the Dáil and the motion was seconded by MacNeill (whose son, Brian, was killed after his capture in Sligo while fighting for the anti-Treatyites, eleven days later). Cosgrave appointed nine ministers, some of whom held more than one ministry. Mulcahy became Minister for Defence as well as Chief-of-Staff of the Army, which drew several protests. The new ministry included every living member of the Provisional Government.

The judgement in the Beaumont case left to Mulcahy, as Minister for Defence, Chief-of-Staff and Commander-in-Chief of the pro-Treaty forces, supreme power to arrest and detain suspects without investigation, charge or trial — a judgement that was to have far-reaching effects in the near future.

An extraordinary situation now existed. The British Government of Ireland Act 1920 had called for two parliaments, a southern and a northern, to govern a divided Ireland. The Bill had united the Irish nationalists in opposition and had given Sinn Féin a powerful common purpose in which it was joined by other Irish organizations to oppose it; the Black and Tans, an army of 60,000 men and the RIC had been bitterly opposed in arms . . . What the Bill originally proposed was what now emerged two years later, with a Civil War raging on the issue.

The spirit of compromise had vanished from the leaders of the pro-Treatyites and was replaced by a ruthless intransigence which refused to consider the anti-Treaty viewpoint at all. An attitude of unswerving allegiance to a rigid policy made that policy into an end in itself. Thus it served, not Ireland's, but Britain's purpose made known in the Government of Ireland Bill. Proclaiming the policy of Collins — the stepping-stone policy — the Provisional Parliament, by their very zeal, betrayed it.

These lost and forgotten documents of de Valera's throw a vivid light on the anti-Treaty position. This was enclosed with his letter of 7 September.[3]

A Chara, As regards our attending the meeting of the Dáil on Saturday. I have considered the matter, and am of the opinion that, both from the point of view of principle and expediency, we as a party, should not attend.

1. The Second Dáil is not dissolved. It is the sovereign authority in the country, in my opinion, at this moment. The assembly that is summoned to meet on Saturday does not pretend to be Dáil Éireann — it is the Provisional Parliament. It has not been summoned by the proper authority, etc., etc. Then there is the oath.

2. So far principle. Now expediency. Our presence at the meeting would only help to solidify all the other groups against us. We would be the butt of every attack. We could not explain — we would be accused of obstructing the business and of 'talking' when we should 'get on with the work'. Our presence there will not promote, but rather retard, peace. Finally, whatever chance there is of union in our own group, it lies more in the direction of abstention than attendance.

3. If we decide, then, as a party not to go, the question remains, shall we issue a statement or should the Army proclaim the meeting, or should we ignore the meeting and say nothing? Strict principle would dictate the second course, but we are not strong enough to maintain the position it would involve. Besides, it is too late to get in touch with Army HQ on the matter. If we issue a statement it will tie our hands, and if at a future time a course other than non-attendance should seem wise we might find ourselves precluded from taking it.

4. Hence, summing up, I am in favour of non-attendance. Let them keep guessing as the reason for the present. If Mr Ginnell thinks he should go that will not be any harm, but, perhaps, an advantage. O'Mahony should certainly go and claim his seat. If he is refused it makes it the Provisional Parliament not the Dáil, and is a violation of the Pact 'subject to' which the elections were decreed. Do Chara, Eamon de Valera.

Now, however, the need for political representation was being felt by others besides de Valera in the Republican movement and, three days after this, he had a pressing document, signed by Oscar Traynor and Peadar O'Donnell among other anti-Treatyite civil and military figures, demanding that the anti-Treaty Deputies meet and set up a Republican Government. De Valera wrote: 'This is no use. If we could maintain a Republican Government, now, after what they did on Saturday, would be the time to set it up. We can't maintain one, I fear.' He maintained this attitude in the face of repeated requests, throughout the day, for him to change his mind. His attitude was that if the Army Executive 'were at hand and would definitely give allegiance to that Government I'd think it wise to try — but again the inability to maintain it.'

Within a few hours, however, he had a letter from Liam Lynch which angered him considerably. The letter underlined that the Army Executive not only was unlikely to give allegiance to a new authority, but considered itself the only proper anti-Treaty administration. It clearly shows how the political and military arms of the anti-Treatyites were drifting apart. The tone of Lynch's letter is that of a supreme commander, which he was, to a somewhat tiresome civilian representative, which de Valera certainly was not. The letter read:

To: Eamon de Valera

The IRA Field GHQ
30th August, 1922

A Chara,
    Your note of the 18th instant, expressing a desire to meet members of Army Executive before the executive meeting was duly received. The meeting was not held as (owing) to difficulty in travelling only some of the members turned up, and in any case as the military situation improved considerably just previous to it, I did not consider it necessary to hold it. I imagine it will be some time before another meeting is called except some unexpected situation arises which warrants an Executive decision. I would however, be only too pleased to have your views at any time on the general situation, and matters arising out of it, and they will receive my earnest consideration.

Mise le meas mor.
Liam Lynch, CS

De Valera was furious, of course, and wrote to Ó Murchadh saying:
This is too good a thing and won't do . . . The position of the political

party must be straightened out. If it is the policy of the party to leave it all to the army, well, then, the obvious thing for the members of the party to do is to resign their positions as public representatives. The present position is that we have all the public responsibility, and no voice and no authority . . . If I do not get the position quite clear, I shall resign publicly . . .

This problem, which was bound to arise and which no one had foreseen or taken steps to prevent, originated in the failure of the anti-Treatyites to prepare themselves for the possibility of Civil War during the threatening period between January and June. Now it was too late to retrieve the reins of total democratic administration from the militarists, who had, so to speak, the bit between their teeth. The attempt, however, was made and de Valera, no doubt influenced by Lynch's attitude, was persuaded to re-consider the question of a new Government.

First a group of influential anti-Treatyites asked de Valera to issue a statement on the anti-Treaty position *vis-á-vis* the 'new' — unconstitutional — Dáil; to discuss the possibility of setting up a joint political and military executive; to convene the Second Dáil (the constitutional elected assembly) as early as possible and to decide on a policy or a possible by-election.

De Valera's reply is a summary of his attitude in mid-Civil War when he had little political support and was seeking a course to bind Republican followers, military and political, together in the best interests of both. His remarks about Rory O'Connor's repudiation of the Dáil are illuminating, as is his acceptance of defeat at the polls. He agreed on an immediate statement.

The position, as I see it, is this: Either (a) the Republican Party must take control, acting as legitimate Dáil, (b) the Army Executive take control and assume responsibility, (c) a joint committee be formed to decide policy for both.

Course (a) would constitutionally be the correct one and most consistent with our whole position . . . I am against it, however. (1) Because we, no more than the others, could not get from the Army (he refers to the Army as a whole) that unconditional allegiance without which our Government would be a farce. Rory O'Connor's unfortunate repudiation of the Dáil, which I was so foolish as to defend even to a straining of my own views in order to avoid the

270

appearance of a split, is now the greatest barrier that we have. (See Chapter 5, Part 1.)

He made two further points under this heading; that of insufficient military strength and the fact that they would be turned down definitely by the electorate in a few months' time in any case because they could not refuse to let the people choose by vote, which would mean turning down the Republic. He preferred (b) — 'but there must be no doubt in the minds of anybody in the matter. This pretence from the pro-Treaty party that we are inciting the Army must be ended by a declaration from the Army itself that this is not so.' He felt that, if his action would not have prejudiced the cause of the Republic, he would have resigned long ago. He did not think course (c) practicable. From Mountjoy, however, came more pressure, from Liam Mellows, who smuggled out a programme for the anti-Treatyites, the first and most imperative object of which was the formation of a Provisional Government of their own, which, as the *de jure* authority in the country, would be a counter to the *de facto* pro-Treaty Government which they considered illegal.

In spite of de Valera's reluctance; in spite of the fact that the Army was in absolute control of anti-Treaty policy and the Party — though held responsible for all anti-Treaty activities — without power, the Army Executive agreed to give allegiance to a government under de Valera's presidency. It was formed — six months too late — on 25 October by anti-Treaty members of the Second Dáil meeting in Dublin. It had a twelve-man Council of State, which could do little more than issue statements on anti-Treaty policy from time to time.

[1] Peter Golden, cousin of Terence and Mary MacSwiney, who had come from the USA.

[2] Dáil means assembly and, without qualification (Dáil Éireann, e.g. Assembly of Ireland) does not necessarily imply succession to the Republican parliaments of 1919 and 1920, although it does became implicit by common usage.

3 This and other quoted documents in this chapter were captured by the pro-Treaty forces and issued as the first White Paper of the Provisional Government in October 1922; now extremely rare.

25

EXECUTIONS AND REPRISALS

In spite of a proposal by Johnson that the midst of a Civil War was no time for a nation to set about enacting a constitution, the Constitutional Bill was presented and passed by the Dáil in October. The Constitution emerged as law for the Irish people and was subordinate to the Treaty which had provoked the Civil War, since there were articles in it vital to the Treaty. Further, if any spark of the bright vision that had been Sinn Féin survived the first bloody months of the war, the new Dáil of the Free State quenched it for good. On 27 September, Mulcahy asked his Parliament for special emergency powers for the Army, a thing that had been hinted at since the session began. It is perfectly clear that the decision to ask for these special powers was taken long before the Parliament convened and was not affected by de Valera's meeting with Mulcahy. Was the purpose to give lawful licence to what would otherwise be considered outrageous military conduct? The effect was to increase the stigma so that not only the Army, but also what claimed to be the national Parliament, became responsible. Another proposal, by Cosgrave, asked that military courts with power to inflict the death sentence on anyone convicted of taking part in, or of abetting any attack on the pro-Treaty forces, or of being in possession of arms or explosives, be set up.

Thomas Johnson, usually suave and incisive, was roused to an extremely violent attack in which he said that the House was being asked to consent to the establishment of a military dictatorship which would give power of life and death over every civilian in the country. Mulcahy's reply was that, with the exception of the sniper and the man who went out with the bomb, the life of the country over a very great portion was normal. This, of course, was nonsense. Mulcahy's purpose appears to have been an attempt to minimize the future role of the military courts.

He said that it was in order to prevent the men from taking upon themselves authority to execute people in an unauthorized way that they asked for powers like these and the danger that such executions would take place was great. It was not unlawful executions, therefore, commonly called murders, which presented a problem to the new 'Government'; it was to arrange matters so that such killings would not be regarded as murder and would be given a legal cloak. The establishment of the courts immediately deprived the anti-Treaty troops of a primary right of warfare and was a major psychological weapon against them.

When Johnson asked if prisoners would be treated as prisoners of war, Cosgrave said: 'No, certainly not.' But a fortnight's warning was given before the military courts came into operation and a general conditional amnesty was offered in the meantime. On 12 October a proclamation announced that the Military Courts would begin to function on the 15th. From that date every anti-Treaty soldier who fought, committed any act of war, carried arms or ammunition, faced death for doing so if captured. And . . . 'to the rigours of the fight was added, for Catholics, of whom nearly the whole army was composed, the penalty of virtual excommunication; many a man was going into danger without absolution, knowing that if he fell in action or was captured and executed, he might be refused the Last Sacrament . . . ' (Dorothy Macardle).

Unfortunately it is a fact that one of the great blots on the conduct of the pro-Treaty party was their treatment of anti-Treaty prisoners and their defiant refusal to better it. As early as July 8 they were denying allegations that prisoners were being ill-treated and in a long statement said that these accusations of ill-treatment were part of a programme of 'organized propaganda on foot to pretend that Irregulars who surrendered . . . are being ill-treated, the object of which is purely political'.

But on 3 July, Diarmuid O'Hegarty, Military Governor of Mountjoy, issued a proclamation to the prisoners in which he announced that they would be treated as 'military captives . . . and that any resistance to their guards or any attempt to assist their own forces, revolt, mutiny, conspiracy, insubordination, attempt to escape or cell wrecking will render them liable to be shot down . . . '

The prisoners refused to accept this in a reply signed by Joe McKelvey as Chief of Staff, IRA. (McKelvey, later executed as a 'war criminal', had been appointed CS in the Four Courts, and was, at this time, unaware that Lynch had resumed office.) Prisoners were, of course, held without charge or trial and this, while not surprising in the early stages, weakened the pro-Treatyites' moral position when they still refused to treat the anti-Treatyites in their hands as prisoners of war, and executed them without trial, charge or status — in several cases men who had been captured *before* the capital offences had been specified or the military courts set up. There were a number of fatalities and woundings, also, when prisoners were fired on by their guards.

One incident launched an abortive inquiry. The priests of Mount Argus, Dublin, complained in public of ill-treatment in Wellington Barracks, and called for a public inquiry.[1] Fr. Smith, Vice-Rector, said that one of their priests was refused admission to a wounded man, Fergus Murphy, on the grounds that there were no wounded prisoners in the barracks. But the priest, in a conversation through the barbed wire with other prisoners, learned that Murphy had been beaten almost to death by rifle butts in the intelligence department.

In the Dáil, Labour Members asked for a public inquiry on the grounds that Fr Smith had established a *prima facie* case on the general question of the treatment of prisoners. Cosgrave replied that Smith was not an impartial person, that an independent inquiry would not be advisable but that a military enquiry would be held. Public opinion, however, was agitated and protest meetings were held, at one of which Fr Kieran O'Farrelly, the priest who tried to see Murphy, read a sworn statement describing the injuries to the prisoner and confirming what Fr Smith had said.

The Dublin City Council on 7 October 1922 formed a committee to inquire into the prison conditions generally, but the Government refused permission to it, to the Dublin Medical Officer of Health or to any other outsiders, to visit the prisoners for any reason. When, in early October, Dublin Corporation decided to institute a sworn inquiry, the Provisional Government announced — with some cynicism, since the purpose of the inquiry was to investigate alleged Government illegalities — that it would be illegal and threatened legal action against it if persisted in. Such an inquiry at that juncture would, of course, have upset the Government plans for military courts and execution of prisoners which were to burst upon the public only a day or two later. The conditions of the prisoners never improved, nor were there any effective results from the inquiry — which was held in spite of these threats. The number of prisoners before the end of the war was in the region of 12,000 and that number increased enormously as the after-war round-up swelled the ranks. Not until they went on general hunger-strike and were subsequently released was the Provisional Government forced to recognize the injustice of their treatment. It was largely due to public pressure in 1923, after the war — the election and the inability to maintain them as a public charge — that steps were finally taken to release them.

The other great blot on pro-Treaty conduct was the campaign of executions which began unannounced and unexpectedly, but with a definite purpose, with the executions of four prisoners, James Fisher, Peter Cassidy, Richard Twohig and James Gaffney on 17 November 1922.[2] Before the shocked members of the inquiry, who had not been intimidated, relatives of the first four prisoners executed said that they had no warning from either Government or the prisoners until they got a telegram: 'Remains of ... have been coffined and buried in consecrated ground. Provisional Government.' Erskine Childers was captured at Annamoe in Wicklow on 10 November, in the house of his cousin, Robert Barton.[3] He was carrying a small, pearl handled .22 automatic which, ironically, had been given to him by Michael Collins.

Ever since the delegation to the London conferences with Lloyd George had split, Childers, the unrepentant Republican who had helped draft 'Document No. 2', had been the object of a deluge of vitriolic propaganda by the pro-Treaty leaders. Griffith had never liked him. Mulcahy and O'Higgins inherited that dislike and, far from dissipating it, built it into a fairytale of which Childers was the terrible ogre; the Englishman, the arch-conspirator, the *ne plus ultra* of brigandage and the ubiquitous commander who led every ambush with diabolical delight. In fact he was a Staff-Captain in the anti-Treaty army in charge of their propaganda — which was never very good.

In October there had been an ominous prelude to the first prisoner killings. An official pro-Treaty bulletin said:[4] 'If prisoners are taken they must not be released until they are incapable of further harm. If executions are necessary they must be carried out with no fear of the chimera of popular reaction.'

The first prisoners shot (a week after Childers was captured) were executed for possessing revolvers. The executions took place on the morning that Childers's trial opened in secret before a military court.

Speaking in Parliament that evening, O'Higgins said he thought it better for the first executions to be average cases: 'If we took, as our first case, some man who was outstandingly active and outstandingly wicked in his activities, the unfortunate dupes throughout the country might say that he was killed because he was a leader, because he was an Englishman, or because he combined with others to commit raids.'

There could be no doubt that Childers was meant nor could there be any doubt as to the fate intended for him . . . the first four executions have been cynically called the 'entrée'. No one knew for what 'outstandingly wicked activity' Childers was being tried, except the Government and members of the Court. It was for the same offence — possession of a revolver, the one Collins had given him. Childers refused to acknowledge the Court or to appeal until persuaded to do so under an application for an order of *habeas corpus* involving eight other men whose names the Government would not disclose. Because Childers was the only prisoner identified and on trial he was persuaded to agree to the application in an effort to save the lives of the other eight men. Although the Government action in refusing the names of the prisoners was condemned by the Master of the Rolls, the application for *habeas corpus* failed, the proceedings in the Dublin High Court finishing late on the evening of 23 November. Childers was shot at dawn the following morning before the public had read the result of the application — and while his appeal was still pending.

Having read a document issued by the Republican Engineering Division, in which the destruction of roads and railways was directed, Mulcahy said: 'The men were executed because they were part of the scheme of destruction which has been compounded in the document just read. Persons who carry on such work had better settle their private business beforehand. Under present circumstances we do not propose, when we get men engaged in ambushing or destroying the life of the country, to endeavour to find out who they are or who their people are before we deal with them.'

Shocked and amazed at this execution policy, Lynch sent a letter to the Speaker of the 'Provisional Parliament of Southern Ireland' on 27 November. In it he said:

The illegal body over which you preside has declared war on the soldiers of the Republic and suppressed the legitimate parliament of the Irish Nation . . . we on our side have at all times adhered to the recognized rules of warfare . . . the prisoners you have taken you have treated barbarously and, when helpless, tortured, wounded and

276

murdered them . . . you now presume to murder . . . the soldiers who had brought Ireland victory when you, traitors, surrendered the Republic twelve months ago . . . we, therefore, give you and each member of your body, due notice that unless your army recognizes the rules of warfare in the future, we shall adopt very drastic measures to protect our forces.

Later the anti-Treatyite authorities issued a list of members of the Provisional Parliament who had voted for the execution of anti-Treaty prisoners — the *'Murder Bill'* — and on 30 November, an instruction was sent to all anti-Treaty battalion OCs ordering that these men should be shot at sight. It ordered that all Free State officers who approved the Bill and who were aggressive and active towards the anti-Treaty forces should be shot at sight, with all the British Army officers and men who joined the pro-Treaty army since 6 December 1921. In all there were fourteen categories of people to be shot. These *'Orders of Frightfulness'*, as they have been called, were the anti-Treaty answer to the execution policy. The Civil War had reached the nadir of bitterness and savagery when, on 6 December 1922, a year after the signing of the Treaty, the Free State came into official existence.

Next day, on 7 December, the Northern Government exercised its right under the Treaty, of 'opting out' of an all-Ireland parliament and refused to nominate a delegate to the Boundary Commission — whose findings, such as they were, in any event they ignored. On 7 December too, Brigadier Séan Hales, a member of the Provisional Parliament who had voted in favour of the executions and who had taken a prominent part in the War of Independence, was assassinated in Dublin. His brother, Tom, was a brigadier in the anti-Treaty army. Padraig Ó Maille, Deputy Speaker in the Parliament, who was with Hales at the time, was wounded.

At dawn next morning, 8 December — the Feast of the Immaculate Conception, a day of particular religious devotion in Ireland — Liam Mellows, Rory O'Connor, Joseph McKelvey and Richard Barrett, who were captured at the beginning of hostilities, were summarily executed without trial or authority — 'as a reprisal for the assassination of Brigadier Seán Hales . . . and as a solemn warning to those who are associated with them who are engaged in a conspiracy of assassination against the representatives of the Irish people.' These reprisal executions excited vigorous comment everywhere.[5]

For any Government, or any body claiming to be a Government, this seems a judicial enormity, an inexcusable departure from its own laws, beyond constitutional explanation. In the parliament that afternoon Johnson said:

'Horror upon horrors. The assassination of Séan Hales was a dastardly thing, murder most foul, but this was murder most foul, bloody and unnatural. These four men had been in the charge of the Government for five months. The Government thought it well not to try them, not to bring them up in the courts, and then, because a man was assassinated — a man whom they held in high honour — the Government of this country announced, apparently with pride, that they had taken out four men who were in their charge as prisoners, and as a reprisal for assassination, they murdered them. These men could not have been engaged in any conspiracy . . . any other prisoner, convicted of any other offence, might be taken out by the government of the country and shot as a reprisal for any other offence by any other person.

Mulcahy in reply made a speech in which he said that they carried out their action with pride: 'The pride we have is deep in our hearts, pride that we are shouldering responsibilities that are very heavy and great.'

Cathal O'Shannon was blunt. He said that the Government was incompetent and unfit to govern the country and that theirs was the crime of treason against the State. And when Cosgrave announced that their policy was one of terror meeting terror — Johnson said: 'I never made any protestation of my religion, but I say now it is a case of Christianity or Nietzsche-ism.'

A few days later the practice, later to become general, was employed of sentencing anti-Treaty prisoners to death and suspending the sentence, which would be carried out if pro-Treaty troops were attacked in the area. The policy of executions was in full swing by the end of January. The number of anti-Treatyites who had been officially executed was fifty-five. The number shot unofficially while in custody continued to grow. Executions on one side were followed by counter-executions on the other. The last official pro-Treaty executions took place on 2 May when Aiken had already declared the 'Cease Fire', bringing the total of 'reprisal' executions to seventy-seven.[6]

A heart-rending selection[7] of the last letters of the four 'Dromboe Martyrs' as they are called — Charlie Daly, Timothy O'Sullivan, Daniel Enright, Seán Larkin — executed on 31 March 1923, is testimony to the types of men these were. Their last thoughts, without exception, were for their families and of thanksgiving that they were able to prepare to meet their Creator. Some of these letters are crude, perhaps, and ill-expressed, but they have a natural dignity and nobility which distinguishes them.

[1] Daily Press, 4 October 1922. While professing to believe the reports of ill-treatment to be propaganda — rather wishful thinking, one imagines, in view of their sources and volume — O'Higgins and Mulcahy made certain efforts to curb ill-treatment of prisoners when it was established. Courts of Inquiry and investigation were held in Dublin and Brigadier O'Daly was removed from his command in Kerry after the incidents there.

[2] Fisher was eighteen years old. The others were not much older.

[3] How the concepts of a few months earlier had changed and hardened may be judged from the fact that Barton, one of those who signed the Treaty and who voted in favour of it in the Cabinet and in the Dáil, was himself imprisoned by the pro-Treatyites at this time. He became a member of de Valera's Council of State on 25 October 1922.

[4] The Free State, October 1922.

[5] 'Murder, foul and despicable and nothing else,' Macardle quotes the New York Nation as commenting.

[6] The pro-Treatyites claim that several of the 'seventy-seven' were executed for reasons other that punitive ones. Two men were executed in Tullamore because of their alleged train robbing activities; in the area of the 3rd Southern Division, according to one source, only two executions were those of IRA men. Unfortunately the documents relating to the trials of the 'seventy-seven', together with evidence relating to the shooting of Michael Collins, were burned by the out-going pro-Treaty administration in the Phoenix Park, Dublin, in 1932, when the first change of Government took place after the Civil War.

[7] The story of the Dromboe Martyrs, McKinney and O'Callaghan (Letterkenny 1959).

26

THE HIERARCHY AND THE WAR

When the Military Courts were still under discussion in the new Parliament the guerilla campaign settled down, in the autumn of '22 and the winter of '22/23, into a steady jabbing by the anti-Treatyites against the pro-Treaty forces. The amnesty offered by the Provisional Government and the peace moves it inspired were indignantly repudiated by de Valera on behalf of the new Republican Government on 9 November. He wrote: '. . . The Government wishes it to be known definitely that there is no truth in these rumours . . . victory for the Republic or utter defeat and extermination are now the alternatives . . . '

It was ironic that, at this juncture when both sides had marooned themselves on islands of impregnable principle, Lloyd George, the real architect of the Civil War, should have been toppled from his Downing Street perch; his defeat due, in the main, it is thought to his handling of the 'Irish Question'. Mr Bonar Law, on 7 November, announced his new Cabinet, the British public were heartily sick of Ireland and the Irish and wished nothing more than to be rid of her completely; no more opportune time (with the Free State still a month away and the Northern Question still open) for a strong settlement of internal Irish differences was presented, or was likely to be. Of course it was missed.

Ambushes, raids, attacks and counter-attacks took place all over the country, several times a day in the cities. On 30 October a spectacular attack was made on Oriel House in Westland Row, Dublin, headquarters of the CID.

Two days later, Mulcahy's house at the Rathmines Road, Dublin, was attacked in an attempt to assassinate him. He was uninjured. One of the attackers, a man called Power, was shot dead. But, within days the anti-Treatyites received a serious set-back when their Chief-of-Staff and GOC in the East, Ernie O'Maille, was wounded and captured at 38 Ailesbury Road, Dublin, home of The O'Rahilly's sister, Mrs Humphries. 'We knew where he was for over a week,' said an

Intelligence Officer with the pro-Treaty troops. When the pro-Treatyites attacked at 7 a.m. one frosty morning, O'Maille concealed himself in a specially-designed wardrobe, in existence since the days of the War of Independence. The raiding party knew of the wardrobe and called on him to come out. He refused and, it is alleged, fired out through it.[1] The troops riddled the wardrobe and O'Maille was seriously wounded. Miss O'Rahilly was wounded in the face — possibly by a gun butt — and Ellen Flanagan, a servant in the house, was wounded in the shoulder. At least one of the women fired on the troops with a revolver, and a soldier, McCartney of the Scottish Brigade,[2] was killed. Number 40 Herbert Park, the home of Madam The O'Rahilly, was also raided and Miss Mary MacSwiney was arrested.[3]

In Cork on the same day Tom Barry brilliantly captured Ballineen and Enniskeen for the anti-Treatyites. Typical of the Dublin city encounters was the attack on Wellington (now Griffith) barracks, attacked in broad daylight on 8 November. When more than twenty men were parading on the square, machine-gun fire was opened on them from across the Grand Canal resulting in more than twenty casualties. An unfortunate and innocent youth named James Spain was pursued by four soldiers, dragged from the house where he had taken refuge, and shot five times. An inquest jury returned a verdict of murder against the Provisional Government. On the following night the anti-Treatyites returned to the attack, this time including Portobello barracks as well. A few days later, a meeting in O'Connell Street, Dublin organized to protest against the detention of Miss MacSwiney, and being addressed by Madame Despard and Maude Gonne MacBride, was fired on by a lorryload of pro-Treaty troops and an armoured car. Fourteen people were wounded and hundreds were hurt in the subsequent stampede.

The foregoing are incidents taken at random: in each county, in each town, every day, similar 'battles' were taking place. The guerilla war, in spite of the less favourable circumstances so far as the anti-Treatyites were concerned, reached a pitch entirely unknown during the British occupation. It strongly suggests even if the British had fulfilled their threat of renewed war — which taking precedent, political expediency and domestic British and world public opinion into consideration, is problematical — that the united Irish Republic, with a sympathetic populace, would have held its own.[4]

On 9 December, Tom Barry mounted a spectacular attack on Carrick-on Suir and a good deal of military equipment was captured.

With Barry, leading the attack, were Brigadier Lacy, William (Bill) Quirke, Michael Sheehan, Michael Sadler and 'Sparky' Breen. About 100 men took part. The pro-Treaty OC Captain Balfe, was held as hostage for two days and on 13 December the garrisons at Thomastown, Callan and Mullinavat surrendered to the anti-Treatyites. The Callan OC, feeling that he had been inveigled into a position of trust in the pro-Treaty machinery under false pretences, nevertheless joined the other side, by that time clearly heading for the end, knowing that by his action he was virtually signing his death warrant. As winter settled on the land and Christmas approached, the anti-Treaty military position, for all such local successes as these, grew steadily worse. Defeat seemed only a matter of time and discouragement spread through the ranks.

In April the Bishops had solemnly condemned the anti-Treatyites for setting up their Army Executive and opposing the Provisional Government which, they said, represented the will of the people.[5] In October they issued a solemn pastoral letter to be read in all the churches of Ireland on 22 October. In it they condemned the anti-Treatyites and accused them of ruination of the country, 'they carry on what they call a war, but which, in the absence of any legitimate authority to justify it, is morally only a system of murder . . . ' It ordered general excommunication of, and deprival of the Holy Sacrament from Republicans who continued to fight. What had been the decision of independent Bishops, now became nation-wide and applied to all anti-Treaty soldiers. They were now denied the solace of their faith which, to a Catholic — as the vast majority of them were — is the most important thing in life. It did not mean that the anti-Treatyites were, *ipso facto,* deprived of their faith and religion. It meant that they were not permitted the Sacraments.

But the anti-Treatyites, holding that they were right and the Bishops wrong, appealed to Rome. The temper of the period is readily judged. The anti-Treatyites, while bowing to the authority of the Church in matters of spiritual leadership, were by no means resigned to the directions of the Bishops in temporal matters. A published protest at the Bishop's references to anti-Treatyites as 'riff-raff, scum, looters, brigands and murderers' says: 'This does not make true men, but it does make men who are true to their faith, very bitter.' At Kilflynn, in Kerry, the following was issued:

Proclamation: Whereas: Our reverend and hitherto respected pastor, Father O'Sullivan, has so much overstepped his sacred office as to use the altar for the purpose of making incendiary statements calculated to cause serious disaffection among the loyal supporters of the Irish Republic, and, Whereas: The aforesaid supporters are liable to be influenced by these statements, it has been decided by the Competent Military Authority to take drastic action against any person or persons who assist in establishing British Authority under the guise of the Free State in Ireland. George O'Shea, J. Caskell . . . Competent Military Authorities.

A committee was formed, with the same Dr Conn Murphy who featured so prominently in the correspondence with de Valera, as organizing secretary, to appeal to Rome on behalf of the anti-Treatyites against the action of the Irish Bishops. It was known as the Catholic Appeal Committee. Its aims were, of course, promptly obscured by pro-Treaty propagandists and Murphy had to publish several disclaimers in the following tones:

. . . We have come together for one purpose — to prepare and present to the Holy See an appeal against the decisions of the Irish Hierarchy, which subject a large number of Irish Catholics to severe spiritual penalties on political grounds. We do not seek any decision for the Holy See on the political issue. What we intend to do is to ask His Holiness not to allow these Catholics to be deprived of the Sacraments of Penance and Holy Communion solely because of their political opinions, and not to permit the clergy to be penalized on the same grounds . . . We say that we have been unjustly penalized on political grounds, and we simply seek to have the penalties removed . . . Conn Mac Murchadha.[6]

This letter brought a reply from Dudley Fletcher who, earlier, had written to the Press appealing for a 'reasonable' attitude from both sides, in which he said:

. . . Surely King George V had as good a claim on the obedience of the Irish people as Ceasar had on the obedience of the Jews of Our Lord's time . . . I can find no evidence that the teaching of the Catechism of the Council of Trent on civil obedience was inculcated in the minds of Irish Roman Catholics, or that they were ever taught to pray for the King and all that are put in authority under him . .

Loyalists welcome the Bishops' teaching as better late than never.

This letter, of course, embodied all that the anti-Treatyites claimed to be fighting against and that the pro-Treatyites claimed was untrue. Its purpose was to quote chapter and verse against the action of the Catholic Appeal Committee in support of the Irish Hierarchy, but all it did was tend to assert something the pro-Treatyites had been denying for months, that the Free State was no more than the Southern Irish Parliament of the Government of Ireland Bill.

In spite of everything, however, the committee's protest was heard in Rome and the Pope sent the Rt Rev. Monsignor Salvatore Luzio to Ireland as a special Papal Envoy. He had been Professor of Canon Law at Maynooth from 1897 to 1910 and was thought to be a good choice. His letters of Credence from the Cardinal Secretary of State to Cardinal Logue said: 'He goes to Ireland by charge of the Holy Father for the object of learning directly, *viva voce* . . . . all news and information that may be useful for the knowledge of the Holy See on the actual condition of affairs in your nation . . . '

Monsignor Luzio was met by the Sinn Féin Peace Committee and appeals came to him from many public bodies asking him for his intervention in the interests of peace. He replied: 'I will give my heart and soul to the movement, and hope to be of service to the Irish People of all sorts . . . '

He saw de Valera and other leading anti-Treatyites as well as many of the Bishops and members of the Free State Government. The latter refused to discuss the situation with him and explained that the monsignor's visit was 'purely a courtesy call'. They refused to consider any peace moves by public bodies, Sinn Féin representatives or representatives of the Pope, except on their own conditions, which they had made clear. Lucio returned to Rome, having accomplished nothing by his efforts.

It is told how, when asked if he had seen the Irish Bishops, he replied: 'No. But I saw seventeen Irish Popes.'

---

[1] The word alleged is used because the author has an indistinct recollection of being told by O'Maille, now dead, that he was shot at while in hiding, without being called on to come out and without firing himself.

[2] One of the ex-British troops who volunteered for service with the pro-Treatyites.

³ The O'Rahilly was killed leading his men in action in 1916. See Miss MacSwiney's remarks quoted on p. 77.

⁴ 'It would have been really impossible (for us) to renew the war successfully,' says Costello. 'There is no denying the fact that we were only able to take one or two barracks. It was the passive resistance of the populace that won. I do think the British would have renewed the war.' On the other hand there is an equally valid opinion which holds that what had been done before could be done again, and with far greater likelihood of success, particularly in view of changed international circumstances and the attention focused on affairs in this country. (The Suez crisis of 1956 and the Yemeni affair of 1964, however, suggest that Britain would have renewed the war if at all possible, had a united Irish Republican front emerged.) But see Churchill's 'note' to the British Cabinet, pp. 16-18.

⁵ It is a curious fact that the Irish Hierarchy, speaking from Maynooth — an institution founded with the help of the British Administration — had been out of touch with the Irish political spirit over the previous 150 years, and, whenever a revolutionary or liberal movement in support of Republican or Nationalist outlook appeared, they invariably opposed it. Catholic Emancipation and, to some extent, the Land League, were the only national movements they were willingly associated with.

⁶ Daily Press, November 1922.

27

CEASE FIRE

By spring 1923 the anti-Treatyites were in a bad way. The days were lengthening, the shelter of night shortening, a summer campaign was before them and many of the leaders were doubtful if their battered and weary troops could face such a campaign, Their position was hopeless. Daily their numbers of dead and wounded, the number of prisoners in jails and internment camps, grew. Columns still in the field were being harassed without rest by superior forces. 'The Republican Itch' and general fatigue were rampant, supplies were scarce, clothing and equipment were unobtainable. The end was inevitable, yet they fought on.

Early in January Liam Deasy had been captured and since then, it seemed, only the intense faith and dynamism of one man — Lynch — prevented the anti-Treatyites' army from moral collapse. On 16 March eleven members of the anti-Treaty Executive attended a meeting in the house of Mr Pierre (Piery) Wall at Knocknaree, Ballymacarbery, Tipperary, to discuss with de Valera his proposals for peace. Lynch, however, still held the view that the Army should fight on. He received some support, while others felt that further resistance was useless and proposed dumping their arms and ending the war; still others were in favour of surrender. Tom Barry proposed that: 'further armed resistance and operations against the Free State Government will not further the cause of the independence of the country.' It was defeated by only one vote.[1]

Deasy was, perhaps, the most brilliant of the anti-Treaty officers; certainly none more sincere or more devoted to the Republican cause than he. Like de Valera, he had the clear, incisive mind of a man who thinks ahead. The fact that he was a soldier and de Valera a politician had not prevented them from arriving at similar conclusions. As GOC, 1st Division of the anti-Treatyite Army he was fully aware of the military situation: also aware of the pro-Treaty plans for wholesale executions — to which the anti-Treatyites would reply with reprisals — he felt that the time had come to take decisive steps to end the war. At the very time when he was planning to make his convictions known to his staff colleagues, he was a sick man captured by pro-Treaty soldiers on 18 January, near Ballylooby in Tipperary, and sentenced to death.

There is no doubt that the sentence made no difference to Deasy, but he was more anxious than ever that the war should cease, now that it was no longer possible for him to place his views before the anti-Treaty Executive. He asked his captors for permission to contact his colleagues. A stay of execution was immediately ordered and he was granted the facilities he desired on condition, however, that they drafted in their own wording, an appeal for unconditional surrender to his colleagues, which Deasy was to sign. He could send whatever letter he liked with the document. As the only means at his disposal for ending the war, Deasy signed the pro-Treaty document on 29 January.

I have undertaken for the future of Ireland to accept and aid in the immediate and unconditional surrender of all arms and men and have signed the following statement: — I accept and will aid an immediate and unconditional surrender of all arms and men as required by General Mulcahy.

Signed, Liam Deasy.

In pursuance of this undertaking I am asked to appeal for a similar undertaking from the following: E. de Valera, Liam Lynch, T. Barry and the other members of the Republican Executive, and for the immediate and unconditional surrender of themselves after the issue by them of an order for surrender of those associated with them, together with their arms and equipment.

Subsequently anti-Treaty prisoners in Limerick and in Clonmel asked that their representatives might be allowed parole to meet the anti-Treaty leaders: 'As we are of the opinion that continued civil strife between brothers in arms would result in a victory for England.' Father — the late Archdeacon — Tom Duggan, who had been nominated by Deasy as intermediary and who had been prominent in peace moves since the outbreak of war, delivered to members of the Free State Government and to the anti-Treaty Executive the documents signed by Deasy. Lynch rejected their contents summarily.

Having moved his HQ to Tower House, Santry, County Dublin, the home of Mr and Mrs Michael Fitzgerald, more and more Lynch had taken on the duties of Commander-in-Chief rather than those of Chief-of-Staff. He did this principally because he was disturbed by the growing tendency that he found, in soldiers as well as in politicians, to consider the anti-Treaty cause doomed, at least from a military point of view. He did not feel this himself and he had a passionate belief in ultimate victory. On 7 December 1922 — the day after the Free State came into being — he had written to Con Moloney, then Adjutant General: 'No terms short of independence can be accepted by the Army or Government . . . ' His mind was set in the final mould and so stayed until the end. On his own authority, he refused to convene Executive meetings because of the fear that the Executive might vote for surrender. Finally he was forced by his colleagues to agree to the Executive meeting *(supra)* of 23 March.

The outcome of that meeting, leaving the Executive divided in opinion, was so indecisive that a second meeting was convened for 10 April. In the interval decisive events were shaping: the pro-Treaty troops had launched a large-scale round-up which was calculated to exterminate the remainder of anti-Treaty resistance by capture or death. Already such notable leaders as Lacy, O'Maille, Deasy, Moylan, together with many more had been killed or captured. Just prior to the 10 April meeting the position had so deteriorated for the anti-Treatyites that only two of the Executive, John Joe Rice and Ted Sullivan — the same who felt that it would have taken 'the whole Free State Army twenty years to dig them out' — felt that resistance could continue. Lynch himself still believed in possible victory. There was some hope of acquiring mountain artillery and he expected this to be decisive. 'His appreciation of the military situation,' says O'Donoghue, 'was more optimistic than the facts warranted.'

He could not and would not face the thought of defeat and collapse of the Republican resistance to the imposition of the Treaty. The farthest he would allow himself to think in such a direction was that the Free State authorities would be compelled to negotiate with the Republicans . . . I feel that in no circumstances would he himself surrender and that he would never allow those under his command to do so.

288

According to Maurice Twomey, a GHQ staff officer in constant association with him at the time:

The meeting was to be held near Goatenbridge at the foot of the Knockmealdown Mountains on the Waterford-Tipperary border and Lynch and his party, which included Frank Aiken and Seán Hyde, stayed at the house of one Michael Condon; Seán O'Meara, Jerry Frewen, Bill Quirke and Seán Hayes, Staff Officers or members of the Executive, were billeted nearby. The following account of what happened that morning, 10 April 1923, though unsigned, is attributed to Aiken:[2]

At 4 a.m. scouts gave the alarm. A column of 'Staters' had appeared on the road moving towards Goatenbridge. We rose and moved to a house higher in the mountainside (that of Mr William Houlihan). Daylight came and, looking to the north we saw in the valley below us three columns of 'Staters'. We were not much alarmed. A report had been received the evening before that a valley to the south-west of us was to be 'rounded-up' and we thought that the forces below us were concentrating to move in on it. About 8 a.m., as we were about to have a cup of tea, a scout from the east ran in to tell us that another column was coming about 1000 yards away across the mountains to our left-rear. Our only line of retreat was thus threatened and, sending word to the scouts watching to the west, we dashed up a glen towards the mountains.

On reaching the head of the glen we halted to await the two scouts who were armed, one with a Thompson and the other with a rifle. We numbered seven — General Liam Lynch and five officers armed with revolvers and automatics, and an unarmed local Volunteer. We were carrying a great number of important papers, which we wished to save at all costs. We were only a few minutes at the head of the glen and no sign of the scouts coming, when the 'Staters' appeared over a rise and our first shots were exchanged. We dashed on again up the mountains, a shallow river bed affording us cover for about 250 yards. When we reached the end of the river bed we had to retreat up a bare, coverless shoulder of the mountain.

This was the chance for the 'Staters'. About fifty of them had a clear view of us between 300 and 400 yards range and they rattled away with their rifles as fast as they could work the bolts. Our return fire with revolvers was, of course, ineffective at this range, but as we

289

staggered up along the mountain, we fired an odd shot to disconcert them.[3] We had gone about 200 yards up the shoulder . . . . when a sudden lull came in the firing. After, perhaps twenty seconds silence in the clear still air of the morning a single shot rang out and General Lynch fell, crying out 'My God, I'm hit.'

Hyde had been helping Lynch, who was nearly exhausted, at the time and they offered a substantial target. The bullet passed behind Hyde and seriously wounded Lynch in the stomach. Aiken and Quirke ran back under fire to help Hyde carry Lynch. The grouping together of the four men was the signal for intense fire from the enemy, but the three men carried him for some distance, repeating an Act of Contrition as they did so.

Lynch was in agony and the carrying hurt him terribly. Several times he told us to leave him down, and at last, after carrying him a couple of hundred yards further, again he told us to put him down and ordered us to go, saying 'Perhaps they will bandage me when they come up.'
[He continues] It would be impossible to describe our agony of mind in thus parting with our comrade and chief . . . His command that we should leave him would have been disobeyed, but that the papers we carried must be saved and brought at any cost.

When Lieutenant Clancy reached Lynch he found an excited soldier covering him with a rifle and shouting that he had captured de Valera. Clancy asked Lynch who he was and was told. Clancy put a field dressing on the wounded man and improvised a stretcher to carry him down the mountainside. A priest, Fr. Patrick Hallinan, attended Lynch on the roadside. Taken to Clonmel by ambulance, where everything possible was done for him, the anti-Treaty military leader, not yet thirty years old, died that evening at 8.45 p.m.

Today a round tower marks the spot in the lonely mountain of Crohan West above Newcastle in Tipperary where he was shot. The death of Lynch was, in effect, the death blow to the anti-Treatyites, depriving them of their military head and of the one man who might have prolonged military resistance.

Suddenly the will to resist in arms any longer deserted anti-Treatyites. Lynch's death spurred the pro-Treaty troops to even more intensive efforts and, in the biggest operation of its kind during the war, the whole of south Tipperary was combed, yielding one result of great importance. On 14 April Austin Stack was captured at Mount Melleray.[5] He had in his possession, and in his own handwriting, a memorandum prepared for the signatures of members of the Army Executive authorizing the President to order an immediate cessation of hostilities and requesting military personnel to hand in their weapons to secret dumps pending the election of a Government, 'of free choice of the people'.

During the next four days blow after blow fell on the anti-Treatyites. Several more of their senior officers were captured or killed, including Ned Somers[6] and Theobald English, killed together in a secret hideout in Tipperary, and generals Frank Barrett and Seán Gaynor, respectively OC 1st Western and OC 3rd Southern Divisions, captured. On the same day Dan Breen and Maurice Walsh were captured asleep in a dugout. On 20 April the adjourned (10 April) meeting was held by twelve members of the anti-Treaty Executive at a Place called Poulacapple in Tipperary. Aiken became Chief-of-Staff in succession to Lynch and, with one dissentient, the meeting agreed to negotiate for peace on the following terms:

(1) The sovereignty of the Irish nation and the integrity of its territory are inalienable.

(2) Any instrument purporting to the contrary is, to the extent of its violation of the above principle, null and void.

An Army Council of Liam Pilkington, Tom Barry, Seán Hyde and Frank Aiken was appointed to meet de Valera and those of his Cabinet not in prison camps. On 27 April de Valera issued a proclamation of the terms and at the same time ordered a suspension of aggressive action by the anti-Treaty troops, to take effect 'as soon as may be, but not later than noon, Monday, 30 April'. De Valera's proclamation opened the way for negotiation and, though Cosgrave refused to negotiate himself, he agreed that Senators Andrew Jameson and James Douglas, who had been approached by de Valera on 30 April for the purpose, should act as intermediaries. They met de Valera on 1 May. Cosgrave gave Jameson and Douglas the following proposals:

(a) All political issues whether now existing or in the future arising shall be decided by the majority vote of the elected representatives of the people;

(b) As a corollary to (a) that the people are entitled to have all lethal weapons within the country in the effective custody or control of the Executive Government responsible to the People through their representatives.

The acceptance of these principles and practical compliance with (b) by the surrender of arms to be the preliminary condition for the release of prisoners who shall be required to subscribe individually to (a) and (b).

Signed in acceptance of the foregoing principles this . . . day of May, 1923.

They were also instructed to inform de Valera that:

(1) Military action against him and his followers would cease when the arms held by them were delivered into the effectual custody of the Irish Free State Executive authorities. The arrangements for the delivery of the arms and the place of their deposit would be made with as much consideration as possible for the feelings of those concerned.

(2) The prisoners to be released on the satisfactory fulfilment of Clause 1, and the signature of each prisoner, before release, to the conditions of the document above mentioned.

(3) The Free State Government would keep a clear field for Mr de Valera and his followers to enable them to canvass for the votes of the people at the next election, provided they undertook to adhere strictly to Constitutional action.

De Valera was told that the pro-Treatyites would not negotiate with the British Government in regard to the oath. On 7 May de Valera submitted counter-proposals, which included the following clauses:

(4) That no citizen who subscribes to the foregoing can be justly excluded by any political oath, test, or other device, from his or her share in the determining (of) national policy or from the councils and parliament of the nation.

292

And:

(d) That pending the election effective control of lethal weapons shall be secured by:

    (1) The strict supervision and control of all arms in the hands of the F.S. forces and their auxiliaries.

    (2) Assigning to the Republican forces at least one suitable building in each province, to be used by them as barracks and arsenals, where Republican arms shall be stored up, sealed up, and defended by a specially pledged Republican guard — these arms to be disposed of after the elections by re-issue to their present holders, or in such other manner as may secure the consent of the Government then elected.

His proposals were rejected in a letter to Senator Jameson on 8 May which said that 'the terms already specified are conditions from which the Government cannot and will not depart'. Agreement could not be reached on the two questions which had been instrumental in starting the war; the oath and the arms of the anti-Treatyites. The other conditions were, as Thomas Johnson said in the parliament on 11 May, 'easily met, and pretty generally conceded'. Johnson added that virtually all de Valera's terms were acceptable to him and he urged the pro-Treaty authorities to begin 'negotiations by action — to suspend all raids and arrests for a period of six weeks'. If that were done he said, peace would come. [7]

Although the negotiations failed, they had shown that both sides were anxious for peace. De Valera's condition that all elected representatives should be allowed to sit in the Dáil without the obligation to take the oath of allegiance would not be conceded by the Free State Government; indeed, it could not be conceded except at the cost of the Constitution. On 13 and 14 May the anti-Treaty Cabinet and Army Council met again. The campaign against their troops had not abated and the situation, from a military point of view, was beyond hope. Their peace proposals being rejected, nothing remained but to bring the war to a conclusion on another basis. The decision was taken to order the anti-Treaty troops remaining in the field to 'dump arms' and 'Cease Fire'. The order was issued by Aiken on 24 May 1923. All over the country harried anti-Treaty Troops hid their arms and the control of the pro-

Treatyites became absolute. Many thousands of prisoners were added to the 15,000 or so already interned and, in the mud of this aftermath of captor and captive, victor and vanquished, finally perished the splendid idea that had been Sinn Féin.

The Cease Fire solved none of the problems which the Treaty brought. It only aggravated them. From the Civil War the pro-Treaty party emerged the stronger with an uncompromising devotion to the Treaty and all it stood for — seemingly for its own sake. There was however, little real strength in their victory. The anti-Treatyites emerged defeated militarily, with their ideal still intact, but still without a civic political programme or common leadership.

A Public Safety Act was passed by the Dáil in June so that anti-Treatyites could be arrested without trial and at about the same time it was decided to hold a general election on 27 August. The Republican position, with regard to campaigning for this, was difficult because, not having accepted the Free State terms — which included electioneering facilities — all their principal men were dead, in jail or open to arrest and imprisonment without trial. Campaigning, therefore, became a matter of great difficulty. They put forward eighty-seven candidates, however — most of whom were on the run — on the Sinn Féin ticket. Eamon Donnelly was appointed Director of Elections and the work was carried on in spite of great opposition.

'Police, military and intelligence agents were used to dislocate the election work of Sinn Féin. Election offices were raided . . . many chairmen and speakers were arrested. At Tubbercurry a man who presided at a Sinn Féin meeting was afterwards dragged from his house, beaten and left on the roadside with broken ribs. At Lixnaw a Republican meeting was fired on and one man was shot dead.'[8]

The Government did not relish or would not allow the Republicans free electioneering under the circumstances. So far as the Government were concerned since de Valera had not accepted their terms, the Republicans (both anti-Treatyites, the militarists, and the civilians who still favoured the Sinn Féin Republican ideal) were disaffected revolutionaries and as such they continued to treat them. The Government were strong, they were victorious and they called the tune, secure in the knowledge that they had made an offer to their opponents which had been rejected.

De Valera was arrested at an election meeting in Clare of which he had said beforehand: 'I will be with them and nothing but a bullet will stop me.' He spent eleven months in prison together with thousands of Republicans, who finally went on hunger-strike in protest at their detention and treatment. Eventually the bulk of them were released after de Valera was released in July 1924.

The election, when it took place in August 1923, provided a painful shock for the Government. Out of a total of 153 seats the Government won sixty-three, the Republicans forty-four and the rest were divided between Farmer, Labour and Independents. Many Republicans were interned and could not vote, but the result showed clearly that, their war conduct apart, the sympathy of a strong minority of the population was still with them.

That election, and the release of the prisoners over the next two years brought to an end the Civil War which, bitter and hateful though it was, is part of Irish history. Out of it came the political spirit and allegiances in Ireland today and from it, too, came some chauvinism and an unawareness by the politicians of the growing generations in the country; generations who never heard of Sinn Féin and for whom this great split means nothing, have grown up; young people who live for today and think for tomorrow; yesterday happened before they had memories.

For them this book may help to fill the great, deliberate gap in Irish history books and, with that gap bridged — with the skeleton taken out, examined and put away in its proper place in the cupboard — they may march onward, disregarding the woeful shadow behind them and old, cracked voices calling them backward, without saying why and wherefore.

[1]O'Donoghue, *No Other Law* , p. 301

[2]*Sinn Féin*, 1 April, 1923

[3]The troops were part of the general sweep, 1500 men were engaged in this area, and, acting on 'information received', were looking for anti-Treaty leaders. Those near Goatenbridge were commanded by Captain Tyler from Clogheen and it was a section of his men, sixty in number, under Lieutenant Laurence Clancy who engaged Lynch's party.

⁴Time and confusion may have linked this shot with the apocryphal 'single shot' that killed Michael Collins, Lynch's opposite number.

⁵The Cistercian Monastery in County Waterford, near Cappoquin.

⁶Who had been a pro-Treaty officer at Callan.

⁷Raids, arrests and executions had not ceased by the pro-Treatyites when de Valera's suspension of hostilities order was published. On 2 May, three days after, two prisoners were executed at Ennis and raids, round-ups and arrests continued. As late as July activity went on. Noel Lemass, captured on 3 July, disappeared until his body was found on 12 October 1923.

⁸Dorothy Macardle. *The Irish Republic*, p. 833. This kind of occurrence is maintained by pro-Treaty sources to have been 'local action' and not policy. However, the general situation seemed to be that even if it was local action it was so widespread as to have the same effect as policy.

SELECT
BIBLIOGRAPHY

OFFICIAL PUBLICATIONS

Dail Eireann, Minutes of Proceedings of the First Dail of the Republic
    of Ireland, Official Record, Dublin 1921.
    Official Reports for 1921 and 1922.
    Debate on the Treaty Between Great Britain and Ireland,
    Dublin, 1922.
    Parliamentary Debates: Official Report, Dublin 1922.
Saorstat Eireann, Official Handbook, 1932.

BOOKS AND EXTRACTS

Barry, Thomas: *Guerilla Days in Ireland,* Dublin: Anvil Books, 1981.
Beaslai, Piaras: *Michael Collins and the Making of a New Ireland,*
    Phoenix Publishing Co. (Dublin), 1926.
Bell, J. Bowyer, *The Secret Army,* Dublin: Poolbeg Press, 1989.
Bennett, Richard, *The Black and Tans,* London: Severn House, 1976.
Blythe, Ernest, *Birth Pangs of a Nation, (Irish Times),* 19/20 Nov. 1968.
Breen, Daniel: *My Fight for Irish Freedom,* Dublin: Anvil Books, 1981.
Brennan, Robert, *Allegiance,* Dublin, 1950.
Bromage, Mary C., *De Valera and the March of a Nation,* 1956.
Caulfield, Max, *The Easter Rebellion,* 1965.
Churchill, Winston: *The Aftermath,* Butterworth, 1929.
Cork's Fighting Story, Kerryman (Tralee), 1949.
Colum, Padraic, *Arthur Griffith,* Dublin, 1959.
Coogan, T.P., *The IRA,* London: Fontana, 1980.
Coogan, T.P., *Ireland Since the Rising,* 1966.
Crozier, F. P. (General), *Ireland for Ever,* Cape, 1932.
Dalton, Charles, *With the Dublin Brigade,* Peter Davies, 1929.
Dublin's Fighting Story, Kerryman (Tralee), 1949.
Forester, Margaret, *Michael Collins: The Lost Leader,* 1971.

Gallagher, Frank, *The Anglo-Irish Treaty*, 1965.
Griffith, Arthur, *The Resurrection of Hungary*, 1918.
Henry, R. M., *The Evolution of Sinn Fein*, 1920.
Holt, Edgar, *Protest in Arms: The Irish Troubles, 1916-23*, 1960.
Hopkinson, Michael, *Green Against Green*, Dublin: Gill & Macmillan, 1988.
Jones, Tom, *Whitehall Diary* (vol iii), 1971.
Kee, Robert, *The Green Flag*, London: Quartet Books, 1976.
Lawlor, Sheila, *Britain and Ireland, 1913-1923*, London, 1985.
Lloyd George, David, *Is it Peace?*, Hodder and Stoughton, 1923.
Longford, Earl of, and O'Neill, T.P., *Eamon de Valera*, London: Arrow Books, 1974.
Lynch, D., *The IRB and the 1916 Rising*, Cork, 1952.
Macardle, Dorothy, *The Irish Republic*, Gollancz — The Irish Press, 1951.
Macardle, Dorothy, *Tragedies of Kerry*, Irish Book Bureau.
McCann: *War by The Irish*, Tralee Kerryman, 1946.
McCracken, J. L., *Representative Government in Ireland*, Oxford, 1958.
MacManus, L, *White Light and Flame*, Talbot Press, 1929.
MacManus, M. J., *Eamon de Valera*, Talbot Press, 1944.
Macready, Gen. Sir Nevil, *Annals of An Active Life*, London, 1924.
Mansergh, Nicholas S., *The Irish Question, 1840-1921*, London: Allen & Unwin, 1965.
O Broin, Leon, *Michael Collins*, Dublin: Gill & Macmillan, 1980.
O'Donoghue, Florence, *Tomas Mac Curtain*, 1958.
O'Hegarty, P.S., *A History of Ireland Under the Union, 1801-1922*, 1952.
Monteith, Robert, *Casement's Last Adventure*.
Neeson, Eoin, *The Life and Death of Michael Collins*, Cork: Mercier, 1968.
O'Connor, Batt, *With Michael Collins in the Fight for Irish Independence*, Peter Davies, 1929.
O'Connor, Frank: *The Big Fellow*, Dublin: Poolbeg, 1986.
O'Donoghue, Florence, *No Other Law*, Irish Press, 1954.
Ó Luing, Seán, *Art Ó Griofa*, Sairseal agus Dill (Dublin), 1953.
O'Malley, Ernest, *On Another Man's Wound*, Dublin: Anvil Books, 1979.
Pakenham, Frank, *Peace by Ordeal*, London: Sidgwick & Jackson, 1972.
Ryan, Desmond, *The Rising*, Golden Eagle Books (Dublin), 1949.
Ryan, Desmond, *Sean Treacy. 3rd Tipperary Brigade*, Tralee: Kerryman, 1945.

Ryan, Desmond, *Unique Dictator* (A study of Eamon de Valera), London, 1936.

Taylor, Rex, *Michael Collins*, London: New English Library, 1970.

Treaty Debates, Government Stationery Office, Dublin.

White, T. De V., *Kevin O'Higgins*, 1948.

Younger, Calton, *Ireland's Civil War*, Muller, 1968.

PAMPHLETS

Collins, Michael: *Arguments for the Treaty*, Martin Lester, Dublin, 1922.

Collins, Michael: *Erskine Childers*.

Gallagher, Frank: *King and Constitution*, Fianna Fáil.

Gibson, Norman: *Partition To-day*, Tuairim.

Gibson, Arthur: *Arguments for the Treaty*, Martin Lester.

de Fuiteoil, Nicolas: *Waterford Remembers*.

de Valera, Eamon: *National Discipline and Majority Rule*, Fianna Fáil Pamphlet No.1, 1936.

de Burca, Seamus: *The Soldier's Song*, P. J. Bourke, Dublin.

O'Higgins, Kevin: *Civil War and the Events which led to it*, Talbot Press (Dublin), 1922.

Keohan, Edmond: *History of Dungarvan*, Waterford News, 1923.

Sceilg (J. J. O'Kelly): *Stepping Stones*, Irish Book Bureau.

Sceilg: *A Trinity of Martyrs*, Irish Book Bureau.

Constitution of the Irish Free State.

Official Correspondence relating to the Peace Negotiations June-September, 1921, Easons.

Sinn Fein Rebellion Handbook, Irish Times.

Correspondence of Eamon de Valera and Others, Government Stationery Office, Dublin.

The Story of the Drumboe Martyrs, McKinney and O'Callaghan, Leitrim.

Iris an Airm (The Army Gazette), 1923.

PERIODICALS AND NEWSPAPERS

So many newspapers and periodicals were consulted that it would be pointless to list them all. Many of those made use of were from the library of the late Dr F. X. Burke of Fitzwilliam Square, Dublin, and were already indexed and filed; and many more were indexed and filed by the author. Below is a list of those found most useful.

The files of *The Irish Times*, the *Irish Independent, The Cork Examiner, The Cork Constitution, The Irish Press* and the *Munster Express*.

An t-Oglach, 1918-21.
Éire, 1923.
An Phoblacht, 1931-2.
Éire Og, 1922.
Evening Herald (Dublin).
Evening Mail (Dublin).
Freeman's Journal.
Irish Bulletin, 1919-21.
Poblacht na h-Éireann, 1922.
New Ireland.
National Observer.
Sgeal Catha Luimnuighe, 1922.
Sunday Independent.
Sunday Press.
Sunday Review.
Sunday Times.
Sunday Express.
The Christian Science Monitor, 1922-3.
The Gael.
The Free State (An Saorstát).
The Observer.

APPENDIX

STATEMENTS AND DOCUMENTS

The manifesto of Sinn Féin as prepared for circulation for the General Election of December 1918.

General Election

MANIFESTO TO THE IRISH PEOPLE

The coming General Election is fraught with vital possibilities for the future of our nation. Ireland is faced with the question whether this generation wills it that she is to march out into the full sunlight of freedom, or is to remain in the shadow of a base imperialism that has brought and ever will bring in its train naught but evil for our race.

Sinn Féin gives Ireland the opportunity of vindicating her honour and pursuing with renewed confidence the path of national salvation by rallying to the flag of the Irish Republic.

Sinn Féin aims at securing the establishment of that Republic —

1. By withdrawing the Irish Representation from the British Parliament and by denying the right and opposing the will of the British Government or any other foreign Government to legislate for Ireland.

2. By making use of any and every means available to render impotent the power of England to hold Ireland in subjection by military force or otherwise.

3. By the establishment of a constituent assembly comprising persons chosen by Irish constituencies as the supreme national authority to speak and act in the name of the Irish people, and to develop Ireland's social, political and industrial life, for the welfare of the whole people of Ireland.

4. By appealing to the Peace Conference for the establishment of Ireland as an Independent Nation. At that conference the future of the nations of the world will be settled on the principle of government by

302

consent of the governed. Ireland's claim to the application of that principle in her favour is not based on any accidental situation arising from the war. It is older than many if not all of the present belligerents. It is based on our unbroken tradition of nationhood, on a unity in a national name which has never been challenged, on our possession of a distinctive national culture and social order, on the moral courage and dignity of our people in the face of alien aggression, on the fact that in nearly every generation, five times with the past 120 years, our people have challenged in arms the right of England to rule this country. On these incontrovertible facts is based the claim that our people have beyond question established the right to be accorded all the power of a free nation.

Sinn Fein stands less for a political party than for the Nation; it represents the old tradition of nationhood handed on from dead generations; it stands by the Proclamation of the Provisional Government of Easter, 1916, reasserting the inalienable right of the Irish Nation, to sovereign independence, reaffirming the determination of the Irish people to achieve it, and guaranteeing within the independent Nation equal rights and equal opportunities to all its citizens.

Believing that the time has arrived when Ireland's voice for the principle of untrammelled National self-determination should be heard above every interest of party or class, Sinn Féin will oppose at the Polls every individual candidate who does not accept this principle.

The policy of our opponents stands condemned on any test, whether of principle or expediency. The right of a nation to sovereign independence rests upon immutable natural law and cannot be made the subject of a compromise. Any attempt to barter away the sacred and inviolate rights of nationhood begins in dishonour and is bound to end in disaster. The enforced exodus of millions of our people, the decay of our industrial life, the ever-increasing financial plunder of our country, the whittling down of the demand for the 'Repeal of the Union' voiced by the first Irish Leader to plead in the Hall of the Conqueror to that of Home Rule on the Statute Book, and finally the contemplated mutilation of our country by partition, are some of the ghastly results of a policy that leads to national ruin.

Those who have endeavoured to harness the people of Ireland to England's war chariot, ignoring the fact that only a freely-elected Government in a free Ireland has power to decide for Ireland the question of peace and war, have forfeited the right to speak for the Irish people. The Green Flag turned red in the hands of the Leaders, but the shame is not to be laid at the doors of the Irish people unless they continue a policy of sending their representatives to an alien and hostile assembly, whose powerful influence has been sufficient to destroy the integrity and sap the independence of their representatives. Ireland must repudiate the men who, in a supreme crisis for the nation, attempted to sell her birthright for the vague promises of English ministers, and who showed their incompetence by failing to have even these promises fulfilled.

The present Irish members of the English Parliament constitute an obstacle to be removed from the path that leads to the Peace Conference. By declaring their will to accept the status of a province instead of boldly taking their stand upon the right of the nation they supply England with the only subterfuge at her disposal for obscuring the issue in the eyes of the world. By their persistent endeavours to induce the young manhood of Ireland to don the uniform of our seven-century old oppressor, and place their lives at the disposal of the military machine that holds our nation in bondage, they endeavour to barter away and even to use against itself the one great asset still left to our Nation after the havoc of centuries.

Sinn Féin goes to the polls handicapped by all the arts and contrivances that a powerful and unscrupulous enemy can use against us. Conscious of the power of Sinn Féin, to secure the freedom of Ireland the British Government would destroy it. Sinn Féin, however, goes to the polls confident that the people of this ancient nation will be true to the old cause and will vote for the men who stand by the principles of Tone, Emmet, Mitchel, Pearse and Connolly, the men who disdain to whine to the enemy for favours, the men who hold that Ireland must be as free as England or Holland, or Switzerland or France, and whose demand is that the only status befitting this ancient realm is the status of a free nation.

Issued by the Standing Committee of Sinn Féin.

DECLARATION OF INDEPENDENCE

Whereas the Irish people is by right a free people:

And whereas for seven hundred years the Irish people has never ceased to repudiate and has repeatedly protested in arms against foreign usurpation;

And whereas English rule in this country is, and always has been, based upon force and fraud and maintained by military occupation against the declared will of the people;

And whereas the Irish Republic was proclaimed in Dublin on Easter Monday, 1916, by the Irish Republican Army, acting on behalf of the Irish people;

And whereas the Irish people is resolved to secure and maintain its complete independence in order to promote the common weal, to re-establish justice, to provide for future defence, to ensure peace at home and good will with all nations, and to constitute a national policy based upon the people's will, with equal right for every citizen;

And whereas at the threshold of a new era in history the Irish electorate has in the General Election of December 1918, seized the first occasion to declare by an overwhelming majority its firm allegiance to the Irish Republic;

Now therefore, we, the elected Representatives of the ancient Irish people in national Parliament assembled, do in the name of the Irish Nation, ratify the establishment of the Irish republic and pledge ourselves and our people to make this declaration effective by every means at our command;

We ordain that the elected Representatives of the Irish people alone have power to make laws binding on the people of Ireland, and that the Irish Parliament is the only Parliament to which that people will give its allegiance;

We solemnly declare foreign government in Ireland to be an invasion of our national right which we will never tolerate, and we demand the evacuation of our country by the English Garrison;

We claim for our national independence the recognition and support of every free nation in the world, and we proclaim that independence to be a condition precedent to international peace thereafter;

In the name of the Irish people we humbly commit our destiny to Almighty God Who gave our fathers the courage and determination to persevere through long centuries of a ruthless tyranny, and strong in the justice of the cause which they have handed down to us, we ask His Divine blessing on this the last stage of the struggle we have pledged ourselves to carry through to freedom.

THE BRITISH OFFER OF JULY 1921

The British Government are actuated by an earnest desire to end the unhappy divisions between Great Britain and Ireland which have produced so many conflicts in the past and which have once more shattered the peace and well-being of Ireland at the present time. They long, with His Majesty the King, in the words of his gracious speech in Ireland last month, for a satisfactory resolution of 'those age-long Irish problems which for generations embarrassed our forefathers as they now weigh heavily upon us,' and they wish to do their utmost to secure that 'every man of Irish birth, whatever be his creed and whatever be his home, should work in loyal co-operation with the free communities on which the British Empire is based.' They are convinced that the Irish people may find as worthy and as complete an expression of their political and spiritual ideals within the Empire as any of the numerous and varied nations united in allegiance to His Majesty's throne; and they desire such consummation, not only for the welfare of Great Britain, Ireland and the Empire as a whole, but also for the cause of peace and harmony throughout the world. There is no part of the world where Irishmen have made their home but suffers from our ancient feuds; no part of it but looks to this meeting between the British Government and the Irish Leaders to resolve these feuds in a new understanding honourable and satisfactory to all the peoples involved.

The free nations which compose the British Empire are drawn from many races, with different histories, traditions, ideals. In the Dominion of Canada, British and French have long forgotten the bitter conflicts which divided their ancestors. In South Africa the Transvaal Republic and the Orange Free State have joined with two British colonies to make a great self-governing union under His Majesty's sway. The British people cannot believe that where Canada and South Africa, with equal or even greater difficulties, have so signally succeeded, Ireland will fail; and they are determined that, so far as they themselves can assure it, nothing shall hinder Irish statesmen from joining together to build up an Irish State in free and willing co-operation with the other peoples of the Empire.

Moved by these considerations, the British Government invite Ireland to take her place in the great association of free nations over which His Majesty reigns. As earnest of their desire to obliterate old quarrels and to enable Ireland to face the future with her own strength

306

and hope, they propose that Ireland shall assume forthwith the status of a Dominion with all the powers and privileges set forth in this document. By adoption of Dominion status it is understood that Ireland shall enjoy complete autonomy in taxation and finance; that she shall maintain her own courts of law and judges; that she shall maintain her own military forces for home defence, her own constabulary and her own police; that she shall take over the Irish postal services and all matters relating thereto; education, land, agriculture, mines, and minerals, forestry, housing, labour, unemployment, transport, trade, public health, insurance and the liquor trade; and, in sum, that she shall exercise all those powers and privileges upon which the autonomy of self-governing Dominions is based, subject only to the considerations set out in the ensuing paragraphs. Guaranteed in these liberties which no foreign people can challenge without challenging the Empire as a whole, the Dominions hold each and severally by virtue of their British Fellowship a standing amongst the nations equivalent, not merely to their individual strength, but to the combined power and influence of all nations of the Commonwealth. That guarantee, that fellowship, that freedom the whole Empire looks to Ireland to accept.

To this settlement the British Government are prepared to give immediate effect upon the following conditions, which are, in their opinion, vital to the welfare and safety of both Great Britain and Ireland, forming as they do the heart of the Commonwealth.

1. The common concern of Great Britain and Ireland in the defence of their interests by land and sea shall be mutually recognized. Great Britain lives by sea-borne food; her communications depend upon the freedom of the great sea routes. Ireland lies at Britain's side across the sea ways North and South that link her with the sister nations of the Empire, the Markets of the world and the vital sources of her food supply. In recognition of this fact, which nature has imposed and no statesmanship can change, it is essential that the Royal Navy alone should control the seas around Ireland and Great Britain, and that such rights and liberties should be accorded to it by the Irish State as are essential for naval purposes in the Irish harbours and on the Irish coast.

2. In order that the movement towards the limitation of armaments which is now making progress in the world should in no way be hampered, it is stipulated that the Irish Territorial force shall within

reasonable limits conform in respect of numbers to the military establishments of the other parts of these islands.

3. The position of Ireland is also of great importance for the Air Services, both military and civil. The Royal Air Forces will need facilities for all purposes that it serves; and Ireland will form an essential link in the development of Air routes between the British Isles and the North American Continent. It is therefore stipulated that Great Britain shall have all necessary facilities for the development of defence and of communications by air.

4. Great Britain hopes that Ireland will in due course and of her own free will contribute in proportion of her wealth to the regular Naval, Military and Air forces of the Empire. It is further assumed that voluntary recruitment for these forces will be permitted throughout Ireland, particularly for those famous Irish Regiments which have so long and so gallantly served His Majesty in all parts of the world.

5. While the Irish people shall enjoy complete autonomy in taxation and finance, it is essential to prevent a recurrence of ancient differences between the two islands, and in particular to avert the possibility of ruinous trade wars. With this object in view, the British and Irish Governments shall agree to impose no protective duties or other restrictions upon the flow of transport, trade and commerce between all parts of these islands.

6. The Irish people shall agree to assume responsibility for a share of the present debt of the United Kingdom and of the liability of pensions arising out of the Great War, the share in default of agreement between the Governments concerned to be determined by an independent arbitrator appointed from within His Majesty's Dominions.

In accordance with these principles, the British Government propose that the conditions of settlement between Great Britain and Ireland shall be embodied in the form of a Treaty, to which effect shall in due course be given by the British and Irish Parliaments. They look to such instrument to obliterate old conflicts forthwith, to clear the way for a detailed settlement in full accordance with Irish conditions and needs and thus to establish a new and happier relation between Irish patriotism and that wider community of aims and interests by which the unity of the whole Empire is freely sustained.

The form in which the settlement is to take effect will depend upon Ireland herself. It must allow for full recognition of the existing powers and privileges of the Parliament of Northern Ireland, which cannot be abrogated except by their own consent. For their part, the British Government entertain an earnest hope that the necessity of harmonious co-operation amongst Irishmen of all classes and creeds will be recognized throughout Ireland, and they will welcome the day when by those means unity is achieved. But no such common action can be secured by force. Union came in Canada by the free consent of the Provinces; so in Australia; so in South Africa. It will come in Ireland by no other way than consent. There can, in fact, be no settlement on terms involving, on the one side or the other, that bitter appeal to bloodshed and violence which all men of good will are longing to terminate. The British Government will undertake to give effect, so far as that depends on them, to any terms in this respect on which all Ireland unites. But in no conditions can they consent to any proposals which would kindle civil war in Ireland. Such a war would not touch Ireland alone, for partisans would flock to either side from Great Britain, the Empire, and elsewhere, with consequences more devastating to the welfare both of Ireland and the Empire than the conflict to which a truce has been called this month. Throughout the Empire there is a deep desire that the day of violence should pass and that a solution should be found, consonant with the highest ideals and interests of all parts of Ireland, which will enable her to co-operate as a willing partner in the British Commonwealth.

The British Government will therefore leave Irishmen themselves to determine by negotiations between themselves whether the new powers which the Pact defines shall be taken over by Ireland as a whole and administered by a single Ireland body, or be taken over separately by Southern and Northern Ireland, with or without a joint authority to harmonize their common interests. They will willingly assist in the negotiations of such a settlement, if Irishmen should so desire.

By these proposals the British Government sincerely believe that they will have shattered the foundations of that ancient hatred and distrust which have disfigured our common history for centuries past. The future of Ireland within the Commonwealth is for the Irish people to shape.

In the foregoing proposals the British Government have attempted no more than the broad outline of a settlement. The details they leave for discussion when the Irish people have signified their acceptance of the principle of this pact.

10 Downing Street, S.W. 1.
July 20th, 1921.

IRISH DRAFT TREATY 'A'

This is the rough draft of the External Association Proposal, embodying ideas and principles agreed upon by the Republican Cabinet, which formed the basis of the Irish offer during the London Conference in 1921.

(Outlines for *ideas* and *principles* only. Wording tentative and rough. Expert draftsmen will be engaged for the wording and form when the principles are agreed upon.)

Recital. Great Britain having, in the name of the British Commonwealth, invited Ireland to enter into association with her and the other states of that Commonwealth, and Great Britain and Ireland being equally desirous to end the ruinous secular conflict between them and to secure the mutual benefits of concord and amity, have resolved to conclude a Treaty of Settlement, Accommodation, and Association, and for that purpose have appointed, the Government of Great Britain . . . : the Elected Government of Ireland . . . who, after communicating to each other their respective full powers, found in good and due form, agree upon the following:

Article I. Great Britain and the partner states of the British Commonwealth recognize Ireland as a sovereign independent state and Great Britain renounces all claims to govern or to legislate for Ireland.

Article II. Ireland agrees to become an external associate of the states of the British Commonwealth. As an associate Ireland's status shall be that of equality with the sovereign partner states of the Commonwealth and Ireland shall be so separately represented in British Imperial Council — Great Britain, Canada, Australia, etc. — and shall be so recognized by those several states.

Article III. In virtue of Ireland's association with the states of the British Commonwealth, citizens of Ireland shall enjoy in each of

310

these states the same rights and privileges as if they were natural born citizens of these states, and reciprocally the citizens of each of these states shall enjoy in Ireland the rights of natural born Irish citizens.

Article IV. Irish citizens resident in the states of the British Commonwealth, and reciprocally citizens of these states, resident in Ireland, shall be excepted from all compulsory service in the military, naval or police forces of the states in which they are resident and from all contributions which may be imposed in lieu of personal service.

Article V. Ireland accepts and the British Commonwealth guarantees the perpetual neutrality of Ireland and the integrity and inviolability of Irish territory; and both in its own interest and in friendly regard to the strategic interests of the British Commonwealth binds itself to enter no compact, and to take no action, nor permit any action to be taken, inconsistent with the obligation of preserving its own neutrality and inviolability and to repel with force any attempt to violate its territory or to use its territorial waters for warlike purposes.

Article VI. Financial article, to be drafted by *Minister of Finance.*

Article VII. Trade article, to be drafted by *Minster of Economic Affairs.*

Article VIII. Constitution and Ulster Question — to be drafted by Mr Griffith.

Article IX. Within fourteen days of the signing of this Treaty, the British Government shall evacuate from Ireland all Military forces and all 'auxiliary police' and all members of their police forces in Ireland recruited since the 1st day of January 1919.

Article X. This Treaty shall be ratified. It shall be submitted on the side of Ireland to *Dáil Éireann*, and on the side of Great Britain to the Parliament of Westminster. Should ratification not ensue, or should either Parliament so determine, it shall be submitted to the peoples of the respective countries, and if the Treaty shall be approved by a majority of the electors, it shall be deemed to have been ratified by the peoples of these respective countries.

For the ratification by the states of the British Commonwealth other than Great Britain, this Treaty shall be communicated by the Government of Great Britain, to the Governors of the Dominion of Canada, Commonwealth of Australia, and the Dominion of New Zealand, the Union of South Africa, and the Colony of Newfoundland, for transmission to the Parliaments of these respective states. Refusal or failure, however, of any of these states to ratify shall not affect the general validity of the Treaty.

Article XI. As soon as ratification of this Treaty shall have been exchanged, the British Government shall communicate the text of Articles to all states with which it entertains diplomatic relations, and the text of the Treaty as a whole to the President and Council of the League of Nations.

The British Government engages to support the securing of the formal recognition of Ireland's perpetual neutrality by the United States of America, by Germany, and by Russia, and by other States with which Great Britain entertains diplomatic relations and which are not members of the League of Nations.

The representatives of the British Commonwealth in the League of Nations engage to support the formal recognition of Ireland's neutrality, integrity, and inviolability by the League of Nations in conformity with the similar guarantee in favour of Switzerland recognized by Article 455 of the Treaty of Versailles of June 28th 1919, and to support an application that may hereafter be made by Ireland for inclusion in the League of Nations.

ARTICLES OF AGREEMENT AS SIGNED ON 6 DECEMBER 1921

1. Ireland shall have the same constitutional status in the Community of Nations known as the British Empire as the Dominion of Canada, the Commonwealth of Australia, the Dominion of New Zealand, and the Union of South Africa, with a parliament having powers to make laws for the peace, order and good government of Ireland and an Executive responsible to that Parliament, and shall be styled and known as the Irish Free State.

2. Subject to the provisions hereinafter set out the position of the Irish

Free State in relation to the Imperial Parliament and Government and otherwise shall be that of the Dominion of Canada, and the law, practice and constitutional usage governing the relationship of the Crown or the representative of the Crown and of the Imperial Parliament to the Dominion of Canada shall govern their relationship to the Irish Free State.

3. The representative of the Crown in Ireland shall be appointed in like manner as the Governor-General of Canada and in accordance with the practice observed in the making of such appointments.

4. The oath to be taken by Members of the Parliament of the Irish Free State shall be in the following form:
   I . . . do solemnly swear true faith and allegiance to the Constitution of the Irish Free State as by law established and that I will be faithful to H.M. King George V, his heirs and successors by law, in virtue of the common citizenship of Ireland with Great Britain and her adherence to and membership of the group of nations forming the British Commonwealth of Nations.

5. The Irish Free State shall assume liability for the service of the Public Debt of the United Kingdom as existing at the date hereof and towards the payment of war pensions as existing at that date in such proportion as may be fair and equitable, having regard to any just claims on the part of Ireland by way of set-off or counter-claim, the amount of such sums being determined in default of agreement by the arbitration of one or more independent persons being citizens of the British Empire.

6. Until an arrangement has been made between the British and Irish Governments whereby the Irish Free State undertakes her own coastal defence, the defence by sea of Great Britain and Ireland shall be undertaken by his Majesty's Imperial Forces. But this shall not prevent the construction or maintenance by the Government of the Irish Free State of such vessels as are necessary for the protection of the Revenue or the Fisheries.
   The foregoing provisions of the Article shall be reviewed at a Conference of Representatives of the British and Irish Government to be held at the expiration of five years from the date hereof with a view to the undertaking by Ireland of a share in her own coastal defence.

7. The Government of the Irish Free State shall afford to His Majesty's Imperial Forces: (a) In time of peace such harbour and other facilities as are indicated in the Annex hereto, or such other facilities as may from time to time be agreed between the British Government and the Government of the Irish Free State; and (b) In time of war or of strained relations with a Foreign Power such harbour and other facilities as the British Government may require for the purposes of such defence as aforesaid.

8. With a view of securing the observance of the principle of international limitation of armaments, if the Government of the Irish Free State establishes and maintains a military defence force, the establishments thereof shall not exceed in size such proportion of the military establishments maintained in Great Britain as that which the population of Ireland bears to the population of Great Britain.

9. The ports of Great Britain and the Irish Free State shall be freely open to the ships of the other country on payment of the customary port and other dues.

10. The Government of the Irish Free State agrees to pay fair compensation on terms no less favourable than those accorded by the Act of 1920 to judges, officials, members of Police Forces and other Public Servants who are discharged by it or who retire in consequence of the change of Government effected in pursuance hereof.

   Provided that this agreement shall not apply to members of the Auxiliary Police Force or to persons recruited in Great Britain for the Royal Irish Constabulary during the two years next preceding the date hereof. The British Government will assume responsibility for such compensation or pensions as may be payable to any of these excepted persons.

11. Until the expiration of one month from the passing of the Act of Parliament for the ratification of this instrument, the powers of the Parliament and the Government of the Irish Free State shall not be exercisable as respects Northern Ireland and the provisions of the Government of Ireland Act, 1920, shall so far as they relate to Northern Ireland remain of full force and effect, and no election shall be held for the return of members to serve in the Parliament of

314

the Irish Free State for constituencies in Northern Ireland, unless a resolution is passed by both Houses of the Parliament of Northern Ireland in favour of the holding of such election before the end of the said month.

12. If before the expiration of the said month, an address is presented to His Majesty by both Houses of the Parliament of Northern Ireland to that effect, the powers of the Parliament and Government of the Irish Free State shall no longer extend to Northern Ireland, and the provisions of the Government of Ireland, Act, 1920 (including those relating to the Council of Ireland) shall, so far as they relate to Northern Ireland, continue to be of full force and effect, and this instrument shall have effect subject to the necessary modifications.

   Provided that if such an address is so presented a Commission consisting of three persons, one to be appointed by the Government of the Irish State, one to be appointed by the Government of Northern Ireland and one who shall be Chairman to be appointed by the British Government shall determine in accordance with the wishes of the inhabitants, so far as may be compatible with economic and geographic conditions, the boundaries between Northern Ireland and the rest of Ireland, and for the purposes of the Government of Ireland Act, 1920, and of this instrument, the boundary of Northern Ireland shall be such as may be determined by such Commission.

13. For the purpose of the last foregoing article, the powers of the Parliament of Southern Ireland under the Government of Ireland Act, 1920, to elect members of the Council of Ireland shall after the Parliament of the Irish Free State is constituted be exercised by that Parliament.

14. After the expiration of the said month, if no such address as is mentioned in Article 12 hereof is presented, the Parliament and Government of Northern Ireland shall continue to exercise as respects Northern Ireland the powers conferred on them by the Government of Ireland Act, 1920, but the Parliament and Government of the Irish Free State shall in Northern Ireland have in relation to matters in respect of which the Parliament of Northern Ireland had not power to make laws under that Act (including matters which under the said Act are within the jurisdiction of the Council of Ireland) the same powers as in the rest of Ireland,

315

subject to such other provisions as may be agreed in manner hereinafter appearing.

15. At any time after the date hereof the Government of Northern Ireland and the provisional Government of Southern Ireland hereinafter constituted may meet for the purpose of discussing the provisions subject to which the last foregoing article is to operate in the event of no such address as is therein mentioned being presented and those provisions may include:

   (a) Safeguards with regard to patronage in Northern Ireland;

   (b) Safeguards with regard to the collection of revenue in Northern Ireland;

   (c) Safeguards with regard to import and export duties affecting the trade or industry of Northern Ireland;

   (d) Safeguards for minorities in Northern Ireland;

   (e) The settlement of the financial relations between Northern Ireland and the Irish Free State;

   (f) The establishment and powers of a local militia in Northern Ireland and the relation of the Defence Forces of the Irish Free State and of Northern Ireland respectively;

   and if at any such meeting provisions are agreed to, the same shall have effect as if they were included amongst the provisions subject to which the Powers of the Parliament and Government of the Irish Free State are to be exercisable in Northern Ireland under Article 14 hereof.

16. Neither the Parliament of the Irish Free State nor the Parliament of Northern Ireland shall make any law so as either directly or indirectly to endow any religion or prohibit or restrict the free exercise thereof or give any preference or impose any disability on account of religious belief or religious status or affect prejudicially the right of any child to attend a school receiving public money without attending the religious instruction at the school or make any discrimination as respects state aid between schools under the management of different religious denominations or divert from any religious denomination or any educational institution any of its

property except for public utility purposes and on payment of compensation.

17. By way of provisional arrangement for the administration of Southern Ireland during the interval which must elapse between the date hereof and the constitution of a Parliament and Government of the Irish Free State in accordance therewith, steps shall be taken forthwith for summoning a meeting of members of Parliament elected for constituencies in Southern Ireland since the passing of the Government of Ireland Act, 1920, and for constituting a Provisional Government, and the British Government shall take the steps necessary to transfer to such Provisional Government the powers and machinery requisite for the discharge of its duties, provided that every member of such Provisional Government shall have signified in writing his or her acceptance of this instrument. But this arrangement shall not continue in force beyond the expiration of twelve months from the date hereof.

18. This instrument shall be submitted forthwith by His Majesty's Government for the approval of Parliament and by the Irish signatories to a meeting summoned for the purpose of the members elected to sit in the House of Commons of Southern Ireland, and if approved shall be ratified by the necessary legislation.

On behalf of the British
Delegation.

On behalf of the Irish
Delegation.

Signed.
D. Lloyd George.
Austen Chamberlain.
Birkenhead.
Winston S. Churchill.
L. Worthington-Evans.
Hamar Greenwood.
Gordon Hewart.

Signed.
Art Ó Griobhtha.
Michael Ó Coileáin
Riobárd Bartún.
Eudhmonn S. Ó Dúgáin.
Seorsa Ghabháin Uí
Dhúbhthaígh.

December 6th, 1921.

Annex

1. The following are the specific facilities required:

Dockyard Port at Berehaven

(a) Admiralty property and rights to be retained as at the date hereof. Harbour defences to remain in charge of British care and maintenance parties.

Queenstown

(b) Harbour defences to remain in charge of British care and maintenance parties. Certain mooring buoys to be retained for use of His Majesty's ships.

Belfast Lough

(c) Harbour defences to remain in charge of British care and maintenance parties.

Lough Swilly

(d) Harbour defences to remain in charge of British care and maintenance parties.

Aviation

(e) Facilities in the neighbourhood of the above Ports for coastal defence by Air.

Oil Fuel Storage

(f) Haulbowline Rathmullen — To be offered for sale to commercial companies under guarantee that purchasers shall maintain a certain minimum stock for Admiralty purposes.

2. A Convention shall be made between the British Government and the Government of the Irish Free State to give effect to the following conditions:

(a) That submarine cables shall not be landed or wireless stations for communications with places outside Ireland be established except by agreement with the British Government; that the existing cable landing rights and wireless concessions shall

318

not be withdrawn except by agreement with the British Government; and that the British Government shall be entitled to land additional wireless stations for communication with places outside Ireland.

(b) That lighthouses, buoys, beacons, and any navigational marks or navigational aids shall be maintained by the Government of the Irish Free State as at the date hereof and shall not be removed or added to except by agreement with the British Government.

(c) That war signal stations shall be closed down and left in charge of care and maintenance parties, the Government of the Irish Free State being offered the option of taking them over and working them for commercial purposes subject to Admiralty inspection, and guaranteeing the upkeep of existing telegraphic communication therewith.

3. A Convention shall be made between the same Governments for the regulation of Civil Communication by Air.

			A.G.
D.LI.G.	B.	W.S.C.	M.OC.
A.C.		E.S.O.D.	R.B.
			S.G.D.

'DOCUMENT NUMBER TWO'

The following is the Counter-proposal drafted by President de Valera as an Amendment to the motion for Approval of the Articles of Agreement. He intended to move the Amendment on 4 January 1922.

That inasmuch as the 'Articles of Agreement for a treaty between Great Britain and Ireland', signed in London on December 6th, 1921, do not reconcile Irish National aspirations and the Association of Ireland with the Community of Nations known as the British Commonwealth, and cannot be the basis of an enduring peace between the Irish and the British peoples, *Dáil Éireann*, in the name of the Sovereign Irish Nation, makes to the Government of Great Britain, to the Government of the other States of the British Commonwealth, and to the peoples of Great Britain and of these

319

several states, the following Proposal for a Treaty of Amity and Association which, *Dáil Éireann* is convinced, could be entered into by the Irish people with the sincerity of goodwill:

Proposed Treaty of Association between Ireland and the British Commonwealth

In order to bring to an end the long and ruinous conflict between Great Britain and Ireland by a sure and lasting peace honourable to both nations, it is agreed

Status of Ireland

1. That the legislative, executive, and judicial authority of Ireland shall be derived solely from the people of Ireland.

Terms of Association

2. That, for purposes of common concern, Ireland shall be associated with the States of the British Commonwealth, viz. The Kingdom of Great Britain, the Dominion of Canada, the Commonwealth of Australia, the Dominion of New Zealand, and the Union of South Africa.

3. That when acting as an associate the rights, status, and privileges of Ireland shall be in no respect less than those enjoyed by any of the component States of the British Commonwealth.

4. That the matters of 'common concern' shall include Defence, Peace and War, Political Treaties, and all matters now treated as of common concern, amongst the States of the British Commonwealth, and in these matters there shall be between Ireland and the States of the British Commonwealth 'such concerted action founded on consultation as the several Governments may determine.'

5. That in virtue of this association of Ireland with the States of the British Commonwealth, citizens of Ireland in any of these States shall not be subject to any disabilities which a citizen of one of the component States of the British Commonwealth would not be subject to, and reciprocally for citizens of these States in Ireland.

6. That, for purposes of the Association, Ireland shall recognize His

Britannic Majesty as head of the Association.

Defence

7. That, so far as her resources permit, Ireland shall provide for her own defence by sea, land and air, and shall repel by force any attempt by a foreign Power to violate the integrity of her soil and territorial waters, or to use them for any purpose hostile to Great Britain and the other associated States.

8. That for five years, pending the establishment of Irish coastal defence forces, or for such other period as the Governments of the two countries may later agree upon, facilities for the coastal defence of Ireland shall be given to the British Government as follows:

   (a) In time of peace such harbour and other facilities as are indicated in the Annex hereto, or such other facilities as may from time to time be agreed upon between the British Government and the Government of Ireland;

   (b) In time of war such harbour and other naval facilities as the British Government may reasonably require for the purposes of such defence as aforesaid.

9. That within five years from the date of exchange of ratifications of this Treaty a Conference between the British and Irish Governments shall be held in order to hand over the coastal defence of Ireland to the Irish Government, unless some other arrangement for naval defence be agreed by both Governments to be desirable in the common interest of Ireland, Great Britain, and the other Association States.

10. That, in order to co-operate in furthering the principle of international limitation of armaments, the Government of Ireland shall not

    (a) Build submarines unless by agreement with Great Britain and the other States of the Commonwealth;

    (b) Maintain a military defence force, the establishments whereof exceed in size such proportion of the military establishments maintained in Great Britain as that which the population of

321

Ireland bears to the population of Great Britain.

Miscellaneous

11. That the Governments of Great Britain and of Ireland shall make a convention for the regulation of civil communication by air.

12. That the ports of Great Britain and of Ireland shall be freely open to the ships of each country on payment of the customary port and other dues.

13. That Ireland shall assume liability for such share of the present public debt of Great Britain and Ireland, and of payment of war pensions as existing at this date as may be fair and equitable, having regard to any claims on the part of Ireland by way of set-off or counter-claims, the amount of such sums being determined in default of agreement, by the arbitration of one or more independent persons, being citizens of Ireland or of the British Commonwealth.

14. That the Government of Ireland agrees to pay compensation on terms not less favourable than those proposed by the British Government of Ireland Act of 1920 to that Government's judges, officials, members of Police Forces and other Public Servants who are discharged by the Government of Ireland, or who retire in consequence of the change of government elected in pursuance hereof;

    Provided that this agreement shall not apply to members of the Auxiliary Police Force, or to persons recruited in Great Britain for the Royal Irish Constabulary during the two years next preceding the date hereof. The British Government will assume responsibility for such compensation or pensions as may be payable to any of these excepted persons.

15. That neither the Parliament of Ireland nor any subordinate Legislature in Ireland shall make any law so as either directly or indirectly to endow any religion or prohibit or restrict the free exercise thereof, or give any preference or impose any disability on account of religious belief or religious status, or affect prejudicially the right of any child to attend a school receiving public money without attending a religious instruction at the school, or make any discrimination as respects State aid between schools under the

322

management or different religious denominations or any educational institution any of its property except for public utility purposes on payment of compensation.

Transitional

16. That by way of transitional arrangement for the Administration of Ireland during the interval which must elapse between the date hereof and the setting up of a Parliament and Government of Ireland in accordance herewith, the members elected for constituencies in Ireland since the passing of the British Government of Ireland Act in 1920 shall, at a meeting summoned for the purpose, elect a transitional Government to which the British Government and Dáil Éireann shall transfer the authority, powers, and machinery requisite for the discharge of its duties, provided that every member of such transition Government shall have signified in writing his or her acceptance of this instrument. But this arrangement shall not continue in force beyond the expiration of twelve months from the date hereof.

Ratification

17. That this instrument shall be submitted for ratification forthwith by his Britannic Majesty's Government to the Parliament at Westminster, and by the Cabinet of Dáil Éireann to a meeting of the members elected for the constituencies in Ireland set forth in the British Government of Ireland Act, 1920, and when ratifications have been exchanged shall take immediate effect.

Annex

1.   The following are the specific facilities referred to in Article 8 (a)

Dockyard Port at Berehaven

(a) British Admiralty property and rights to be retained as at the date hereof. Harbour defences to remain in charge of British care and maintenance parties.

Queenstown

(b) Harbour defences to remain in charge of British care and maintenance parties. Certain mooring buoys to be retained for use of His Britannic Majesty's ships.

Belfast Lough

(c) Harbour defences to remain in charge of British care and maintenance parties.

Lough Swilly

(d) Harbour defences to remain in charge of British care and maintenance parties.

Aviation

(e) Facilities in the neighbourhood of the above Ports for coastal defence by air.

Oil Fuel Storage

(f) Haulbowline and Rathmullen — To be offered for sale to commercial companies under guarantee that purchasers shall maintain a certain minimum stock for British Admiralty purposes.

2. A Convention covering a period of five years shall be made between the British and Irish Governments to give effect to the following conditions:

(a) That submarine cables shall not be landed or wireless stations for communications with places outside Ireland be established except by agreement with the British Government; that the existing cable landing rights and wireless concessions shall not be withdrawn except by agreement with the British Government; and that the British Government shall be entitled to land additional submarine cables or establish additional wireless stations for communication with places outside Ireland.

(b) That lighthouses, buoys, beacons, and any navigational marks or navigational aids shall be maintained by the Government of Ireland as at the date hereof and shall not be removed or added to except by agreement with the British Government.

(c) That war signal stations shall be closed down and left in charge of care and maintenance parties, the Government of Ireland being offered the option of taking them over and working them for commercial purposes subject to British Admiralty inspection and guaranteeing the upkeep of existing telegraphic communication therewith.

(The following addendum concerning N.E. Ulster was to be proposed as a separate resolution by the President.)

ADDENDUM NORTH-EAST ULSTER

Resolved:

That, whilst refusing to admit the right of any part of Ireland to be excluded from the supreme authority of the Parliament of Ireland, or that the relations between the Parliament of Ireland and any subordinate Legislature in Ireland can be a matter for treaty with a government outside Ireland, nevertheless, in sincere regard for internal peace, and in order to make manifest our desire not to bring force or coercion to bear upon any substantial part of the Province of Ulster, whose inhabitants may now be unwilling to accept the national authority, we are prepared to grant to that portion of Ulster which is defined as Northern Ireland in the British Government of Ireland Act of 1920, privileges and safeguards not less substantial than those provided for in the Articles of Agreement for a Treaty between Great Britain and Ireland signed in London on December 6th, 1921.

THE IRISH ARMY COMMANDS IN MARCH 1922

1st Northern Division	Donegal— Four Brigades. Commandant Joseph Sweeney	pro-Treaty
2nd Northern Division	Tyrone and Derry — Four Brigades. Commandant Charles Daly	anti-Treaty
3rd Northern Division	Belfast, Antrim and Nth Down — Three Brigades. Commandant Joseph McKelvey	anti-Treaty

4th Northern Division and	Armagh, West and South Down North Louth — Three Brigades. Commandant Frank Aiken	non-partisan, afterwards anti-Treaty
5th Northern Division	Monaghan, East Cavan and South Fermanagh. Commandant Dan Hogan	Pro-Treaty
1st Eastern Division	Meath, Westmeath and Kildare — Nine Brigades. Commandant Seán Boylan	pro-Treaty
Dublin No. 1 Brigade (Independent)	Commandant Oscar Traynor	anti-Treaty
South Dublin Brigade (Independent)	Commandant Andrew Mc Donnell	anti-Treaty
North Wexford Brigade	North Wexford and South Wicklow. Commandant Joseph Cummin	pro-Treaty
South Wexford Brigade	Commandant Thomas O'Sullivan	anti-Treaty
Carlow Brigade	Commandant Liam Stack	pro-Treaty
Midland Division	Longford, Leitrim and Fermanagh. Commandant Seán MacEoin	pro-Treaty
First Western Division	Clare and South Galway. Commandant Michael Brennan	pro-Treaty
Second Western Division	South Roscommon, South and East Mayo, North Galway. Commandant Thomas Maguire	anti-Treaty
Third Western Division	North Roscommon, Sligo, part of Mayo. Commandant Liam Pilkington	anti-Treaty
Fourth Western Division	North and West Mayo, parts of Sligo and Galway. Commandant Michael Kilroy	anti-Treaty

First Southern Division	Cork, Kerry and Waterford and West Limerick — Ten Brigades. Commandant Liam Lynch	anti-Treaty
Second Southern Division	Kilkenny, Limerick and part of Tipperary — Five Brigades. Commandant Earnan O'Malley	anti-Treaty
Third Southern Division	Leix, Offaly and part of Tipperary — Five Brigades. Commandant Michael McCormick	pro-Treaty

TEXT OF THE FOUR COURTS PROCLAMATION

Oglaigh na hÉireann

PROCLAMATION

Fellow citizens of the Irish Republic;

The fateful hour has come. At the direction of our hereditary enemy our rightful cause is being treacherously assailed by recreant Irishmen. The crash of arms and the boom of artillery reverberate in this supreme test of the Nation's destiny.

Gallant soldiers of the Irish Republic stand rigorously firm in its defence and worthily uphold their [*sic*] noblest traditions. The sacred spirits of the Illustrious Dead are with us in this great struggle. 'Death before Dishonour' being an unchanging principle of our national faith as it was of theirs, still inspires us to emulate their glorious effort.

We therefore appeal to all citizens who have withstood unflinchingly the oppression of the enemy during the past six years to rally to the support of the Republic and recognize that the resistance now being offered is but the continuance of the struggle that was suspended by the truce with the British. We especially appeal to our former comrades of the Irish Republic to return to that allegiance and thus guard the Nation's honour from the infamous stigma that her sons aided her foes in retaining a hateful domination over her.

Confident of victory and of maintaining Ireland's Independence this appeal is issued by the Army Executive on behalf of the Irish Republican Army.

(Signed)

Commdt.-Gen. Liam Mellows, Commdt.-Gen. Rory O'Connor, Commdt.-Gen. Jos. McKelvey, Commdt.-Gen. Earnan O'Maille, Commdt.-Gen. Seamus Robinson, Commdt.-Gen. Seán Moylan. Commdt.-Gen. Michael Kilroy, Commdt.-Gen. Frank Barrett, Commdt.-Gen. Thomas Deerig [*sic,* Derrig], Commdt. T. Barry, Col. Commdt. F Ó Faolain, Brig. Gen. J. O'Connor, Commdt. P.O. Rutiless.

28th June 1922.

RESOLUTION ON SECRET MILITARY COURTS

The following Proclamation was issued on 10 October 1922, after the granting of Special Emergency Powers to the Provisional Government's Army.

To All Whom It May Concern:

1. With a view to the speedy termination of the present state of armed rebellion and insurrection, and the restoration of peace, order, and security, the Government, with the sanction of Dáil Éireann, has sanctioned the doing by, or under the authority of, the Army Council of all of the following matters or things:

    (a) The setting up of Military Courts of Committees for the inquiring into charges against persons in respect of any of the offences hereinafter mentioned, provided, however, that every such Military Court or Committee shall include as a member thereof at least one person nominated by the Minister of Defence and certified by the Law Officer to be a person of legal knowledge and experience.

    (b) The inquiry by such Military Courts or Committees into the cases of persons charged with any of the offences following, that is to say:

(1) Taking part in, or aiding or abetting any attacks upon or using force against the National Forces.

(2) Looting, arson, destruction, seizure, unlawful possession, or removal of, or damage to, any public or private property.

(3) Having possession without proper authority of any bomb, or article in the nature of a bomb, or any dynamite, or gelignite, or other explosive substance, or any revolver, rifle, gun or other firearm or lethal weapon, or any ammunition for such firearm.

(4) The breach of any general order or regulation made by the Army Council and the infliction by such Military Courts or Committees of the punishment of death or of penal servitude for any period or of imprisonment for any period or of a fine of any amount either with or without imprisonment on any person found guilty by such Court or Committee of any of the offences aforesaid provided that no such sentence of death be executed except under the counter signature of two members of the Army Council.

(c) The removal under authority of the Army Council of any person taken prisoner, arrested, or detained by the National Forces to any place or places within or without the area of jurisdiction of the Government, and the detention or imprisonment of any such persons in any place or places within or without the area aforesaid.

(d) The regulation and control of the sale, possession, transfer of, and dealing in, revolvers, rifles, guns and other firearms.

2. By regulations made the 2nd day of October 1922, the Army Council have provided for the trial by Military Courts of civilians charged with the offences specified in the preceding paragraph and for the infliction upon any civilian convicted by a Military Court of any such offence, of any of the following punishments according to the nature and gravity of the offence:

Death
Penal Servitude,

329

Imprisonment,
Deportation,
Internment,
Fine.

3. It is provided by the said regulations that they shall come into force upon and shall apply as from such date as the Army Council shall determine and announce by proclamation.

4. By proclamation published the 3rd day of October 1922, the Government announced and proclaimed as follows:

AMNESTY OFFER

(1) Every person who is engaged in such insurrection and rebellion against the State as aforesaid, or in such armed opposition to the National Forces as aforesaid, or who has been guilty of any offence against the State directly arising out of such insurrection, rebellion, and armed opposition aforesaid, and who, on or before the 15th day of October, 1922, voluntarily delivers into the possession of the National Forces all firearms, arms, weapons, bombs, ammunition and explosives, and all public and private property, now unlawfully in his possession, and quits all lands or buildings unlawfully occupied by him, and who, on or before the 15th day of October, 1922, voluntarily ceases to take any part in, or aid or abet, such insurrection, rebellion, or armed opposition, shall be permitted to return unmolested to his home, and to every such person we hereby offer, assure and proclaim a full amnesty and pardon for all such insurrection, riot, rebellion, and opposition and offences as aforesaid.

(2) Every such person may deliver any such firearms, arms, weapons, ammunition, explosives and bombs, and any such public property as aforesaid, to the Officer Commanding the nearest Military position or station, or to any such person as shall be nominated by him.

SIGNED ON BEHALF OF THE GOVERNMENT
OF SAORSTÁT ÉIREANN.

LIAM T. MAC COSGAIR,
President of Dáil Éireann.

Know then, and it is hereby announced and proclaimed as follows:

(1) After the 15th day of October, 1922, we, the Army Council, will exercise all the powers and do all the matters and things in the first paragraph of this proclamation mentioned, or any of them, according as the same shall to us seem necessary or expedient.

(2) The said regulations as to the Trial of Civilians by Military Courts made by us, the Army Council, on the 2nd day of October, 1922, shall come into force and apply as from the 15th day of October, 1922.

Given at General Headquarters, Portobello Barracks, Dublin, and published this 10th day of October, 1922.

Signed on behalf of the Army Council,

Risteard Ua Maolcatha, General
Commander-in-Chief.

UNITY PROPOSALS OF MAY 1922

We, the undersigned officers of the IRA, realizing the gravity of the present situation in Ireland, and appreciating the fact that if the present drift is maintained a conflict of comrades is inevitable, declare that this would be the greatest calamity in Irish history, and would leave Ireland broken for generations.

To avert this catastrophe we believe that a closing of the ranks all round is necessary.

We suggest to all leaders, Army and political, and all citizens and soldiers of Ireland the advisability of a unification of forces on the basis of acceptance and utilization of our present national position in the best interests of Ireland; and we require that nothing shall be done which would prejudice our position or dissipate our strength.

We feel that on this basis alone can the situation be faced, viz:

(1) The acceptance of the fact — admitted all sides — that the majority of the people of Ireland are willing to accept the Treaty.

(2) An agreed election with a view to

(3) Forming a Government which will have the confidence of the

whole country.

(4) Army unification on above basis.

> Tom Hales
> S. O'Hegarty
> Seán Boylan
> Owen O'Duffy
> Micheál Ó Coileáin
> Dan Breen
> H. Murphy
> F. O'Donoghue
> R. J. Mulcahy
> Gearóid O'Sullivan

THE PACT

Between Collins and de Valera 20 May 1922
We are agreed:

(1) That a National Coalition panel for this Third Dáil representing both parties in the Dáil and in the Sinn Féin organization be sent forward on the ground that the national position requires the entrusting of the Government of the country into the joint hands of those who have been the strength of the national situation during the last few years, without prejudice to their present respective positions.

(2) That this Coalition panel be sent forward as from the Sinn Féin organization, the number from each party being their present strength in the Dáil.

(3) That the candidates be nominated through each of the existing party Executives.

(4) That every and any interest is free to go up and contest the election equally with the National-Sinn Féin panel.

(5) That constituencies where an election is not held shall continue to be represented by their present deputies.

(6) That after the election the Executive shall consist of the President, elected as formerly; the Minister for Defence, representing the Army; and nine other ministers — five from the majority party and four from the minority, each party to choose its own nominees. The allocation will be in the hands of the President.

(7) That in the event of the Coalition Government finding it necessary to dissolve, a general election will be held as soon as possible on adult suffrage.

THE CONSTITUTION OF SINN FÉIN

As adopted by the Árd-Fheis which met in Dublin on 25 October 1917.

I

(1) The name of this organization shall be Sinn Féin.

(2) Sinn Féin aims at securing the International recognition of Ireland as an independent Irish Republic.
Having achieved that status the Irish people may by referendum freely choose their own form of Government.

(3) This object shall be attained through the Sinn Féin Organization.

(4) Whereas no law made without the authority and consent of the Irish people is or ever can be binding on their conscience. Therefore in accordance with the Resolution of Sinn Féin adopted in Convention, 1905, a Constituent Assembly shall be convoked, comprising persons chosen by the Irish Constituencies as the supreme national authority to speak and act in the name of the Irish people and to devise and formulate measures for the welfare of the whole people of Ireland.

Such as:

(a) The introduction of a Protective System for Irish industries and

Commerce by combined action of the Irish County Councils, Urban Council, Rural Councils, Poor Law Boards, Harbour Boards, and other bodies directly responsible to the Irish people.

(b) The establishment and maintenance under the direction of National Assembly or other authority approved by the people of Ireland of an Irish Consular Service for the advancement of Irish Commerce and Irish interests generally.

(c) The re-establishment of an Irish Mercantile Marine to facilitate direct trading between Ireland and the countries of Continental Europe, America, Africa, and the Far East.

(d) The industrial survey of Ireland and the development of its mineral resources under the auspices of a National Assembly or other national authority approved by the people of Ireland.

(e) The establishment of a National Stock Exchange.

(f) The creation of a National Civil Service, embracing all the employees of the County Councils, Rural Councils, Poor Law Boards, Harbour Boards, and other bodies responsible to the Irish people, by the institution of a common national qualifying examination and a local competitive examination (the latter at the discretion of the local bodies).

(g) The establishment of Sinn Féin Courts of Arbitration for the speedy satisfactory adjustment of disputes.

(h) The development of transit by rail, road and water, of waste lands for the national benefit by a national authority approved by the people of Ireland.

(i) The development of the Irish Sea Fisheries by National Assembly or other National authority approved by the people of Ireland.

(j) The reform of education, to render its basis national and industrial, by the compulsory teaching of the Irish language, Irish history, and Irish agricultural and manufacturing potentialities in the primary system, and, in addition, to elevate to a position of dominance in the University system, Irish agriculture and economics.

334

(k) The abolition of the Poor Law System and substitution in its stead of adequate outdoor relief to the aged and infirm, and the employment of the able-bodied in the reclamation of waste lands, afforestation and other national and reproductive works.

II

A Special meeting of the Executive may be summoned on three day's notice by the President on requisition presented to him signed by six members of the Executive specifying the object for which the meeting is called, In case of an urgent emergency the President shall call all members of the Executive to an emergency meeting, and may take action in the name of the Executive in case he secures the approval of an absolute majority of the entire Executive, the section taken is to be reported for confirmation at the next ordinary meeting of the Executive.

III

That where Irish resources are being developed, or where industries exist, Sinn Féiners make it their business to secure that workers are paid a living wage.

That the equality of men and women in this Organization be emphasized in all speeches and leaflets.

INDEX